OFF THE BOOKS

Vesco: and the Looting of IOS

OFF THE BOOKS

ROBERT A. HUTCHISON

064318

William Morrow and Company, Inc.
New York

Library of Congress Cataloging-in-Publication Data

Hutchison, Robert A., 1938–
  Off the books.

  Includes index.
  1. Citibank (New York, N.Y.)—Corrupt practices.
2. Banks and banking—Corrupt practices. I. Title.
HG2613.N54F674 1986   364.1′68   85-21376
ISBN 0-688-04881-1

Printed in the United States of America

First Edition

1 2 3 4 5 6 7 8 9 10

BOOK DESIGN BY RICHARD ORIOLO

For Daphne,
Tamara,
and
Chloe,
three wonderful
people

Acknowledgments

During the two years it took to research and write *Off the Books,* I traveled to a dozen cities in Europe, the United States, and Canada, seeking information, reviewing documents, and interviewing, or attempting to interview, more than one hundred persons. Some were not helpful, but others became genuinely interested in the project, often contributing ideas and suggestions as well as their knowledge of events and situations. Because of the sensitiveness of the subject and the shyness of bankers for public attention, most of the people who helped me unravel this story have no wish to be named. Among those who can be mentioned, I owe special thanks to my agent, Peter Shepherd, of Harold Ober Associates; my editor, Bruce Lee, and his former assistant Elizabeth Terhune. I would also like to thank Nora Hui, whose enthusiasm helped get the project started; Washington attorney Frederic Townsend, whose request under the Freedom of Information Act brought most of the documentation into the public domain; Geneva currency expert Gerald Staines, for help in understanding the technicalities of foreign exchange trading; psychologist François Schlemmer, who gave me the courage to keep going during a most difficult moment; former Citibanker Jean-Michel Ennuyer, for explaining the mindset of a foreign exchange trader; Dingell subcommittee staff director Michael Barrett, Jr., for his time and counsel; former SEC attorney Irwin Borowski, who was concerned that I "get it right"; and former SEC director of enforcement Stanley Sporkin, for his most valuable insight. Finally, I am grateful to the Fund for Investigative Journalism, Washington, D.C., whose grant made possible some additional research that otherwise could not have been undertaken.

Geneva, June 25, 1985

Contents

III
THE COVER-UP

IV
THE INVESTIGATION

V
THE LEAK

VI
THE UNRAVELING

Introduction

Citibank/Citistate

At 3:44 A.M. on October 6, 1976, in a darkened office on the fourth floor of Citibank headquarters at 399 Park Avenue, a telex machine suddenly lit up and started to chatter. Before the second hand on the wall clock above the machine had traveled halfway around the dial, the telex finished transcribing a partially coded message from the Citibank foreign exchange trading room in Frankfurt, some four thousand miles away.

ATTN MR VICTOR LEE
PLS BOOK FOR US
CITIBANK FRANKFURT BUYS FROM NASSAU BAHAMAS
6 MIO POUNDS STERLING AGAINST US DOLLARS AT 1.6660
HO PASS THE ENTRIES AND ACC LONDON
I HOPE WELL REC.

The "I hope well received" was not acknowledged. Due to the time-zone difference, trading had just begun in Frankfurt, while in New York it was still the middle of the night. Consequently, the message remained unattended on the receiving machine for the next five hours.

The message was in any event a pro forma booking instruction, and, unlike normal currency transactions between banks, which it was designed to resemble, did not need instant attention. In this "Victor

Lee" telex, Citibank Frankfurt was informing head office that it had
"bought" £6 million from Citibank Nassau for $1.666 per pound.
The traders in Frankfurt knew that the Nassau branch had no foreign
exchange desk, and for this reason, they had not contacted Nassau
directly.

Minutes later, the silence in the Eurocurrency department at Citibank headquarters was interrupted as a further message came in from
Frankfurt indicating that the purchase of the £6 million was a "spot"
deal with a value date (i.e., delivery date) of October 8, 1976. Because the back office work in any foreign exchange transaction takes
longer than the actual dealing, which can be concluded by telephone
or telex in a matter of seconds, the value date for spot deals is usually
two days after the contract date. The supplemental message read:

ATTN MR VICTOR LEE
REMEMBER THAT POUND STERLING TRANSACTION CITIBANK
FRANKFURT AT 1.6660
VALUE MUST BE OCTOBER 8, 1976

Five hours later, at 8:43 A.M., as the trading rooms in Europe were
closing for the day and the first foreign exchange dealers in New York
were coming to work, the telex on the fourth floor at 399 Park Avenue came alive again:

ATTN. VICTOR LEE
CITIBANK AG FRANKFURT SOLD TO NASSAU STG. 6 MM
AGAINST DLRS AT 1.6525 VAL OCT. 8, 76
HO PASS DLRS ENTRIES / CITIBANK LONDON
POSITION SQUARED
PROFIT DM 200,000.—
TOTAL PROFIT FRANKFURT DM 900,000.—

A clerk eventually ripped all three messages off the machine and
passed them to the back office for processing. It was routine. The
clerk knew that "Victor Lee"[1] was a code indicating that the buy
and sell orders required special treatment. Later in the day, the processing department would type up confirmations of the trades on Citibank Nassau forms showing a Nassau postal address but New York
telephone and telex numbers.

---

[1] Although "Victor Lee" was a code that signaled a "parked" or "special transaction," such
a person did exist. The real Victor Lee joined the Eurocurrency department in September 1976
as a junior trader. His job was to write up the "tickets" on which the incoming "parking"
transactions were recorded and transmit them to the operations department for processing.

On New Year's Day 1979, a friend and I were walking along a deserted beach at Casey Key, south of Sarasota on Florida's Gulf coast. The friend had driven down from Washington, D.C., with his four children for the holidays. The sun was warm and an offshore breeze gently rolled the waves onto the beach. I was vacationing in Florida with my family. We had arrived two weeks before from Geneva, Switzerland, where I worked as a financial journalist for the *Sunday Telegraph* of London and the *Financial Post* of Toronto. We planned to spend a month on Casey Key while I wrote a series about Michele Sindona, the Italian banker who turned out to be, with New Jersey businessman Robert Vesco and Swedish match king Ivar Kreuger, one of the biggest crooks of the century.

My friend asked if I knew about a foreign exchange scandal brewing in Switzerland. The newspapers had reported that American banks in Geneva and Zurich were suspected of speculating against the dollar on a massive scale. A *Washington Post* reporter by the name of Larry Kramer had been there and broken the story.

A few days before, the *Post* had carried one of Kramer's reports from Geneva, which indicated that the Swiss were focusing their probe on Citibank but that they might broaden it to include other foreign banks. Kramer reported that Citibank could owe the Swiss as much as $50 million in back taxes and penalties on undeclared revenues from foreign exchange speculation.[2]

This was the first I had heard of a Citibank inquiry, and it interested me. As a reporter, I had covered some of the great foreign exchange scandals of the 1970s—among them the 1974 Lloyds Bank affair in Lugano, in which a junior trader lost the bank $60 million; the June 1974 Bankhaus Herstatt collapse in Cologne, caused by more unauthorized currency dealing; and the downfall, also in 1974, of the Sindona empire, with its important foreign exchange frauds.

I replied that I didn't know about the Citibank case. But as we walked along the sand we discussed the turmoil in the foreign exchange market, the plight of the falling dollar, and how difficult it was for someone like myself, paid in dollars, to continue living in Switzerland. Many American expatriates quit Europe during the 1970s and returned to the United States because it had become too expensive for them to live abroad.

A Montrealer, I had moved to Geneva in 1959, when the U.S. dollar bought 4.32 Swiss francs. The dollar remained around this level

---

[2] "Banks Fear Swiss Probe Will Widen," by Larry Kramer, *The Washington Post*, December 22, 1978.

until 1971, when its exchange rate began to "float" against other currencies. By 1978, two years after the "Victor Lee" telex, the dollar reached its historic low against the Swiss franc. One dollar then purchased only 1.50 Swiss francs.

My friend, who worked at the Federal Energy Regulatory Commission (FERC), found the foreign exchange market, floating exchange rates, balance of payments deficits and interest-rate differentials all very puzzling. Why was the dollar taking such a beating? It must be costly, he reasoned, for American companies that needed to maintain large staffs abroad. It was, I agreed, but also it made American products more competitive in the international marketplace. On the other hand, imports became more expensive. It has been estimated that a 1 percent drop in the dollar added $1 billion to the U.S. balance-of-payments deficit. For banks, which made the market in foreign exchange, huge profits are earned in trading currencies. The more the market fluctuates, the larger the potential for profits—and losses—becomes. It is a fascinating and risky business.

Our discussion ended there and I thought nothing more about the Swiss probe for at least a year, as I was involved at the time in major litigation arising from a series I had written concerning a group of shady characters making a living on the Côte d'Azur by bilking wealthy investors. Because they were Monaco-based, I had named them the "Monte Carlo Syndicate," which did not endear me to the Monegasque authorities. But the Monegasques did end up taking steps to expel the syndicate members.

My friend changed jobs at the end of 1979 and returned to the Securities & Exchange Commission (SEC), where he had previously worked. I read in the newspapers that the Swiss probe of Citibank's dealings ended "inconclusively" in 1980. That didn't surprise me. The ways foreign exchange traders have for rolling over positions, breaking them up, switching and swapping, pairing, parking, going short or long, spot or forward, made it virtually impossible for outside inspectors to reconstruct any bank's foreign exchange book over a prolonged period.

The Citibank case remained out of mind until mid-September 1982, when I opened the *International Herald Tribune* and the headline "Citicorp Denies Executives Directed Illegal Transactions" caught my eye. The story, from Washington, concerned the hearings that a congressional subcommittee was holding to determine why the SEC had not initiated proceedings against Citicorp after a staff report found that it had engaged in improper foreign exchange dealings. The author of the SEC report was Thomson von Stein, with whom I had shared that New Year's Day walk almost four years before.

My interest was again aroused and I began the research that led to this book. In conducting my research, in early 1984 I asked the SEC's public affairs office to arrange interviews with von Stein, his co-investigator Robert Ryan, and John Fedders, the director of enforcement who had recommended to the commission that it drop the Citicorp case. Word came back that Fedders would see me, and a meeting was scheduled. I phoned von Stein and asked if he and Ryan would also be present. Nobody had informed him of the meeting, so he wrote Fedders seeking guidance.

In his memo, von Stein told Fedders that we had known each other for a dozen years, that he had stayed at my home when he visited Switzerland and, likewise, that when I came to Washington I sometimes stayed with the von Steins.

When I met Fedders a few days later he was hopping mad. Being such a close friend of von Stein, he asked, did I think I could write an unbiased and balanced account of the Citicorp case? I indicated that I thought I could.

"Well," he huffed. "I hope you mention in your book that you are friends and that your families are also on friendly social terms." I said that probably I would, and we proceeded with our interview, in which Fedders came across, after his initial bristling, as a dedicated public servant, a fighter, ambitious, not too tactful, and dogmatically committed to his beliefs.

Listening to John Fedders defend his "prosecutorial discretion" in recommending that the commission not proceed against Citicorp reminded me somewhat of Richard Nixon defending his reasons for ending the dollar's convertibility into gold. Both were convinced their decision was right, but neither foresaw the storm it would create.

In August 1971, pressure against the dollar had become enormous. In three days of hectic activity in foreign exchange, European central banks had been forced to take in billions of U.S. dollars in exchange for their own currencies. It seemed that nobody wanted to hold dollars anymore, and Washington feared that the foreign central banks would ask the U.S. Treasury to redeem the excess dollars for gold— literally all the gold in Fort Knox.

Rather than face a run on the nation's monetary reserves, on August 15, 1971, President Nixon announced the "suspension" of the dollar's convertibility into gold. At a stroke, and without consulting

America's trading partners, he ended the Bretton Woods agreements, which had defined the shape and rules of the post-World War II monetary system. In its place, since international trade does not and cannot come to a standstill, there devolved a non-system, extremely difficult to regulate, based on "floating" exchange rates.

Explaining his decision to the nation, Nixon said, "I am determined that the American dollar must never again be a hostage in the hands of international speculators."

He asked: "Who gains from these crises? Not the working man, not the investor, not the real producers of wealth. The gainers are the international speculators. Because they thrive on crises, they help create them."

Convertibility had been the sacred cow of the Bretton Woods system. It gave the system its symmetry, as the gold-dollar exchange rate of $35 an ounce was the "reference" marker to which all other currencies were pegged.

Nixon's action removed the central peg from the system. Many astute traders, not only the gold bugs, had long felt that bullion, at $35 an ounce, was undervalued. Conversely, this meant that the dollar was overvalued. Left to the "free" market forces, the dollar began its long downward float. The foreign exchange market went into wild gyrations, and trading volume soared as speculators rushed in and out of a spectrum of currencies.

Nixon implied that the "international speculators" were faceless, evil gnomes working for the system's destruction. A fact he didn't mention was that the world's biggest currency speculators were the world's biggest banks. And New York's Citibank would distinguish itself in the years ahead as the biggest speculator of all.

Up to the 1960s, banks rarely dealt in foreign exchange for their own account, and the system remained stable. But chronic payments imbalances by some countries—notably the United States—growing inflation, and a host of other factors gradually destabilized the system. Wobbly exchange rates encouraged banks to expand their foreign exchange trading, and over the next decade the foreign exchange market grew in volume by ten or twenty times.

When, in 1973, all governments joined in a generalized system of floating exchange rates, the idea was to allow countries with chronic payments problems more flexibility in adjusting their exchange rates to economic policy. This became an excuse for some countries to continue with undisciplined policies, which, logically, would lead to a devaluation of their currencies. Rather than wait for this to happen over a period of years, foreign exchange traders went into the market and, by continually "hitting" a currency, accomplished it within a matter of months.

The trade boom of the 1960s had left large international banks with more short-term funds at their disposal than central banks had reserves. Therefore it became possible for major banks, when they saw an adjustment coming, to "hit" successively a series of currencies and bring about a much broader realignment of the market. It was rough work, and frequently the adjustments they achieved "overshot" the targets of the monetary authorities.

By then even the smaller commercial, regional, and private banks had learned of the profits to be made by "hitting" a currency. To be sane in a world of madness was madness itself. Not to join a herd of traders "hitting" a currency, and so bring about a devaluation of that currency, was considered madness by most foreign exchange traders. They were in business to make money, not to implement the economic or fiscal policies of any nation. The biggest casualty in this free-for-all was the system itself. Central banks were no longer in control.

The early-morning "Victor Lee" telex between Citibank Frankfurt and head office would never have been disclosed publicly except for the persistence of a junior trader in Paris by the name of David Edwards who had the temerity to accuse the chief trader there of enriching himself at Citibank's expense.

What was first known within Citibank as the "de Laet affair"— after the chief trader whom Edwards denounced—became the "Edwards affair" when the young trader was unable to prove his suspicions that de Laet (pronounced DeLatt, to rhyme with hat) was "on the take." Edwards later uncovered evidence that Citibank encouraged its chief traders in Europe to "cook the books" in order to avoid local taxes and exchange controls. Ultimately, after Edwards took his discovery to Citibank's board of directors and, finally, to the SEC, it became the "Citibank affair." It tarnished the image not only of America's largest banking institution, but of the chairman, Walter B. Wriston, who had guided the bank to its preeminence.

Wriston had made Citibank the largest, most aggressive, and most arrogant of all international banks. In his twenty-four-year reign as president and then as chairman, he created a multinational monster that led all other banks in exploiting the regulatory freedom of the vast Eurocurrency market. In the process, Citibank became the larg-

est dealer in Eurocurrency deposits, the world's largest foreign exchange dealer, and the world's largest private lender. As Wriston
presciently observed in a speech delivered in June 1979, "The Eurocurrency market proved conclusively that, although the world may
still be divided politically, it is one economically and financially."

What Wriston was really saying is that in the age of electronic
banking, money can be placed anywhere in the world within seconds,
freely crossing international time zones, where national regulators are
unable to follow because they are prohibited from reaching beyond
their own frontiers.

While John Fedders was relatively open in discussing his reasons
for recommending that the SEC proceed no further in its Citibank investigation, I found that Citibankers themselves preferred to remain
mute on the subject. According to Charles B. Young, who had been
the bank's senior officer in Paris when Edwards blew the whistle,
Citibank adopted a corporate policy not to talk about the Edwards affair, judging it a "no-win situation." Even retired Citibankers preferred to respect corporate policy in this regard, pointing out that their
pensions were paid by the bank.

An effective screen was erected between the writer and the insti-
tution. Access to the key corporate players, including Wriston him-
self, was denied by the bank's principal attorneys, Shearman & Sterling.
In Zurich, as in Toronto, Paris, New York, Milan, London, and
Brussels, Citibank's doors were closed to me when it was learned that
I was writing about the Edwards affair.

Because of Citibank's policy, dialogue used in this book to describe certain meetings has been reconstructed without the assistance
of all the participants. In some cases, I relied on testimony before the
SEC or on existing notes and minutes made by some of the parties to
the meetings. As for the institution itself, I was permitted to submit
questions to a panel consisting of Citicorp general counsel Patrick
Mulhern, Shearman & Sterling senior partner Joseph T. McLaughlin,
and associate attorney Henry Weisburg. I met with them for three hours
at their Citicorp Center offices on May 30, 1984, but thereafter,
scheduling problems on both sides prevented further meetings and a
process of submitting written questions was adopted.[3] This continued
over four months, during which forty-five questions were tabled. Most

---

[3] Shearman & Sterling refused to meet with the author alone. "We would feel more comfortable
with your editor present," Mr. McLaughlin announced.

received replies that varied in length from one word to a few sentences. Shearman & Sterling also provided some documents. A final list of sixteen questions, however, apparently tried their patience to the breaking point, and answers to them were refused.

The bulk of Citibank's internal documents used in this book were obtained through a Freedom of Information Act request filed with the SEC by Frederic Townsend, a Washington attorney with Ralph Nader's public interest group, and from the public record of the House Committee on Energy, and Commerce's subcommittee on investigations and oversight.

David Edwards, when I first contacted him, was reluctant to talk. He felt he already had been sufficiently scarred by his Citibank affair and didn't want to relive any part of it. But gradually he opened up and gave a warm, personal and, on occasion, emotional rendering of events, as best he could recall them. During some of the more difficult sequences, I could hear his stomach grind as he came to grips with the issues again.

Citibank and its attorneys denied acting unethically, dangerously, or illegally. Others, including some former Citibankers, expressed the view that the bank's conduct was shocking, its behavior irresponsible, its policies such as parking destined to lead to a weakening of the monetary and banking systems, and the attorneys deserved censure for covering it up. Few had mixed opinions about what had happened, though all agreed that something had gone wrong: either with the bank's management and control mechanisms or, depending from which angle they viewed the problem, with an abusive use of investigative power by the SEC and an unwarranted extension of that agency's regulatory jurisdiction. The Citibank affair, as it unfolded, had all the makings of a first-class mystery story centered on one of the most arcane and complex areas of banking—foreign exchange trading.

Researching the facts unveiled the secrets of currency trading and how major banks, appraising the economic fundamentals underlying international trade, commerce, and capital movements, can influence the exchange rates of national currencies. Foreign exchange traders, who operate today in a marketplace shrunk by microchips and megabytes to the size of a TV monitor, make the market in currencies, determining at what price they are bought or sold. In doing this, it is true, they facilitate a transfer of goods and services between countries with different economic systems and standards. While this was once the main function of foreign exchange trading, it is no longer so.

While foreign exchange trading has become a major profit item on the balance sheets of some banks, much of the dealing serves no useful economic purpose, and indeed actually destabilizes the system. In today's markets, a currency's value can fluctuate by as much as 5 percent in a single trading session, which renders international trade too uncertain for stable growth.

With such extraordinary swings, the complex and fast-moving foreign exchange market can easily be used for "transfer pricing"—that is, the marking up or down of a unit, in this case the price of the U.S. dollar, as it crosses international frontiers in order to direct some profits to the most advantageous tax location.

How does this work? Take the example of a widget maker in Lyons, France. He manufactures widgets for 20 French francs apiece and sells them across the country for 30 francs each. He learns, however, that a large manufacturer of widgets exists in New Jersey, and because of advanced manufacturing techniques, the New Jersey manufacturer produces a superior item for the equivalent of 10 francs. With shipping and customs included, the French widget merchant figures he can import the American model for a total unit cost of 16 francs. This means he can make 4 francs more per unit selling imported widgets than selling his own domestically produced widgets. It also means he will pay higher taxes to the French government on higher profits.

A friendly banker suggests that the Lyons merchant should set up an import-export company in the Bahamas that buys the American widgets, then sells them to the Lyons merchant for 20 French francs apiece. The Bahamian company keeps the 4-franc profit; the widgets, however, never pass through the Bahamas because they are shipped directly from New Jersey to France. As far as the French tax authorities can tell, the Lyons merchant continues to make the same profit he would otherwise have shown on the sale of domestically produced widgets. This is because the extra profit is "booked" in the Bahamas by transferring there the markup on each imported widget. Multinational corporations often do this when they sell in one market goods they have produced in another market. It is perfectly legal if structured in a manner that respects local law and custom.

If transfer-pricing can be done with widgets, or for that matter with crude oil, cars, computers or cosmetics, it can also be done with currencies. Although Citibank denied it was doing this, my two years of research have proven that it was. What remained to be solved was whether Citibank's technique for shifting trading revenues from a high-tax country to no-tax Nassau by using the foreign exchange market and arbitrarily fixed exchange rates was legal.

My search for the facts took me, in September 1984, to a Milan courtroom, where eleven Citibank officers and employees were to be criminally tried for violating, through the parking of open foreign exchange positions, Italy's strict exchange control laws. Until then there had been no adjudication in any court of law, which enabled Wriston and Citibank's lawyers to claim to the House Commerce and Energy subcommittee that no country had ever found the practice illegal. This was a half truth at best: it conveniently ignored that in the United States the Office of the Comptroller of the Currency had ordered Citibank's board of directors to cease and desist; in Switzerland, the authorities had also censured Citibank, collecting in the process several million dollars in unpaid taxes and fines; in France, as in Germany, Citibank avoided potential litigation by agreeing to pay several million more dollars in back taxes and penalties to the fiscal authorities. But, it was true, no legal judgment existed condemning Citibank for breaking the rules of good banking conduct.

A few weeks before the Milan trial opened, Shearman & Sterling's McLaughlin had written me that only "some inquiries in Italy remain pending," neglecting to mention—or perhaps assimilating "some inquiries" with formal criminal charges—that an indictment had been issued two months before. The case was handled by Dr. Luca Mucci, one of Milan's most experienced and most respected prosecuting magistrates. Three years before, Mucci had revoked the passport of Roberto Calvi, chairman of Banco Ambrosiano, whose bank was then in the early stages of difficulty. Because of his Vatican connections, Calvi was called "God's banker." In spite of Mucci's restraining measures, Calvi acquired forged papers, fled to London as Ambrosiano collapsed, and a week later was found hanging from Blackfriars Bridge.

Prosecutor Mucci had spent four years investigating the Citibank case and described it as one of the most important to be brought under Italy's law 159 on the illicit export of capital. His indictment alleged that at least nine of the eleven defendants had conspired in 1976 to create "fictitious" foreign exchange transactions in order to transfer $2 million in trading profits from Milan to tax-free Nassau. If found guilty, they risked a maximum of two years' imprisonment and the bank could be fined six times the amount involved.

An investigation by a Bank of Italy inspector, who was to be called as a witness at the trial, suggested that the volume of Citibank's parking during 1976 alone exceeded $350 million. But Mucci had structured his case around only ten transactions, which, he said, were the clearest examples of Citibank's transfer-pricing techniques.

The defendants included two former Citibank branch managers in Milan, Baron Hans von Fluegge, a West German national then residing in Düsseldorf, and Philip D. Sherman, an American who had been shifted to Frankfurt. They also included Francesco Redi, a former head of Citibank's Treasury operations in Milan, who was by then the head of Citibank in France, and Redi's former assistant, Franco Riccardi, who was the current head of Citibank's Treasury in Milan, as well as four other traders, and a secretary who handled the telex confirmations. Two years before, Redi had been proposed for the job of managing director of the state-owned Banco di Roma, but the nomination was withdrawn when news of Dr. Mucci's investigation was published in the Italian magazine *L'Espresso* showing a picture of Redi under the headline *"Evado e vengo."*[4]

The trial opened on Friday, September 21, 1984, in the seventh section of Milan's criminal court, which is housed in the city's Palazzo di Giustizia, a monumental edifice built during the Mussolini era to reflect Italy's reborn grandeur. There was pandemonium next door in the fifth section courtroom, where the first of a series of criminal trials issuing from the collapse of Banco Ambrosiano, Italy's biggest postwar banking scandal, was also commencing. In courtroom No. 7, no seats had been provided for the public; apparently, no one was expected. As the lawyers and defendants waited outside the courtroom for the three judges—a court president and two assessors—squads of khaki-uniformed *carabinieri* led manacled prisoners by chains through the hallway to one of the other criminal courts. These defendants were all from the lower classes, most of them young men in their twenties, wearing rough clothes and yet attempting to look dignified despite their desperate situation.

The three Citibank judges finally appeared, almost an hour late. They took their seats under a fresco of a barefoot maiden in a white robe holding a sword in her right hand and a book marked CORPUS JURIS in her left. Cold gray marble lined the walls and the floor had not been swept since the last trial. After the judges came the prosecutor, Dr. Mucci, splendid in a black silk robe with gold tassels and cords dangling from each shoulder, and the defense counsel, at least ten of them, including two of Italy's most famous trial lawyers. The de-

---

[4] *"Evado e vengo"* is a play on words that, loosely translated, conveys the idea: "I evade the law and I am rewarded." The article appeared in *L'Espresso,* December 26, 1982.

fendants were called to appear. Only six presented themselves, neatly dressed in business suits, shoes shined, unmanacled, and unguarded by any armed *carabinieri*. Francesco Redi had remained in Paris, Baron von Fluegge was too busy in Düsseldorf, and Rafael Moreno Valle, a vice-president since transferred to New York, sent a telegram expressing his regrets for being indisposed. In addition, two local traders were absent—one was said to be "missing," while the other had remained "at home," allegedly claiming he had not been served notice of trial.

The court president, Dr. Renato Caccamo, seemed indifferent. He pondered whether due process had been respected in serving the defendants. Defense counsel demanded that the case be dismissed. After an hour's discussion of procedure, Dr. Caccamo ordered its return to the prosecutor's office for verification that notice of trial had been duly served. That meant Mucci would have to begin the process of serving the defendants all over again. The trial was adjourned and no date was fixed for its resumption.

Mucci was outraged. With twenty-three years' experience in criminal prosecutions, he was not known for making mistakes. Any appeal would take at least six months and require tremendous work. Wriston and Citibank's attorneys, meanwhile, could continue to maintain that no court of law had ruled parking illegal. There was no adjudication.

According to a study prepared for Citicorp's board of directors in October 1979, Citibank accounted for 9.08 percent of the total foreign exchange business contracted throughout the world.[5] The same survey estimated that the total volume of trading in the foreign exchange market amounted to $20 trillion annually, with Citibank accounting for $1.8 trillion of this. By extrapolation, Citibank was admitting that its daily trading volume was around $7.2 billion, or more than one and a half times its capital and reserves. This meant that each day Citibank was at risk in the foreign exchange market for an amount equal to 150 percent of its capital funds.

There is good reason to suspect that Citicorp's figures are far too low. Shearman & Sterling, in a 1978 study prepared for the bank, estimated that the total annual volume of the foreign exchange market was $50 trillion. A 1983 study by a Geneva-based firm, Staines Currency Investment Management S.A., estimated that the volume went as high as $62.5 trillion.

[5] See Appendix I for Citibank's list of the major foreign exchange dealers and estimate of their share of the market.

By comparison, the international reserves of the United States at the end of 1978 were $18.6 billion, of which $16 billion was held in gold and SDRs, the so-called "paper gold" created by the International Monetary Fund.[6]

Citicorp in 1978 declared record foreign exchange revenues of $105 million, which represented 25 percent of total profits, though only 3.6 percent of total income for the year. Its capital funds were then $4.7 billion. Viewed from another perspective, Citicorp was admitting that it risked, on an annualized basis, $1.8 trillion, a figure equivalent to 380 times its capital and reserves, to produce a profit of $105 million. Was Citicorp, therefore, employing a prudent risk-to-profit standard?

Wriston had set the standard himself when, in the early 1970s, he announced that henceforth Citibank's target for annual growth in earnings would be 15 percent. These increased earnings had to be generated somehow. Foreign exchange seemed like a logical growth sector.

The parking of foreign exchange positions—in other terms, the hiding of open positions from the authorities—enabled Citibank to engage in unprecedented speculation. The bank's participation in raids against the dollar or the pound sterling led automatically to accentuated swings in the foreign exchange market. Was this responsible banking?

Citicorp's internal documents reflect that, during the late 1970s, Citibank made the bulk of its foreign exchange profits in Switzerland, not from commercial transactions but from speculative transactions in amounts that far exceeded the limits set for safe and orderly trading by the Swiss central bank. Speculative trading can be defined as the taking of very substantial positions and making profits on them from favorable price movements. The only way in which Citicorp was able to take these very substantial positions was by parking.

Citibank's European branches had a practice of deliberately buying and selling positions at the same price, from the Nassau branch, which in fact had no foreign exchange department. Certain internal memoranda reviewed by the author indicated that the number of transactions in which the purchase and sale of positions were made at identical prices far exceeded the number of transactions that were done to shift profits offshore. This confirmed that in Europe most of Citicorp's foreign exchange profits were derived from the parking, or off-booking, of positions which exceeded local central bank limits.

Although the SEC's investigation of the bank's foreign exchange

---

[6]Source: *Federal Reserve Bulletin*, May 1979; table: U.S. Reserve Assets.

practices concentrated on the European branches, Citicorp's own 1979 survey confirmed that parking, and more specifically the purchase and sale of currencies at "tailored forward rates," was regularly practiced at least at ten other branches in Asia and the Middle East.

In addition, the survey—carried out in twenty-two countries by the internal inspectorate—found that serious breaches of the bank's prudential controls had occurred at eight locations. Citibank treasury heads in Japan, Hong Kong, Singapore, and Malaysia kept hidden profit reserves, while in Mexico the internal auditors uncovered the existence of "unbooked" foreign exchange contracts. As a result, the board passed a resolution reaffirming that hidden profit reserves were a no-no. The board also directed branches that wanted to continue parking to obtain local legal opinions to determine whether the practice was legally defensible under existing regulations in the countries concerned.

In 1979, Citicorp's foreign exchange profits fell to $6 million.

In May 1980, Citibank senior vice-president Paul Austin, who was then the treasury officer responsible for foreign exchange policy, told von Stein that the bank had stopped all parking.[7] It was not clear whether Austin was referring to Citibank's parking from Europe, or parking worldwide. In spite of that affirmation, Citicorp's foreign exchange earnings in 1980 rose to $164 million. Austin's statement was difficult to reconcile with the fact that the bank had recently opened a new booking center in Bahrain.

In 1981 Citicorp's foreign exchange profits increased to $265 million. In 1982, they were $241 million, and in 1983 they reached $274 million, indicating a dramatic increase in the volume of trading. Citicorp's capital and reserves were then $5.9 billion.

Day-to-day activity on the foreign exchange market, meanwhile, was marked by increasing exchange-rate volatility and a surging U.S. dollar, which, according to the *Financial Times* of London, "defied gravity." By January 1985, the dollar purchased 2.60 Swiss francs, almost twice the amount of Swiss currency it had purchased at its low point in 1978. The U.S. currency baffled experts. It remained strong in spite of a $230 billion budget shortfall and a current account deficit of $130 billion forecast for 1985. Ominously, the dynamics of the market had shifted to a new crisis configuration. The true shape of an unfettered foreign exchange market having emerged, with under 5

---

[7]Re: Citicorp, HO 1100, SEC Division of Enforcement, Report of Investigation, February 1981, page 95.

percent of the transactions bearing any relationship to international trade or long-term capital flows, the question which some currency experts were asking was, Will the monetary system survive the next major crisis?

Part I

THE WHISTLEBLOWER

Chapter 1

To Be a Citibanker

*Despite the multiplicity of values, there are certain rules
of conduct which guide our staffs around the world.*

—LETTER TO CITICORP INVESTORS, 1975 ANNUAL REPORT

One winter weekend when he was twenty-five, David Edwards drove
from London to Glasgow to meet a girl friend. The event was not of
itself earth-shattering, except that, arriving a day early for his rendez-
vous, David visited Clydeside, where he saw his first oceangoing ship.
Being an enterprising Texan, that night he found the only poker game
in Glasgow, of course in the Gorbals. He put up £200 and doubled
his stakes, decided to quit while ahead, only to have his winnings
lifted from him at knife point in the alleyway outside. After grappling
with his assailant in the early morning snow, David awoke in the hospital twelve hours later suffering from a concussion and knife wounds,
which, fortunately, did not pierce his rib cage.

The point of the story, which David was telling as we lounged in
the sun on the edge of a swimming pool in Dallas fifteen years later,
was to demonstrate how far this precocious prairie boy had come in
life. David Edwards, in 1968, was about to be hired as a clerk by a

British merchant bank. By 1983, he was managing $4 million in other people's money from a suite of offices at the Plaza of the Americas in downtown Dallas, getting up at 5 A.M. to tune in to the European markets, putting in twelve hours a day on the screens and telephone, hedging his clients' positions in the bond, bullion, commodities, and currency markets.

Not bad for someone who had been born in the north Texas town of Wichita Falls and who had spent a good part of his boyhood on his grandfather's farm in east Texas. During the first twenty-two years of his life, David had virtually never set foot outside of Texas, which covers about the same percentage of the earth's surface as France. The exceptions were occasional trips to Oklahoma, on the far side of the Red River, twenty-five miles north of Wichita Falls, or into western Louisiana with his grandfather to shoot wild geese. He had gumption, you might say. For as long as anybody could remember David had wanted only to be a banker. To make this point, he remembered that on his sixteenth birthday one of the neighbors on Pembroke Lane gave him a book with an inscription that alluded to his dream of one day traveling the world as an American banker, inventing new ways to finance trade and turn the wheels of international commerce.

David's interest in high finance and desire to travel were kindled by his grandfather, Thomas Elbert Edwards, a barrel-chested automobile distributor who ran out of customers and money in the Depression. After attempting to recycle himself as a traveling salesman, Thomas Edwards decided to invest the last of his cash in a small farm and work the land. He found 154 acres for sale near Ben Wheeler, population 200, little more than a widening in the road about two hours' driving time to the southeast of Dallas, and moved there with his wife and stacks of books that reached the ceiling.

As a young man—about the time of the Spanish-American War—Thomas Edwards joined the U.S. Navy and served as an aide to the admiral of the Atlantic fleet. While on sea duty he had crossed the Atlantic and sailed into the Mediterranean, visiting the ports of Europe and North Africa. He awed David with descriptions of London, Paris, Berlin, and Rome in the early 1900s and of a visit to St. Petersburg before the Bolsheviks took over.

Thomas Edwards had two sons: Thomas Elbert, Jr., who, to distinguish him from his father, was known as Bobby, and David senior. Bobby graduated from Annapolis and became a wing commander, flying off the carrier USS *Enterprise* in the early days of World War II. He dropped a bomb down the smokestack of a Japanese destroyer, flew ground-support missions over the beaches of Guadalcanal, and was decorated for his exploits, receiving the Navy Cross on the flight deck of the *Enterprise* from Admiral Chester Nimitz in person. Returning from patrol in 1943, Bobby's twelve-plane flight encountered a pack of Japanese Zeros. The first ten planes got back on board the *Enterprise* safely, but the eleventh aircraft crashed into the conning tower of the *Enterprise* and the pilot was trapped in his cockpit. The flight deck obstructed, Bobby was last seen flying south, the pack of Zeros on his tail, as the *Enterprise* steamed northwards. He was reported missing in action, and no trace of him was ever found.

Thomas Edwards's second son, David senior, became an engineer with the Douglas Aircraft Company. He married Katherine Tarry, the daughter of Wichita Falls merchant J. P. Tarry, before being transferred to the Douglas plant at Long Beach, California. The first of their four children, David, was born in 1944. Three years later, they returned to Wichita Falls, a rail junction and milling center, with stockyards and grain elevators, and a population at the time of 45,000. David senior helped run the Tarry Moving & Storing Company. The Edwardses and the Tarrys were staunch Methodists; they went to church most Sundays and sat in the family pew. Attendance sometimes seemed more a social event than an act of devotion, though for David junior Sunday School remained an obligation.

David's grandparents never recovered from the loss of Uncle Bobby. David and his youngest brother, Mark, went to live with them in Ben Wheeler for a while, helping with the crops and tending the forty head of cattle. They lived pretty much like hermits. No television then, and the nearest neighbors were miles away, but the little wooden farmhouse was crammed with books. Grandfather Edwards sparked David's interest in reading. "You didn't live in a small town anymore once you learned to read," David said.

David's interest quickly turned to politics. At the age of twelve he was out ringing doorbells for Adlai Stevenson. This led to a part-time job as a campaign helper for the Democratic Party in Texas. He liked the action and became close to the chairman of the executive committee of the Texas Democrats, Dallas attorney Eugene Locke. In fact, said David, he became one of Locke's "surrogate sons." With interests in oil, construction, and real estate, including a 25,000-acre ranch in Big Bend County, Locke was a powerhouse in the state.

Locke had been John Connally's roommate at college. He was also a close friend and confidant of Lyndon B. Johnson, participating strongly in Johnson's 1960 campaign for the vice-presidency. In 1962, when David first went to work for him, Locke was the manager of John Connally's successful gubernatorial campaign.

A major disaster occurred in David's life that year. His father had founded an oilfield service company, Advanced Oil Tools, Incorporated. The oil recession of the early sixties sent Advanced Oil Tools down the tubes, and David senior faced personal bankruptcy. As the eldest son, David had a strong sense of family responsibility. He gave up his undergraduate studies at the University of Texas in Austin and returned home to help his father get back on his feet financially. There were times, David said, when he dreaded answering the doorbell. Even attending church became an ordeal, for fear of running into one of his father's creditors. In time all debts were paid, but it was a harrowing experience for young David. He swore it would never happen to him and decided the best way to safeguard against it was to learn a good, solid profession. David redoubled his resolve to become a banker.

He worked as a night clerk at the Catalina Motel and kept the books for thirty-two neighborhood stores to pay for his courses at Midwestern State University in Wichita Falls. The work ethic, integrity, and honesty ran strong in the Edwards family. Outwardly, this gave David an appearance of confidence, while inwardly he was a bundle of nerves.

Engaging and considerate, David had the gift of making people want to help him. There was a touch of cockiness about him too, which, rather than detracting from his charm, enhanced it. He projected an image of well-mannered wholesomeness and enthusiasm, which reflected his belief that the spirit of capitalism had made America strong.

After graduating from Midwestern in 1967 with a bachelor's degree in business administration, David made his first trip on a commercial airliner. He bought a ticket to New York City and flew there for interviews with several investment banking firms on Wall Street. He returned sadly, empty-handed, and enrolled that autumn at the University of Texas in Austin, deciding a master's degree in economics would render him more credible as a prospective banker.

Gene Locke returned to Dallas that December after spending three years as a troubleshooter for President Johnson in Asia. When Johnson had learned in 1965 that President Ayub Khan of Pakistan was about to conclude a treaty with the Chinese, he furnished Locke with an open checkbook and sent him as U.S. ambassador to Islamabad. Locke's mission was to inform Ayub Khan that any deal with Peking would be dimly viewed by Washington. Ayub got the message, and Locke, thinking his mission over, prepared to return to private law practice. Instead, to establish a clear channel of communication with Saigon that would give him accurate assessments of the military situation there, Johnson asked Locke to serve as deputy ambassador to South Vietnam under veteran career diplomat Ellsworth Bunker. Locke accepted, but a year later, the communications problem resolved, he packed his bags and came back home, only to be pressed into service a final time.

Big John Connally had given up the governorship of Texas to become Secretary of the Navy. Johnson wanted to keep control of the governor's mansion in Austin in the family, so to speak, and he asked friend Gene to seek the gubernatorial nomination in the Democratic primary. Locke's three-year absence from Texas politics had put him out of touch with the party's grass roots, and this was a heavy handicap. One of the people he called upon to help him in the primary was his "surrogate son," David Edwards. Locke was defeated in the May 1968 primary by the lieutenant governor, Preston Smith, and soon after, he retired from politics. Before taking leave, David asked Locke for his help in becoming a banker.

Locke provided David with letters of introduction to three blue-ribbon New York banking houses. That summer David returned to New York, copies of Locke's letters in hand, and did the rounds. At Morgan Stanley, a senior partner looked David up and down—his wardrobe consisted of one suit and two sports coats—and said, "You're from what's-it-called Falls, and you want to work abroad. My, that takes gall."

At Lehman Brothers he was told to go work for Citibank and come back to see them in five years. David was feeling depressed by the time he was ushered into the boss's office at White Weld, Incorporated, the Eurobond specialists. John Cravans sent him to see David Mulford, a junior associate who had just spent three years with White Weld Limited in London.[1]

"Mulford impressed me no end," said David. "Much like myself, he came from a small town in the Midwest. He had been to Oxford, where he got a Ph.D. in African studies, and he was making it big in international banking."

Mulford wasn't going to hire David. But he told the young Texan two things that made eminent sense. First, he had to master some special discipline that would make him irresistible to banks. Second,

[1] David Mulford became Assistant Secretary of the Treasury for International Affairs under Donald T. Regan and played a key role in the Reagan administration's efforts to resolve the Latin American debt crisis.

he should go to London, where the Eurodollar action was, and polish his credentials by getting a degree from the London School of Economics. David had never heard of the LSE, but he asked around and what he learned made him think it was better suited to turning out left-wing radicals than international bankers. He appreciated, however, that attending the LSE might knock some of the prairie dust off him.

David returned to Texas and within weeks he was making plans to go to London. That summer it seemed like America had gone mad. For security reasons, President Johnson could only make public appearances on military bases, and in the spring Martin Luther King was assassinated. Although he had grown up a Democrat, David was in many ways a political reactionary. He abhorred creeping socialism and took no part in antiwar protests or civil rights demonstrations. He approved of Johnson's decision not to seek reelection. He preferred Robert Kennedy over Senator McCarthy for the Democratic presidential nomination. He came close to tears when he heard on the morning news a few days before leaving for New York that a Palestinian by the name of Sirhan Sirhan has assassinated Robert Kennedy. Sirhan was the same age as David. "I did it for my country," Sirhan had shouted when collared and disarmed. Some country, David thought.

At the beginning of October 1968 David withdrew his savings of $15,000 from the bank, converting it into traveler's checks, packed everything he owned into three suitcases, and bought a one-way ticket to London. Before leaving, he went to say goodbye to his grandmother, Lilly-Bess Tarry. "Mark my words, David," she told him. "You'll travel the world in search of a black orchid. But in the end you'll come home and find it here, right in your own backyard."

Differing opinions exist, but many regard the LSE as the birthplace of modern economics. The alumni included John F. Kennedy, pop star Mick Jagger, U.S. Federal Reserve Board chairman, Paul A. Volcker, and economist Harold Wilson, the Labour Party leader who was three times prime minister during the sixties and seventies. The LSE also gave shelter, as teachers or students, to others like Bertrand Russell, George Bernard Shaw, Professor Lionel Robbins, Professor James E. Meade, and Nobel laureate Friedrich August Hayek. Its academic standards were highly enough rated that some considered a LSE degree as guaranteed achievement in any domain.

Within a week of arriving in London, David registered as a postgraduate and began preparing for a degree, which he never completed. He concentrated on writing a three hundred-page thesis on the

Eurodollar market, calculating that it would give him access to the management of any bank in London. He had, by then, modified his goal. He wanted to become the only American merchant banker in the City, the square mile of London from the Temple law courts to Aldgate, between the Thames and the Barbican, that is centered on the Bank of England and contains the institutions that traditionally have financed British industry and much of the world's trade.

While conducting his research, David met Drew Bockman, a girl from Texas who had gone to undergraduate school at Georgetown and, like David, was following the LSE's external program. She had gotten to know a group of expatriates living at Oxford, including Rhodes scholar Bill Clinton, the future governor of Arkansas, and she introduced David to them. David found Oxford stimulating, and he rented a small apartment in the town while continuing his research on the origins of the Eurodollar.

His research taught him that the honor of creating the first Eurodollars belonged to the Communists. Indirectly, Mao Tse-tung was responsible. As a consequence of Mao's seizing of power in 1949 and founding the People's Republic of China, the U.S. Treasury froze all Chinese assets in American banks. The Russians recognized the dangers to themselves hidden behind this show of American pique and withdrew their dollar balances from New York, lest one day Washington should retaliate against them in similar fashion.

A Belgian banker by the name of Louis Franck noticed that the Russians settled their foreign trade accounts with the dollars they kept on deposit at Moscow Narodny Bank in London. Franck then headed Samuel Montagu & Company, a merchant banking firm known for its bullion dealing, which meant that he was well placed to observe that as soon as the Russians cleared a trade bill through Moscow Narodny, they replenished their supply of dollars by selling bullion on the London gold market. While the dollars sat on deposit at Moscow Narodny, they led an idle existence and played no role in the international capital markets. This, Franck supposed, was also true for other dollar balances that were accumulating outside of the United States in the early 1950s. Franck decided to tap this pool of "Eurodollars" by organizing, in 1963, the first syndicated Euroissue. It was a $20 million Eurobond issue in favor of the Kingdom of Belgium. The market had been waiting for the innovation of just such an instrument. It was an instant success, and the formula devised by Franck was quickly copied by other issuers, beginning a revolution in international finance.

David's first choice for employment became Samuel Montagu &

Company, and once again he solicited Gene Locke's aid. Several years before Locke had tried to interest Louis Franck in a Texas-based mortgage banking business, without success. The two had, however, remained in touch. Now Locke sent the Belgian banker a letter warmly recommending the young Edwards. David also wrote chairman Franck a three-page letter introducing himself and asking for a meeting. After a month there was no response. Irked, David went to the Montagu offices at 114 Old Broad Street, around the corner from the Bank of England, and asked to see the chairman, not realizing that Franck had recently retired and been replaced by David Montagu.

The porter behind the brass doors asked coolly whether the chairman was expecting his visit. "He should be," David replied. The porter rang through to the chairman's office and, when the secretary came on the line, handed the phone to David so that he could introduce himself.

The secretary was polite, but obviously taken aback. "Where are you from, Mr. Edwards?" she asked, meaning which company was he with.

"From the state of Texas, ma'am," David replied with all the pomp he could muster.

"Oh." Pause. "Are you in London for long?" she asked again, flustered.

"Sure am," David answered, to which the secretary volunteered that Mr. Montagu was in Paris and not expected back until late the next morning. "I can give you an appointment for two o'clock tomorrow afternoon. Would that be all right?"

"Fine," said David.

The next day he returned with his three hundred-page study of the Euromarket and a copy of his letter to Mr. Franck, which he presented to David Montagu together with the news that he wanted a job and was not about to take no for an answer.

"I came to London at my own expense," he explained. "I've paid the ante and now I want to play in this game."

David Charles Samuel Montagu, son and heir of the Third Baron Swaythling, an Eton old boy, graduate of Trinity College, Cambridge, and a former Guards officer, was so impressed by the Texan's gumption that he sent him to see two of his directors, Ken Bennett, head of the domestic banking department, and Michael Conolly, a senior member of the international department. Neither was interested in hiring a green young American.

"Why should we train you?" Bennett asked. "You're going to stay around long enough to learn how we do things here, then return home and go to work for some large American bank."

David protested. "No, no, you've got it wrong. I'm here to stay. I plan to live in London for the rest of my life."

David's enthusiasm finally won them over. Samuel Montagu & Company hired him and David started under Bennett in the credit department, where he remained for the first six months; then he spent four months in the foreign exchange trading room. When he stepped through the door of Montagu's trading room, David knew he had found his niche in the bank. "I sort of stuck to the walls, and they couldn't get me out of there," he recalled.

His tour of the bank continued, however, and he was soon assigned to the corporate finance department under another Montagu director, Michael Andrews. Even so, David spent the mornings in the trading room, entering the precious metals and currency transactions into a master ledger. In the 1960s merchant banks were among the biggest dealers in the foreign exchange and precious metals markets, and the mechanics of their trading fascinated David. Montagu's handled most of the Russian bullion selling and was an agent for the Vatican in its extensive foreign exchange operations.

In addition, the bank had its mystery clients, like "Deux Cents," a Polish egg exporter from Paris who was one of the largest private speculators in foreign exchange. David recognized the egg merchant's voice whenever he got him on the trading room phones, because "Deux Cents" spoke in a heavily accented voice and conspiratorial manner. When "Deux Cents" visited the bank he was always shabbily dressed, but he kept kilograms of gold in the Montagu vaults as margin for his trading. "Deux Cents" also dealt through Union Bank of Switzerland, though under another name, until his sudden death in January 1974. Unfortunately for Union Bank, the "Deux Cents" estate proved uncollectible and the big Zurich-based bank admitted losing $50 million when it liquidated "several hundred million dollars" in open positions that the egg merchant had built up just before his death. Montagu's escaped walking on eggshells because it held the gold.

David stayed with Montagu's for two and a half years, of which a little more than one was spent full-time in the trading room. Telerate screens had not yet been introduced, and a junior trader, as David eventually became, was given the job of calling other banks to get their rates. Most of the day David was on the phone to Frankfurt, Hong Kong, New York, or Zurich asking for updates, which he handed to the senior traders. David's workout as a junior trader was not without bumps. Finally, he resigned from Montagu's in early 1972.

David soon learned that Montagu alumni populated the banking world. Months later, half the board of directors resigned, including David Montagu, who became chairman of the newly formed Orion Bank in London. Michael Conolly went to International Westminster Bank. Michael Andrews also left and became managing director at Brandts Limited, a small merchant bank, partly owned by Citibank, which in the mid-1970s dissipated its entire working capital in a series of loan disasters.

On the London cocktail circuit David had met Citibank's senior officer—known as the "senof" in Citispeak—for U.K. operations. Richard Vokey was one of chairman Walter Wriston's bright young protégés. He did an impressive job expanding Citibank's business in Britain during the 1960s and was regarded as hot corporate property at head office until, a decade later, he resisted transfer. This was dimly viewed on the fifteenth floor at 399 Park Avenue and in the early 1970s Vokey resigned to become deputy chairman at Hill, Samuel, another merchant banking house. Whle still London senof, Vokey gave David an introduction to the head of Citibank's International Banking Group in New York. David left Montagu's and London in February 1972. The following month he was hired by Citibank as an executive trainee in the newly formed international money market division. He was given a starting salary of $13,000 per annum, which over the next two years was raised to $32,000.

In 1969, while David was still at Montagu's, First National City Bank of New York, as the Citi was then known, had passed its archrival, the Chase Manhattan, to become the largest bank in New York City, and the second largest in the nation, with assets of $22.8 billion. The Chase had assets of $22.1 billion. As the race between the two giants continued into the 1970s, the Citi progressively widened the gap, acquiring in the process a reputation for luring the brightest recruits by offering top salaries. It was a tough, aggressive environment in which to work, but young Citibankers who made the grade were encouraged to think that they were the élite of an industry.

The International Staff Handbook that David Edwards received when he joined the international money market division described Citibank as "the fastest growing financial organization on the international scene." This growth, it said, was largely due "to the imagination and talents of Citibank staffers."

The foreword to the handbook added: "Granted, Citibank has developed many new ways of doing banking. But other banks have been quick to follow our lead. What makes Citibank different from these other financial institutions—and better—is the staff Citibank employs. Citibank is committed to employing the best people available to do the job that must be done.''

Citibank was founded in 1812 as The City Bank of New York. After 1865 it adopted the name of National City Bank of New York and rose rapidly to become, toward the end of the century, the largest bank in the United States. National City began its international vocation in 1914, when it opened the first overseas branch of any nationally chartered U.S. bank, in Buenos Aires. The following year it opened branches in Rio de Janeiro, Montevideo, São Paulo, and Havana. In the twenties, its overseas expansion progressed rapidly under the aggressive, tub-thumping management of chairman Charles E. Mitchell. The bank, through its affiliated National City Company, engaged in high-pressure selling of stocks, many of which went to a fraction of their par value in the Great Crash of 1929. Mitchell was pilloried by the Senate Banking and Currency Committee as the banker who did most to bring on the Great Crash. He was forced to resign from National City in 1933 and was indicted for tax fraud, though later acquitted.

Mitchell's reputation as one of the architects of the 1929 bust dogged the bank for years afterward. But having limped through the thirties, National City entered the postwar period a sleeping giant, its name tarnished, no longer the nation's number-one bank, but its financial position sound and its world network of branches largely intact and open for business.

In 1946, Walter B. Wriston, five years out of Wesleyan University and a master of international law from Fletcher School of Law and Diplomacy at Tufts University, became a junior inspector at National City. In 1956, after the merger with First National Bank of New York, Wriston became head of the combined First National City's European division, which then consisted of branches in London, Paris, and Frankfurt. In 1959, under the chairmanship of James Stillman Rockefeller, Wriston was put in charge of the entire overseas division. He was appointed president in 1967, when his mentor, George S. Moore, left that position to take over from Rockefeller as chairman. Wriston succeeded Moore as chairman in 1970.

Wriston made Citibank the world's largest bank. In the process, he became the premier American banker. One of his first steps was to centralize under one profit center the bank's worldwide foreign exchange and money market operations, which were, by the nature of currency swaps and interest-rate differentials, two closely related activities.

The new profit center was called the international money market division (IMMD). The IMMD was part of the treasury division, although under Citibank's "matrix" system of management, which shaped the Citi structure of the 1970s, operational control was run through the international banking group (IBG), which was responsible for managing the foreign branch network, then consisting of 300 offices in 60 countries. IBG accounted for 60 percent of the institution's net income.

The person designated to run the IMMD was a veteran overseas divisionnaire with the aristocratic-sounding name of Freeman H. Huntington. Free, as his colleagues called him, began as an office boy at National City Bank in the Depression, married the typist at one of the branches where he served, and worked his way through the ranks to command the largest branch in Brazil, at Sao Paolo. Recalled to head office, Free was promoted to senior vice-president.

By the time David Edwards joined the IMMD, First National City Bank's assets had increased to $42.5 billion. Deposits totaled $34.9 billion, and loans outstanding were $26.6 billion. It had 32,000 employees and more financial resources at its disposal than the monetary reserves of a score of smaller nations. Three years later it would officially contract its name to Citibank, after its parent holding company, Citicorp, incorporated in the state of Delaware.

Huntington put David to work with Paolo Cugnasca, a trader brought in from the Milan branch to develop a centralized funding section for Eurocurrency loans. The Cugnasca section became known as the Eurocurrency department. In fact it was a desk at head office to which Bahamian extraterritorial status was unofficially assigned. Huntington's IMMD now proposed that European branches use this "Nassau desk," even though it was located in New York, as a booking center for Eurocurrency loans. In practical terms, if the Citibank branch in Frankfurt had a client who needed a French franc loan, the Citibank treasury in Frankfurt would fund the loan by borrowing the francs in the interbank money market out of London. The francs could be delivered anywhere and did not need to be cycled through Frankfurt, where the transaction would be taxable.

This service offered a double attraction. First, revenues earned on loans booked through the Nassau desk escaped all taxation, as no taxes are collected in the Bahamas. Second, the deposits used to fund such loans avoided reserve requirements and liquidity ratios traditionally imposed by central banks to ensure that commercial banks under their jurisdiction have adequate cash at hand to meet their obligations. European central banks and the U.S. Federal Reserve require the commercial banks they regulate to "freeze" a percentage of their deposits—in the case of the U.S. Federal Reserve, 12 percent of demand deposits and 3 percent of longer-term deposits—in a safe-keeping account that can only be unfrozen as customers withdraw their deposits. In the Bahamas, however, no deposit reserves exist for offshore money and no liquidity ratios are required.

Within months, $2.5 billion in "nonresident" European loans were shifted to the Bahamas, via the Nassau desk. The borrowers, lenders, and financial intermediaries were spread through many jurisdictions, so the question of where the loans should have been booked was debatable.

In the autumn of 1972, Freeman Huntington sent David on a European tour to teach the branches overseas how to book their loans through Nassau and still credit themselves with the business. David enjoyed having his own "dog and pony show," flying everywhere first-class. But in the midst of his triumph the market circumstances changed drastically.

In March 1973, the monetary system fell apart. The dollar was officially devalued for the second time in two years, and floating exchange rates were introduced. Senior management assumed that the finance officers of the bank's 480 multinational corporate clients—the heavy profit-earners—would need professional counseling to cope with unstable exchange rates. Hedging of currency exposures was not yet within the normal skills of most corporate treasurers.

Citibank set up a corporate counseling department within the IMMD. David was transferred to the new department. His boss, vice-president John S. Barnett, devised an "international finance and hedging model" with which to wow corporate customers. His idea was that corporate customers would feed information into the model and get back an analysis of their problems with a recommendation for solving them. They would also receive foreign exchange forecasts and information on new foreign exchange regulations as and when central banks introduced them. The scheduled kick-off date for the new program was December 1973, and David was told to go out and sell it.

Barnett couldn't stand David. He gave him a scathing personnel review. David asked Huntington to transfer him out of Barnett's department. "We had a personality clash and couldn't get along," he said. He told Huntington he wanted to become a foreign exchange trader.

"I want to go into a trading room in order to fully comprehend the, if you wish, discipline of money-market management," he explained.

Huntington consented to transfer David to Paris with the understanding that if things worked out, after a year or eighteen months David would be made the treasurer of another Citibank branch and given his own trading room to run. This was exactly what David wanted.

Treasury is the heart of a bank. To quote from a Citibank document, "The Treasury is responsible for the funding, money market and foreign exchange operations of Citicorp activities in each country."[2] If short of liquidity, the branch's treasury must go into the money market and borrow. But if the branch has excess liquidity, treasury is responsible for placing it in the market at the best available rate of interest. The foreign exchange department is part of treasury. If the Paris branch needs Deutsche marks to lend a client with business in Germany, treasury must buy or borrow those Deutsche marks to fund the loan. If treasury buys them, it is a foreign exchange operation. If treasury borrows them, it is a money market transaction. In either case, the bank ends up with a foreign currency risk. Treasury is responsible for deciding whether or not to "cover" the exchange risk by completing a compensating operation in the forward market. Running the treasury is a complex art and one of the least understood in banking.

Citibank opened its branch in Paris during World War I. But Citibank never managed to gain a real foothold in the French market. In 1973, the Paris branch ran into serious problems. Head office's answer, a year later, was to throw men and money into the breach, hoping that the added resources would produce the desired effect. David Edwards, an added resource, joined the Paris task force in November 1974.

[2]Citibank document 3573: Institutional Reporting Requirements, April 1974.

Chapter 2
Les Cambistes

*There is no quicker way to make a trader take
unreasonable risks than to make him feel that he has to
produce a given profit.*

—FREEMAN H. HUNTINGTON, SENIOR VICE-PRESIDENT,
CITIBANK N.A., MARCH 17, 1977

Citibank's offices at 60 Champs Elysées were a monument to the halcyon days of Charles E. Mitchell. Intended as the Continental headquarters of National City, construction of the six-story building began in 1929, as stock markets were soaring, and finished in 1933, during the depth of the Depression. It had monumental bronze doors, a marble banking hall, and a grand staircase leading to the executive offices, operations platform, and trading room on the second floor. The building was imposing and so well situated that in 1940 the Nazis requisitioned it as the Paris headquarters of their Propaganda Ministry.[1]

In April 1974, a new senior officer, Charles Bellamy Young, was

[1]Citibank sold its building on the Champs Elysées in April 1978 but continued to occupy the premises for another five years until moving, in 1983, to a new Citicenter at La Défense, the huge commercial and business complex to the north of Paris.

sent to replace the existing area chief. Young, a thirty-three-year-old vice-president, arrived in the French capital as part of what Citibank insiders termed an "accordion move," a phenomenon that from time to time rippled through the bank's worldwide management structure. Accordion moves sometimes took months to unravel. Part of the 1974 series sent the Paris head of treasury, Jean-Claude Coulon, to Johannesburg, which for a foreign exchange manager was like being sent to Siberia. Head office left Young the task of finding a successor for Coulon.

Jean-Michel Ennuyer, who had been the chief trader under Coulon, was a logical choice for the head of treasury. But Ennuyer, who fully expected the promotion, had a major drawback. He tended to treat his dealing limits lightly.[2] The Paris trading room was notorious in the Citibank network for its lax controls. Under Coulon there had been a breakdown in record-keeping procedures, particularly in the liability ledgers, and Paris had lost money in its foreign exchange trading in 1973. A major target of the 1974 shake-up was to upgrade the Paris treasury staff. And so another note in the accordion shuffle was the transfer to Paris that June of the chief trader from Citibank's branch in Antwerp, a Belgian by the name of Jean-Pierre de Laet.

Young got on well with de Laet. The Belgian was more diplomatic and less excitable than Ennuyer. Young promoted de Laet to the head of treasury over Ennuyer.

Ennuyer, who remained chief trader, thoroughly disliked de Laet. Born in the ex-Belgian Congo, now Zaire, of modest parents, de Laet became a clerk at Citibank in 1967, quickly working his way into the retail exchange department. To earn extra cash before being promoted to the currency trading department, he moonlighted as a door-to-door insurance salesman in the evenings. He was, according to Ennuyer, insecure, stubborn, and not too smart, with no respect for bank or customer. But he was a first-rate trader, although he only had one specialty, and that was selling the dollar.

"He would sell, sell, sell when the dollar was going down, but was nowhere to be found when the dollar started going up," Ennuyer remarked.

Late one afternoon, Jean-Michel was closing the books for the day when he noticed that de Laet had a large open position against the dollar. The dollar was strong that afternoon, rising against the French

---

[2] Notes of Arthur G. Natvig, vice-president, comptroller's division, Paris, February 5, 1975; Citibank document 4680.

franc. Ennuyer tried to reach de Laet for instructions, but couldn't find him. A six-figure loss was in the cards if the trend continued; only a small one if he sold the position immediately. He elected to sell, recording it in the daily trading ledger. Next morning when de Laet found out, he had the loss entered onto Jean-Michel's dealing blotter. Ennuyer was furious.

This was the atmosphere David Edwards found when he joined the Paris trading-room staff in mid-November 1974. Huntington had promoted him to senior assistant manager and he qualified for a special overseas living allowance, which in practical terms meant he could bank his salary and still live like a prince on the allowance. The personnel office found him an apartment on the Left Bank, near the Eiffel Tower, and the prospect of an American bachelor living in the French capital with a pocketful of money and a rising career made David feel he had a corner on the best of all worlds.

The stress in the trading room had been particularly heavy that summer. The West was in the deepest recession since World War II. The foreign exchange market, after a year of coping with floating exchange rates, experienced one of its worst upheavals. The oil exporting countries had quadrupled the price of their crude and were building up a record surplus of $68 billion for the year. Before these petrodollars could be recycled, a major liquidity crisis, marked by soaring interest rates, brought about the collapse of a string of European and American banks owned or controlled by Italian financier Michele Sindona.

The first shock came in May 1974, when Franklin National Bank of New York, at the time the nation's nineteenth largest, disclosed it was having treasury problems. Franklin, which was the centerpiece of Sindona's American empire, reported foreign exchange losses of $60 million for the first five months of that year and was uncertain whether it could stay afloat long enough to unwind the rest of its forward contracts. Finally, in September 1974, the Federal Reserve Bank of New York stepped in and took over the outstanding portion of Franklin's foreign exchange book, which totalled $800 million. Two weeks later Franklin became the biggest banking bust in U.S. history.

Before Franklin expired, on June 24, 1974, Bankhaus I.D. Herstatt, West Germany's largest private bank, collapsed. Herstatt's foreign exchange losses were estimated at $522 million. Its failure almost brought foreign exchange trading to a standstill. In many countries, government reaction was to increase supervision of foreign exchange activity. The object was to curtail speculative forward dealing by imposing new statutory limits on the banks. The limits were expressed either as a percentage of capital and reserves or in absolute terms by requiring banks to "square"—i.e., cover—their open positions at the end of each trading day.

Charles Young was ambitious. He had previously been part of a small financial control unit at head office that prepared performance analyses for the bank's two senior officers, chairman Walter B. Wriston and president William I. Spencer. As Young explained, this gave him exposure at the highest level and also showed him how top management worked. He realized that his performance as senof in Paris would be judged on the turnaround in revenues he could produce.

Young consulted his executive team and decided that the Paris trading room should earn $250,000 each month—$3 million per annum.[3] Young counted on his treasury for up to 50 percent of the branch's total earnings. As Young was facing Wriston's blunderbuss if he failed to perform, he had no reservation about putting others who worked under him in the same field of fire, although in foreign exchange this was a chancy proposition.

De Laet had a staff of ten traders working under him. During normal days they handled about one hundred transactions, which meant that they fielded or initiated perhaps a thousand phone calls and telex transmissions with other dealers around the world.

Foreign exchange traders belong to a narrow fraternity. There are not more than four thousand of them in the world. Few outsiders understand their business, and none is permitted to penetrate their inner circle, the International Forex Association.

Trading tends to begin slowly around the start of public banking hours and peaks in mid-afternoon. When the market really heats up, the trading room is filled with the tension of split-second decisions. To suit the speed of their dealing, traders use a jargon of their own— for example, dollar deposits are "dollie-deps," Swiss francs are "Swissies," and a three-day currency swap is referred to as "spotnext."

Traders can lose several hundred thousand dollars by miscalculating a change in the rates by a few "pips." Therefore they are generally agile young men with high IQs, and because it is such a nerve-grinding business, a trader is considered "old" at forty; most end up with back office or supervisory jobs long before they are fifty. In their prime, according to Wriston, the best are "like lions in a den." They

[3]Citibank document 4682.

deal routinely in eight-figure amounts and commit their banks to risks that most vice-presidents with twenty years more service have no authority to handle.

De Laet, when he arrived from Antwerp, inherited overnight position limits ranging from $1 million when dealing Italian lire against French francs to $10 million when dealing U.S. dollars against French francs, and an overnight limit for all currencies combined of $35 million.[4]

Position trading limits—the so-called "overnight limits"—set by head office for each respective branch were often in conflict with the policies of local central banks which sought to dampen or stop altogether foreign exchange speculation. The Bank of France, for example, did not permit *any* overnight positions to be held against the French franc. Therefore, if de Laet wanted to keep a speculative position against the French franc for longer than his daylight trading hours, he had to find a way to off-book the open position, either at another Citibank branch or with a "friendly" bank in another country.

De Laet was annoyed at having David Edwards injected into his domain. But as Edwards was evidently close to Huntington, de Laet had to tolerate his presence. So he put Edwards to work on the dollar-French franc desk, also known as the dollar/Paris desk.

From his time at Montagu's, David appreciated the peculiarities of interbank dealing. A trader whose rates are solicited by another bank never knows whether the counterparty, if in the money market, is a borrower or lender of funds, or, if in the foreign exchange market, a buyer or seller of currency. Convention requires that when solicited for a quote, a trader must announce *both* his bid and offered rates simultaneously. Convention also requires him to deal if the counterparty accepts one or other of the quoted rates. Therefore, understanding the psychology of the marketplace and the mindset of the counterparty is important.

Deals are usually concluded in increments of $5 million, by telephone or telex, within a matter of seconds. A typical "spot" transaction done over the telephone might sound as follows: Jean-Michel Ennuyer, chief trader at Citibank Paris, wants to sell dollars for Deutsche marks. He dials the Morgan Guaranty trading room in New York, where the call is answered by Fred. Jean-Michel has never met Fred, but he has dealt with him a thousand times over the phone and recognizes his voice.

---

[4]Recommended 1975 Foreign Exchange & Liquidity Limits for France; Citibank document 4702.

> JEAN-MICHEL: Hi there, pal! CitiParis here. What's spot dollar/mark?
> FRED: 25/30.

This means to Jean-Michel that Morgan Guaranty will buy dollars at DM 2.7125, the so-called bid rate, or sell them for marks at DM 2.7130, the offered rate. However Fred has only given Jean-Michel the "tics"—also called "pips"—which are the thousandths of a decimal point, leaving off the 2.71, which is referred to as the "big figure." Fred still does not know if Jean-Michel is a buyer or a seller.

> Jean-Michel: I give you 10 at 25.

This indicates that Jean-Michel likes the DM 2.7125 bid rate and sells Fred $10 million for marks.

> FRED: Okay, my friend, Done.
> JEAN-MICHEL: Thanks pal. Frankfurt my marks.
> FRED: My dollars myself.

The deal concluded, they hang up. Each trader quickly enters the trade on his desktop "blotter," a sheet with his running position on it, and then writes up a "ticket," which means filling in a printed form outlining the transaction for his back office, so that it can send out a confirmation and transfer the funds.

By "Frankfurt my marks," Jean-Michel was telling Fred to send DM 27,125,000 to the Citibank Paris account at Citibank Frankfurt, and by "dollars myself" Fred was saying transfer the $10 million to Morgan Guaranty in New York. As it was a "spot" transaction, the "value date" for delivery of the funds was in two days' time.

If trading were slow and Jean-Michel not under pressure, he might have engaged Fred in some small talk to find out what the Morgan Guaranty trader thought of the market, thereby extracting extra intelligence from him, or, alternately, he might have fed Fred some clues—real or false—as to his trading position. The lottery aspect of foreign exchange dealing was underlined by the fact that many traders also made a side-book over the telephone on their favorite sporting events, such as rugby matches, the Tour de France cyclist race, World Cup soccer, or international ice hockey championships. This unofficial bookmaking ceased in the later 1970s, however, when some traders ended up owing more than $100,000 to the pool and couldn't pay.

While it was clear to Jean-Michel that David had little practical experience as a trader, he was impressed by the Texan's talents as a showman. These were apparent when Jean-Michel visited head office in 1973 and met David for the first time. David had invited Jean-Michel, a stranger to New York, back to his West Side apartment for drinks.

Jean-Michel remembered David making three phone calls during the hour they spent there. The first was to Texas to check on an oil-drilling venture. He made the second to a friend who was a foreign exchange trader in Tokyo, to see how the dollar was doing in tomorrow's market, fourteen time zones away. The third was to Brazil to inquire about a million-dollar commodity deal.

Impressive, Ennuyer concluded of David's telephone posturing. David had a flair for the dramatic and a good sense of timing, which underlined the Frenchman's feeling that here was a rising star in the Citi galaxy. David, ten years later, could not remember the event and, to underline his skepticism, said he had never telephoned Brazil in his life.

Ennuyer, a tall, angular young man with dark hair, thick glasses, and a perpetually agitated manner, was two years older than David. He spoke machine-gun English with a Maurice Chevalier accent and, like most *cambistes,* was highly articulate and complex of character.

Edwards was, in many respects, his opposite. Blonde, slate-eyed, he was, at an even six feet, not quite as tall as Ennuyer. After three months laboring at it, he spoke French with an atrocious American accent which, to his credit, he was constantly seeking to improve.

In spite of their opposing cultures, Jean-Michel and David got on well together. Politically, they were both conservatives, or at least antisocialist. And they were both gamblers, with the throb of the marketplace in their veins.

Jean-Michel had studied economics at the Institute of High Commercial Studies on the boulevard Malesherbes in the center of Paris. He was an avid reader of philosophy, preferring the works of Hegel, a student of military strategy (Karl von Clausewitz and Napoleon), and a lover of Marcel Proust, the turn-of-the-century writer whom Ennuyer considered to be France's greatest novelist. His credentials meant that he had no difficulty in landing a job as a foreign exchange clerk at Société Genérale, France's third largest bank. He joined Citibank in 1970 as a trainee under Jean-Claude Coulon.

Coulon was convinced that one day Ennuyer would make a great trader. To give him experience, he sent Jean-Michel with his wife to Milan for two months to work under Francesco Redi, the treasury head of Citibank's Milan branch. Redi teamed him up with another young trader, Paolo Cugnasca, who had not yet been transferred to New York, and the two became fast friends.

"He taught me the business," Jean-Michel said of Cugnasca. "He's quite a guy: super-smart and super-cynical."

David had also become good friends with Cugnasca when they worked on the Nassau desk. Paolo, he agreed, was an excellent teacher.

After David had been in Paris a few months, Jean-Michel was closing the books one afternoon when the trading room clerk informed him that they were long $10 million. Jean-Michel was astounded. The dollar was under pressure and weakening by the minute. He checked with David, who had been speaking with Freeman Huntington in New York that day. David said Free had told him to buy the dollar.

"So he did," Jean-Michel said. "It was a disaster."

David recalled another trading blunder. The Citibank trader in the foreign exchange pit at the Paris Bourse called him one afternoon to report that the dollar was sinking. "Aw shit," David said, more to himself than the pitman, and slammed down the phone. At the close of trading, the pitman called back to confirm he had bought dollars.

"You did what?" David shouted.

"But you said *achète* (buy)," affirmed the pitman.

That evening David walked into Chuck Young's office and said, "I've got a funny story to tell you, but it's going to cost a quarter of a million dollars to hear."

Young heard the story, but he was not amused.

Chapter 3

The "Inspector-General"

You can't win in this game unless you get the whole team in there . . .

—WALTER B. WRISTON, AS QUOTED IN *Euromoney*, OCTOBER 1983

The Paris trading room was located on the second floor at 60 Champs Elysées. It was a drab, L-shaped room, next to the operations platform, a large, open area for about thirty credit officers and administrative staff. Access was from the platform, through the short end of the reversed L, where four domestic money-market traders manned a cluster of desks, each with a push-button switchboard, called a *tableau de change*, on top of it.

Jean-Pierre de Laet's office was off to the left of the money-market section so that he could keep an eye on traffic through the room. The main part of the room, where four foreign exchange traders and four deposit dealers had their desks and switchboards, was around to the left and formed the back of the reversed L. It was twenty feet wide and thirty feet long, with a bank of telex machines along the right wall. The far end of the room was a panel of ceiling-to-floor windows

that gave onto the rue de la Boétie, a side street off the Champs Elysées. In spite of the windows, the room was stuffy, with a pall of cig-
arette smoke clinging to the ceiling.

As the chief trader, Jean-Michel Ennuyer had his desk in the center
of the room. David Edwards was given a chair next to Pierre Lasseur,
a spot currency trader. David spent his first several weeks in the Paris
trading room struggling with French, noting words and expressions
in a leatherbound exercise book, while he sat at Lasseur's elbow,
watching him trade.

"I was sort of a privileged person in the room. I was not one of
de Laet's employees, and because I couldn't speak the language, I
wasn't a threat to anyone," he said.

David's transfer to Paris meant that his career path was on an upward track. He was confident, even, that he had reached the fringe of
"corporate property," a reservoir of talent from which candidates for
fifteenth-floor status at 399 Park Avenue were chosen.

"I really had no boss in Paris and could do pretty much what I
liked," he explained. Of course, he was learning to manage a treasury operation. All this entailed, really, was sitting there for eighteen
months without making waves, and if Huntington kept his word, at
the end of this formative period he would be promoted to vice-president and given his own treasury to run, hopefully someplace like Singapore or Rio de Janeiro.

One of Huntington's tasks as head of the IMMD was to create a
career path for American university graduates that would take them
through the trading room to senior management levels. It was a source
of uneasiness at head office that the top currency trading positions in
the overseas network were held by foreigners. While it was acknowledged that foreigners had a flair for currency trading, they were, in
some general way, perceived to be cast from less certain metal.

The bank's crusty old-guard comptroller, Bernard T. Stott, who retired in 1973, had voiced concern that some foreign traders were
downright sneaky. One in particular had entered Citibank legend for
exceeding his trading limits by more than a billion dollars. His name
was Carlo Bordoni. He came to Citibank with the highest credentials
and was made a manager of the newly opened Milan branch in 1963.
When his unauthorized dealings were uncovered a year later, it took
a team of internal auditors and foreign exchange experts several months
to unravel them. In fact, Bernie Stott was never fully certain that the
bank didn't lose money as a result of the Bordoni caper. But Bordoni, described by one of Stott's inspectors as a "slippery genius,"

did not want to rip off the bank for personal gain. He was "only" trying to corner one part of the Eurodollar market, which was still a fledgling affair in the mid-1960s. "It was pure megalomania," the inspector commented.

Bordoni left Citibank in December 1964 and went on to even greater excesses. He opened his own money-broking firm in Milan for a while, then worked for the rising financier Sindona as general manager of Banca Unione, building that Milan bank's foreign exchange department into one of the biggest players in the game before its collapse in 1974. Bordoni helped Sindona plot the 1972 acquisition, through a Liechtenstein holding company, of Franklin National Bank. When Wriston, visiting London at the time, learned that Bordoni had been named a director of Franklin New York, he cabled Jack Conlin, Citibank's chief foreign exchange trader in New York, with instructions to cease dealing with Franklin. Placing Franklin National on a stoplist probably saved Citibank from trouble two years later, when the Sindona empire collapsed.

Wanting to train American talent for the bank's trading rooms around the world was well and fine, but Huntington found that few American university graduates had the patience or aptitude needed to make an accomplished foreign exchange trader. David Edwards was an exception. Unfortunately, Edwards quickly realized he had been, in his words, "dealt a bad hand" by drawing a posting to Paris. It had a reputation for being a sloppy place, the "junk pile" of the European network.

Edwards regarded Jean-Pierre de Laet as "a good mechanic," and said he was "the fastest arbitrageur I ever saw." He observed that de Laet spent a lot of time in the side office speaking on the phone in Flemish to his Belgian broker, Jan Debeuckelaer. Moreover, de Laet was abrasive and filled with "little-guy complexes."

"Anybody six feet tall didn't bother with them. I mean, it was hard for me to get personally upset about Jean-Pierre. He was five-foot-four and wore lifts. He came to work in brown suits and pink polyester shirts. I had no ego problem with him," Edwards remarked.

Six months after taking over the treasury in Paris, de Laet had a rebellion on his hands. In early 1975, speculation spread through the trading room that de Laet dealt almost exclusively with two foreign exchange and money market brokers because they were kicking back a share of their commissions to him.

Edwards watched carefully how de Laet traded. One day while de Laet was punching out a telex to one of the brokers, Edwards noticed that de Laet's bid rate for a Eurodollar placement was a sixteenth of a point higher than the market rate. This indicated to David that de Laet was offering the broker a sweetheart deal to increase his kickback revenue.

The same month that Edwards moved to Paris, Huntington organized in London a two-day conference of European treasury heads. Such meetings were usually held twice annually and they afforded Citibank's senior foreign exchange traders an opportunity to compare notes about operating procedures and regulatory controls.

Participants at the November 1974 conference included Ernst W. Brutsche, vice-president in London; Edgar A. Giger, vice-president in Zurich; Fritz Menzel, vice-president in Frankfurt; and Francesco Redi, vice-president in Milan. These four were the acknowledged stars of Huntington's team of foreign exchange traders, with Brutsche and Giger the two outstanding among them. Giger had the largest overnight dealing limit of any Citibank trader. It was $75 million, compared to $65 million for Menzel, $30 million for Brutsche, and $20 million for Redi. Also present was Jean-Pierre de Laet, newly promoted from manager to regional vice-president.

The agenda included a review of dealing limits, the installing of a high-speed data-transmission system between the European branches and head office, and a discussion of new foreign exchange reports requested by the U.S. Treasury.

The London meeting was also attended by Citibank's "inspector-general" of foreign exchange accounting, Arthur G. Natvig. A vice-president in the comptroller's division, Natvig was then only eighteen months from retirement. He had been sent to London by the new chief comptroller, Stephen C. Eyre, as a prologue to a special audit of European treasury operations, which was then being planned. Eyre, at the prompting of Wriston, wanted to make sure that Citibank was committing none of the excesses that caused the collapse of Franklin National Bank and Bankhaus I.D. Herstatt.

In the wake of the Franklin and Herstatt disasters, the U.S. Treasury wanted to improve its monitoring of the foreign exchange market. A letter explaining the new monitoring directives was sent to the chief executive officers of banks across the country. In due course Wriston received such a letter, together with a questionnaire on Citibank's dealing procedures.

Wriston, it was said at the conference, considered the new requirements another intrusion by government into the affairs of commercial banks, and he was in favor of ignoring them. He already regarded the banking industry as overregulated.

"We have gone back to the Fed to see if we can't avoid this," Huntington told the conference. But the prospects for changing the rules, he said, were not promising. Natvig thought the bank should comply, as it was preferable "to avoid troubles with Washington on an issue we cannot win, especially as there are new people—perhaps not entirely compatible yet—on the committees there just now."[1]

Natvig kept a business diary everywhere he went, typing his notes on a portable typewriter and annotating them with his meticulous handwriting. The fact that he kept such a complete diary was perhaps the only failing of this otherwise model corporate personality.

From Crown Heights in Brooklyn, Natvig had joined National City Bank in 1931, straight out of high school. He started as a clerk, going to Brooklyn College at night to learn accounting. After serving in the U.S. Army and the Merchant Marine during World War II, he returned to Citibank, becoming an inspector, which kept him on the road.

A bachelor, in a sense Natvig had married the bank, living out of a suitcase as he traveled around the world, springing surprise audits on branches from Amsterdam to Tokyo, stopping along the way in places like Bahrain, Sao Paolo, and Kuala Lumpur.

Physically, he was bland, with fair hair, blue eyes, and glasses, and of medium height. But his ferreting mind suited the job. Foreign exchange fascinated him and he probed every aspect of it, enjoying himself like a kid in a sandbox in spite of his sixty years. His health a problem, he asked to be seconded on the projected survey of European treasuries by Edwin L. Pomeroy, an assistant comptroller who became his dauphin.

Pomeroy was an Englishman. Shortish and stout, though by no means portly, like Natvig he was a bachelor and when asked his place of residence, replied, "Of no fixed address," because he too lived from a suitcase.

Natvig enjoyed his role as diarist. At the November 1974 conference, the finance division complained that collecting the data for the U.S. Treasury reports would cost $500,000 a year. Considering that the bank was taking in foreign exchange profits of between $6 million and $7 million a month in the second half of 1974,[2] Natvig thought a half-million-dollar annual expense was small change. He also found it astounding that after Herstatt, with the dollar under new pressure,

---

[1] Arthur Natvig's notes, New Report to Treasury on Foreign Exchange, FHH, November 12, 1974 (London Treasurers' Conference); Citibank document 3034.
[2] Arthur Natvig's notes; Citibank document 3029.

Citibank traders were making record foreign exchange profits.

As Huntington was exhorting his treasury heads to be more aggressive, Charles Coombs, the chief foreign exchange expert of the Federal Reserve System, was expressing his concern to the Federal Reserve's open market committee that "disorderly conditions" in the exchange market were weakening the financial system and damaging world trade.[3]

The open market committee, which consists of the seven Federal Reserve governors, the president of the Federal Reserve Bank of New York, and four additional members rotated from among the presidents of the other eleven Federal Reserve banks, determines the flow of credit in the United States. In 1962, the open market committee was also entrusted by the U.S. Treasury with protecting the dollar from excessive exchange-rate fluctuations, a task that became increasingly difficult under a floating-rate regime.

Exchange rates are the linchpin of the financial system. Although few people give them much thought, in times of peace they are *the* central factor determining whether there is prosperity or recession. They set the price at which goods and services are exchanged between nations. They determine how the assets and liabilities of a country are valued and how international claims and debts are measured.

Stable but flexible exchange rates are a prerequisite for economic growth and expanding world trade. Big banks, however, make big money in volatile foreign exchange markets. Citibank, the world's largest foreign exchange dealer, was a dramatic example. Nineteen seventy four's disorderly markets provided Citibank with unprecedented foreign exchange earnings of $79 million. For Citibank, earnings of this magnitude more than compensated for a U.S. inflation rate of 9.4 percent and a dollar that declined during the year against all major currencies except the yen and the lire.[4]

The last item to be discussed at the November 1974 conference was "Parking Foreign Exchange Positions."

Natvig's notes mentioned that "increasing regulatory restrictions . . . make it necessary for us to do more 'parking' of positions. . . .

"Switzerland is already 'parking' in Nassau for some weeks. We (and in particular to the statutory auditor PMF) should avoid discuss-

[3] Robert Solomon, *The International Monetary System, 1945–1981*, (New York: Harper & Row), 1982, p. 341.

[4] Changes in Output and Prices, 1963–79; Table 1, page 8, International Monetary Fund Annual Report 1980; and International Financial Statistics, 1978, published by International Monetary Fund, Washington.

ing this with anyone outside the Bank because it will be thought that we have an advantage over the Swiss banks or in some way are 'getting by' on our small capital in Switzerland.

"There is some problem as to where to take profits, as obviously we have some choice and prefer to take them in a low-tax point, but have to consider legal and statutory requirements. Huntington will discuss with tax counsel in NY. A system will be worked out to permit the European branches to park in Head Office. It can then be decided whether or not it will really be at Head Office or in Nassau. . . ."[5]

The PMF referred to Peat Marwick Fides, the Swiss affiliate of Peat Marwick Mitchell, the biggest of the big eight international accounting firms. Peat Marwick was Citibank's independent auditor, and Peat Marwick's Swiss affiliate acted as the statutory auditor of the bank's Swiss operations with a dual reporting responsibility to the bank and the Swiss banking authority.

This was not the first mention of parking inside Citibank, although it was the first that Natvig, ill with cancer and just out of the hospital, had heard of the concept. Parking had been discussed at a previous treasury conference in New York the year before. Milan had parked since the late 1960s so that its foreign exchange book would conform with the figures it reported to the Italian authorities. Zurich started parking after Milan, probably in 1972, and not "some weeks ago," as Natvig believed.

While Natvig didn't like parking, he had to tread lightly. He was conscious of being a team player. Pulling together as a team was a frequently repeated theme of Citi life. It was regarded as the essence of competitiveness and success. Team spirit was frequently stressed in internal publications. When a vice-president of the finance division sent a circular to division heads and senofs describing "Matrix Allocations," typed in capital letters at the bottom of the first page was the reminder that GLOBAL ESTEEM IS EARNED AS A TEAM.[6]

From Natvig's notes and subsequent reports, it was clear that knowledge of parking was to be restricted to a few team members. And this worried Natvig. He feared that keeping something secret from some team members and not others would breed suspicion, even threat of blackmail. He later pointed this out, but to no avail.

After the London conference, Natvig returned to New York with a

[5] Arthur Natvig's notes, "Parking" or "Selling" our Positions Abroad (London Conference), November 13, 1974; Citibank document 2191.
[6] Citibank document 2999.

suitcase full of notes. He went to see Stephen Eyre to discuss the format of the special audit of European treasuries that Eyre wanted done. The comptroller had assigned Natvig the project not only because he was the bank's specialist in foreign exchange accounting, but also because he got along well with the treasury heads, the people he was supposed to police. He was interested in their problems and they talked freely with him.

Natvig was modest about his skills. In a memo to a vice-president in the finance division, he wrote: "Something more basic than just modesty makes me chary of being referred to as an expert in foreign exchange. . . . I would much prefer to be characterized as someone with an abiding and continuing interest in exchange accounting and, I hope, with an understanding of the risks—which I think must be adequately reflected by our exchange accounting system."

The vice-president had asked Natvig for his view on whether Citibank should "breakout"—i.e., identify more clearly—in the financial statements its foreign exchange trading profits. Natvig's answer was no.

He concluded: "I feel it would be useful to avoid [publishing] too much detail on exchange earnings. Can you imagine the glee with which *The New York Times* would editorialize (and how impossible it would be to rebut effectively) if it should find Citibank taking a position against the dollar in times of stress?"[7]

When Eyre wanted to be primed for the 1975 annual general meeting of shareholders, he asked Natvig to prepare answers for the more probable questions on foreign exchange he might have to face. Natvig's efforts to capture the spirit of what Eyre wanted demonstrated the degree of schizophrenia that reigned inside the bank on this important issue. Here are some excerpts:

"Speculation?
"Nobody knows quite what speculation means in exchange trading. If you mean do we take substantial positions, the answer is yes. If you mean do we take positions without giving full consideration to the risks as we see them, the answer is no."

The institutional aim in a public forum was to play down the speculative aspect of currency trading and build up the commercial aspect

---

[7]Natvig memorandum to James M. Hoppe, vice-president, finance division, re: Public Reporting of Foreign Exchange Trading Profits, May 26, 1974; Citibank document 3025–3028.

of the business. But if the question of whether the bank should be taking positions for its own account arose, Natvig proposed to meet it head on. He coached Eyre to reply:

"If a bank avoids taking positions it merely drops out of the market, deferring to other banks willing to take on this function."

And if asked, "Do we ever take positions against the U.S. dollar?" Natvig thought Eyre should reply:

"We are basically a dollar bank with dollar capital and a dollar balance sheet: and a strong sound dollar is in our interest. But if we anticipate a fall in the value of the dollar, we could not prevent it from falling by taking long dollar positions in our overseas branches. You have to remember that a currency rises or falls in the exchange market on its own strengths and weaknesses (purchasing power, stability, interest rates, etc.), and that while positions taken by the banks have a *stabilizing* influence on the timing and rapidity of changes, they neither cause nor prevent changes in the rates over the long term."[8]

As Edwards later pointed out, Natvig's replies suggested a skillful blending of fact and wishful thinking. Citibank's trading policy was not to *stabilize* the market but to make profits, and Citibank, which controlled as much as ten percent of the foreign exchange trading on any given day, was bound to accentuate rate changes—i.e., move the market further than otherwise might have been the case. While true that Citibank traders could neither cause nor prevent rate changes over the long term, in the short term they could play havoc with the rates and frequently did, because they earned their profits from trading.

Natvig's prepackaged answers played down the speculative and destabilizing aspect of trading for profit. Eyre obviously understood the imperative, and the risks, of this double standard. In giving Natvig last-minute instructions for the European survey, Eyre said he wanted to know what Citibank traders were doing to "bend either our own rules or the new regulations. . . ." This was discussed at a meeting in Eyre's office on January 30, 1975, when the comptroller set the guidelines for the Natvig/Pomeroy mission.

---

[8] Excerpted from Natvig's memo to Stephen C. Eyre, re: Annual Stockholders Meeting—Probable Questions; and Foreign Exchange Operations, January 22, 1975; Citibank documents 3632–3637; emphasis added.

He wants to know generally what is going on in exchange in Europe other than the normal commercial exchange activity. This would mean capsulizing what each branch does:

- Generation of funds for loaning or disposal of these funds.
- Turnover in deposit/placement business and why.
- Summary of the new regulations for each country, and what will be
  - their impact on operations and earnings
  - the efforts to bend either our own rules or the new regulations (if done) to adhere to our institutional goals. Here he stresses again that we are the industry leader.[9]

Eyre feared that if Citibank, the leader among American banks in the foreign field, was caught doing something wrong, the repercussions would be severe and could have global consequences for the banking system. "This would be true not only of any substantial exchange losses or irregular accounting, but also of any clashes with host governments or central banks abroad," Natvig quoted the comptroller as saying.

While Eyre accepted that adherence to Citibank's institutional goals might make it necessary to "bend either our own rules or the new regulations," he stressed that "our exchange departments have to be super-pure, like Caesar's wife." But bending rules and being super-pure were not generally compatible.

Natvig and Pomeroy selected Paris as their first destination. When they arrived there, Jean-Pierre de Laet was in the midst of stifling a trading-room mutiny led by Jean-Michel Ennuyer. Although the conflict was raging, the "inspector-general" and his dauphin never noticed the unrest. De Laet knew he had to remove Ennuyer to restore cohesion to his staff, and he was waiting for the appropriate moment. "There was a lot of overt, absolute conflict between them," David recalled. And that was the absolute truth.

[9] Arthur Natvig's notes, January 30, 1975—Guidelines for Exchange Survey in Europe; Citibank document 2807.

Chapter 4

"Paris Doesn't Park"

In fact, Paris may occasionally park. . . .

—ARTHUR G. NATVIG, MARCH 1975

Stephen Eyre originally estimated that Natvig and Pomeroy would need three months to complete their survey. But he allowed they could stretch it to six if necessary. Traveling separately, Natvig delayed by a medical problem following surgery, they arrived in Paris at the beginning of February 1975. The Paris staff had booked them into a dusty little hotel in the eighth arrondissement, off the Champs Elysées.

Natvig attributed Paris's history of treasury problems to chaotic bookkeeping. He noted that Jean-Pierre de Laet had improved controls by introducing a system of manually kept "white cards." They showed the daily inflow and outflow of funds by currencies for each trader and gave a running account of the trading room's profits and losses. At the close of each day, the white cards were collated and the information channeled into two streams: the position book, which showed the accumulated profits (or losses) for the month, and the daily summary sheets, which went only to the treasury head and the senof. As the summary sheets also included deposit and loan balances excerpted from the general ledger, they monitored the branch's liquidity.

The white-card system was old-fashioned. But it worked, and it was only intended as a temporary measure. Automation was around the corner with the delivery, in the second half of the year, of a NCR 399 computer. The 399 would put Paris in line with the other European branches as far as computerized bookkeeping was concerned.

Natvig and Pomeroy concurred that de Laet had given "a new sense of organization, discipline, policy and direction to the Treasury and dealing room." They regarded de Laet's changes as a positive effort "to substitute rational and reliable records for the old 'back of an envelope' systems which existed before.

"The old systems not only resulted in loss of opportunities, but also led to substantial losses in 1973 when the accounting virtually collapsed and obliged the dealers to trade 'blind,' " Natvig noted in his French work papers.[1]

In spite of the improvements, Natvig mistrusted de Laet and felt that tighter controls were still needed. He found discrepancies of up to $6 million—"hardly close enough"—between the daily summary sheets and the monthly liquidity reports to head office. Moreover, the liquidity reports that went to head office were different from those that went to the French regulatory authorities at the end of every month. "We don't like sending one set of figures to New York and a different set to the banking authority," he observed.[2] The reports were different because de Laet resorted to window dressing by exchanging liquidity in the form of back-to-back deposits with other Citibank units, thereby presenting a more conservative picture of the branch's deployment of resources.

"It is clear that a window-dressing transaction can do what its name suggests: defeat the whole purpose of liquidity reports by showing a liquid position within the MCO limits when in fact the branch is way outside its limits," Natvig reported to Eyre.[3]

Another practice Natvig didn't like was de Laet's "after-hour dealing." He appreciated that a certain amount was required because the

---

[1] Citibank document 4680–4681.
[2] Citibank document 2338.
[3] Ibid. MCO stands for Maximum Cumulative Outflow. An MCO limit controls the mismatched maturity risk, also known as the gap risk, which occurs when contracts to sell a given currency mature earlier than contracts to buy that currency. An MCO limit seeks to avoid a situation whereby a branch does not have sufficient currency on hand to meet its delivery obligations. At Citibank, the MCO limit restricts every dealing room's cumulative outflow for each currency separately and all currencies combined on a daily basis.

Paris market closed an hour before London and six hours before New York. But Natvig wanted it kept to a minimum, as he found it "an impediment to good operations."[4]

Then there was that other "problem" named Jean-Michel Ennuyer. "Recently," Natvig reported, "during the absence of the Treasury Head, he considerably exceeded his daylight limit and thereby sustained a substantial loss (FF 1.5 million) in trading $ against FF on one day."[5]

During February 1975, the month that Natvig and Pomeroy spent in Paris, disorderly conditions dominated the foreign exchange market. Representatives of the U.S. Federal Reserve traveled to London that same month to stitch together a swap network of $600 million in foreign currencies to stop the dollar's decline. Natvig and Pomeroy noticed the tension in the marketplace, but they were oblivious to the tension in the Paris trading room.

Natvig was easily tired after his operation and understandably kept his workload to a minimum. He never set foot inside the trading room during his February 1975 visit to Paris. Both he and Pomeroy accepted de Laet's criticism of Jean-Michel Ennuyer without questioning the senior trader himself. Nor did they meet with the other traders, either at work or over a glass of beer in their local hangout, the Café Elysées-Express, in the rue Ponthieu, behind the bank. They held themselves aloof, out of touch.

Within weeks, Ennuyer was moved out of the trading room and became a "platform officer," handling credit relations with the bank's big corporate customers. Life on the platform, however, wasn't for Ennuyer. He candidly admitted he was a gambler, likening himself to Alexis Ivanovich, hero of Dostoyevsky's short story *The Gambler*.

"My big metaphysical concern is to beat the market. I don't care about the money," he said later. "To do that takes certain panache. De Laet doesn't know what the word *panache* means."

Finally, missing the action of the market, in October 1976 Ennuyer left Citibank and joined the staff of one of the oldest foreign exchange and money brokering firms in France, Raymond Peter S.A. These little-known institutions first made their appearance in the major European marketplaces in the 1920s as go-betweens with banks, for which they receive a brokerage commission. There are not more than two-score of them in the world, and they maintain direct tele-

[4]Citibank document 4681.
[5]FF 1.5 million was then equivalent to about $337,500.

phone lines into the trading rooms of the banks they deal with. Each firm covers a number of currencies; each major currency is covered by several brokers, giving banks a choice.

Brokers play a controversial role in the marketplace. Critics accuse them of artificially creating business to collect a commission. Credit Suisse in Zurich frowns upon dealing with them. But in a classic sense they do fulfill a useful function, disseminating information, acting as intermediaries, and negotiating contracts at rates acceptable to buyer and seller or borrower and depositor.

Some traders use brokers only for certain types of transactions— for example, when dealing in minor currencies. Rather than contacting hundreds of banks to find the best rate, they leave it to the broker and get on with other business. Brokers never disclose the identity of their assignor until the terms of a transaction have been agreed to by a counterparty. It also happens that a trader might want to conceal his dealing strategy from the marketplace and therefore uses a broker to accumulate or liquidate all or part of a position.

If, for example, the dollar/Deutsche mark trader at Citibank Zurich wanted to contact a specific broker, he would push a button on one side of his desktop console, activating a direct line into that broker's office. Likewise, if the broker wanted to contact the dollar/mark trader at Citibank Zurich, the designated button would light up on the trader's console. With push-button entry into the dealing rooms of his clients, a fast broker can contact a dozen different banks within minutes and have their reactions to a given transaction. After checking the market and perhaps negotiating with a few banks, the broker might revert to his assignor with a firm commitment to deal, but on slightly modified terms. Only if the two banks agree does the broker tell each the name of the other. He then sends out a confirmation and a bill for his brokerage commission—in the order of one thirty-second of a percentage point on each side of the deal—to both counterparties.

With the development of the Eurocurrency markets in the 1960s, brokers expanded their business to include the placing of Euro-deposits. Usually this is handled by a different team, working in a different room of the same brokering firm. Even though Credit Suisse, as well as some other big banks, remains skeptical, the broker system has its merits. Notably, it assures a speedy and anonymous passing of market information and generally facilitates the trading process. Because of his dealing skill and contacts in the market, Ennuyer was good at this work, but de Laet had other preferences and never passed any Citibank business in his direction.

Natvig reported to Eyre that the Bank of France had forbidden any "overselling" of the French franc. He realized it was possible to avoid this restriction by "parking" oversold French franc positions with another Citibank branch outside the country. But both Young and de Laet told Natvig: "Paris doesn't park." De Laet explained this more fully to Natvig: "If Paris has an excess overnight position, it will sell it (or cover by buying), usually dealing with another branch. If Paris takes the position back the next day, this is just by chance, because there is no obligation or gentleman's agreement; and in any event it would be done at a good rate at the time of taking the deal back." [6]

De Laet and Young were not entirely forthright with Natvig on this point. And the "inspector-general" was perhaps too naïve in accepting a statement that he had every reason to doubt. According to one Citibank document, Paris parked a $370,000 foreign exchange loss in Nassau during 1975.[7] Moreover, head office had approved a $200-million parking limit on money-market deposit transactions for Paris that year.[8]

Natvig later amended his notes with a small handwritten annotation: "In fact Paris may occasionally park . . ."

Three years later, a special audit by Citibank's outside accountants, Peat Marwick Mitchell, determined that Paris had destroyed much of its parking documentation for the period prior to 1976. A review of the records in Nassau, however, indicated that Paris parked at least eleven positions with Nassau during 1975, for a total contract volume of $144.7 million.[9]

[6] Arthur Natvig's French work papers; Citibank document 1717.
[7] Citibank document 1049.
[8] Recommended 1975 Foreign Exchange & Liquidity Limits for France; Citibank document 29A.
[9] SEC interoffice memorandum from Ian Dingwall, staff accountant, to Robert Ryan, special counsel, re: Citicorp, a review of Peat Marwick Mitchell's work papers, April 4, 1979.

Chapter 5

But Zurich Does Park

*The banking authorities know that all Swiss banks do
it. . . ."*

—HANS H. ANGERMUELLER, CITICORP VICE-CHAIRMAN, AS
QUOTED BY SEC STAFF, january 4, 1980

At the beginning of March 1975, Natvig and Pomeroy flew to Zurich
to meet Edgar Giger, the "master of the Swiss franc."

Citibank's head of treasury in Zurich was six feet tall, with a push-
button mind, rapid and precise. He came to Citibank in December
1971 from a small cantonal (state) bank that was not an important
dealer in foreign exchange. Citibank's dealing limits were the biggest
in the business. As soon as Giger got his hands on them, he became
one of the key players in the game. And with Citi's name behind him,
he developed an aggressive dealing style all his own.

"Sometimes Eddie would enter the markets with a bang, opening
full limit against the dollar. Then he would pull back as other traders
came in. Baschnagel and the chief traders at the other big Swiss banks
thought he had unbelievably large limits. They were big, but also he
used them to maximum effect. With his tactics, he could move the

70

market," Edwards, a student of Giger's trading, explained.

In 1974, a year of unparalleled turmoil in the foreign exchange market, Giger's trading department earned $24.8 million—more than one-quarter of Citibank's total exchange profits for the year.[1] Foreign exchange trading was the Zurich branch's most important activity, accounting for more than 80 percent of Citibank's pre-tax earnings in Switzerland. Although Natvig and Pomeroy were unaware of any IMMD shift in policy, a decision had been taken in 1973 to pay less taxes in Europe so that, for "political reasons," more taxes could be paid in the United States. Huntington, therefore, was pushing Giger to off-book more of his trading profits through Nassau, as a matter of corporate policy. But Giger was concerned that if too much of his foreign exchange profits were siphoned off to Nassau, it could cause problems.

In a "strictly private and confidential" letter to Huntington, he explained that "a lot of people in the organization in Switzerland have access to [our] profit and loss statements, and I would definitely not like to see comments being made outside the organization [that] we are swinging profits to other countries by booking artificial rates on foreign exchange positions.

"As of the end of August [1973] our profit for Switzerland before taxes was $9.2 million; after taxes $7.6 million and, from this, exchange profits amounted to $7.5 million. You can definitely see that the bank covers more or less the taxes and what is over is being made by our exchange operations. . . .

"Should we take these exchange profits away by switching over to another country, eg. Nassau, a lot of questions will arise among local staff, and this is the only reservation I have in this respect.

"However, should you decide that, for tax purposes, we should book positions elsewhere, we will definitely follow your instructions."[2]

This letter, written eighteen months before the two assistant comptrollers arrived in Zurich, was important in understanding what was happening inside the organization. It indicated that line management wanted to maximize profits by avoiding taxes in Europe. But as this entailed the transfer of profits to a tax haven by simulating real foreign exchange transactions, it had to be kept hidden from all but a few individuals inside the organization. This was an apparent breach

[1] In 1974, Citicorp's reported income from foreign exchange trading was $89.4 million.
[2] Letter from Edgar A. Giger to Freeman Huntington, September 21, 1973; Citibank document 7424–7425.

of the bank's own internal controls and policies. The "inspector-general" and his dauphin did not realize this was IMMD policy, although within the next few weeks, as they progressed with their European survey, it became apparent to them.

If the bank's own control staff didn't know about what amounted to a sophisticated transfer-pricing scheme—used in one form or another by multinationals to achieve the most favorable tax treatment—it was doubly certain that the Swiss authorities were kept in the dark as well. What the Swiss were aware of, however, was the high volume of foreign exchange trading on the interbank market in Zurich, and this worried them. The Swiss National Bank was concerned that the speculative dealing by major traders was pushing the Swiss franc to unrealistic heights and undermining Zurich's soundness as a world financial center.

Early in 1975, therefore, the Swiss National Bank required all commercial banks operating from Switzerland to square their *long* Swiss franc positions at the close of each day. Under the new regulations, open positions *against* the Swiss franc, whose strength was hurting the country's export and tourist industries, were still allowed, as well as positions in other currencies that did not involve a delivery of Swiss francs, but in no case could a bank carry open overnight positions that exceeded 40 percent of its capital and reserves.

Citibank had capital and reserves in Switzerland in 1975 of SF 107 million ($43.8 million with the dollar at SF 2.445). The 40 percent rule meant that its overnight positions could not exceed SF 42 million, equivalent to about $17.2 million. But Huntington had accorded Giger an overnight limit of $75 million—almost five times larger than the local statutory limit.

After checking into the Carlton Hotel on Bahnhofstrasse, the most expensive shopping street in Europe, Natvig and Pomeroy went to Citibank's Zurich trading room. It was located over a furniture shop at 16 Saint Peterstrasse, around the corner from the hotel. They reported back to Eyre that because Giger camouflaged the full extent of his trading by "parking" with the Nassau desk, the new Swiss National Bank restrictions had not "significantly" cut trading profits. During the first two months of the year, Giger's trading profits averaged just under $1 million a month.

Natvig kept a lot of the dealing activity while in the Zurich trading room to see how Giger coped with the new restrictions. At the time there were half a dozen traders in Zurich. Each had his own desk, with a telephone switchboard and a large blotter in front of him. Most deals were completed by telephone, rarely by telex.

The traders jotted down the completed deals on their blotters so that they had a running tally of their overall position literally staring them in the face and could tell when they were approaching their dealing limit. They also filled out deal tickets, listing the counterparty and exact amount of the currency purchased or sold, the rates agreed upon, and the transfer arrangements. They were required to time-stamp the deal tickets before sending them to the back office for processing.

Giger set the dealing strategy. He also dealt on the phones himself while overseeing his staff, approving all big trades with a knowing nod, and listening for price swings or bumps in the market.

The day before—Tuesday, March 4, 1975—the dollar had dropped to SF 2.39. Zurich was short the dollar, so everything was peaches and cream. But suddenly the dollar started to rise. The change was so rapid that at one point the potential loss on the position was $900,000.

Giger's traders managed to turn the position—not quickly enough, complained Giger, who was attending a meeting in Geneva that day— and lowered the loss to $700,000. The dollar's unexpected strength was attributed to rumors out of Berne, the Swiss capital, that the government was preparing new legislation to require banks to report all foreign exchange transactions over $5 million.

At the end of the day, Zurich had a sizable long position in the dollar, which it sold to head office at SF 2.45. Giger kept a "hidden" profit reserve by overstating his cost-of-cover at the month-end reporting date. Head office knew about this "psychological cushion" and tolerated it, although the practice was forbidden by the internal *Accounts & Procedures Manual*. Natvig termed it an "anathema to sound bookkeeping." Until Tuesday's debacle, the hidden profit reserve was around $2.3 million, so it easily absorbed the loss. What follows is adapted from Natvig's log.

Wednesday, March 5, 1975—dollar opened strong at SF 2.4450. Giger, back from Geneva, started building a long position. His strategy after a turn in the market is to go along with the change, but if the turnaround is not sustained, take a new loss and start over again. By late in the day he was $30 million long; the dollar then ran out of strength. He decided to keep the position overnight, expecting unfavorable new from Bonn which would weaken the Deutsche mark. His longer-term view expected the dollar to resume its downward slide in the absence of encouraging economic news from the U.S.

Thursday, March 6, 1975—dollar found no support; the long position was sold in quiet trading, with no basis to force action. The sale resulted in a loss of another $600,000. Hidden profit reserve now under $1 million. Giger took a short position of $50 million which he parked overnight with Nassau.

Friday, March 7, 1975—end-of-the-week trading is always calm: dollar opened weak, then edged upwards on little volume, closing at SF 2.4620 to 60, not good news with a heavy oversold (short) position. The week had been disastrous. We were wrong three times. Hidden kitty virtually out of funds. Late news from New York showed dollar minimally firmer. Giger decided to keep short position until Monday, but had he covered at Friday's closing, the loss for the week would have been $1,310,000.

Monday, March 10, 1975—dollar opened strong at SF 2.48, but closed lower at SF 2.4700 to 2.4740. If it continues to weaken on Tuesday, Giger will cover, trying for a SF 0.01 profit per $, leaving about $200,000 in the kitty.

Tuesday, March 11, 1975—dollar weakened, closing at SF 2.4690 to 2.4710. Giger made some money on in-and-out trading. But he didn't cover the $50-million short position, even though the price momentarily went to SF 2.4670 (the break-even target). He decided to wait until tomorrow when he hopes to buy at SF 2.4570. If he does, he'll have a profit of $250,000 in the kitty.

Wednesday, March 12, 1975—dollar remained soft all morning: Giger covered the $50 million at about SF 2.46, for a profit of $200,000. Later he went back in, building a $27 million long position, with the dollar rising to over SF 2.48 at close. A rumor on Bahnhofstrasse that the Federal Reserve was going to stop U.S. banks from dealing against dollar was denied late in the day, so Giger figured on Thursday he'd close out the long position and go short again. He was now convinced that the long bear market in the dollar was nearing an end, but until there was some good news from the U.S., he predicted the dollar would hover between SF 2.45 and SF 2.50.

Thursday, March 13, 1975—market opened strong with dollar nudging SF 2.50 on a small deal. But no support. Long position sold for a $20,000 profit and changed to a short one on rumors of large yen purchases by Arab oil exporters. Late in day Giger changed back to a $23 million long position at another small profit on belief that some Swiss banks were short and didn't want to stay uncovered over weekend.

Friday, March 14, 1975—dollar weakened on news that Saudi riyal might revalue. Giger covered long position at another small profit. At noon (when Friday activity tends to die) he had a short position at cost not too different from present market of SF 2.4830 to 60. Estimated profit in kitty was $200,000. Giger decided to keep the short position over the weekend.[3]

Natvig closed his log and, with Pomeroy, moved to Milan to see what was happening there. But he left Zurich with misgivings, which he expressed to Eyre in a "private and confidential" letter, dated March 24, 1975.

He reported that because of the new Swiss regulations, Zurich frequently parked its excess dollar positions—"long or short, and from, say, $10 million to $50 million"—with Nassau.

To avoid drawing attention to them, he suggested that parked deals be handled no differently from other foreign exchange transactions and that they should be done at rates that fell within the prevailing market range for the day.

"This will mean mainly that realistic rates will be used on the reversals (vs. the original parking rate used at present), which will mean that Nassau will take profits and losses. It will also mean that the telex messages will be done in a more normal way, i.e., referring to purchases or sales rather than to parking," his letter stated.[4]

With these suggestions, Natvig began to formulate an institutional policy for handling parking transactions in a manner that would be virtually impossible to detect.

He was particularly concerned that the statutory auditors in Switzerland, Peat Marwick Fides, might stumble over the practice and report it to the Swiss National Bank. Therefore parking had to be hidden not only from the regulatory authorities but from the bank's own auditors.

"Simple parking as presently done would probably be looked on (if detected by the authorities through the statutory auditor) as a means of circumventing local regulations; and as such it would doubtless be specifically forbidden to the detriment of future profits. Although management thinks it most unlikely, detection could conceivably also involve restrictions on the Bank's overall Swiss activities, and possibly also some sanctions or reprisals against its senior officers," Natvig observed in his Swiss work papers.[5]

[3] Excerpted from Citibank document 2148–2149.
[4] Citibank document 1726.
[5] Suggestion to Restructure the Nassau Parking Operation; Citibank document 1728–1729.

Chapter 6

Milan and Frankfurt Also Park

Ordinarily we park $5 million to $10 million two or three times a week. When we expect to leave the parking open for a week or more we park with Nassau. But Nassau is known as a place for doing illegal entries, so we avoid, particularly when the parking is expected to be left for only a few days, and/or if the amounts are not too large; and in these cases we park with a Citibank branch in Europe.

—MILAN FOREIGN EXCHANGE TRADER, APRIL 1975
(CITIBANK DOCUMENT 1747)

As you are well aware [Citibank] Germany is right now limited to open exchange positions of 30 percent of our paid-in capital, i.e., positions in the equivalent of DM 28 million. Inasmuch as we sometimes carry bigger exchange positions, it has become a general practice to park such positions with . . . Nassau.

—FRITZ MENZEL, VICE-PRESIDENT, CITIBANK FRANKFURT,
AS QUOTED IN CITIBANK DOCUMENT 2190, MAY 18, 1975.

In Milan, Natvig and Pomeroy discovered a second use for parking. They had watched Giger transfer his excess overnight positions from Zurich to Nassau. This also happened in Milan: the traders there placed their excess positions in Nassau to "comply" with Bank of Italy restrictions. But in addition, the two assistant comptrollers learned that the Milan traders sometimes off-booked trading profits through the Nassau branch.

This off-booking of profits in tax-free Nassau was done by simulating foreign exchange contracts that deliberately "lost" money for Milan. Although Paris and Zurich did the same, Natvig and Pomeroy had not remarked on it, either because they did not realize the significance of it or, as in Paris, it was purposely kept hidden from them.

At the Milan offices in the Piazza della Repubblica they were able to study the practice for the first time and discover how it worked. As their survey progressed, however, they confirmed that substantially the same practice was followed at other branches. They were told that the "parked" profits, although booked offshore, were credited to Milan through the management information system (MIS). This computer-based aid subsequently was described by one Citibank director as "an internal management score-keeping device." The tax authorities in Italy were not shown the MIS reports. Kept by a special accounting unit at head office, they resembled, suspiciously, a second set of books.

Apart from the risk of being caught and having to pay substantial penalties, Natvig and Pomeroy were beginning to feel uneasy about some of the administrative aspects of parking, particularly when it involved the transfer of profits. From Milan, Natvig wrote Eyre to point out that the existing procedures for parking were unsafe because they bypassed the bank's internal system of prudential controls.

"How is it possible to have an independent control over net overnight positions under a parking arrangement?" he asked. "Strictly speaking, you can't, because you don't want to tell the control department about parking to restrict this information to as few people as you can. Even so, they wouldn't be able to recognize which contracts are parked unless we tell them. *The only way is to keep senior management informed;* and this can be done effectively only when senior management understands exchange operations in detail. The people in the trading room all know about it, and if anything badly out of line were done, supposedly they would speak up."[1]

---

[1] Citibank document 1749; emphasis added.

From Milan, Natvig and Pomeroy went to Frankfurt, where Fritz Menzel, the local head of treasury, had some constructive thoughts on how better to disguise parking. By the time they arrived in London in mid-May for the next treasury conference, they had a clear idea of what was wrong with parking and how to correct it. On May 15, 1975, they discussed their suggested reforms with the treasury heads and Freeman Huntington, whose insecurity and lack of decision were beginning to worry Natvig. The outline of their discussion went to Eyre.

In addition to sending their recommendations to Eyre, Natvig kept the comptroller informed through frequent telephone conferences. Eyre discussed the Natvig/Pomeroy proposals with Huntington. But Eyre was not a line officer and consequently could not initiate changes in policy. His duty was to report to the board of directors, or at least to the chairman of the board, any matter that he perceived to be potentially troublesome. The record shows that Eyre reported Natvig's views to Wriston. Natvig himself, at a comptroller's conference in Jamaica some months later, even spoke in person to Wriston about parking.

In spite of his warnings, Natvig noted that senior management had taken a policy decision to continue parking. This he thought was folly itself, because "all auditors worldwide have been alerted to ways of hiding foreign exchange deals by the Franklin National, Sindona and Herstatt affairs." Nevertheless, senior management decided that the profits were sufficiently material to outweigh the risk of being caught.

"The solution can be seen as one of philosophy, accounting, or wording, and it seems that the chance of serious problems could be reduced by changing some of the details of what we are now doing," Natvig observed after talking with Eyre.[2]

Natvig's apprehension of trouble with local regulators, which everyone thought unlikely, was well founded. When Giger returned from the London conference to Zurich he was summoned to the Swiss National Bank offices in Borsenstrasse for a little chat. The national bank had heard through the grapevine that Eddie "has somehow broken the rules and taken large positions against the dollar." Giger thought the complaint was sparked by another Swiss bank out of jealousy over the "exceptional foreign exchange earnings," which showed up when the 1974 financial statements for the Zurich branch were published.[3]

[2] Natvig's notes: "Parking" of Foreign Exchange Positions; Citibank document 3934.
[3] Natvig "Private and Confidential" letter to Stephen Eyre, re: Parking of Positions, May 22, 1975; Citibank document 2201.

Natvig reported to Eyre that "Giger was able to reply satisfactorily, but he also got a warning to the effect that if anything 'funny' is going on, *the banking authority would have no hesitation in lifting Citibank's license.* "Both Giger and John Fogarty, the Swiss senof, considered this "just sword rattling."[4]

Edward L. Palmer, chairman of Citibank's executive committee, visited Switzerland a few weeks later and was questioned by bankers he met about Citibank Zurich's large foreign exchange earnings. Giger confirmed that the profits were made by selling the dollar. But here Natvig rallied to his support. "It must be said that the banks do not cause the dollar to go up and down. They are merely the marketplace. Citibank, for all its resources, could neither support the dollar effectively nor cause it to decline (even the Fed can't achieve this except to level out short-term fluctuations)."[5]

Brutsche had previously told Natvig that "Giger practically had a shouting match with the Swiss National Bank . . . without reaching any conclusions. He is lying low, not doing too much, although . . . still taking some daylight positions which he sells to Nassau at night."[6]

Giger's successes were now becoming a burden, drawing attention not only to his trading creativity, but also to his lifestyle. Natvig informed Eyre that Giger traded in precious metals for his own account, which he thought was all right.

Natvig also reported to Eyre that Giger had recently bought a new home for about $300,000, which, he said, did not "compare unfavorably" with his annual salary of $80,000.[7]

The home, in one of Zurich's quieter residential districts, was unimposing from the outside but was described as "palatial" by other Citibankers who had seen the inside. The floors were laid with Carrera marble, the living room was dominated by a massive antique desk with two telephones on it, and a sixty-foot swimming pool was set in that part of the basement where a sliding wall opened onto a garden patio.

Natvig also mentioned that Giger had made a good deal of money on his precious metals speculation by taking a position in gold just before it went through the roof. "My feeling is why not? It would be nicer if he just bought or sold gold spot, with delivery, rather than futures, but since the Bank does not deal in gold what harm can there

---

[4] Ibid., emphasis added.
[5] Natvig's notes: Conversation with Stephen Eyre, June 20, 1975 (by telephone from New York); Citibank document 1722.
[6] Ibid.
[7] Ibid.

be unless he truly gambled, which I doubt and could not explore without a more specific mandate. . . . Obviously he has no right to use his position in the Bank to buy or sell positions in gold, but he should be able to buy gold as I can buy stocks."[8]

"My opinion of Giger is tops, number one, and that while we all know the line around conflict of interest is a hard one to draw . . . in this case I experience no discomfort."[9]

On July 18, 1975, Natvig recorded that Johnny Robertson, the head trader in London under Brutsche, had told him, "Giger seems happy again, which to him means that he is back in the market. . . . I called Glanzman [in Zurich] for confirmation. He said that Giger and Fogarty went to the banking authority about six weeks ago, and were told plainly that they have been bidding up the SF, and they will have to keep volume down. As far as Glanzman is concerned, he is still lying low, or at least he said the profits are still down."[10]

[8]Ibid.
[9]Ibid.
[10]Natvig's notes: "Giger laid low for a while"; Citibank document 1724.

Chapter 7

The Natvig/Pomeroy Report

Off-booking. *I don't know that term.*
—WALTER B. WRISTON, JUNE 28, 1983

June 1975 was another crisis month for international banking. Zaire, the world's second largest exporter of copper, stopped servicing its $2 billion in foreign debt. In the early 1970s some 130 American, European, and Japanese banks, attracted by estimates of rising copper revenues, had rushed to lend the government of President Mobutu Sese Seko somewhere between $250 million and $850 million—the banks were reticent about disclosing the exact amount. In 1974 a sharp decline in world copper prices led to a reduction of Zaire's foreign exchange revenues and the country instantly fell behind in its payments, notwithstanding that President Mobutu, who kept a dozen wives in regal splendor and owned a $2 million property above Lausanne, in the foothills of the Swiss Alps, personally had enough funds in his private Swiss bank accounts to meet interest payments on the national debt for several years.

Zaire's indebtedness was a mere molehill in terms of the 1982 world debt crisis. Nevertheless, it caused uneasiness in bank boardrooms, offering bankers a premonition of the huge debt overhang building up in the third world. Citibank, which a few years before had incorporated First National City Bank (Zaire) S.A.R.L. in Kinshasa, was Zaire's biggest commercial creditor. However, its loan exposure was small—Citibankers said unofficially it was about $20 million—compared to what the bank would commit to Brazil or Mexico over the next six years. But Wriston was firm: there must be no default, as that would require the bank to classify its loans to Zaire as nonperforming, necessitating a special accounting provision against losses.

There had been relatively few defaulting nations since World War II—Cuba, Liberia, and North Korea were exceptions—and until 1975 none had occurred under the new floating-rate technique whereby banks funded and syndicated loans themselves on a six-month rollover basis. A default would set a dangerous precedent that other debtor nations might be tempted to follow, thereby provoking the ultimate ruin of the banking system. Call it something else if necessary, but in principle, default was to be excluded from the banking lexicon. Wriston proposed that a special working party be formed among creditor banks to deal with the problem.

Zaire thus became the first third world nation to be tailored with a debt rescheduling program by major Western banks. Vice-chairman Al Costanzo and the New York law firm of Shearman & Sterling represented Citibank on the rescheduling committee. Zaire did not live up to the agreement, which was twice renegotiated over the next five years and ended up costing the banks $500 million in fresh loans. But there was no default. This was important: after all, it was the principle that mattered. As Wriston pointed out, even if Citibank lost all its 1975 Zaire loan position, it would only represent a third of what the bank wrote off as a result of the 1970 Penn Central failure. Nevertheless, nonperforming foreign loans were mounting in the bank's portfolio and by the end of 1975 a total of $355 million was at risk under this rubric. This was in addition to the $300 million in worldwide loan losses that had to be written off that year. The bank's capital at year-end 1975 was $2.7 billion.

That same month, Ed Pomeroy returned to New York, leaving Natvig in London to draft the report on the state of Citibank's European treasuries. The ''inspector-general'' saw a lot of the local treasury head, Ernst Brutsche, during that summer. If Giger was the master of the Swiss franc, Brutsche was the king of the Eurodollar. He ran Citibank's Eurodollar book virtually single-handedly from London.

Brutsche was known as a straight-shooter whom most traders instinctively liked. In April 1965 he was the number two trader at Citibank in Frankfurt when Keith Woodbridge, the former head treasurer for Europe, picked him to replace Marcel Herremans, Citibank's dealer in Brussels. Herremans had just been fired as the man responsible for the largest foreign exchange loss ever disclosed by Citibank. The Brussels debacle was brought on by the huge interest-rate differential that existed in 1964 and 1965 between the dollar and sterling. It was generally thought that the Bank of England, through devaluation, would have to let interest rates drift lower to stimulate the domestic economy and that the U.S. Federal Reserve would have to accede to the marketplace and allow interest rates in the United States to rise.

Herremans, under pressure from his senof to increase trading-room profits, started to buy spot sterling and sell it at a discount for dollars one month forward; simultaneously, he sold spot sterling and bought it back six months forward, still at a discount. But his four-legged operations left him with a five-month gap between the mismatched maturities. To square his book, at the end of one month he bought spot sterling and sold it five months forward. His anticipation was that the differential in interest rates would narrow and the effective five-month swap, on which he earned 3 percent, he could undo at 2 percent or less.

Herremans's view of the market was correct. The British and U.S. authorities, however, persisted in maintaining the wide interest-rate differential longer than anyone thought they could. Sterling interest rates even went up for a while, and Herremans kept on doubling his forward position in hopes of making back the losses. While increasing the aggregate total of his contract book, he appeared to be keeping within the "open" overnight limit by selling short-dated contracts. Citibank, at the time, had no maturity gap limit. Consequently, the resident inspector completely missed the fact that Herremans's actual foreign exchange book exceeded $800 million, a horrendous amount even by 1984 standards. The danger of maturity gaps in foreign exchange positions, so evident thereafter, until then was given little consideration by bank managements.

Herremans used First Boston as his principal counterparty, and one day the head trader there casually remarked to Citibank's head trader in New York that the volume of trades out of Citi's Brussels branch was huge. The head trader in New York alerted Woodbridge and together they descended on Brussels to find out what Herremans was up to. Struck by the sheer size of the gap exposure when reported to him, Wriston ordered a clean-up squad to square the positions. Citibank's cost-of-cover loss was $8 million.

Brutsche did so well in rebuilding morale in Brussels that five years later he was appointed vice-president and moved to London to take over the treasury function there. His mastery of the Eurodollar market was such that at their May 1975 London conference, the European branch treasury heads agreed to "regionalize" all Eurodollar money market activity through Brutsche's trading staff in London. Under this arrangement, London was to look after the other European branches by taking from them or selling to them Eurodollars at preferential rates. In exchange, the branches were not to compete with London in the international market, but they could continue to deal deposits in their own domestic market.

De Laet, however, persisted in taking short-term Eurodollar deposits from outside the Paris market. Widening the spread between the lending and borrowing rates—i.e., increasing his profit margin—he would place them back in the market with a longer maturity. Occasionally, Brutsche found that Citibank Paris was competing with London for the same deposits, and this made him mad. He complained to Natvig, who noted that de Laet was making money for the Paris branch by going against the London agreement. "This is a direct result of senof's profit pressures on the trader, and Huntington [must] put a stop to it," Natvig remarked.

"It will have to be explained to the Paris treasurer that he has a lot to lose if he doesn't have the institutional sense to avoid screwing London.

"Huntington hasn't yet asked the senofs for approval of the regionalization plan, and he should. This omission has created a difficult situation: Young forces the Treasury head to violate the spirit of regionalization."[1]

Brutsche thought Huntington was weak and indecisive. The IMMD, he told Natvig, lacked management. He complained that there was "no sense of purpose throughout the group. No feeling of where we are or where we want to be." Staff selection was haphazard. Consequently team spirit was low, and there was an absence of balance and efficiency. "Top supervision," he concluded, "is vulnerable, lacking professional expertise."[2]

[1] Arthur Natvig's notes: June 3, 1975 (Brussels) Re: Regionalization & Paris; Citibank document 3582.
[2] Arthur Natvig's notes: IMMD—HO (EWB June 29, 1975); Citibank document 3768.

Brutsche and Giger ran the major part of the bank's foreign exchange book between them. Other Citibank traders alleged that sometimes the two of them coordinated their market strategy, consulting over the phone on a Sunday and then advising the rest of the network of their "outlook." If it was to "hit" the dollar, they would build their short positions before lunchtime on Monday. This invariably caused a reaction in the market as traders at other banks, seeing the movement, sensed the beginning of a trend. In the afternoon they would call Huntington and tell him the dollar was under pressure in Europe. Huntington would give the green light to alert the bank's corporate customers. The rest of the afternoon would be spent enticing the multinational clients to hedge against a fall in the dollar. On Tuesday they would start covering their short positions and, if the dollar showed resistance to further decline, reverse them to catch the rebound.

Natvig finished drafting the Survey of European Treasuries at the end of July 1975 and forwarded it to Eyre, who called him to New York to discuss "enriching" the front page and sending only it to senior management. Eyre didn't want to overtax them with detail.

Natvig protested. "There is already so much condensed information that further shortening can only cause omission of essentials," he told Eyre.

The report was sixteen pages and came during a period when the tremendous fluctuations of exchange rates made currency trading hazardous. Just how hazardous was appreciated by Brutsche. On August 7, 1975, the U.S. Treasury decided to issue $6 billion in bonds to sop up some of the excess dollars in the European market. The dollar deposit rate immediately firmed on expectations of higher interest rates. Brutsche narrowly avoided being caught with an open $600 million deposit gap. Having borrowed the $600 million for a month, which he then loaned out for six months, he risked having to repay the thirty-day deposits with higher-interest money. Brutsche sensed something was stirring and, Natvig reported, started covering his maturity gap a few days before the change in rates occurred, with the result that he had almost no exposure when the news came over the wire.

With positions of $600 million at risk, a report on exchange and money market dealing could hardly be rich enough. But Natvig, the two-fingered typist, did not tend to verbosity on paper. His sparsely worded one-page summary that preceded the main report only ran twenty-five lines.

SURVEY OF EUROPEAN TREASURIES
London, Frankfurt, Zurich, Paris, Brussels, & Milan
EXCHANGE AND MONEY MARKET DEALING
February–July 1975

1. Personnel: This is a business of people and skills. Incumbent staffs are excellent, but there is some understaffing, and senior back-ups are lacking.
2. Dealing environment has changed.
3. Regulation has become more extensive and more restrictive.
4. Foreign exchange positions are now being parked at other Citibank units abroad. Some changes in handling are recommended to reduce problem potential.
5. Effectiveness of operating and control procedures and the direction in which they are evolving are generally satisfactory.
6. Credit: Bank lines have been reexamined after Herstatt failure. Adherence to limits reasonably good considering the need for instant responses in swift-moving money markets. Clean risk control needs continuing attention and further refinement. Increasing computerization is enhancing credit control.
7. Liquidity reports sent to Head Office (OD 348) are not all prepared on the same basis. The instructions need clarification.
8. Some changes in liquidity controls and reporting suggest themselves: reporting on two levels may be desired (separate for funding and liquidity evaluation), and swap limits could be eliminated.
9. Country exposure: Suggestions have been sent to Head Office to help realign the objectives of this new approach to cross-border risk, separately for (1) normal customer risks, and (2) money market risks.
10. Round-trip transactions: Summary of confidential deals arranged by the European branches to improve ratios, minimize reserves, reduce taxes, off-book special operations, etc.

On August 28, 1975, Eyre sent the Natvig/Pomeroy survey, with a brief covering note, to Citicorp chairman Wriston; Citibank president Bill Spencer; chairman of the executive committee Ed Palmer; and Citicorp vice-chairman Al Costanzo. Copies also went to George Vojta, in charge of the international banking group; Don S. Howard, senior vice-president, finance; and Freeman Huntington.

The survey reported that in the aftermath of the Franklin National and Herstatt collapses, Citibank's relative standing in the marketplace had been enhanced. But new central-bank regulations and a more stringent enforcement of them "now prevail in most countries" and are "generally aimed at curtailing exchange trading and speculation."

The most visible effect on European trading, the survey noted, "has been the growth of parking of positions." The survey defined parking as the "off-booking of positions at other Citibank units." It continued:

"Off-booking permits traders to comply with the letter (if not the spirit) of the locally imposed limitations on maximum overnight positions, while institutionally they take larger positions up to their Head Office-approved limits."

Natvig and Pomeroy listed their suggestions for restructuring parking to make it more difficult to detect. They proposed that

- formatted telex messages be introduced which could be kept in regular files as it would no longer be necessary to segregate them;
- all deals be routed through head office rather than Nassau because the mere mention of a Bahamian destination raised suspicion of tax evasion;
- all deals should be done at "realistic market rates"; deals structured at "artificial rates just to off-book profits" should be discontinued;
- records and running-balances of each branch's parked positions should be kept at head office in the interest of better control and avoidance of "double-counting" of limits. "Confidential records" of MIS adjustments should be made as simple as possible if they were to remain with the branches.

The last six pages of the survey concentrated on "round-trip" transactions. They headed this section: Summary of Confidential Deals Arranged by the European Branches to Improve Ratios, Minimize Reserves, Reduce Taxes, Off-Book Special Operations, etc. Natvig considered round-tripping, although not stated in the report, as "obfuscatory" but smart.

The authors explained that a variety of round-trip transactions were done by the European branches for the following reasons:

- window-dress local balance sheets to improve ratios (e.g., liquidity, capital adequacy, etc.);
- avoid or reduce obligatory reserves;

- reduce tax liability for bank and customers;
- fund and borrow from the DM "Jersey Pool";
- fund and lend through Nassau-Germany.

Strictly confidential treatment was necessary for these transactions. They warned that if discovered, the bank would probably be hit with tax claims and penalties and ordered to desist. But they thought that other banks in Europe were up to the same tricks, and therefore they supposed that Citibank was not alone in incurring this risk. Natvig and Pomeroy made no recommendations to stop any of the questionable practices, only recommendations to disguise them more skillfully.

On September 4, 1975, Wriston returned the Natvig/Pomeroy report to Eyre with the hand-written notation:

Steve:
Be certain to follow up on these points.

s/WW

Wriston did not make clear which points he had in mind, or what he intended by "follow up." If he meant, "clean up," he didn't say it. In any event, Eyre did nothing for the next three weeks. And he received no acknowledgment from Spencer, Palmer, Costanzo, Howard, or Vojta. Finally, on September 23, 1975, he dashed off a note to Natvig:

Dear Arthur,
I received back from Walt Wriston the memorandum I had sent him with the results of your European study. He asked specifically that I follow up on the resolution of the points mentioned. To be sure I don't miss anything on the follow-up, I would appreciate any thoughts you might have on the formalization, timing and implementation of the follow-up program.

Natvig and Pomeroy by then had commenced a similar survey in the Far East. It was not until October 2, 1975, when he was in Singapore, that Natvig found time to compose a four-page letter to Eyre setting out his thoughts on a follow-up program.

At a comptroller's division conference in Jamaica the following January, Wriston acknowledged a more than passing awareness of the problems of parking when he told Natvig he didn't see how head office could be criticized for taking a Swiss franc position in Nassau, "even if our Swiss dealer does it. Of course, if we undo at the same rate as we originally did the deal, we are looking for trouble, and should avoid."[3]

[3] Arthur Natvig's notes: WW/Parking, January 10, 1976; Citibank document 1688.

Chapter 8

How It Is in the Big Time

No matter how many limits, guidelines, controls, or reports are established, the integrity of a foreign exchange operation really comes down to the people involved.

—FREEMAN H. HUNTINGTON, MARCH 17, 1977

David Edwards felt a sense of professional pride in being a foreign exchange trader, and also a sense of loyalty to the institution he worked for. He figured that if you didn't take pride in your work, you were either no good at it or dishonest.

Jean-Pierre de Laet was good at what he did. He was, according to Edwards, one of the best spot traders in the business. But Edwards had become entangled in the rumor campaign about de Laet. This was the source of his suspicion that de Laet was using the bank's name and resources to his own advantage. Edwards became convinced that the Paris treasury boss was taking kickbacks from brokers, and, also, that he was trading, with the weight of the Citi behind him, for his own account. Both were against Citibank's code of ethics.

While Edwards despised de Laet's trading ethics, the Belgian felt even less warmly toward the brash Texan trainee. De Laet hardly tolerated Edwards in his trading room. He disliked the way Edwards short-circuited communications with head office. When Huntington called from New York, the IMMD head preferred to talk with Edwards, the only member of the Paris trading staff who spoke perfect English. If Edwards could place himself so well with Huntington, de Laet was insecure enough to fear that he might also undermine relations with Chuck Young.

Young, at thirty-five, was an eleven-year veteran of Citibanking. Eminently sociable, he was upwardly mobile, obviously a banker for all seasons. He had a Jimmy Stewart smile, was about six feet all, with a glint of boyish mischief in his blue eyes and the self-assurance of a very debonair but aging Ivy Leaguer. He had charm and was possessed of easy manners which, with slightly graying hair and a good tailor, rendered him as smooth a package as any Hollywood screen caster could have imagined.

Young was recruited into the Citibank foreign service in 1964, three days after his twenty-fourth birthday. Just weeks before, he had received his master's degree from Johns Hopkins School for Advanced International Studies in Washington.

A Yale graduate, class of '62 (he majored in European history), he was born and raised in Middletown, Connecticut, home of Wesleyan University, Wriston's alma mater. He was of Irish, British, and German descent, the perfect ethnic cocktail for a Citibanker. In the summer of 1963 he had married Carol Ann Lombardi, a political science major at Manhattanville College. That same year he took the State Department entrance exams and passed, but was turned down on the oral exams a year later. "It was the first and only exam I ever failed," he remarked.

He and his wife had considered joining the Peace Corps, but while at the School for Advanced International Studies he became disillusioned by the bureaucracy in Washington, which Wriston referred to as "Disneyland on the Potomac," and decided against a career in government service. In his final year he was interviewed by recruiters from a number of major corporations. First National City Bank of New York, Chase Manhattan, and Texaco extended job offers. "I never felt quite comfortable with the Texan oil company mentality," he recalled almost twenty years later. His focus shifted to banking and, more particularly, to the international side of banking.

In those days, Wriston was still head of Citibank's international division. But the chairman and the president of the bank were both Yale graduates, which impressed Young. After talking with another Yale alumnus who had opted for a Citibank career, and who made it sound like a go-ahead place, Young decided to join Wriston's foreign legion.

After being posted as manager to the tiny branch in the Hotel Tequendama in Bogotá, where his biggest business was "cashing checks for airline hostesses," in 1971 Young, his wife, and their first child were transferred to the Far East. Then in September 1972, he was transferred to the bookkeeping department in New York.

Until then a contender for higher management position, Young now faced being buried in the sub-strata at head office and faced certain oblivion. Fortunately, he had a friend in New York. His name was George J. Vojta, a senior vice-president who was being groomed as one of Wriston's understudies.

Young had met Vojta, whose name means "rising sun" in Finnish, in the Far East. They were both Yale graduates. Vojta, five years older than Young, had spent a year at Yale Divinity School before switching to political science. He joined Citibank in June 1961 after receiving his master's degree in international relations. He served Citibank in the Philippines, Singapore, and Pakistan. He was in charge of the Citi's flourishing Japanese operations when Young first met him. But in December 1971 Vojta returned to New York as the senior corporate planner. Two years later he became head of the international banking group.

Edwards believed that Vojta may have lobbied on Young's behalf to win him a transfer to the financial control department. But Vojta said this was "not really so. Chuck made his own way." In any event, after some months Young was assigned to a unit that reported directly to Wriston and Spencer. The unit's mission was to brief the two top executives on the bank's performance, evaluating new investments and analyzing the financial results. Young got a lot of visibility in this position, and by early 1974 he had worked off the black mark. Vojta offered the rehabilitated Young a choice of senior officer in Iran or Singapore. Young had the gall to turn both down. Then Vojta proposed the job of senof in France and Young said, "Yes!"

Young's immediate concern in Paris was to expand the branch's commercial clientele. French corporations, nervous about the staying power of the French franc, had a large appetite for dollars. Young figured Citibank could help by providing them with Eurodollars in almost limitless quantities.

Young sent his branch officers into the headquarters of major French corporations to drum up business. UTA, the French air transport company, used Citibank's services to finance the acquisition of a DC-10 aircraft. The Paris branch participated for $6.5 million in a syndicated loan to Elf-Aquitaine, the large French oil company, to help finance its North Sea drilling operations. It granted a ten-year Eurocurrency loan of $68 million to Compagnie Générale Maritime so that this major world shipping company could purchase six new vessels. Another $95 million loan went to the Société Nationale des Chemins de Fer Français as partial financing for its modernization program, and $24 million was loaned to Charbonnage de France.

During the summer of 1975, while Natvig and Pomeroy were completing their European survey, Edwards began to formulate his suspicions of de Laet more clearly. He noted that de Laet routed the larger transactions through the Antwerp firm of Debeuckelaer & Cie., whose managing partner, Jan Debeuckelaer, had been de Laet's schoolmate in Antwerp. Most of the time, it seemed to David, there was no need for a broker, particularly not one located in the Flemish port city, which, although a world center of the diamond trade and the seat of the oldest stock exchange (founded in 1460), was not a center for foreign exchange. But David was aware that brokers sometimes encouraged traders to use their services by offering to return a part of the commissions to them. Banks frown upon this practice, but it is still done, through secret channels.

David suspected Debeuckelaer was paying kickbacks to de Laet through an account at Credit Suisse in Zurich. He assumed that the account was registered in the name of some obscure Liechtenstein or Panamanian trading corporation set up for the purpose and that de Laet used the account as a cover for his own clandestine dealings in the foreign exchange and money markets. David once observed that de Laet drew a check on Credit Suisse, which made him think hidden payments were routed through the big Zurich bank.

David also believed that the Paris treasury head occasionally dealt through Debeuckelaer at rates that were outside the normal market spread for the day. If this was so it would mean to David that de Laet loaned Eurocurrencies through Debeuckelaer & Cie at rates that were *below* the market's bid rate or, alternately, he borrowed funds *above* the market's offered rate.

David was distracted by de Laet's dealings, and it undermined his concentration. He wrestled with the problem throughout the summer and into the autumn. Finally, when de Laet went to New York in mid-October 1975 to attend a treasury conference, David decided the moment had come to report him.

On Monday, October 13, a gray and windy day in Paris, the currency market had performed erratically. The Middle East was astir again as President Ford signed a Congressional resolution authorizing the stationing of two hundred U.S. technicians in the Sinai to monitor the Israeli-Egyptian disengagement. The week before, heavy fighting between Christian and Moslem factions in Lebanon had forced Citibank to close its offices in Beirut, and by Monday all staff and dependents had been evacuated to Athens.

The market was still lingering on the week-old words of Secretary of the Treasury William E. Simon, who warned Congress that the federal government's massive borrowing—$80 billion projected for fiscal 1976—was "crowding out" private corporations and home buyers by making access to the nation's capital markets too expensive for them.

And New York City was facing bankruptcy.

Those were the negative factors affecting the fate of the dollar that day. On the positive side, King Khaled of Saudi Arabia announced the formation of a new cabinet, retaining pro-Western Sheik Ahmed Zaki Yamani as his petroleum minister. And Kuwait asked foreign oil companies to cease paying for their crude in sterling and to make payment exclusively in U.S. dollars.

Other OPEC countries were exposed to follow Kuwait in insisting on dollars, which ensured strong demand for the U.S. currency in the months ahead. But for the moment the reverse occurred. The dollar weakened in the day's trading. David lost $75,000 for the bank on short-date swaps, buying dollars one week forward and rolling them over for spot delivery. The loss was fortunately small, and David thought nothing of it. All summer had been a good trading market and he had made money for the bank.

During the summer David had run into Michael Conolly, one of his former superiors at Montagu's. Conolly was now general manager of International Westminster Bank in France. David liked Conolly, who was something of a father figure in banking for him. He invited Mike and his wife to his apartment for drinks and home-cooked Mexican food. The offer was reciprocated and David would occasionally drop by the Conolly apartment, which was only a few blocks away, for some friendly chit-chat or to play with the two Conolly children, who thought David was a real cowboy because he carried a silver bullet in his pocket. David mentioned his friendship with Conolly to Chuck Young, who said he would enjoy meeting the pin-striped Brit. So David arranged for Conolly to invite them to lunch on Tuesday at the International Westminster offices in Place Vendôme.

Tuesday, October 14, looked like another hectic day in the market. David came in at 7:30 A.M., picking a copy of the *International Herald Tribune* off Cathy Lewis's desk on the platform. The headlines told him that French President Valéry Giscard d'Estaing was off that morning to Moscow for meetings with Leonid Brezhnev, while in Zaire General Mobutu was preparing to celebrate the tenth anniversary of his rise to power. A Brookings Institution study from Washington foresaw no threat of a capital crisis if federal deficits were held to $60 billion for the remainder of the decade. However, data from the Office of Management and Budget projected a minimum federal deficit of $165 billion by 1980.[1]

A Congressional Budget Office report released the same day concluded that default was a near certainty for New York City by December unless federal aid was forthcoming. This reminded some traders of a confidential study by federal bank regulators leaked to *The New York Times* a few weeks before. It indicated that one hundred of the nation's 14,000 banks would be in serious difficulty if New York City defaulted.

The Dow Jones was hovering around 835. Gold declined at the morning fixing in London to $141 an ounce. The outlook for the dollar looked equally grim until Sheik Yamani, visiting Bonn, told newsmen that his country favored extending the current nine-month freeze on higher oil prices to the end of 1976. This sent the dollar soaring. In Paris it gained sharply to FF 4.4275. In Zurich it reached SF 2.6825, and in Frankfurt it tipped DM 2.5950.

At noon David walked across the platform to Chuck Young's office and together they left the bank for their luncheon with Mike Conolly. It was raining and miserably overcast, but lunch was pleasant in the International Westminster private dining room. David was amused by how typically British it seemed, with elegant Chippendale furniture in the center of Paris, overlooking the seventeen-century square, with its Mansart facades and Napoleon's column made from 1,200 bronze cannons captured at the Battle of Austerlitz.

Young was in good spirits, and on the way back to the bank after lunch, in the chauffeur-driven Citroën, David decided to bring the de Laet matter to the senof's attention. He certainly hadn't been agoniz-

---

[1] In November 1983, the Congressional Budget Office predicted the federal budget deficit for fiscal 1984 would be $185 billion. Beyond 1984, the congressional agency predicted a steady rise in the deficit, reaching $250 billion by 1988.

ing over it, but it seemed that the moment was propitious.

"Chuck, something's been eating my craw and I'd like to talk to you about it," he said.

It was spontaneous, and neither suspected the conversation that followed would impact his career with more or less disastrous effects. Young invited David to his office.

They marched up the monumental marble staircase and into Young's office, which had been used by Paul Joseph Goebbels, the club-footed Nazi propaganda minister, on his wartime visits to Paris. Large double doors led into the richly paneled room with high ceilings and windows that looked onto the Champs Elysées. It was furnished with the monarch of all leather couches, some lounge chairs, a coffee table, and a very large desk.

When David was seated, he told Young: "This guy you've got as head of treasury is a crook. He's screwing the bank." David had a laundry list of de Laet's misdealings and he went through it for Young.

"I told Young I had substantial reason to believe that Jean-Pierre de Laet was involved in, one, taking kickbacks from a Belgian foreign exchange and money-market broker, two, that he was taking foreign exchange positions on his own account, and, three, that he was lending Eurocurrencies below the bid rate and borrowing Eurocurrencies above the offered rate in order to increase his kickback income," Edwards later testified.

"I felt compelled to come forward not only out of a sense of outrage over the nature of the practices, but also because I was certain that the kickback scheme was often influencing the tenor of the branch's deposits, thus affecting our funding strategy—that is, putting the liquidity of the bank in jeopardy."[2]

When David finished running through his list, Young looked at him and said, "David, why don't you go out of the room, come back in, and wink, and ask me, 'Don't you know how it works in the big-time money market?"

David was taken aback. "But that's not the point," he tried to tell Young.

Young got mad. "Damnit, David. What is the point?"

"Don't you understand what's happening? Chuck, I've agonized over this too long to wink and forget it."

"But if you don't forget it, I'll have to call for an investigation."

[2]David Edwards's testimony before the Securities & Exchange Commission, April 7, 1978, page 11.

Until then, the possibility of an investigation hadn't crossed David's mind. As far as David was concerned, the matter could have ended there. He just wanted it off his chest. However, Young insisted that if David didn't back off, he would have to ask the comptroller to step in.

David got mad at what he considered was Young's unprofessional attitude and said, "Yes, let's have an investigation. We want to clear this up."

As far as David was concerned, the documentary evidence to support the last of his three allegations existed in the trading-room files. The inspectors from the comptroller's division only had to compare actual market rates with the rates listed on the deal tickets for the transactions de Laet closed with the broker Debeuckelaer. From such a comparison it would quickly become apparent whether de Laet was favoring the broker with sweetheart rates.

David assumed that the bank's inspectors could verify the first two allegations by discreetly monitoring de Laet's behavior, analyzing not only his trading habits but also how he conducted his financial affairs: with whom he banked, how he invested his money, and how he spent it.

Young threw his hands in the air. "Enough!" he said. "We'll talk about it tomorrow."

David never imagined he would draw that kind of a reaction. "I thought I could go in there and say what I had to say and feel relieved. Instead, I left the room feeling shellshocked."

"Pat, I want you to conduct an aggressive and thorough investigation."

—RICHARD M. NIXON, AS QUOTED BY ACTING FBI
DIRECTOR L. PATRICK GRAY III, JULY 1972

David Edwards brooded over an impression that Chuck Young was protecting de Laet. In the weeks ahead it caused him to make some damaging remarks that did not help his cause. He maintained, however, that he had no intention of doing anything to place the bank, or his career, in jeopardy. His only motivation, he said, was to protect the bank from potential scandal.

On Thursday, October 16, 1975, Young called David to his office for a second meeting. De Laet was still attending the treasury conference at head office, and currency trading in Europe had been at a virtual standstill most of the day as the exchanges waited word of a possible default from New York City. Default was averted in the final hour because the city's teachers offered to purchase Municipal Assistance Corporation bonds with $150 million of their pension fund savings. The bulletin that carried the news signaled a sharp rally for the dollar.

Five months before, the major New York banks had helped precipitate the crisis by refusing to lend the city another penny. Earlier in the week, however, the banks had relented and agreed to roll over, or refinance, $59 million in city notes that fell due that Friday. U.S. banks held $3 billion in New York City bonds and could afford a default even less than the teachers. But the teachers, proportionate to their financial resources, shouldered a much larger share of the burden.

When David arrived at Young's office he was surprised to find Will Derby there. Derby, a vice-president, was the branch operations officer and Young's principal hatchetman. He seemed friendly enough, but David didn't trust him. David called him Mr. Tough Guy. The meeting began in a chummy manner, the "I'm okay, you're okay" stuff that Young was so good at conveying. David, however, was on his guard, watching for a setup.

"I was told we were there to discuss ways to categorically prove that de Laet was on the take. I began the meeting by asking Mr. Derby if he also suspected de Laet," he later wrote to one of the bank's senior comptrollers.

Derby spoke no French. But he told David that he had heard the trading-room rumors about de Laet. He showed David the monthly ledger cards indicating how much the bank paid in commissions to each foreign exchange and money market broker. The name of Jan Debeuckelaer & Cie. was the only broker on the cards to appear all in capital letters. Derby said he had been watching payments to Debeuckelaer & Cie. to see if he could detect any basis for kickbacks.

Derby also mentioned that the bank had instructions to pay Debeuckelaer through Banque Belge Limited in London rather than at the broker's business domicile in Antwerp.[1] He said this procedure, which was unusual, had been requested by de Laet.

"We're going to solve this thing real quick," Derby promised. "Now, what's your proof?"

David had none.

"Look, you just can't come in here without a smoking gun," he said.

Derby was matter-of-fact, round like a pressure cooker, and constantly popping Tums tablets. According to David, Derby suggested

[1] Banque Belge Limited, the British subsidiary of Société Générale de Banque S.A., Belgium's largest commercial bank, was founded in 1909. In 1982 it reported total assets of $500 million. Its vice-chairman was Lord O'Brien of Lothbury, former governor of the Bank of England.

three ways of getting proof: breaking into de Laet's home to search for incriminating evidence; approaching the Belgian broker and offering to go on the take himself; or confronting de Laet while wearing a hidden tape recorder.

"If you're going to raise a problem, you have to bring a solution," Derby told him.

"I rejected their suggestions," David said, "and stated that if they continued their tactics I would be tempted to take the matter to the U.S. Senate Committee on Multinationals."[2]

Edwards later said he made this threat to stave off further pressure to "commit incriminating acts." The meeting ended abruptly, but on Friday Young summoned Edwards to another meeting. Derby was again present, and he took the lead.

"David, we have to document these charges. We need a handwritten statement from you," Derby told him.

Young then suggested that David work on it over the weekend and deliver it to his apartment at 6 P.M. Sunday. But Edwards figured it would be foolish to rush into something like that and, before leaving, said he'd think about it.

That same day Wriston joined David Rockefeller, chairman of the Chase, and Ellmore C. Patterson, chairman of Morgan Guaranty Trust Company, in warning the Senate Banking Committee in Washington that a default by New York City would adversely affect the world money markets and exert a downward pull on economic activity. After listening to the three bankers, the committee recommended extending $4 billion in federal loan guarantees to the city, a move later confirmed by Congress, and the crisis was deferred.

The fact that neither New York City nor Zaire had actually gone bust underlined Wriston's belief that governments made good clients. Whether debt-ridden or not, governments were voracious consumers of credit and required a variety of high-fee services. Wriston said it made good sense to be a good banker to the governments of countries where the bank did business. In Citibank's case, this was especially wise because two-thirds of the bank's earnings came from outside the United States.

Wriston decided that to deal effectively with governments, Citibankers needed stature within the communities in which they worked. Senofs were encouraged to entertain and travel first-class. They re-

---

[2]David Edwards, memorandum to Eugene Sweeney, regional comptroller for Europe, November 14, 1977.

ceived weighty allowances and their offices became courts; their residences comfortable. They appointed their own council of ministers. They became the princes of the Citi.

The senof in London moved into a magnificent townhouse by Eaton Square, haunt of shipping magnates and Saudi royals. The senof for Pakistan took over a many-servanted palace that rivaled the British High Commissioner's residence for Raj-like splendor. In Paris, the senof was given an apartment in the Palais Royal that was originally intended for the deputy governor of the Bank of France.

The Palais Royal was an eighteenth-century palace built by Louis-Philippe II, Duc d'Orléans, who after the Revolution became king of the French. Young's apartment was situated at the northern end of the Palais Royal gardens, an elongated quadrangle enclosed by the four elegant wings of the palace.

David, when he arrived at Young's apartment on Sunday evening, October 19, 1975, was ushered upstairs to the library. Impatient, Young asked for the statement. Having already threatened to take his tale of corruption in the Paris trading room to the U.S. Senate committee investigating the behavior of multinationals, David now made his second blunder. He told Young that on the advice of counsel, he was not prepared to make a written statement. But he said he was willing to talk to anyone at the bank whom Young suggested.

Young was flabbergasted that Edwards would consult an outside attorney for an internal matter. He interpreted it as evidence of hostile intent. In fact David had only talked the matter over casually with a friend, Bob Simpson, a lawyer with the firm of Donovan Leisure in Paris. Simpson had advised David to give the bank an opportunity to correct the situation without putting a document on record. By submitting a written statement, he was escalating the conflict and this should only be undertaken, Simpson advised, if David wanted to change his career and become the Ralph Nader of banking.

Young was visibly tense. Although David didn't know it—no one had informed him—the comptroller, Stephen Eyre, was coming to Paris that week. Eyre was bringing with him the regional comptroller for Europe, David Allars, who was based in London. Edwards later assumed that Young was nervous because of Eyre's visit. He had done such a whiz-bang job of turning the French operation around that David supposed the comptroller wanted to make sure there were no nasty surprises and that the branch's earnings were as represented by Young and his staff.

Certainly Young didn't want any loose cannon rolling around when

Eyre was on deck. He asked Derby to check the broker slips for abnormal payments and write a memo detailing his findings. Derby, no accountant, found nothing to support the allegations, but Young didn't tell David so. Young now suggested that David contact Allars at his hotel, the George V, first thing Monday morning and make an appointment to see him.

David did this and arranged to see Allars in his suite at the hotel, around the corner from the bank, at 5 P.M. on Monday. He went to the meeting, he said, "very much with cap in hand." Allars had brought his wife to Paris with him, and Mrs. Allars was in the bedroom changing into an evening dress when David arrived at the door.

Allars asked Edwards to sit down and explain what he thought de Laet was up to. David ran through the kickback scheme in fifteen minutes. The Antwerp broker, he said, paid the kickbacks into a secret bank account, probably at Credit Suisse in Zurich. David supposed de Laet did his personal trading in foreign exchange through the Zurich account.

David further mentioned to Allars that he suspected de Laet had run up substantial losses in his personal trading. David thought de Laet was covering these losses by prostituting the bank's liquidity in order to increase his kickback income. David also thought that Jennifer James, a trading assistant with IMMD, might be able to shed light on these activities because de Laet had given her a check drawn on Credit Suisse.[3] James had been a trainee in Brussels when de Laet was a junior trader there and they remained in touch even though she had been transferred to New York.

David assumed Allars understood everything. He sketched in how de Laet might operate a secret trading account through the Antwerp broker. But Allars was skeptical. He thought the scheme too cumbersome. He recorded in his notes that David offered to approach Debeuckelaer to see if the Belgian broker would offer him kickbacks, something that David categorically denied having proposed. In any event, Allars felt that the Credit Suisse account was the most promising lead and said he would follow it up with his own contacts at the big Zurich bank. He estimated it would take him a month to complete his inquiries, and he would let David know the outcome.

David was reassured that the matter was out of Young's hands. He told Allars he thought Young had been naïve in his handling of

[3] Jennifer James is not a real name but is used by the author to protect someone who may have had no direct dealings with de Laet.

de Laet. But Allars made the same observation of Edwards. "A sincere individual, but green behind the ears. De Laet drives him hard," he reported to Eyre.[4]

Allars was convinced that David had acted in good faith. For example, David had expressed concern that his allegations would put de Laet under a cloud and that worried him. Allars wrote four key words on top of his notes: *Evangelist / Marbles / Judgment / Balance.*[5]

After his meeting with Allars, David was given the impression by Young that the comptroller's division was going to mount a big investigation and wanted David out of the way in case de Laet became suspicious. Young therefore transferred David out of the trading room, assigning him to "special projects." David was given a desk in the platform area.

While Young wanted David to believe his best interests were being served, behind David's back he angled to have the troublesome trader transferred out of Paris. He asked David not to discuss the de Laet affair with anyone at head office and especially not with Camille Legerie, the energetic resident inspector who was forever running up and down the back stairs with ledgers in hand, an accounting demon with, as far as Young was concerned, a pocket calculator for a mind. Young had not forgiven Legerie for giving the Paris treasury operation a scathing review in his last inspection report, evaluating its overall performance as below standard. Young didn't want David activating Legerie's critical sense once more. Legerie was also one of the few people who took David's allegations seriously.

To work himself back into favor, David proposed to develop a new discounting procedure for a type of commercial instrument known as banker's acceptance. Young thought this was a good idea.

Widely used for short-term trade financing, a banker's acceptance is a draft drawn on a bank by an individual or firm. The maturity is usually from 30 to 180 days. An acceptance substitutes the credit of a bank for that of the drawer. David worked on the project for three months before coming up with a formula whereby Paris covered the drafts by having head office tap on its behalf the Federal Reserve's discount window in New York. The dollars borrowed from the Fed would then be changed into French francs by a "forward swap" spanning the term of the acceptance. The scheme, as structured by David, was innovative but simple, and it worked.

[4] David Allars's handwritten notes; Citibank document 893.
[5] Allars's handwritten notes; Citibank document 896.

Allars, meanwhile, spoke with Young and Derby about the allegations and about Edwards's overall performance in Paris. Derby told him that Edwards had not been a good trader and had lost $75,000 for the bank when de Laet was away in New York attending the treasury conference. Derby thought Edwards feared being berated by de Laet for his loss and sought to deflect de Laet's fury by casting doubt on the treasury head's personal integrity. Young suggested that Edwards should move on. "Future dicey. His overall performance not that good. Delicate situation," Allars noted.[6]

Back in London, Allars asked Brutsche for his opinion of de Laet. Brutsche considered de Laet a good trader, but reported that he had been under pressure at home as well as in his new job at the bank. His marriage was breaking up.

They discussed de Laet's dealing for his own account with the kickback income received from the broker, as outlined by Edwards. Brutsche, for whatever reasons, avoided opening this Pandora's box, and Allars, after listening to him, concluded: "It would not be easy to pull any largescale manipulation in the manner described by DE. In view of the technical difficulties too many people would have to be in on the act. However manipulation of brokerage is certainly possible—on basis of business volume, not rigged deals."[7]

Camille Legerie ran his own analysis of the commissions paid to Jan Debeuckelaer and the transactions that they covered. His findings were not conclusive. For him, at least, there was doubt. David, moreover, furnished Legerie with an example of de Laet using off-market rates. He reported this to Allars.

Allars, meanwhile, made his own list of commission payments by Citibank Paris to the Antwerp broker and examined the contracts to which they related to see if he could detect any sham deals. None showed. His contact at Credit Suisse in Zurich supposedly ran de Laet's name through the computer to see if he had an account. If de Laet had one, it was not registered under his name. Allars did find that de Laet kept an account with Banque Nationale de Paris, which he checked out. It ran only small balances. Nothing exceptional. He checked on the Antwerp broker. "No unfavorable information. Looks okay," he noted.

A few days later, Camille Legerie called Allars to report that Young and Derby had talked to Edwards again and told him to stop "stir-

[6]Citibank document 896.
[7]Citibank document 893.

ring." No particular significance was attached to Legerie's call, and in fact, Young later explained that he was intent on smoothing over the disruptive aspect of the "Edwards affair" and wanted to get business back on a normal footing, free of any feelings of recrimination or suspicion.

Allars, for his part, described de Laet as shrewd and egoistical, but he uncovered no evidence that the Belgian was dishonest.

Allars returned to Paris in mid-November. Over lunch at *D'Chez Eux,* a restaurant near David's apartment, Allars unveiled the results of his month-long investigation. "Even though they had found eleven to thirteen checking accounts in de Laet's name, none had been directly credited by any of the brokerage houses with whom Citibank Paris did business," Edwards later wrote in a memo to Allars's successor in London.

On the way back to the office after lunch, Allars volunteered that had he found the slightest scrap of evidence to substantiate the allegations, de Laet would have been immediately suspended and placed on a blacklist.[8] David wondered whether this was a warning that he might be the next candidate for the blacklist. He was getting nervous.

Allars reported to Eyre a few days later that the matter was closed. "Our investigations have produced no positive indications or leads of any wrongdoings:

no account with Swiss banks in name JPD
staff account ok
checking account with BNP ok
no account with Banque Belge in London
no concentrations in dealings with broker
mostly, the counterparties are Grade A names
brokerage paid to JD (the Antwerp broker) appears reasonable and in order.

Edwards admits he jumped up too quickly. He remains convinced that JPD is on the take, but has no positive means of substantiating his belief at this stage.

I questioned him again closely on the technical aspects of the manner in which JPD was supposedly siphoning off funds, and he admitted that it involved a rather difficult and cumbersome handling procedure. Also, he was not entirely consistent with respect

[8] Source: David Edwards's SEC testimony, p. 15.

to our first conversation (Jennifer James; prostitution of liquidity).

Also, he has not been a successful trader, and has been removed from direct trading responsibility for that reason alone. Possibly he was diverting attention.

I am convinced that Edwards is sincere (not malicious), but he comes across as someone naive and immature—in the nature of an evangelist whose balance is not quite right.

> *Solution:* Remove the cloud from JPD (although we shall keep him under observation).
>
> *Edwards*—Keep him on the Special Projects and handle him delicately. He could do us harm.[9]

---

[9]Memo from David Allars to Stephen C. Eyre, November 19, 1975; Citibank document 905/7.

Part II

THE SCHEME

Part 1

THE SCHEME

Chapter 10

Olsen's Tip

The first people aware of a trader who is exceeding bounds are usually other traders.

FREEMAN H. HUNTINGTON, MARCH 17, 1977

The Café Elysées-Express, at 54 rue Ponthieu, is a small and noisy corner establishment with a zig-zag bar and a restaurant in the back under a moonscape ceiling. Whoever chose the decor came up with a model of modern bad taste in interior design. To the right of the door on the way in stood an electronic pinball machine whose sound effects regularly punctuated the din of conversation from the bar. Gottlieb's God of War, imported from Chicago. Boom! BAM!

David Edwards found it was the perfect machine for working off his frustration. Boom! BAM! Another strike for justice. The cause was good. But David was under a cloud. He was accused of using bad judgment. Boom! BAM! He had been right about de Laet and would prove it. Only it would take time.

Boom! BAM! Swoosh-Bang! Tok-tok-tok. Three free games.

"Ça alors," said a Frenchman from the bar.

"Encore un bière," David ordered. He wondered how thorough

the investigation by David Allars had been. In early December 1975, Young had asked him to lunch. Young told him flatly that he had compromised his career. Young suggested that David would be better off professionally to leave Citibank. David had felt a knot in his stomach. He had been tempted to dump the rest of his lunch into Young's lap. But he restrained himself.

In spite of Young's efforts to convince him to resign, he continued to work on "special projects," hoping to reingratiate himself with the Paris team, wondering above all how he might salvage his reputation. A figure slipped around the corner from the rue de la Boétie. It was almost 7 P.M. The figure hurried across the street toward the bar. David could tell by his gait that it was Ole Olsen, a Danish trader who worked for de Laet. Olsen looked excited.

"What's up?" David asked as Ole came through the door.

"I don't understand," Ole said. "J.P.'s upstairs on the telex right now losing a pile of money to Nassau. But if I lose $50,000 in a day, he goes crazy."

"Bingo," said David. The pinball lights started blinking on and off in his head.

"De Laet's shifting money to Nassau at phony rates," he muttered to himself. "So that's the game."

David realized that Nassau's book profit (Paris's book loss) on the simulated transaction would be credited back to Paris on the internal Management Information System (MIS). The scenario suddenly became clear: de Laet was transferring profits to no-tax Nassau with his after-hours trades. As this increased the branch's MIS'sed earnings, thereby improving Young's posture at head office, David reasoned that the Paris senof would turn a blind eye to de Laet's other chiseling.

A few weeks later, in April 1976, David first heard mention of the term *parking* as related to the off-booking of foreign exchange positions. John Gardner, a former British tax inspector who became Citibank's European tax director out of London, turned up to "sprinkle a little holy water" on David's bankers' acceptance deals. De Laet introduced Gardner to Edwards on the morning of the tax director's arrival in Paris. David suggested he and Gardner meet for a drink after work. They were sitting on the terrace at the Hilton and Gardner pulled out a memo he had just written to George Putnam, the senof in London.

"Have we got problems!" he exclaimed.

David remembered that the memo was headed, "£10,000 fine, and/or two years imprisonment." It detailed how Citicorp International Bank Limited avoided reporting income "parked" in Nassau. Gardner claimed he and a colleague had dreamed up a parking scheme in 1974 to compensate for large real estate losses incurred by the London branch. The scheme allowed London to meet its projected earnings in spite of the losses. Then Brutsche adapted the parking procedure to shift interest revenue to Nassau.

Brutsche did this by lending Eurodollars to Nassau at call at about 3 percent. He took the same funds back again as six-month money, paying 7 percent, with London losing the 4-percent differential to Nassau. Brutsche then informed the MIS department in New York. They debited Nassau's account on the twentieth of each month and credited London's unofficial books, the MIS set, with the difference.

This maneuver "allowed Citibank to reduce its taxable income in the UK by moving some of its earnings to Nassau, then having them reappear in New York," David reported.

It became a problem, however, when other branches learned about parking and soon it was "epidemic," Gardner said. "Now," he remarked, "they're doing it all over Europe."

Gardner, according to David, felt the bank was subjecting itself to possible blackmail. "If we ever have a treasurer who is in trouble, we have to stick by him through thick and through thin, for the parking of positions has gotten completely out of hand. All European branches are doing it."

"What we are doing," David remembered him saying, "is a criminal offense."

When Gardner testified about this meeting five years later, he said, "As I can recall, we didn't discuss anything of that at all. When asked what he had discussed with Edwards, he replied, "I really cannot remember."[1]

"The Gardner meeting made the whole thing crystal clear to me—that nobody was going to do much about the de Laet thing because that's the way they wanted it. I had gone from feeling naïve to down in the dumps. I was in a box. I thought that maybe everybody was on the take. But I still couldn't drag myself away from it. It was like being married and not being able to get a divorce," David recalled.

"That was an awfully hard winter for me. They almost broke me. And I had worked like hell on the bankers' acceptance project, getting it all wrapped up in three months, in hopes of working my way back onto the team. Young was holding me on a string, and I was working so hard to get back into his good graces."

[1] John Gardner, testimony before the SEC, January 21, 1981; page 161.

Chapter 11

De Laet's
"Have a Nice Weekend"

We have a policy that Nassau will always deal with overseas branches as . . . call it a last resort, if you will.

—DONALD S. HOWARD, CHIEF FINANCIAL OFFICER,
CITICORP, MARCH 27, 1980

Just before noon in New York on Friday, June 11, 1976, the telex machine on the fourth floor of 399 Park Avenue received a message from the Citibank trading room in Paris.

06/11/76 1127 EDT
423712 FNCB UI
CITIFX C 650153F

HI HI THERE FRIENDS MOM PSE

ATT MR BOB WEXLER CITI NASSAU
FROM TRADERS DEPT CITI PARIS

PLEASE BOOK FOR US THE FOLLOWING TRANSACT
CITI NASSAU BUYS FROM CITI PARIS DOLLARS 6,000,000

AGAINST F FRANCS AT THE RATE OF 4 7275
VALUE THE 15 OF JUNE
PSE DEBIT OUR ACCOUNT

CITI NASSAU SELLS TO CITI NEW YORK DOLLARS 4,000,000
AGAINST F FRANCS AT THE RATE OF 473 75
VALUE THE 15 OF JUNE

CITI NASSAU SELLS TO CITI BRUSSELS DOLLARS 2,000,000
AT THE RATE OF 473 75 AGAINST F FRANCS

PLEASE M I S TO US

FF 60,000 REPRESENTING THE 100 PIPS ON THE 6,000,000
THESE 60,000 F FRANCS MAKE DOLLARS 12,500 WITH THE
RATE OF 473 00

SO NOW THE TOTAL AMOUNT TO BE M I S TO US IS
DOLLARS 77,000

TKU VM FOR YOUR HELP
REGARDS
JP DE LAET VP

WELL RECEIVED PSE + +
WELL RECEIVED +

OK PALS MANY THANKS INDEED HAVE A NICE WEEKEND
SEE YOU MONDAY
BIBI F N[1]

It was 5:45 P.M. in Paris by the time the message cleared the trading room there. The local foreign exchange market had closed almost two hours before, and at 60 Champs Elysées most of the staff had already gone home for the weekend. Jean-Pierre de Laet was alone in the trading room, bent over the telex keyboard, operating the machine himself. He had just "lost" $12,500 to Citibank Nassau.

De Laet had planned and executed the transaction in three parts to make its true intent almost impossible to detect. He addressed it to "Bob Wexler" because that was one of two codes, known only to a small number of insiders, used to signal that it was a parking job requiring special treatment. The other was "Victor Lee."

The deal appeared perfectly normal—except there was no foreign

---

[1]Citibank document 7022. "BIBI F N" is shorthand for "bye-bye for now."

exchange trader at the Nassau branch. But had Nassau a trader, he could have been a man sitting under a palm tree on the beach for all it mattered to the mechanics of the operation. Nassau was never intended to exercise any control over the transaction. The "parkor"—in this case de Laet—instructed the "parkee"—i.e., the Nassau desk in New York—precisely how to book the deal, subtract the profit and move it on. Paris dictated the rates, the amount, and the timing; the IMMD, acting on Nassau's behalf, obliged.

From de Laet's instructions, Huntington's IMMD staff knew that the transaction was only a quick pass-through on Nassau's books. In the first leg, de Laet instructed Nassau to buy from Paris $6 million in French francs at a rate of 4.7275. While the rate was artificially fixed, it was near enough to the trading range for the day to be virtually impossible to spot. As the accounting entries criss-crossed the Atlantic, de Laet jiggled the rates, increasing them by 100 pips, so that Nassau was left with a profit. Around the twentieth of each month, the cumulative profits parked in Nassau were reported to New York and entered onto Paris's MIS ledger.

In the second leg, the $6 million was split into two lots and sent on its way again, minus the 100 pips: $4 million "sold" to New York and $2 million "sold" to Brussels. This complicated procedure made it harder to track should the French tax inspectors stumble across it in the Citibank Paris files.

The second leg was to be completed at Tuesday's value date of June 15. De Laet could then close the triangle by bringing the original French franc position, less the 100-pip profit, back onto his books as and when needed.

So far that month, as the last part of the telex indicated, Paris had "lost" $77,000 to Nassau—income that should have been reported to the French fiscal authorities.

Multinational U.S. corporations like Citicorp pay U.S. taxes on their worldwide income no matter where it is booked. But to avoid double taxation, the Internal Revenue Service allowed multinational concerns to apply a credit of up to 46 percent—the U.S. corporate tax rate—on income taxes paid to foreign fiscal authorities. Citibank's foreign earnings, however, were greater than its domestic earnings, which meant that its foreign tax credits were so large that if the parent Citicorp used them all, it would pay no U.S. taxes at all. Wanting Citibank to be perceived as a good corporate citizen, senior management set a minimum level for U.S. taxes it intended to pay, and this solely for political reasons, regardless of the excess of foreign tax credits. The level was around $20 million.

Vice-chairman Costanzo later explained this to the Securities & Exchange Commission with considerable frankness when he said: "You know, we said, 'No matter what comes, we're going to pay $20 million,' or whatever. And we'd have this kind of a goal. Therefore our objective was to reduce our foreign taxes so that, in effect, we did not reduce our U.S. tax bill below that policy level, if you wish. So that, in effect, it's never been a situation that we have foreign tax credits we couldn't use. But it's been more one of we're at the margin and we want to manage this so that we don't reduce our U.S. tax bill to levels we consider undesirable."[2]

This was a curious admission by Costanzo, for it meant that it had become politically more desirable for Citibank to launder some of its foreign profits through Nassau before consolidating them in the earnings mainstream. For de Laet, the operation achieved a double goal. By "losing" money to Nassau, he was not only shielding the bank from full French taxation, he was also increasing the earnings that Paris reported to head office.

This placed de Laet in a curious position. He was violating French exchange and fiscal controls by parking in Nassau, though apparently he had no qualms about doing it. Obviously, he had the satisfaction of knowing that head office condoned it. The "wash" through Nassau was a good deal for the bank, for IBG, for IMMD, for Charles Young, and for himself.

His after-hours trading complete, de Laet closed the telex for the weekend and left the office. He took pride in his work and was satisfied with his week's performance. He walked up the Champs Elysées to where, that morning, he had parked his green Jaguar. Ahead of him was a forty-five-minute battle with traffic, around the Etoile, down the avenue de la Grande Armée to the Port Maillot, en route for Saint Germain-en-Laye, on the northwestern outskirts of Paris, where he rented a large, modern villa.

He knew it was going to be another tense weekend at home with his wife and ten-year-old son, Alain, and that come Monday morning, it would be a relief to get back to the bustle of the trading room.

Graziella de Laet, a plain-looking housewife who had once been proud of her husband's success, now suspected he was having an affair with dark-haired Moroccan-born Esther Rebibo, who worked as a trading assistant at the bank. Graziella's once secure world had turned into a nightmare of doubt and bitterness.

Later she would file for divorce.

[2]G. Albert Costanzo, testimony before the SEC, July 11, 1980, pp. 78–79.

Chapter 12

Huntington's Moot Issue

*The U.S. Government is well aware that its financial
credibility and power rests to a very large extent on the
role and behavior of its banks abroad.*

—*Far Eastern Economic Review*, MAY 9, 1975

Toward the end of June 1976, Freeman Huntington's secretary called
David Edwards from New York to inform him that Huntington was
coming to Paris.

As soon as David heard the news, he knew he was in trouble. Not
often did a senior vice-president leave a busy schedule at head office
to visit one of his flock in the field.

Huntington stopped over in London and met with David Allars, who
reviewed for him the "Jean-Pierre de Laet affair," which in fact had
become the "David Edwards affair." Allars went over the allegations
that Edwards had first brought to Young's attention seven months
previously. He set them out as he understood them, which was not
quite the way Edwards had originally expressed them:

Eurobook in a mess (gaps)
de Laet taking massive positions

de Laet on the take (kickbacks from brokers, deals at inflated rates to the benefit of broker and de Laet).

Allars also mentioned Edwards's threat to take his whistleblowing to Washington, by denouncing the corruption in the foreign exchange market to the Senate Committee on Multinationals, and his breaking confidence by discussing his charges against de Laet with persons outside the bank (a reference to Robert Simpson).

"There is no choice," Allars noted, without finishing the phrase. "But Edwards should not be made to feel that any . . . offer [of a treasury post] has been withdrawn because of the de Laet affair."[1]

With David's fate hanging by a thread, Huntington arrived in Paris looking remarkably fresh and rested for a man who was under stress and who had less than eighteen months to live. He was only staying in Paris for the day, he explained, because he wanted to be back in New York for the weekend to see the tall ships, in bicentenary homage, sail up the Hudson.

They spent all afternoon together in the second-floor conference room next to Young's office. David, in spite of the underlying gravity of the visit, was pleased to see Huntington. "He was like a great-uncle to me," he said. And David badly needed an ally.

"Look, Free, I've been putting up with these clowns since October and I'm fed up with them," he said. It was the first time he had been able to talk to Huntington about what he felt was going on in Paris. And for the first time, he broadened his accusations to include Young, whom, he said, was covering for de Laet because the head of treasury used his off-booking talents to help the senof increase the branch's earnings.

"This thing is bigger than you know," David exclaimed. "Hell, de Laet's just the tip of the iceberg."

Huntington seemed interested. David explained the process de Laet employed for "losing" money to Nassau by engaging in fake foreign exchange transactions. Once this basic concept was mastered, it opened the door to many other ploys of similar intent. David mentioned that de Laet sometimes used funny swap rates to transfer profits from the world corporation group to treasury. Citicorp France was a multitude of different operations, and David maintained that de Laet was screwing one division for the benefit of the senof's profit area.

"I'll look into it," Huntington promised.

[1]David Allars's notes: Huntington, June 22, 1976; Citibank document 902.

David felt encouraged. He trusted Huntington.

After three hours, both men were drained. As David folded away his papers, Huntington patted him on the shoulder and said, "Hang in there, boy. We'll get to the bottom of this."[2]

Before going on annual home leave that summer, David took ten days off to travel to the Mediterranean coast with Bill Clinton and his wife, Hilary. Clinton, whom David had met eight years before at Oxford, had recently gone to work for the Democratic National Committee and was enthusiastic about Jimmy Carter's chances to become President. He wanted David to work with him on the Carter campaign. They squeezed into David's white Peugeot 504 and drove to the Costa Brava and then to the Côte d'Azur. The more David thought about it, the more he liked the idea of an unpaid leave of absence to work on the Carter election campaign. He still didn't think his career in jeopardy, but it would give him breathing space and allow time for the dust to settle.

Back in Paris toward the end of July, David saw Young and told him he was going on home leave in August. He also took the opportunity to badger Young about why he had not received a salary review in over a year. Young, he said, had promised him one.

Young responded, according to David, "Because in October 1975 you were not a team player."

On his way through New York, David stopped at head office to see Huntington. The IMMD boss had not talked to David since their Paris meeting. David wanted to know if Huntington had uncovered anything about the parking practices they had discussed in Paris and what management's reaction had been.

The issue, as David now conceived it, had shifted from de Laet's misdealings to focus on "cooking the books in Paris" and whether Young and de Laet were "parking positions in Nassau in order to meet their budgeted earnings."[3]

David estimated that Paris was netting $3 million more per year on its MIS reports than the branch was in reality earning. This, he figured, was why Young didn't want him rocking the boat. In fact Paris received MIS'ed earnings in 1976 of $821,657, still a considerable amount.[4]

---

[2] In May 1984, Citibank's general counsel, Patrick J. Mulhern, stated that if Edwards mentioned parking to Freeman Huntington in June 1976, Huntington never informed senior management of Edwards's new allegation.

[3] David Edwards, testimony before the SEC, April 7, 1978, page 19.

[4] Citibank document 1049.

Huntington this time conceded to Edwards some knowledge of position parking, and he agreed that head office should do something to stop it. But he claimed he could find nothing to indicate that Young was manipulating the books. He was restive, and David sensed that he didn't want to be tied down.

Realizing his career would be compromised if Huntington distanced himself from the crusade, David lost patience. "Look, Free, it's time for the bank to stop killing the messenger who brings the bad news," he said. "Damnit, this investigation is being covered up to protect Young."

After a moment's silence and only Huntington's sad eyes for comfort, David asked if he could have an unpaid three-month leave of absence to do volunteer work for Jimmy Carter's election machine. To his surprise, Huntington thought this a wonderful idea.

"Great!" he said, which to David sounded like "Solution!"

Huntington promised that while David was raising campaign contributions for Carter, he would devote more time to the Paris problem.

David was again hopeful that Huntington would act. By the same measure he was concerned that he had, in fact, shown faulty judgment in pursuing the Paris conspiracy with such doggedness. The first serious doubts were setting in, and with them, a gradual decline in self-confidence.

David spent the next three months working with the Carter election committee, including one week barnstorming the Southeast with Bert Lance. After Carter's election triumph, he returned to New York, hoping that Huntington had dealt with the problem.

Huntington, however, was in the hospital recovering from a heart attack. David, sensing a return to Paris would not be wise until he had seen his boss again, extended his leave of absence for another two months. He went back to work for the Carter committee as a member of the transition team.

When finally he saw Huntington toward the end of January 1977, David thought the tall and slender head of IMMD, who normally displayed a florid complexion and a keen sense of humor, looked like death warmed over. Huntington informed him he was still looking into the Paris situation, but meanwhile had decided to transfer David to Amsterdam. This, he said, entailed a promotion to assistant vice-president and, also, a rise in salary.

"You should be happy, boy," Huntington assured him.

But David was deeply upset by this turn of events. He was hardly listening when Huntington told him to pack up his affairs in Paris and be in Amsterdam as quickly as possible. He was galled by the thought that for Huntington the subject was now a moot issue.

David went back to France on February 1, 1977. He spent the next two weeks packing and putting his 8,000 pounds of household effects into storage. Then, before leaving Paris, David decided to go to see Young. A contact in Washington had told him that one of Citibank's executive vice-presidents, James Farley,[5] had made derogatory remarks about him, insinuating that he was morally dishonest. David suspected Young was behind the remarks and that the Paris senof was mounting a slander campaign against him. David found his nemesis sitting at the Goebbels desk, more belligerent than ever. With his usual directness, David asked Young if he was trying to have him blacklisted.

Young had every reason to feel cocky. The new resident inspector, Neville Armstrong, had just completed a full inspection of the treasury area, including foreign exchange and money market operations, and given it a clean bill of health. In his report, Armstrong concluded that "Management, in all the areas reviewed, by virtue of their experience and in-depth knowledge of operations, provide a high quality of direct supervision and continually endeavor to improve efficiency."

The previous inspection by Camille Legerie, two years before, had evaluated treasury's performance as below standard. Armstrong, in his 1977 review, accorded it the highest overall rating of four, which was "above acceptable level." His remarks on de Laet were flattering: "Under the supervision of the experienced Treasury Head, the area is functioning smoothly. Although occasional exchange contracts are closed, resulting in excesses over Bank lines, adherence to lines and limits in general is at an above acceptable level. The competence and efficiency of the staff mean the Bank's exposure in this highly volatile market and the related risk elements are properly managed and controlled.

"The substantial time and effort devoted to this area, coupled with the implementation of the NCR 399 systems, have resulted in a marked improvement in the overall standard of operations since the last inspection. The previous problems regarding Liability Ledger, interest accruals, controls over records, and daily check of exchange posi-

[5]James D. Farley was a member of Citicorp's executive committee. In 1976 he was in charge of the merchant banking group, which handled international loan syndications.

tions/profits have been eradicated, while penalty interest claims and overdraft interest on "nostro" accounts have been reduced to a minimum. In conjunction with the above, the increase in the experience level of the staff and the overall tightening of controls, the exceptions revealed are of a non-serious nature and are at a manageable level." [6]

The Paris branch had customer deposits of $60 million, deposits from other banks of $502 million, and deposits from head office or other branches of $1.1 billion. Its foreign exchange book totaled $516 million, which was well within the aggregate contract limits. [7] So Young should have felt very secure.

However, seeing Edwards was like waving a red flag in front of Young. "Every time this guy came forward, he would send my blood pressure to about 260," Young told the Securities & Exchange Commission three years later.

" 'You drew your gun and didn't shoot'," David quoted Young as sneering. " 'Now we're going to shoot you.' "

Young, according to David, advised him to get out of banking.

David exploded and was about to lunge across the desk at Young, but caught himself just in time. He settled back into his chair and switched to an accusatory approach.

"You know you're up to things you shouldn't be doing," he told Young. "I believe de Laet is still on the take, only it's being covered up because you guys are violating the law."

"What are you talking about?" Young asked.

"Your exchange dealings with Nassau. You're in violation of French exchange controls and tax regulations."

"David, believe me, we've been operating here for a long time. We don't have a problem. Yes, there are a lot of complicated regulations. But I don't think we have a problem."

Young, David said, reverted to his "I'm okay, you're okay" routine. But David did not let himself be influenced by Young's sudden show of conviviality and continued to point an accusing finger. "If I'm not given someone to talk to within the bank, to reopen this whole damn investigation and clear my name, then I'm going to take it outside the bank," he again threatened.

At first, David said Young responded by telling him that if he had any loyalty to the bank or his profession he would keep his suspicions internal and not broadcast them to the outside world. Young ex-

---

[6] Resident Inspection Report, January 14, 1977; Citibank document 3919–3920.
[7] Annex to Resident Inspection Report; Citibank document 3921.

plained that since 1973, the bank's incremental growth in foreign exchange earnings came from position parking in Nassau. Finally, Young offered to have the investigation reopened if David would abide by the findings of a new arbiter. That depended, David replied, on who the arbiter was. Young, he said, suggested Edwin Pomeroy. Pomeroy had taken over from Arthur Natvig, retiring that month, as the "inspector-general" of foreign exchange accounting.

David had nothing to lose. He thought this was acceptable and said so. There the matter rested for another month, while David moved to his new posting in Amsterdam.

David drove to Holland on St. Valentine's Day. The staff in Amsterdam found him an apartment on the Herengracht, near the center of the city. Young, meanwhile, did two things. First, he called his immediate superior, Robert F. B. Logan, who was in charge of IBG's Division III. Young told Logan that Edwards should be fired.

A high school graduate from Berwickshire, in southeastern Scotland, Logan joined Citibank in 1960. Ten years later he was appointed senof in Frankfurt, where he remained until April 1976, when he became head of Division III, the unit responsible for overseeing Citibank's operations in Europe and Canada.

When senof in Frankfurt, Logan had been aware of parking because it was used by the head of treasury, Fritz Menzel, on a broad scale. But in February 1977, Logan for the first time was confronting the problem on an institutional level.

Logan did not have the authority to fire Edwards. He told Young, however, that one way or another, he wanted a clean resolution of the "Edwards affair" within sixty days.

"My God, here we are almost a year and a half after the original allegations and we have not fired either one or the other," was how Young interpreted Logan's reaction. The point was that you didn't impugn another teammate's integrity without something happening. Somebody goes: if de Laet was innocent, Edwards should be fired; or vice versa. "The second time we were going to resolve this cleanly," Young remarked.

Chapter 13

Logan's Concern

Parking *is not in our lexicon anymore.*

—STEPHEN C. EYRE, MARCH 12, 1980

Four days after David Edwards moved to Amsterdam, and ten days after Charles Young recommended he be fired, Robert Logan, the head of Division III, hosted a conference of senior area officers at Düsseldorf. One of the reasons for the February 18, 1977, conference was to ask the European senofs to obtain legal and tax opinions from local counsel on "the appropriateness of parking" so that the matter could be reviewed in detail at a meeting in London the following month. Logan denied that either conference was called in reaction to Edwards's disclosures about parking. In later testimony, he said he did not hear of Edwards until two years after the Düsseldorf meeting.[1]

Logan, a fairly direct person given to sudden bouts of irritability, was definitely concerned about the dangers of parking. But his efforts to assemble a fair review by outside counsel of foreign exchange parking was frustrated by delay on the part of the European senofs

[1]Robert Logan, testimony before the SEC, March 19, 1980, page 13.

123

and treasury heads. Only the Milan senof immediately did anything to satisfy Logan's request. Other senofs complained that it was a waste of time and money, as they knew well enough the laws and regulations in their jurisdictions. Finally, Brussels, Frankfurt, Paris, and Zurich obtained opinions in time for the follow-up conference in London, but judging from the minutes, it is unlikely that these opinions were ever delivered into Logan's hands—at least not until some months later.

The London conference was described as tense, with diverging views surfacing between the field commanders and head office. The minutes, prepared by Logan's assistant Saleem Muqaddam, the financial comptroller for Division III, stated that Logan was concerned that "the institution could be taking unnecessary and unknown risks by *transferring of exchange positions* between countries. He indicated that this question had to be addressed in detail and a system put in place to handle our trading activities in such a way that

1) the reputation of the institution would not be at risk, or
2) would not create any monetary risk in the marketplaces where we operate."[2]

Logan had asked Huntington to attend the London conference since it primarily concerned the activities of his IMMD staff. Huntington flew to London from Montreux, Switzerland, where, the day before, he had given the last public address of his life. His speech, to the Association of International Bond Dealers, was about the risks and controls of foreign exchange dealing. On such an arcane subject he was clear and just technical enough without being overbearing.

Huntington spoke highly of the traders he worked with, stressing that no matter how comprehensive the limits, guidelines, or controls, the integrity of a foreign exchange operation really depended upon the people involved. Professional traders, he said, welcome controls since they provide a framework in which to work. "But the greatest control over exchange trading activity is the quality of the people in the dealing room—their professional integrity, experience, loyalty and professionalism. The real key is a good trading staff buttressed by a tough internal control policy," he told his audience in the Swiss lakeside resort city.

When he addressed the senofs and treasury heads in London, Hun-

---

[2] Division III ACO/Treasurer meeting held in London on March 18, 1977; Citibank document 546–553; emphasis added.

tington appeared to have some doubts about the integrity of Citi-bank's parking system. This contrasted ever so markedly with his bold suggestion in Montreux that traders actually "welcome" controls. In London they were discussing how to make the avoidance of con-trols—albeit state rather than institutional controls—more "appro-priate," which in Citispeak meant more "legal." Echoing Logan's sentiments, he told his London audience, "We might just be naively doing something which may not be appropriate."[3]

Ernst Brutsche also attended the London meeting, having flown in from New York to provide support for Logan, who feared resistance from the field. Brutsche was regarded as one of the fathers of parking because of his reciprocal deposit scheme between London and Nas-sau. At its height, this round-tripping scheme had reached a volume of $1,500 million and, because of the interest-rate differential it ex-ploited, was another technique for the London treasury to "lose" money to Nassau.[4]

Brutsche was now senior vice-president in charge of the newly constituted treasury division at head office. Francesco Redi had re-placed Brutsche as head of treasury in London in another "accordion move" that began in the summer of 1976. Redi's former assistant, Francesco Riccardi, had taken over as head of treasury in Milan. Both were present, as were Jean-Pierre de Laet from Paris, Fritz Menzel from Frankfurt, Jean Levy from Brussels, and Reggie van Leer, head of treasury in Amsterdam.

The minutes continued:

"After discussion, it was the general consensus that the *transfer-ring of positions* to Nassau or any other offshore center should be stopped unless it was cleared by legal and tax advisers as an accept-able business procedure. *As an alternative, it was decided that a 'World Foreign Exchange Trading Unit' would be established in Mr. Brutsche's area in New York.*"

To accommodate existing exchange controls in Europe, the senofs and treasury heads agreed that "new trading limits . . . be estab-lished for each country. The limit in local trading will be the one le-gally permissible under local law and *the excess limit will be available for trading through the intermediary of New York.*"[5]

Thus there was to be a two-tiered system of limits: one shown on

[3] Saleem Muqaddam, testimony before the SEC, August 14, 1980, page 112.
[4] See Chapter 10, pages 109–111.
[5] Citibank document 546–548; emphasis added.

the local books and another—the difference between the statutory limit and the full position limit approved by head office—to be kept on record in New York only.

In closing the conference, Logan once again requested that copies of legal and tax opinions be forwarded to Muqaddam as quickly as possible.

Afterward, Brutsche summed up the "general consensus" as being more smoke than fire. "The meeting didn't cause any major, basic changes to be made. It was more a question of tidying up controls."[6]

The world foreign exchange trading unit was never set up. After months of hesitation, it was abandoned for a simpler process, more easily controlled from within the IMMD. But both solutions underlined the essentially cosmetic concern that Citibank management paid to the problem. In official Citispeak, *parking* was to be replaced by *transferring of positions* or some other equally innocuous catch phrase.

The minutes made no mention of the Edwards affair. But Neville Armstrong, the resident inspector in Paris, told David three months later that "[your] accusations . . . against Jean-Pierre de Laet . . . came up at that conference." Armstrong was confirming that the Edwards affair had been let out of the bag and was creating a malaise throughout the Citibank trading network.

As a postscript to the London meeting, Logan and Huntington agreed to jointly send out a "tidying up" letter confirming the "consensus" that had been reached between the treasury and divisional factions. Huntington accepted the task of drafting the letter. By July 1, 1977, nothing had crossed Logan's desk, either from Huntington or from the lawyers. Logan dictated a curt note to Muqaddam:

"I am no longer willing to wait on countries . . . fumbling around getting tax opinions, etc. These matters have to be dealt with correctly and without delay.

"Please set up a very short timetable with all the [senofs] to make sure that we have here in the Division the outside [legal] and internal tax advisors' opinions, together with country action plans for my review.[7]

Logan also instructed Muqaddam to write a draft of a "tidying up" letter as he now feared that if left to Huntington, it would never get done.

The opinions that eventually came to Logan's office were anything

[6]Brutsche, testimony before the SEC, March 20, 1980, page 23.
[7]Citibank document 7615.

but reassuring. The Brussels opinion, supplied by Liedekerke Wolters Waelbroeck & Kirkpatrick, was bland. It noted that "the Belgian authorities forbid, in principle, all . . . banks to have foreign currency exchange positions against Belgian francs." While refraining from discussing the legal consequences of parking, two of the firm's senior partners, Jacques Liedekerke and John Kirkpatrick, stated that any profits derived from such transactions, even though in theory forbidden, were nevertheless subject to Belgian tax treatment.[8]

The Zurich attorney, Dr. Stefan Kraft, a noted expert on Swiss banking law, covered the subject in four pages. He summarized his findings neatly. "My question as to whether the transactions discussed are normal arm's length transactions has been answered negatively ('not 100% normal arm's length') and my question as to whether they would have to be considered as a method for evading Swiss regulations has been answered in the affirmative. Accordingly, there is a certain risk exposure not only in the area [of banking law], but also in the field of taxation."[9]

The Frankfurt opinion, produced by the law firm of Feddersen, Kemmler, Weiskopf, differed significantly from the Zurich opinion. But the Frankfurt attorneys were given conflicting facts. Dr. Kraft in Zurich was told that they were sham deals—that is, *not at arm's length*. The Frankfurt attorneys were told that the deals *were at arm's length*.

"The information that we have obtained from you gives no reason for the assumption that the FX-trading could be deemed sham transactions or of a fiduciary nature. . . . Based on your judgment that the conditions under which Citibank AG Frankfurt trades with Citibank N.A. Nassau are market conditions, we do not see any tax exposure for Citibank AG from the transactions described above."[10]

Studio Legale Guglielmo Gulotta in Milan concluded that parking was a violation of Italian exchange controls for which the penalties included imprisonment. In a second opinion, the Gulotta law firm concluded that parking profits in Nassau was tax fraud, also a criminal offense.[11]

Citibank Paris consulted a tax expert associated with Peat Marwick Mitchell in France. He gave an accountant's opinion of the tax consequences of parking. According to Pomeroy, after talking with him,

---

[8]Citibank document 1534–1535.
[9]Citibank document 1657–1660.
[10]Citibank document 1528–1532.
[11]Citibank documents 415–422. Citicorp general counsel said that following receipt in February 1977 of the Italian opinion, "we immediately moved all our trading in lira to London."

the expert "seemed more concerned with the possible appearance of non-adherence to the spirit of [French] exchange control." But the Peat Marwick associate pointed out that "without the attention of the authorities being specifically brought to it, it was unlikely that the situation would be discovered. . . ."[12]

[12]Citibank document 308–309.

Chapter 14

Sweeney's Song

First National City Bank is known in the trade as 'Fat City'—it is the nirvana, the brightest and best in global banking, the most profitable banking institution in America, the gaudy go-go queen of a traditionally discreet and somber industry.

—*Far Eastern Economic Review,* MAY 9, 1975

After his last meeting with Young, David Edwards began to realize that corporations do not react like individuals.

"They should have fired me, but they didn't," he admitted. But he made the mistake, he said, of thinking that Citibank was eventually going to act like an individual and show some integrity. It never happened.

David had been in Amsterdam a little more than a month, temporarily assigned to the trading room under Reggie van Leer, when Ed Pomeroy walked into the office. Pomeroy said he had heard that David wanted to talk to someone from the comptroller's division. They made an appointment to meet for a drink that evening.

Pomeroy had come to town with Arnold Claman, another vice-president in the comptroller's division. Claman, who looked more like an FBI agent than a banker, specialized in loss recoveries. He was in Amsterdam to see about recovering a $3 million loan that the branch had made to a spot trader in the Amsterdam oil market.

After work, Pomeroy took David to a little bar he knew, around the corner from the bank. David ordered a Heineken and Pomeroy a Bols gin. They spent the next two hours going through, as David described it, "the whole song and dance," except that when David came to the bit about parking, Pomeroy stopped him: "Let's not get into that. I'm here to discuss Jean-Pierre de Laet." But David kept on anyway, mentioning that he now suspected there was a cover-up to protect Young and "hide the manipulation of the books and the parked positions."

When David had finished, to his astonishment, Pomeroy asked if he would mind retelling the story to Arnold Claman. David said that was fine by him, and the next evening, March 24, 1977, the three of them met in the lobby of the Hotel de l'Europe in Nieuwe Doelenstraat. It was an awkward place for a confidential conversation, and David found Claman an awkward person to deal with. He was big, with a broad face, thick neck, and the manners of an Irish cop.

Pomeroy encouraged David to tell the whole story. After describing de Laet's misdealings, he mentioned Nassau and was about to launch into the institutional aspects of parking when he had second thoughts and glanced at Pomeroy for direction.

"You can mention it," Pomeroy assured him.

So he opened the sluice gates and it all poured out: why he believed senior management wanted the lid kept on parking and therefore were not going to do anything about putting a cat among the pigeons in Paris. But David, as usual, was not talking specifics, only generalities, or, as he called them, "policy issues." David figured that any meaningful investigation would uncover the details behind his generalities, because meaningful evidence—the telltale confirmations, deal tickets and brokerage slips—were lying all over the Paris trading room.

Claman's response was an even, "Don't worry. I'll look into it and get back to you as soon as possible."

Claman hardly inspired confidence in David, but as David commented, "I wasn't given a lot of choice." He waited three weeks for some reaction from the assistant comptroller, and when none came, he called Claman in New York. Claman didn't sound surprised by David's call. In fact David was very much on his mind. He had just received a letter from Pomeroy, asking what he had done with "the

Edwards file.'' The file was sitting on top of his desk.

"Have you looked at the Edwards file yet, or talked with Free?'' Pomeroy inquired. "Young said he told de Laet about the allegations. Edwards won't be happy. Allars is against asking de Laet about all the deals, accounts, gifts, etc., *as we might be embarrassed by what we found,* but unable to do much at this stage,'' Pomeroy wrote in his letter of April 18, 1977.[1]

Claman told David he had spoken with Huntington and that they would work something out. As a matter of fact, Claman said, he had David's personnel file in front of him at that very moment. After Claman mentioned the personnel file several more times, David asked: "But what's my personnel file got to do with this? I mean, it's not relevant to the question.''

There was silence, and then Claman suggested that if David would forget about Paris, he and Freeman would look after him.

David got the message. "Obviously, I wasn't going anywhere with this guy.'' He remembered shouting some smart-aleck remark over the phone at Claman—his misadaptation of a line from the Tom Stoppard play *Rosenkrantz and Guildenstern Are Dead,* which came out, "If you can't play that flute, what makes you think you can play me?''—and slamming down the receiver.

The pressure was working on David's nerves. He was edgy. His car had recently been broken into and a suitcase containing documents stolen. He had no idea who was responsible. But it wormed its way through his imagination, and he felt isolated and vulnerable.

He said he had gone into Chuck Young's office on that fateful Tuesday in October 1975 feeling like "the most confident guy in the world. If you know the truth and you know what's right and what's wrong, you just do what you have to do, and I *was* confident that what I was doing was right.

"I thought that if I kept on going up the ladder, at some point someone would shake my hand and say, 'David, you did the right thing.' ''

In Amsterdam he had confided his fears and his secrets to Jonathan Elkus, the number-two officer in the branch. David needed someone to whom he could turn for advice. Elkus, like Edwards, was a new man in Amsterdam, having only recently been transferred from Hong Kong, where he had spent four years during which he had lived through a similar experience.

During his stay in Hong Kong, Elkus had uncovered what he de-

[1] Citibank document 530–531; emphasis added.

scribed as "a pattern of deteriorating loans." When he investigated further, he found that the root of the problem was a questionable lending practice relating to the integrity of some of the larger borrowers, who were often connected in one way or another with senior branch officials, and to the quality or even existence of collateral for the loans.

Elkus reported the questionable loans to his superiors. At first he was ignored, but when he persisted he was threatened with transfer or dismissal. Next, he went to the regional auditor, who recommended he talk with the assistant comptrollers in New York. Elkus waited for his next home leave and brought with him a suitcase of documents showing the deteriorating loans. Back at head office, he found the assistant comptrollers lacked fervor and this caused him to seek a meeting with George Vojta, who had just taken over IBG.

"What should I do?" Elkus asked Vojta, after explaining the Hong Kong situation.

"Follow your conscience," Vojta advised.

Subsequently, Elkus talked the matter over with the senior vice-president in charge of Asia, which he had previously avoided doing because he anticipated a lack of response. As anticipated, the senior vice-president dismissed the allegations as totally unrealistic.

Meanwhile, without informing Elkus, Vojta contacted the comptroller's office and asked for a special audit. As a result, a task force of internal auditors finally went to Hong Kong. After an inspection that lasted several weeks, they adversely classified loans amounting to tens of millions of dollars—in all, about one-third of the branch's loan portfolio. Over the succeeding months, about $25 million of the classified loans had to be written off as uncollectable.

When Elkus heard how Arnold Claman had reacted to Edwards's story of corruption in Paris, he sensed the same thrust of injustice that had almost cost him his career. He felt he understood the soul searching that Edwards was going through.

"You must go to the top," he counseled Edwards.

With Edwards in his office, Elkus called Stephen Eyre in New York. When Eyre came on the line, Elkus explained why he was calling. Edwards could hear only one side of the conversation, but once his name was mentioned, he sensed Eyre's reply: "Oh no, not that nut again."

In fact, Eyre asked Elkus: "Is he [Edwards] shooting off his mouth again?"

Elkus thought he convinced Eyre that Edwards's allegations were serious and that Edwards was not, as Eyre seemed to think, a troublemaker. In any event, Eyre was sufficiently aroused to take action. He called Eugene Sweeney, the regional comptroller in London who had recently replaced David Allars, and told him to contact Elkus. That evening Elkus received a call from Sweeney, who wanted to know the background to the Edwards affair. Elkus explained that it sounded as if Edwards had been badly treated and was likely to do something drastic—like take his story to the press—unless given a fair hearing inside the bank.

"It would be bad if he was driven into going outside the bank, as he is reaching the point of desperation," Elkus told Sweeney.

The next day, Sweeney called Edwards and arranged to see him in Amsterdam later in the month.

A couple of days before Sweeney arrived in Amsterdam, Pomeroy wrote Allars in New York with some pointed advice: "I don't want to give Edwards the slightest excuse for saying continued inaction on our part led him to spread the word about de Laet. Look at his file to see if he has a legitimate grievance re salary. Then talk to Free about the best way of unloading the guy. . . . His attitude may have hardened since then, but I still think we owe him something or at least shouldn't screw him purely because he brought up the allegations about de Laet."[2]

Sweeney and Edwards met in a private breakfast room at the Hotel de l'Europe and shared what David described as the longest breakfast of his life. David was reasonably practiced at his "song-and-dance act" and once he had finished, he said Sweeney told him: "This is a terrible story."

Sweeney, according to Edwards, would reopen the investigation if Edwards agreed not to "break the bottle" by taking his allegations public. Edwards said Sweeney also agreed that there existed strong *prima facie* evidence indicating the Paris books did not accurately reflect the real profit-and-loss position, and that, if this in fact were the case, the practice should be stopped.

Sweeney asked David to come to London to talk with a "multiple currency expert." If David was able to satisfy the expert that Citibank's control system was not finely enough tuned to pick up the irregularities he described, then Sweeney said he would "open the books of the Paris branch for a historical investigation."[3] Furthermore, according to David's SEC testimony of a year later, Sweeney agreed

[2] Citibank document 529.
[3] David Edwards, testimony before the SEC, April 7, 1978, page 22.

that the London meeting would be held in complete confidence. Not even David Allars would be told of it, because David feared that Allars somehow had been coopted into the cover-up. David also testified that Sweeney warned him to concentrate on the de Laet corruption charges and not to mention the parking of foreign exchange positions.

The London meeting took place on June 13, 1977, at the regional comptroller's offices on Old Brompton Road. When David arrived that Monday at 9:30 A.M. he found a different Eugene Sweeney. He was still the same natty dresser with the "CPA appearance," but his attitude had changed. David suspected that Sweeney had talked to Allars in the meantime and that Allars had screamed at him: "What the hell are you doing encouraging that guy? He's caused us enough trouble as it is."

Sweeney introduced David to the only other person present, the "multiple currency expert." His name was Neville "Sach" Armstrong who, to David's horror, was Citibank's resident inspector in Paris. The offices, almost next door to Harrod's, were spartan, with a blackboard that David used to illustrate his explanation of de Laet's bookkeeping gymnastics.

David had further refined his presentation for the Old Brompton Road meeting. He explained that the irregularities in the Paris treasury fit into three concentric rings. He went over, briefly, the kickback ring and then spent the next two hours explaining how de Laet and Young "cooked" the books, which was the second ring.

One of the methods involved the booking of future interest income as foreign exchange income and then returning it to the interest account at a later date. This procedure allowed the Paris treasury to bring forward anticipated earnings, even though a reasonable risk existed that they might never materialize.

Armstrong, according to David, agreed that this procedure was beyond the detection capabilities of the monitoring process used by a resident inspector. Armstrong admitted he had noticed symptoms of this practice, but said they could only be picked up by a more thorough audit of the treasury operation.

Every time David felt he was beginning to reach Armstrong, Sweeney would interject, "Now, Sach, hold it. Don't be too hasty."

De Laet, David said, performed most of his magic through the swap process.[4] Swap transactions in Paris were not time-stamped, allowing

---

[4] A "swap" is the combination of a "spot" foreign exchange trade (for immediate delivery) with a reciprocal "forward" foreign exchange trade (delivery sometime in the future) by which, in effect, two contracting parties "swap" currencies for a specified period of time.

a trader to pass a spot sale in the morning while withholding the second part of the swap, the forward purchase, until the close of the market so as to benefit from a knowledge of the day's trading range.

Of course this was extremely helpful when structuring non-arm's length deals. It allowed the trader the full benefit of hindsight. De Laet, David charged, frequently used artificial rates in his swap transactions with head office and other Citibank units.

Again, Armstrong agreed. He said that when he questioned de Laet about unforeseen earnings, the treasury head would reply, "It's all in the swaps."

David explained that the Paris branch was able to get away with hiding these irregular practices because of the accounting gyrations used by de Laet for booking "interest" entries on transactions structured to avoid the special French surtax on foreign exchange earnings.

Just before lunch break, Sweeney asked David if anyone could corroborate his allegations about de Laet. David said he thought Jean-Michel Ennuyer might be able to, and also Jan Dil, a Dutch trader who had worked under de Laet and was then the chief trader for Citibank in Toronto.

After lunch, David wiped the blackboard clean and announced, "Let's go into the third concentric ring: the parking of positions in Nassau."

"Hold it, David," Sweeney interrupted. "You promised you wouldn't go into that."

David denied he had made any such promise. They spent the next hour arguing about that and also about whether Young, as senof, could block what David described in later memoranda as a "historical investigation."

The whole purpose of the meeting, David maintained, was to open an investigation into the parking of positions in Nassau by Paris. Before adjourning, David insisted that in the minutes of their meeting they agree on the three areas that David had covered: kickbacks, cooking the books, and parking. Sweeney was reluctant to record anything about cooking the books and refused all mention of parking.

"If you bring this matter up, it will not go in your favor," David said Sweeney warned him.[5]

In the end, Sweeney made no minutes, only a few handwritten notes, which he kept for himself. As they left the Old Brompton Road office, after seven hours of discussion, Sweeney said, "We'll get back to you."

[5] Edwards, SEC testimony, page 27.

David had heard that song before.

He never heard from Sweeney again.

David returned to Amsterdam downcast. On Wednesday, June 15, 1977, Jon Elkus came to his office to hear how things had gone in London. "Terrible," David said. The phone rang. David answered, motioning to Elkus to stay. It was Jean-Michel Ennuyer calling from Peter S.A., the foreign exchange brokers in Paris.

"Jesus, David, what have you done to de Laet?" Ennuyer wanted to know. Ennuyer said he had just finished an hour-long phone conversation with de Laet, who was up in arms over David's treachery in London. De Laet wanted Ennuyer to make a statement denying he had witnessed any irregularities while chief trader under de Laet. He said de Laet offered him a six-month 50 million French franc placement as inducement, with promise of more business daily, if he agreed. David's heart sank.

That night David drove down to south Holland with a Dutch girl friend. At 9 P.M. he called Sach Armstrong at his home in Paris and complained that he and Sweeney had broken their promise to keep the London meeting secret.

"Sach," David said, "I am a little disturbed. I got a call this morning from Paris."

"From whom?"

"A fellow there who tells me that you evidently must have gone back to Paris and told Jean-Pierre de Laet I had talked to you in London and you must have outlined everything to Jean-Pierre that I told you."

"No, not at all."

"Well, de Laet called him this morning and spent over an hour on the telephone with him outlining it all blow by blow. I am outraged!"

"I have spoken to Mr. Young."

"You told Young? Don't you think that was a fairly irresponsible move?"

"No."

"Why?"

"Because I was advised to speak to Mr. Young by Mr. Sweeney."

"Gene Sweeney told you to talk to Chuck Young?"

"Well, Chuck Young knew the meeting was taking place."

"He did?"

"Yeah. . . . And of course when I got back yesterday, he asked to see me. And Gene had given me the okay to go ahead and speak to Mr. Young."

"Well, I am a little surprised, because Gene Sweeney asked me not to talk to anybody about this."

"Look, David, I don't think you should be talking to me. I am not in charge of this investigation. I am just obeying orders. It is as simple as that. . . . You should be talking to Sweeney."

"Sweeney is in Athens. I cannot get hold of him."

"Well, you should not be talking to me . . ."

"We agreed in the room that we would continue to keep this in our group—meaning the three of us."

"Young was aware the meeting was taking place."

"Before it happened?"

"Before it happened."

"Did you tell Young?"

"No."

"Sweeney told Young?"

"I don't know, but Young was aware the meeting was taking place."

"Yoohoo! What a surprise! I think they are covering it up again. . . . As the resident inspector in France, you went back and told Chuck Young that I suspected him of cooking the books."

"No, I did not say that."

"Yeah?"

". . . Let's draw this conversation to a close. I don't know how you got my number, and I am very annoyed that I have been called."

"Is that right?"

The conversation lasted another few minutes before finally it was broken off with a hint by Armstrong that since their London meeting, people at "a pretty high level in head office" had become involved.

Eight days later, on June 13, 1977, David received a telephone call from Freeman Huntington, who ordered him to New York immediately.

When David arrived at head office, Huntington told him: "I want to talk to you about two things. They may or may not be related. The first is you have to shut up. You can't go on. You are not allowed to go back to London to talk to the comptrollers.

"The second is what are you going to do for a job?"

David had two days of discussions with Huntington, during which he pleaded for a reopening of the investigation on a higher level. David said he wanted someone else to assume responsibility and if it was recognized that he had acted in good faith, then he hoped for some measure of rehabilitation.

"After all, I'm not trying to undermine the institution. I'm only trying to get it to follow the law, which should be in the bank's best interest and consistent with its policy,'' he said he told Huntington.

Huntington sighed and said he would see what could be done to get David a hearing at the executive management level. But he added that such a meeting couldn't be arranged immediately because of the July Fourth holiday. He suggested that David go home to Texas while he worked on setting it up. He provided David with an air ticket. While in Texas, David called several times to head office. Each time, Huntington told him he was still working on it.

Finally, David returned to New York on July 25. When he walked into the office, Huntington told him he was scheduled to see George Vojta on the afternoon of July 27.

Chapter 15

The Second Denial

I can categorically state that at no time, nor in any way, did I suggest, direct, or participate in any cover-up.

—H. R. HALDEMAN, MAY 31, 1973

On March 31, 1977, two weeks after Logan's conference in London, George Vojta wrote to all division heads, ACOs,[1] and senofs:

Each ACO/Senof will audit local tax plans and exposure to assure that booking and tax procedures adopted during recent years will stand up under rigorous legal and regulatory scrutiny . . . . Each country is expected to review its business activities to assure compliance with local business practice and regulations, the Corporate Policy Manual and U.S. Federal Reserve Regulations.[2]

Until then, Citibank's *Accounts and Procedures Manual* only required that traders comply with foreign exchange limits set by head

[1] ACO was a new rank in Citi command, standing for area corporate officer, and it was awarded to senofs in countries, like France, Switzerland or West Germany, with more than one branch.
[2] Citibank document 7921–7922.

office. But in the March 1977 edition, under foreign exchange trading, a new sentence was added:

> Limits imposed by local authorities (banking and other regulatory agencies) will be closely observed, and if these are more restrictive than those imposed by the Bank, they will supersede the Bank's requirements.

These instructions were generally disregarded, and the system adopted at the London conference earlier that month prevailed. Senior management in Switzerland, for example, introduced the London procedures, splitting the Swiss overnight limit into two categories—the local position limit and the New York position limit. This enabled Switzerland, which had a $75 million overall limit approved by head office, to show an "official" limit of $20 million, which was in line with the statutory regulations enforced by the Swiss National Bank, when in fact it was allowed to take overnight positions totaling another $55 million on its New York approval sheet.

When David Edwards returned from Texas at the end of July 1977, the first person he saw was Paolo Cugnasca, whose office was close to Huntington's on the fourth floor. David used Cugnasca's office as his base whenever visiting head office. The Italian trader was no longer in charge of the Eurocurrency desk, but ran Citicorp's worldwide capital hedging unit. Cugnasca was well aware of David's problems. "Don't fight City Hall," he counseled David. "It's not worth it."

When David said he had a meeting with Huntington, Cugnasca warned: "David, be careful with Freeman. He's not the friend you think he is."

A spiral staircase connected the IMMD offices on the fourth floor with the IBG offices on the fifth floor. Huntington walked David to the staircase when he went to see Vojta. "Good luck, boy," Huntington said. "Come and see me when it's over."

Vojta had the big corner office that had previously been occupied by Al Costanzo before he was moved to the vice-chairman's suite on the fifteenth floor. Vojta was Citibank's great conceptual thinker. He saw the world as Wriston saw it. He did his best to set David at ease, telling him he had acted quite properly in raising a question of corporate concern about the conduct of a bank officer in Paris. He said every conceivable line of inquiry would be used to look into the charges and asked if David would abide by the results of his investigation. David said he would.

"How did it go?" Huntington wanted to know after David returned to the fourth floor.

"Fine," said David.

But nobody told him that Vojta was only weeks away from reassignment.

Huntington supplied David with an airplane ticket back to Texas, where he remained for several weeks awaiting the outcome of Vojta's inquiries.

Before leaving that afternoon, David noticed the IMMD was a beehive of activity. But David was not told the reason for the commotion. He was virtually an outsider, no longer even a contender for the team. The activity, in fact, was related to the distribution of the "tidying-up" letter that Saleem Muqaddam had drafted for Logan's and Huntington's signatures. The letter had been four months in the works. It was marked STRICTLY PRIVATE AND CONFIDENTIAL and went to all Division III ACOs, senofs, and heads of treasury.

July 27, 1977
Re: *Foreign Exchange Positions Off Local Books*

Gentlemen:
Effective immediately no foreign exchange positions off local books may be booked at branches other than New York. The booking of new foreign exchange positions off local books with Citibank New York will take place according to the procedures outlined below. With regard to foreign exchange positions off local books currently outstanding and/or advised on or before 8/8/77, detailed procedures are also outlined below.

1) *Reporting Procedures*
Overseas branches will inform International Foreign Exchange & Funding in New York by phone of all deals to be booked. Information will be given over (212) 559 8414 or (212) 559 3003. All contracts will be booked with Citibank New York.

2) *Overnight Limits*
Overnight limits in excess of limits set by local authorities will be transferred to the International Foreign Exchange & Funding—Policy & Coordination in New York. International Foreign Exchange & Funding will control usage of each limit versus outstanding contracts.

Page two of the letter dealt with internal housekeeping and was purely technical. The letter closed by naming the two coordinating officers who were to act as the parking lot attendants. They were Paolo Cugnasca and Gerhard Isele, another member of Huntington's IMMD staff.[3]

In late August 1977, David was summoned back to New York. David was filled with misgivings when he learned that by order of Walt Wriston, Tom Theobald had replaced Vojta as head of IBG. The great conceptual thinker had been put in charge of Citicorp's long-range planning, which meant that he was a general with no troops to command.

David went directly to see Huntington, who informed him that Vojta had decided there was no substance to his allegations.

"Vojta said to tell you, 'The chapter is closed.' "

"I'd better hear it from him," David said.

David spent the next several hours with Vojta in his new office going over the charges. David thought Vojta became short-tempered with his persistence. Vojta, after all, had reviewed the charges with an intradivisional team that included, in addition to Huntington, the chief auditor, the head of international audits, the senior foreign exchange comptroller, the auditor in charge of fraud and defalcations, and the head of Division III. This second round of inquiries had focused on de Laet's trading practices, as Vojta regarded parking more an operational than ethical problem of trying to accommodate national regulations with the realities of trading in the international marketplace.

After examining the charges one more time, the experts had returned to Vojta with a pooled report that concluded there was still no proof that de Laet had acted dishonestly. Vojta now tried to impress upon David it was time to put his concerns behind him and concentrate on getting on with his career.

Vojta also informed David that he was being transferred to a newly formed government business unit at head office. He said he found David quite enthusiastic about the change. He had read a paper David had written while "recuperating" in Texas on expanding the role of small businesses in government-backed development projects and felt it was constructive.

Huntington indicated that the new assignment was only temporary. He told David to go back to Amsterdam and pack up his affairs there before reporting to the new unit. But not wanting any trouble with

[3]Citibank document 1507–1509; also, 5268–5270.

Young, Huntington forbade David to retrieve his household goods, still in storage in Paris. David flew to Amsterdam on September 10, 1977. While he was there, he received the news that Huntington had died.

David was now an orphan at Citibank.

Chapter 16

Theobald's Promise

All employees must have a keen appreciation of our responsibility to the public in every country in which we operate. Collectively, we must earn public confidence in the integrity of our institution—in terms of its purposes and plans, its business transactions and its actions within the community.

—CITICORP *Ethical Standards Desk Book,* JUNE 1976

The new head of the international banking group, Thomas C. Theobald, was a thirty-nine-year-old Harvard Business School graduate who had been with Citibank since 1960. By November 1977, Theobald was commanding the most direct pathway to the chairman's office. Wriston had gone to the helm of Citibank from command of the international division, as had George Moore before him. Theobald was following the same route, which made him the third or fourth most powerful figure within the Citi structure.

Theobald was thin and aesthetic looking, but clammy. He had none of Wriston's sarcasm or wit. When a Citi executive announced he was off to see Wily Walt, his colleagues would warn him, "Watch out for the hooks." With Theobald, it might have been, "Don't slip on the ice."

Arthur Natvig remembered meeting Theobald one day in Citicorp's executive dining room on the 38th floor. He had gone there for lunch. If executives were unaccompanied, custom required them to take a seat at the large oval common table in the center of the room. Natvig found himself seated next to Tom Theobald.

"Nice day, eh?" Natvig said, turning toward his neighbor, who had already ordered.

He got back a grunt. A distinctly chilly grunt. He tried two more questions, was rewarded with one more grunt, and decided to give up, spending the rest of his lunchtime in silence.

Edwards returned from Europe at the end of October 1977 and moved, temporarily, into Cugnasca's office. Paolo was on vacation, deer hunting in Vermont. After a few days, Ernst Brutsche told him he was being shifted out of treasury to a newly formed government lending and export promotion unit headed by Bob Terkhorn, Vojta's former chief of staff. David refused the transfer and instead spent the next ten days composing two letters, one to Theobald, asking for his help, and the other to Eugene Sweeney, the regional comptroller for Europe. While working on them, he received a memo from Terkhorn confirming his transfer to the payroll of the government unit. He was asked to initial an attached copy of the memo to indicate his acceptance. Instead, he boldly wrote across it: "Unacceptable. I plan to remain in the treasury group until we are able to resolve this," and returned the memo to Terkhorn.

On November 14, 1977, David sent his letter of last resort to Theobald.

Dear Mr. Theobald,
I am writing to ask your assistance as the Head of the International Banking Group in Citibank, therefore as my ultimate superior, in resolving the following problem.

On Friday, November 4, 1977, I learned from Ernst Brutsche, SVP, and Bob Terkhorn, VP, that George Vojta, EVP Planning, had issued instructions on the previous day, November 3, for my reassignment to the permanent US Staff assigned to the Government Division. This is not the assignment I had been led to expect by Freeman Huntington and Bob Terkhorn as recently as September of this year. Aside from my disappointment over such an unexpected reversal of the Bank's position resulting in my virtual demotion into an area in which I have no expertise, I am greatly distressed by what I take to be the cause of Mr. Vojta's action.

The way in which this change in assignment has been handled is consistent with the manner in which I have been treated over the past twenty-six months, since I first discovered and began to try to bring to light questionable activities involving the Bank's Paris branch, including the receipt of kickbacks by an officer of the branch; the "cooking of the books" by the management; and the illegal parking of foreign exchange positions in Nassau in order to meet budgeted earnings.

Since I first brought up the matter, as I then knew it, in Paris over two years ago, I have been subjected to illogical job transfers and denied official performance reviews. I have also been denied the opportunity to work in my field of expertise and have been slandered both within and outside the Bank. Yet never once have I been accused of wrongdoing or incompetence, having been evaluated in 1975 as one with a very promising career in the Treasury Division. Moreover, from the beginning of this episode, I have tried to act in a manner beneficial to the stockholders and directors of Citicorp and within the official channels of the Bank.

More important, the issues and evidence I have discussed have never been refuted by any reasonable standards. The Bank's investigation, at least as it has been reported to me, has been largely chimerical. On the other hand, if files to which I have no access reveal or imply that the investigation corroborates my allegations, then the Bank's treatment of me becomes all the more indefensible.

Mr. Vojta's latest change of my status places me one step away from professional oblivion. It is totally unacceptable to me, especially in view of the fact that I have yet to receive adequate answers to questions for which Mr. Vojta took full responsibility at our meeting on July 27th of this year. Therefore, I do not think it is in my best interest or those of the Bank to leave the Treasury Division for new duties until I have received at least a candid assessment of my position in the Bank.

The hard truth is I am being punished within the Bank for taking action that was justified by what I saw going on in Paris and what I took to be official policy of Citibank—simply to follow the law and to terminate any illegal activities.

Was I wrong to do what I have done? I think not. Would the Bank have been better served if I had participated by conspiracy of silence in the illegality? I think not. Would our Bank have been better off if I had brought these problems to the attention of the appropriate public officials rather than my superiors within the Bank? No.

I know you are beginning a new position. From what I can gather, many if not all of these practices which I brought to light may have ceased. None the less, I think you should know that to the best of my knowledge:

1. There has been no formal historical investigation of the accounting practices of Citibank Paris in the face of such strong symptomatic indication that the practices were not in accord with the Citibank Accounting & Procedures Manual and the Securities & Exchange Commission Reporting Requirements in spite of the fact that I provided these indications to the Head European Comptroller and to the Resident Inspector of Citibank Paris, both of whom agreed with my conclusions at the time.
2. Citibank's official policy on its practice of parking foreign exchange positions in Nassau remains unclear.
3. I have been denied an official review for the past 2½ years, depriving me of my only means of documenting this affair in my personnel record.
4. My proposed transfer cannot be justified in view of my expertise, my interest, and my performance during the period I was allowed to perform, but only on grounds of a great bureaucracy's discomfort with the bearer of bad but true news.

I have enclosed for your information a letter of this date to Mr. Eugene Sweeney, VP, who was involved in my long attempt to set things right. The letter sets out as succinctly as I can the train of events, based on my notes and recordings which has led me to this impasse in my career.

I hope you will give this matter serious consideration and that you will see fit to rescind my transfer order and give me the opportunity to serve in a capacity in which I am able to work effectively and advance the interest of Citibank.

Sincerely yours,
David Edwards,
Assistant Vice-President

The letter that David sent that same day to Eugene Sweeney detailed his two-year quest to have the Paris treasury investigated. In it, he claimed that his transfer to the government unit was "clearly a

retaliatory demotion for what I have done and said, although no one
has effectively refuted the accuracy of any charges or the propriety of
the manner in which I have raised them.''

Theobald's reaction was instant. He did precisely what was required of him. He had never heard of Edwards before and had no
idea with whom, among Citibank's 25,000 employees, he was dealing. First, he spoke with Terkhorn, who confirmed that Edwards had
refused his new assignment, which was to develop new forms of export financing. Terkhorn urged Theobald to see Edwards. Next,
Theobald demanded explanations from Young, Derby, and Sweeney.
He also spoke with Eyre and fixed a meeting for 10:30 A.M. Wednesday, November 16, 1977, to be attended by Eyre, Allars, Pomeroy,
Logan, Terkhorn, and Vojta.

At the meeting, Eyre assured Theobald that two previous investigations had turned up no evidence to support Edwards's charges. But
Eyre agreed to send Pomeroy to Paris one more time to investigate
further. Theobald also wanted Jean-Pierre de Laet's file reopened, this
time to probe those potentially embarrassing "deals, accounts, gifts,
etc." which Allars, six months previously, had not wanted to disturb.

While waiting for replies from Young, Sweeney, and Derby, later
in the day Theobald called Edwards to his office—the same one, with
the same sofa, desk, and coffee table, that Vojta had occupied only
weeks before.

"There he was," David later said, "one smooth rattlesnake with
nothing but ice in his heart."

Instant antipathy distanced the two men.

"Why did you write all these things?" David claimed Theobald
demanded.

David was taken aback. He still expected someone high up on the
ladder one day would shake his hand and say, "Edwards, you did the
right thing!" He certainly hadn't expected Theobald to be so aggres-
sively negative in the opening seconds of their meeting. Theobald didn't
wait for an answer. He waved the Terkhorn memo with David's *Unacceptable* scribbled on it. "And this?" he asked. The ice had melted;
Theobald was fuming.

David stood his ground. Why, he wanted to know, hadn't he received any answers to his questions? Finally, according to David,
Theobald grumbled that he was getting the answers. To lay the matter
to rest once and for all, he had asked the "chief partner in charge"
of Peat Marwick Mitchell, Citibank's outside auditors, to undertake
an independent inquiry.

David understood that this new inquiry would focus on parking. Theobald promised to give him a written summary within a month. The meeting lasted twenty minutes. David was stiffly ushered out.

When asked by SEC investigators eighteen months later what had been discussed at this meeting, Theobald said he doubted the subject of parking ever came up.[1]

[1] Thomas C. Theobald, testimony before the SEC, May 16, 1980; page 13.

Chapter 17

Cugnasca's Papers

Citibank has never been happy just to maintain a "market share." We want those few extra points that prove we are the best international bank.

—CITIBANK'S AREA CORPORATE OFFICER IN HONG KONG, AS QUOTED IN *Citibanker,* JUNE 1983

Following his meeting with Theobald, David returned to Paolo Cugnasca's fourth-floor office, which, in Cugnasca's absence, had become his last foothold in treasury.

If Theobald kept his word, the kind of high-powered investigation that David had been insisting on for the past two years would finally get rolling. David felt certain that only such an inquiry, truly independent and led by the senior partner of Peat Marwick, would vindicate him and save his career. He settled into the chair behind Cugnasca's desk and began going through the drawers in search of pad or paper on which to write his notes of the Theobald meeting. More particularly, he wanted to write Theobald a six-liner confirming his eagerness to cooperate in the investigation.

In one of the drawers lay a folder. Out of curiosity, David removed it and started going through the documents it contained. The first one was a 21-page report marked CONFIDENTIAL, which turned out to be a parking manual. It had been drafted by Cugnasca at the end of 1975. In June 1976, as Huntington visited Paris, the manual was circulating in its original draft among the treasury heads of Division III. At the time, Huntington had conceded only the faintest knowledge of parking and promised David he would look into the matter. But here was a primer, prepared for Huntington's use, that proposed the standardization of parking procedures and the recording of parked positions on a centralized set of books.

An introduction helpfully defined parking. "Nassau Branch is used by Overseas Branches as a vehicle to book Foreign Exchange transactions for their account. The Branch initiating the transaction (Parking Branch) transfers to Nassau (by means of a Foreign Exchange contract) its (or part of its) total overnight Foreign Exchange Position.

"Typically, this is done either to comply with local regulatory requirements, or to transfer (taxable) profits generated abroad to a tax-haven area."

The manual underlined that Nassau was only an accommodating branch. It held no responsibility for the positions parked with it, and "all profits/losses deriving from these transactions are allocated to the Parking Branch via MIS." Parking telexes were to be sent to the Eurocurrency department of the IMMD at head office, using one of three indicated telex numbers, and not directly to the Nassau branch. For more effective control and identification, telex messages were to follow a standardized format.

"The nature of these Parked Positions is such that under no circumstance the Parking Branch can indicate the related transactions as 'Parking.' " The manual gave several examples of typical formatted messages. Before closing, it stressed, "Again, the responsibility for Parked Positions lies solely with the Parking Branch, while Nassau only acts as a booking unit. . . . Naturally, no mention of Parked Positions will be made." [1]

David stayed late that Wednesday evening and photocopied the confidential parking file. He also looked into the credenza next to Cugnasca's desk and found that it contained thousands of trading tickets, confirmations, and head office approvals for parking transactions. These led him to an operations storeroom on the sixth floor that

[1] The Cugnasca Report; Citibank document 7032–7053.

was crowded with boxes marked "Parked Positions—Germany"; "Parked Positions—France"; "Parked Positions—Switzerland"; and so on, through the fiefdoms of Division III. The boxes contained the parking telexes sent from the European branches to head office.

David suspected this new evidence was the tip of an iceberg. He supposed the full dimensions of the iceberg were known only to a small ring of people. He wondered how far up the command ladder knowledge of parking went. Leery after being told so often that "parking is not in our lexicon," or words of similar intent, he decided to keep the find to himself until he had a clearer idea of what Theobald's strategy would be.

On Friday, November 18, 1977, Young replied to Theobald with a memo claiming that Edwards was a liar:

> I not only didn't tell Edwards he shouldn't complain, I decided to investigate. I told Derby to check the deal slips with the Antwerp broker. On October 16, 1975, Derby and I met again with Edwards. I told him going to Washington would make people question his judgment. On November 16, 1975, Derby and Guido Vollenwieder said the Antwerp broker didn't get out-of-line rates. I didn't say in December 1975 he should leave Citibank. . . .
>
> Although Paris got MIS earnings from Nassau in 1975/76, none of these MIS earnings resulted from Paris deliberately losing money on its books. Edwards didn't get a review by me in July 1976 as he was on New York's payroll. He believed James Farley, executive vice president, had described him as a 'crook' in talking with an official from Washington seeking information about Edwards. . . . I didn't say incremental earnings since 1973 were from foreign exchange parking. Later, Conolly from Natwest called me. . . . The Ennuyer incident occurred the day we removed him from the dealing room. Ennuyer did give me a memo re: the manipulation of the cost-of-funds report. De Laet denied both allegations. On October 13, 1975, Paris lost $75,000 as a result of Edwards's trading decision.[2]

A few days later Will Derby sent Theobald his version of the October 1975 meetings. "I deny saying I heard rumors the previous year that Jean-Pierre de Laet was taking kickbacks. I didn't show Edwards the monthly ledger cards showing commissions to the Antwerp bro-

---

[2] Excerpted from Citibank document 508–519.

ker. I didn't say the broker was being paid in London at de Laet's request. I didn't suggest he break into de Laet's house or tape de Laet.''[3]

Sweeney's memo was a few days longer in coming. He also complained of being misquoted by Edwards. "I didn't say there's a strong case that the Paris books were wrong. I didn't say an investigation couldn't or shouldn't be done. In sum, David Edwards's letter is full of inaccuracies.''[4]

Cugnasca later said a malaise had crept over treasury's operations. But the malaise was not David Edwards; it was parking. Francesco Redi, Brutsche's successor as head of treasury in London, identified the problem in a letter he had written to Huntington a year earlier. Setting out his fears about parking, he said the bank was exposing itself to the following possibilities:

1. Severely upsetting the local Central Bank;
2. Exposing ourselves to blackmail, for example by some unhappy staff member;
3. Violation of internal foreign exchange limits through parking of positions with other branches [a probable reference to "double parking," which had bothered Arthur Natvig].

"One should question at this point whether it is worthwhile wasting the expertise we have been building up in the field over the last fifteen years, and [determine] what are the alternatives to avoiding a substantial reduction of foreign exchange earnings in the Institution," Redi suggested.[5] Huntington never replied.

Pomeroy arrived in Paris a few days after the November 16 council of war in Theobald's office. His investigation focused not on whether Young and de Laet had "cooked the books," but, foremost, on discrediting the character of David Edwards and, collaterally, on the old question of kickbacks.

On November 22, 1977, Pomeroy met with Jean-Michel Ennuyer. Young had requested the appointment, and when Ennuyer heard that it was related to Edwards's allegations against de Laet, he said he would come immediately. According to Pomeroy's notes, a major part of the meeting was devoted to a description of the brokerage business

[3] Excerpted from Citibank document 346–347.
[4] Excerpted from Citibank document 298–299.
[5] Francesco Redi, letter to Freeman H. Huntington, June 29, 1976; Citibank document 7054–7055.

in Paris, and a "picture of wide corruption was painted," which he thought was "perhaps somewhat exaggerated for our benefit." His notes continued:

The following points *specifically* related to Edwards memo [to Sweeney] of 11/14/77 were discussed.

Although Edwards repeats . . . that he had mentioned Ennuyer as being able to corroborate any contention that de Laet was on the take from brokers, Ennuyer confirmed that he had no substantive evidence, although he clearly conveyed impression that he believed the allegations to be true.

We were unable to get clear confirmation of the phone call which Edwards maintains Ennuyer made to him on the morning of 6/15/77. Ennuyer only mentioned a half-hour call which Edwards had made to him in the evening about this time.[6] Ennuyer claims to have told Edwards that there was no purpose in making allegations of kick-backs unless he could back it up with proper evidence. He claims to have given similar advice to Edwards in the past.

Ennuyer did not recollect de Laet giving him a substantial deal that day . . . with a promise of more to come daily. He confirmed Chuck Young's statement that as a result of a chance encounter with Young he had already discussed increased use of his company for FF dealings.

Ennuyer did not have any firm recollection of approaching Young on the subject of de Laet's manipulation of the books or of sub-mitting a handwritten report to him (page 7) although Young does now have some recollection of such an incident. Ennuyer claims that de Laet was manipulating the books by incorrectly reflecting the cost of swaps to show an improved funding cost. (Later in the day, de Laet, with the support of one of the traders, R. André, accused Ennuyer of doing the same sort of thing to cover exchange losses.)

Ennuyer claimed that A. Dangé formerly in the trading room but now working with him could supply us with more positive infor-mation of de Laet taking kickbacks, but he later seemed to back away from this. The fact that Dangé had more information was supposedly based on his assumption that he must have more infor-mation because he worked with de Laet for longer. . . .[7]

---

[6] Whether Ennuyer made the phone call had no bearing on the main issue, which should have been to determine if in fact Paris was "cooking the books." No mystery existed for Ennuyer. In an interview in November 1983, he confirmed having made such a call to Edwards at the time indicated.

[7] Citibank document 296–297.

Pomeroy did not contact Alain Dangé and never ascertained whether the former Citibank trader had "more positive information." He did, however, get in touch with Michael Conolly. Young arranged and attended the meeting.

David thought Conolly—who was fifteen years his senior—"an awfully nice guy." He said, "I liked Mike and had him over to my apartment in Paris and introduced him to all my friends. I felt I could trust him and that he was an older figure to whom I could turn for advice."

Following the October 1975 introduction by Edwards, Conolly and Young had become close friends. Their families shared a summer cottage and their children went to the same school. Conolly became caught in the middle of two friendships.

Before leaving Paris for his new posting in Amsterdam, David had called Conolly and suggested they meet for farewell drinks. Conolly accepted and David had confided in him about his conflict with Young. As he talked he became intensely emotional, Conolly recalled. "David had a strong puritanical streak in him, and some issues he really took to heart," he said.

David unfolded his story of corruption in Citibank's Paris trading room and asked Conolly for advice. He was depressed and was considering returning to Texas to see if his trading experience would gain him employment with one of the expanding regional banks there. Conolly suggested that David should speak with Young, but David replied that he had done so without results.

Sufficiently disturbed by David's story and trying to be helpful, Conolly phoned Young in March 1977 to relate what David had told him. Conolly's conversation with Young did not last long, and afterward, Young informed head office of its tenor.

Pomeroy's notes stated that the "main purpose" of the meeting with Conolly "was to establish what Edwards had told him as he is the only person whom we know Edwards to have spoken to outside the bank on these matters."

In addition to containing a number of errors, including the misspelling of Conolly's name, Pomeroy's notes presented a richly colored portrait of an unstable Edwards. When later Conolly was shown the notes, he was upset. Pomeroy, he said, had substantially misrepresented his intentions in passing on to Young what David had told him.

"Conolly has known Edwards since they worked together in Samuel Montagu in London. Conolly regarded him as good company but incompetent professionally although never under his (Conolly's) supervision,'' the notes began.

Pomeroy briefly described Conolly's recollection of the March 1977 meeting, and then continued: "Sometime after March 1977 (probably July 1977), Edwards raised the subject again with Conolly and mentioned cover-up by the Bank because of involvement in moving profits offshore. Edwards claimed to have discussed the matter with Wriston who did not show much concern. Edwards expressed willingness to leave the Bank if only he could get out with his reputation clear.''

But Conolly hadn't been in Paris in July 1977. He spent the month vacationing in Majorca, Spain, with his family. Moreover, Edwards had already left Europe by then, having been called back to New York by Huntington on June 23, 1977. Conolly had no recollection at all of another 1977 meeting with Edwards. The notes continued:

> Conolly's recommendation (unasked for) was that we should ease Edwards out as a danger to banking because of his loose tongue but thought we should do so gently to save complications. We explained this had been our plan.
>
> Although our original hope was that Conolly would come forward as a witness in the case of a defamation suit, he made clear his unwillingness to do so as, apart from being a friend, he obviously feels that he might be next to be denounced with resultant embarrassment to Natwest. He also mentioned the 'wild look' that comes into Edwards's eyes when he gets going on these matters and Young and I both sensed some fear on Conolly's part of physical violence if Edwards learnt that Conolly was willing to confront him.
>
> Conolly said that he had been surprised by Edwards's fairly free-spending ways. On a couple of occasions he asked what his salary was and got a different answer each time. Conolly thought both figures low in relation to his apparent expenditure but understood that he was getting money from certain oil ventures.[8]

On December 5, 1977, David learned from Terkhorn that Peat Marwick Mitchell "had given the bank a clean bill of health." On December 7, 1977, Pomeroy, back in New York, questioned Jennifer

---

[8] Citibank document 294–295. Conolly said the notes were inaccurate in several respects. He denied, among other things, having suggested that Edwards should be "eased out," that Edwards was a danger to banking, or that Edwards had "free-spending ways."

James, the trading assistant who had once worked with de Laet in Brussels, on her alleged dealings with the Paris treasury head. Pomeroy's memo of the meeting, which was held in the presence of another Citibank officer, stated, "James denies Edwards's charges of trading for her own account."[9] Edwards, however, said he had never alleged any such thing.

Late in the afternoon of Friday, December 14, 1977, with rain padding against the windows at 399 Park Avenue, Theobald asked Ernst Brutsche to bring Edwards to his office.

Brutsche had been given the task of convincing David to resign voluntarily. But David wasn't having any of that. Once seated on the sofa, Theobald thrust a letter into his hands that demanded his resignation.

Theobald's six-paragraph letter was brutally direct:

I have discussed with a number of Citibank senior officers the allegations which are made in your November 14 letter to me . . . to the effect that (1) Jean Pierre de Laet . . . was involved in taking kickbacks from foreign exchange and money market brokers, (2) the Paris branch engaged in improper accounting practices characterized by you as the branch management "cooking the books," and (3) the Paris branch engaged in placing foreign exchange positions in Nassau in violation of French regulations.

As you are to some extent aware, and have been informed by your supervisors, these allegations have been the subject of intensive investigations by Citibank's Comptroller's Division and others since you first made them more than two years ago. In the course of investigating your charges we repeatedly requested you to provide us with any evidence you might have to substantiate your allegations. Yet, neither our investigators nor you have to date been able to provide any substantive, factual corroboration of the allegations which you have made.

We believe that you must be aware, and indeed you have been informed of, the extremely serious implications of your allegations, especially when viewed in the light of your inability to furnish substantiation. These considerations are particularly acute since these unsubstantiated accusations have been directed not only against a fellow officer but against the institution itself.

[9]Excerpted from Citibank document 292.

The letter stated that Edwards's continued employment was harmful to "the best interests of Citibank," and consequently, his "immediate" resignation was demanded. It then ended with a protective request: "Needless to say, should any evidence come to your attention hereafter which would tend to substantiate your allegations, we would urge you to bring it to our attention." [10]

As David finished reading, Theobald added a personal comment, comparing Citibank to a club. "He told me you get along by going along, and anything that threatens the club from within must be expelled," David recalled.

By then David realized nobody higher on the ladder was going to shake his hand, and he also was aware that he would never become executive vice-president. "There was no threat to my job," he said. "I no longer had a job." This produced a levitating effect, for it meant he no longer needed to take anything Theobald said seriously.

David replied that Charles Stillman junior would turn in his grave if he could hear Citibank described as a club. Stillman, the son of Captain Charles Stillman, a former Mississippi river pilot and gun-runner, acquired control of National City Bank in the mid-nineteenth century and made it the largest and most go-ahead bank of the day. Certainly Stillman had not achieved his success by treating the Citi as a social establishment. "This is not a club, it's a goddamn bank," David said.

They were seated on the couch, talking very genteelly. "Theobald never raised his voice. But the forcefulness of his words told me he would have killed me if he could." Theobald controlled his temper masterfully until David started quoting from Citibank's code of ethics.

"I wrote that code!" Theobald exploded.

"But who guards the guards?" David asked.

Whereupon Theobald got up and stomped out of his own office.

---

[10] Thomas C. Theobald, letter to David Edwards, December 14, 1977.

Chapter 18

Citibank's
Code of Ethics

"I don't know what you mean by parking."

—THOMAS C. THEOBALD, MAY 16, 1980

The *Desk Book on Ethical Standards* was the bible by which Citi-bankers were supposed to abide. It listed the standards of behavior expected of the directors, officers, and staff members in the ninety-three countries where Citicorp operated. It was a confidential docu-ment—"the information contained herein should not be released in whole or in part to non-Citicorp parties without the approval of the Secretary's Office"—and a committee on good corporate practice was its guardian.

In the foreword to the 1976 edition, Walter Wriston claimed that Citicorp's reputation for integrity had been built by "the men and women who work here now, and who have worked here in the past."

Wriston added that the policy statements contained in the *desk book* were "the foundation of Citicorp's corporate 'conscience.' "

The cornerstone of that "conscience" was the so-called corporate mission, which was reproduced on page one:

The mission of Citicorp is to be the most competent, profitable, and innovative financial service organization in the world.

This was expanded a few paragraphs later:

It is the intent of Citicorp management that the law of the countries where our business activities are conducted be known and obeyed. Above the minimum level required by law, it is Citicorp's policy to adhere to the highest standards of integrity, to be applied consistently throughout the world. Our internal ethical standards are the result of shared moral convictions and our international experience. Rationales such as "everyone in the market does it" or "our competitors do it" cannot be countenanced as permitting deviations from our standards. Through consistent and continuous compliance with these standards, Citicorp has earned a reputation for excellence and integrity while achieving outstanding business success. This reputation for integrity, retained by generations of Citibankers, must be maintained and defended. No business plan or individual proposition can be accepted if there is a risk of impairing that reputation. All employees are encouraged to communicate freely with their supervisors in cases where any question regarding ethical standards or the maintenance of our integrity could arise.

These were standards in which David Edwards believed. He considered them part of the institutional fabric. Wriston warned that "willful failure" to comply with the bank's ethical standards "may be grounds for dismissal, because the hard earned reputation of our organization can be tarnished by individual members whose acts are contrary to the precepts of law or ethics." Wriston's foreword listed seven absolute commandments, which were supposedly inviolable and commonly were referred to by the staff as Citibank's code of ethics:

- We will act toward others in a manner in which we desire them to act toward us.
- We will accept individual responsibility for our actions without seeking refuge or anonymity behind the Citicorp reputation, or that of any smaller group acting on Citicorp's behalf.
- We will conduct our personal and business dealings in accord with the letter, spirit and intent of relevant laws and regulations.
- We believe in the free enterprise system and the appropriateness of earning a profit from providing fair and efficient service to our customers.

- We will conduct our business in other countries in a manner which recognizes Citicorp's status as a guest which is subject to the host's wishes as to its continued presence.
- We will be completely candid with our fellow employees in all business matters so that decisions will be reasonable and based upon all relevant facts.
- We will not, directly or indirectly, use the reputation or resources of Citicorp to enhance our personal opportunities for material gain.

Chapter 19

Edwards's Blue Book

Should any evidence come to your attention . . . which would tend to substantiate your allegations, we would urge you to bring it to our attention.

—THOMAS C. THEOBALD TO DAVID EDWARDS, DECEMBER 14, 1977

As far as Edwards was concerned, Tom Theobald's strategy was now perfectly clear. Edwards's response was to spend the next six weeks preparing a 106-page report containing his best evidence of the sham foreign exchange deals that Paris and other European branches used to park, in Nassau, their open positions above statutory limits and also to off-book the extra profits these positions generated.

In early January 1978, while Edwards was assembling his report, an assistant comptroller in Europe came to the conclusion that Zurich's foreign exchange procedures deviated from the bank's "normal requirements" in three ways:

1) "parking" of foreign exchange positions . . . in excess of limits established by Swiss banking authorities.

2) pricing contracts with head office . . . so that the profits from these positions are recorded outside Switzerland.

3) holding back a portion of monthly profits as an unofficial reserve.

The assistant comptroller, Brian deFreytas, wrote David Allars, with a copy to Ed Pomeroy, asking if head office had approved these operations.[1]

The reply by Allars to this inquiry is not known. But the answer is known: Huntington and his superiors at head office had approved the operations. After starting timidly to park in 1973, the volume of the foreign exchange positions off-booked by Zurich through the Euro-currency desk in New York quickly became enormous and therefore material to Citibank's overall earnings. At the end of November 1977, the last month for which deFreytas had figures, Citibank Zurich had oversold the dollar by a record $90 million, buying Deutsche marks for $20 million, yen for $19.6 million, and Swiss francs for $50 million. These positions were parked with International Foreign Exchange & Funding, the old Nassau desk, in New York.[2]

Throughout 1977, the foreign exchange market had been in turmoil, with the dollar falling by 14 percent against the Swiss franc, 9.6 percent against the yen, and 8.8 percent against the Deutsche mark. The market's turbulence reflected the general feeling of economic uncertainty that accompanied the decline of American prestige in the world. By parking their excess positions to escape national controls, which were designed to limit speculation, Citibank traders were capitalizing on the market's instability and, by so doing, accentuating the swings in exchange rates and adding to the general uncertainty.

This was not without risk. Citibank's foreign exchange earnings fell considerably for the year and were only $13 million, down from the record $79.7 million in 1974, and also 26 percent below the previous year. Inflation in the United States, after hovering for a time around 6 percent, was moving upward again as the dollar weakened. The U.S. currency recovered modestly at year end, but in January 1978, after an unexpected upward blip, it sank like a stone, and with it the American stock markets.

Edwards, meanwhile, answered Theobald's letter of December 14, 1977, announcing that he had no intention of resigning. "Please be

[1] Citibank document 1755 (also 3991).
[2] Citibank document 418A.

assured that there is an abundant supply of very disturbing evidence,''
he advised Theobald. He enclosed a copy of the June 11, 1976, parking telex from Jean-Pierre de Laet to Citibank New York as a sample.[3]

"If you would give me the courtesy of a full hearing, I would be
glad to discuss this matter in greater detail. I have not spent five and
one-half years at Citibank to see my effectiveness as a banker jeopardized by a breakdown in communications between a senior bank
official and myself. I look forward to an interview with you," Edwards's letter to Theobald stated.[4]

This time around, Theobald did not bother to answer. But Edwards
had already retained Geoffrey Shields, an attorney with the Chicago
law firm of Gardner, Carton & Douglas, to help him negotiate an
honorable withdrawal. On January 27, 1978, John E. Hoffman, Jr.,
a partner with the New York law firm of Shearman & Sterling, Citibank's attorneys, replied for Theobald with a letter to Shields denying a further meeting.

Ignoring the copy of the de Laet parking telex that Edwards had
sent Theobald almost three weeks before, Hoffman's letter stated:
"While Mr. Edwards was repeatedly asked to substantiate his allegations, he has not done so and Citibank's own investigators have not
been able to provide any substantive factual corroboration of the allegations Mr. Edwards has made."

It added: "[I]f you or your client have evidence which would tend
to substantiate Mr. Edwards' allegations, I urge you to submit it to
us, or if you do not wish to part with such documentary material, I
urge you to submit a summary so that we can determine whether the
meeting you have requested would be likely to lead to fruitful further
inquiries."[5]

By then Edwards had completed his analysis of the material uncovered in the sixth-floor storeroom. From the thousands of transactions
in the boxes marked "parked positions" he had selected four typical
deals, complete with dealing tickets and confirmations, and translated
them from the dealers' dialect into layman's language.

To show that the four examples were not isolated cases, Edwards
included in his report copies of Cugnasca's parking manual, Redi's
letter to Huntington reacting to the Cugnasca manual,[6] an example of

---

[3] See Chapter 11 for a full text and description of the telex.
[4] Letter from David Edwards to Thomas C. Theobald, January 9, 1978.
[5] On February 8, 1978, Hoffman wrote Shields a second letter in which he referred to the de Laet parking telex as "an internal Citibank telex communication reflecting a foreign exchange transaction some eighteen months ago."
[6] See Chapter 17, pages 150–158.

MIS adjustments, and a dozen requests to Huntington for approval of "special transactions" between Milan and Nassau, and Paris and Nassau, the latter being run through Banque Belge in London. He prefaced this with his letters of November 14, 1977, to Sweeney and Theobald. He made a dozen copies and bound them together in blue binders. This assemblage of material, highly embarrassing to Citibank, became known as the Blue Book.

"For the past two and a half years, I have raised the issues contained in this report again and again. Repeatedly, I have been told that these matters were being investigated, and yet I have had to prod my superiors to carry on with their investigations. I have been told that no evidence exists to support my assertions.

"The following are four examples of the use of Nassau by Citibank branches for parking profits earned in Europe. These are not isolated cases. Indeed, there is evidence in them of their being merely routine transactions in the ongoing parking of funds," the introduction to this analysis stated.

Example A described Paris's June 1976 parking in Nassau of a $12,500 taxable profit. This was the same transaction that Edwards sent to Theobald on January 9, 1977.

Example B was a series of three "Victor Lee" telexes that detailed Frankfurt's transfer to Nassau, on October 6, 1976, of a DM 200,000 ($82,000) profit. Edwards explained that the three telexes relating to the purchase and sale of £6 million by Frankfurt were part of a chain of similar "trades" by which the German branch deliberately *lost* money to Nassau. The last of the three telexes referred to a total profit position of DM 900,000 ($370,000 at then prevailing exchange rates) that it had off-booked that month with Nassau.

The Frankfurt-Nassau "deals," like the Paris, Milan, and Zurich examples, were not real deals in any accepted sense, but accounting transactions. No payments were made into or out of a clearing bank— either Citi London for Frankfurt's pounds or Citi New York for the dollars. Still, Citi Frankfurt deducted the $82,000 from its real earnings.

Example C described how in September 1976 Milan used Amsterdam and London to park a $5 million position that was progressively liquidated, resulting in the transfer to Nassau of a $29,700 profit.

Example D, the most complex, with sixteen pages of back-up documentation, recorded the transfer of a $1 million taxable profit from Zurich to Nassau in December 1976. The Zurich example began with these instructions, directed to New York:

2866

FNCB ZURICH BUYS FROM NASSAU USDOLS 35 MIO AG SWISS AT 2.4543
VALUE DECEMBER 8
H O FOR DOLLARS AND ACCT FOR SWISS

2872

THIS WILL SQUARE OUR POSITION WITH YOU IN DOLL SWISS AND
LEAVE YOU WITH A PROFIT OF SFRS 563,500.—WHICH WE BUY FROM
YOU AT THE RATE OF 2.4500 AND SELL YOU USDOLS 230,000 VALUE
DECEMBER 8, AND WHICH AMOUNT YOU WILL HAVE TO CREDIT TO
FNCB ZURICH VIA M.I.S. VALUE DECEMBER 8

The 2872 telex indicated that the purchase of $35 million by Zu-
rich from Nassau, referred to in the first (2866) telex, was part of a
series. This particular transaction squared a long dollar position that
Zurich already had outstanding at the Nassau desk in New York, and
it left Nassau with a SF 563,500 profit.

The 2872 telex informed New York that Zurich purchased the SF
536,500 from Nassau at a rate that translated Nassau's Swiss-franc
profit into a $230,000 profit. It ended with instructions to credit the
profit to Zurich's MIS account. This pattern was repeated in a second
set of instructions telexed simultaneously:

2867

FNCB ZURICH SELLS TO FNCB NASSAU US DOLS 35 MIO AG DMKS AT
2.3990 VALUE DECEMBER 8
H O FOR DOLLARS AND ACCT FRANKFURT FOR DMKS

2873

THIS WILL SQUARE OUR POSITION WITH YOU IN DOLL/DMKS AND
LEAVE YOU WITH A PROFIT OF DMKS 647,500.—WHICH WE BUY
FROM YOU AT THE RATE OF 2.398148148 AND SELL YOU USDOLS
270,000.—VALUE DECEMBER 8, AND WHICH AMOUNT YOU WILL
HAVE TO CREDIT TO FNCB ZURICH VIA M.I.S. VALUE DECEMBER 8

The 2867 and 2873 telexes, combined with the 2866 and 2872 telexes, brought the total to $500,000 in profits parked with Nassau. The
exchange rate of DM 2.398148148 used in the 2873 telex was obviously contrived, and a dead giveaway as such to any bank inspector, because it was carried to the billionth decimal place when normal
rates are only taken to the thousandth decimal place. The Zurich trader,
however, did this to round up the amount of his profit to the precise
$500,000 figure.

The series closed with three more transactions, bringing the total profit transferred by Zurich to Nassau for that week to $1 million. And then the charade resumed, with Zurich giving the opening positions that it wanted booked through the Nassau desk for the following week, value December 15. What Edwards did not understand was that he had stumbled across Eddie Giger's end-of-quarter profit transfers to Nassau. Such large profit transfers were, to that extent, not an everyday occurrence.

Edwards was not aware that in August 1975 Natvig and Pomeroy had completed a survey on European treasuries that went to Wriston and that recommended, among other things, the use of formatted telexes to better disguise parking deals and that "all deals be done at realistic rates. . . ."[7] Wriston had told Eyre, "Be certain to follow up on these points." While the sample deals that Edwards included in the Blue Book showed that the suggestion to use formatted telexes had been adopted, more than a year later artificial rates were still being used. Citibank's outside directors, members of the audit and examining committees, to whom responsibility for dealing with the Blue Book allegations would be given, were likewise unaware of the 1975 Natvig/Pomeroy survey. This key document was never given to them.

Finally, Edwards wrote an introductory letter to the Blue Book dated January 31, 1978. Not until February 8, 1978, however, did he send copies of the Blue Book to Citibank's policy committee, and to Dr. Lawrence E. Fouraker, dean of the Harvard Business School, who was chairman of Citicorp's audit committee and Citibank's examining committee; Walter Hanson, senior partner of Peat Marwick Mitchell; Henry Harfield, a senior partner at Shearman & Sterling; and John Hoffman.

He claimed in his transmittal letter that he was solely interested in preserving "Citibank's unique position in the world of banking" by exposing practices that "are not consistent with the tenets of sound banking on which the corporation is built." He also sent a copy to Walter Wriston, with a covering note:

"The enclosed material should be self-explanatory. I am sure you are aware of the questions I have raised. If you want to ask me about this report, please feel free to contact me at my extension—8413—or at my home—107 East 36th Street."

[7] Natvig/Pomeroy Report, page 4, Citibank document 1687.

Chapter 20

The Third Denial

Citibank . . . has built its business . . . on the bedrock of institutional integrity.

—WALTER WRISTON, JUNE 28, 1983

On February 9, 1978, one day after he sent out his Blue Book and almost six years after joining Citibank, David Edwards's career as an international banker was terminated.

His reward for being a whistleblower was addressed to his parents' home in Wichita Falls. It came from the desk of the future vice-chairman and author of Citibank's code of ethics, Thomas C. Theobald.

Theobald's letter and Edwards's Blue Book actually criss-crossed in the mail. This demonstrated, according to Citibank general counsel Patrick Mulhern, that the Blue Book was not the cause of Edwards's firing.

Wriston was subsequently quoted as saying: "Edwards was dismissed because he was totally incompetent." [1]

---

[1] "An Interview with Walter Wriston," *Executive* (Cornell's Graduate School of Business Review).

Theobald's letter only mentioned that Edwards had acted "in a manner detrimental to the best interests of Citibank." It made no reference to the de Laet parking telex that Edwards had sent Theobald one month before. The de Laet parking telex actually demonstrated that the troublesome Texan possessed some documentary proof to support his allegation that Paris was "cooking the books." When confronted with the reality of Edwards's proof, which the bank, after all, had requested, it reacted capriciously by slamming the door.

February 9, 1978

Mr. David Edwards
131 Pembroke Lane
Wichita Falls, Texas

Dear Mr. Edwards:

I have received your letter of January 9, 1978, responding to my letter of December 14, 1977, and rejecting our request that you voluntarily terminate your employment with a letter of resignation. We have already informed you of our conclusion that you have acted in a manner that is detrimental to the best interests of Citibank. Under these circumstances, we now advise you that your employment with Citibank is terminated, effective immediately.

We will credit your account for the amount of $1,192.43. As per the attachments, this amount represents a refund of the hypothetical tax charged during 1977, the balance of your housing allowance less $2,872.00 outstanding advances from July and August 1977. We will also pay for the shipment of your household goods from Paris to Wichita Falls, Texas.

Very truly yours,
s/Thomas C. Theobald

There was, Edwards concluded, no justice in being a whistle-blower.

Part III

THE COVER-UP

Chapter 21

Scenario

> *"I quite agree with you," said the Duchess; "and the moral of that is—'Be what you would seem to be'—or, if you'd like it put more simply—'Never imagine yourself not to be otherwise than what it might appear to others that what you were or might have been was not otherwise than what you had been would have appeared to them to be otherwise.'"*

—LEWIS CARROLL, *Alice's Adventures in Wonderland*

After receiving his copy of the Blue Book in early February 1978, Lawrence Fouraker, dean of the Harvard Business School and a director of both Citibank and its parent Citicorp, contacted Stephen Eyre, the comptroller, and asked what it all meant. Fouraker had heard indirectly about David Edwards on at least two occasions.

Fouraker was chairman of two committees of the board: Citicorp's audit committee and Citibank's examining committee. These bodies were responsible for supervising the independent audits of Citicorp and continuously examining the affairs of Citibank, particularly by monitoring the periodic inspections conducted by the bank's principal regulator, the Comptroller of the Currency. In this capacity, he worked closely with Eyre, whom he had come to know well.

Eyre had mentioned to the dean sometime before that he had been troubled by an attack on the integrity of the chief trader in Paris. The chief trader, he said, had been accused by another employee of accepting kickbacks, which allegations the internal auditors had investigated and found to be unsubstantiated.

Then, in November 1977, Tom Theobald told Fouraker about an unusual problem he was having with an employee who refused reassignment. The employee in both instances, Fouraker subsequently learned, was David Edwards.

The audit and examining committees generally met in joint session at least once a quarter, and membership consisted of outside directors. In 1978 they were John W. Hanley, chairman of Monsanto Company; John P. Harbin, chairman of Halliburton Company; H. J. Haynes, chairman of Standard Oil Company of California; C. Peter McColough, chairman of Xerox Corporation; Charles M. Pigott, president of PACCAR Incorporated; Dr. Eleanor H. B. Sheldon, president of the Social Science Research Council; William E. Simon, former secretary of the U.S. Treasury; Darwin E. Smith, chairman of Kimberly-Clark Corporation; and Franklin A. Thomas, president of the Ford Foundation.

Eyre was the only staff member who reported to and assisted the committees in their deliberations. Then fifty-five, he was a Yale graduate who had been with Citibank for thirty-one years. Before taking over as comptroller in 1973, he headed the Canadian and Caribbean division, which was part of IBG.

In theory, Eyre was supposed to alert the committees to any activity or area of the bank that he considered problematic or capable of materially disturbing the financial well-being of the institution.

The audit and examining committees met prior to a full board meeting on Tuesday, February 21, 1978, on the twenty-third floor at Citicorp Center. Beforehand, Wriston spoke with Fouraker. "Here is a bunch of allegations about the bank, and I think the audit committee and the board should hold an investigation," he said, handing to the dean his copy of the Blue Book, which he had read for the first time the night before.[1]

What else Wriston told Fouraker was not disclosed, except that he wanted the investigation to determine "what, if anything, in this book

[1] Walter Wriston, testimony before the SEC, July 9, 1980, page 45.

is so.'' Wriston didn't think much of the Blue Book. He called it a "mishmash of all kinds of allegations," which he said were not consistent with his impressions of how the bank conducted its foreign exchange operations.

But clearly, much was at stake in the Edwards allegations. The potential penalties ranged from loss of banking license in some of the countries concerned to fines of up to six times the amounts involved, with criminal proceedings against officers and directors a likely follow-up. The investigation, therefore, had to leave no doubt that the charges were unsubstantiated, and to achieve this with necessary impact, it had to have authority, independence, and depth.

Fouraker, with Eyre's help, informed the audit and examining committees of the situation and suggested that Shearman & Sterling, Citicorp's outside general counsel, be hired to review the charges and proceed further if required. Management generally assumed by then that Edwards was going to stir up as much trouble as he could and a strong, credible defense of the bank's foreign exchange policy was therefore imperative.

The audit and examining committees asked John E. Hoffman, Jr., a senior partner with Shearman & Sterling, to proceed with an internal investigation. According to Xerox chairman Peter McColough, the committees initially requested that Hoffman develop a methodology for determining whether a pattern of illegality was apparent in Citibank's foreign exchange operations. McColough, however, didn't know at that time, and still didn't know more than a year later, who Jean-Pierre de Laet was, which makes it unlikely that he ever read the Blue Book.

Internal investigations had become a common occurrence following Watergate, when a number of major corporations were discovered to have made illegal contributions to President Nixon's reelection campaign. The illegal contributions, also bribes and illicit commissions, became referred to generically as "questionable payments."

The Securities & Exchange Commission began enforcement proceedings against some of the companies named by the Watergate special prosecutor's office. But the SEC soon recognized that many more public corporations had made "questionable payments" than it had the manpower to investigate. The SEC, therefore, invited corporations to assist its enforcement efforts by voluntarily disclosing whether they had engaged in any of these activities. This became known as the SEC's "voluntary disclosure program."

The program had four essential elements: (1) an investigation by persons of unquestioned integrity to determine the necessity for public disclosure; (2) a statement of corporate policy condemning questionable payments; (3) the passing of a board resolution forbidding all recourse to them; and (4) making appropriate disclosure by filing a Form 8-K report with the SEC.

Hundreds of corporations responded to the program and retained outside counsel to investigate whether their management had used secret slush funds, maintained off-the-book accounts, or proffered bribes to government officials, politicians, or political organizations. Their findings were filed with the SEC as public disclosure documents.

As long as the SEC's division of enforcement was satisfied the internal investigation had been conscientious, it accepted the public cleansing of the corporation's dirty linen without initiating enforcement action or demanding injunctive relief. Some internal investigations became models of disclosure and integrity. Others were less so but still passed muster. Shearman & Sterling had conducted a number of internal investigations, both for regular clients and companies with which it had no prior relationship. The firm was therefore experienced in their preparation and presentation.

Hoffman recommended to the audit and examining committees that they authorize him to retain Peat Marwick to assist in the investigation—he preferred to call it a "special review." He explained that the form for these undertakings had, by 1978, been pretty well standardized. The basic incentive for embarking on such an enterprise was to head off an investigation by the SEC or any other government agency. Hoffman had no need to remind the committees that an official investigation was more disruptive and damaging than one done by the corporation's own counsel.

A leading authority on internal investigations was John M. Fedders, then a partner with the Washington law firm of Arnold & Porter. He had written extensively about them, explaining how best they could be turned to a company's advantage. "Although a voluntary internal investigation initiated by a corporation does not preclude a government agency from initiating a similar investigation, a government agency rarely will duplicate a corporation's internal investigative effort," he explained in one of his texts.

He cautioned, however, that such a preclusion only applied "if the internal investigation is thorough and complete and there is no evidence of a cover-up or whitewash."

Hoffman was concerned about the SEC's division of enforcement. Fedders wrote that the securities agency tended not to investigate if convinced that corporate counsel was doing a thorough job.

"The SEC staff recognizes that if a corporation conducts a voluntary investigation and makes public disclosure, there is little necessity for an SEC investigation and an enforcement action . . . , especially where the SEC *is informed in advance* that a company, not yet under investigation, will proceed in accordance with the SEC's program," he explained.[2]

But Fedders, who later became the SEC's director of enforcement, also advised that "no law firm should be selected to conduct an investigation *about matters on which it previously has rendered legal advice.*"

Shearman & Sterling had counseled Citicorp on how to handle David Edwards's termination and meet his demands for compensation. This alone placed in doubt its ability to act as an independent and fully open-minded investigative counsel. But Fouraker said Shearman & Sterling's lack of suitability for the job was considered and rejected.

Hans H. Angermueller, Citicorp's senior executive vice-president for legal affairs, reported the committees' decision to the board of directors at its lunchtime meeting, which followed. The minutes of the full board session brushed over the "tax evasion charges by an ex-employee" in six lines, recording only that "Peat, Marwick, Mitchell & Co. and outside counsel are to review a sampling of the charges and proceed further if required."[3]

"More specifically," Hoffman later said, "we were to find out what parking really was and its consequences under the relevant local laws."[4]

Two factors weighed heavily in the decision to retain Shearman & Sterling. The first was the almost incestuous nature of the relationship between the firm and the bank. [The board meeting and the meeting of the audit and examining committees that preceded it were held in a Citibank conference room on the twenty-third floor at Citicorp Center. Hoffman's office was located in the same building, seven floors higher.] The second was the high degree of confidence that the directors placed in Hoffman.

Hoffman had the reputation of being a top-notch litigator. He had been with Shearman & Sterling since joining the bar in 1961. He rep-

[2] "Corporate Criminal Responsibility—Conducting an Internal Investigation," by John M. Fedders, Chapter 62, *Criminal Defense Techniques* (published in 1979); emphasis added.

[3] CITICORP—Minutes of a Regular Meeting of the Board of Directors held at Citicorp Center on Tuesday, February 21, 1978, at 1:00 P.M.; Citibank document 7426–7427.

[4] Statement by John E. Hoffman, Jr. before the Subcommittee on Oversight and Investigations of the Committee on Energy and Commerce, House of Representatives, June 28, 1983, page 4.

resented Citibank in the complex international claims litigation that resulted from the 1974 failure of Bankhaus Herstatt and later did a masterful job on Citibank's behalf in the financial negotiations that led to the January 1981 release of fifty-two American hostages in Iran. As a litigator, Hoffman said he was trained "first to get the facts, and then make judgments—not the other way around."

Shearman & Sterling was the third largest law firm in the United States. Founded in 1873, it was also one of the oldest. The firm had 370 attorneys working for more than 2,000 clients in the U.S. and abroad. Citicorp, however, was by far its largest client. *The American Lawyer* estimated that 30 percent of Shearman & Sterling's roughly $65 million in annual revenues came from Citicorp or business related to Citicorp activities.[5]

The relationship between Shearman & Sterling and its biggest client had existed for more than a hundred years. The firm's cofounder, John Sterling, had been a Manhattan neighbor and close friend of the great Citi patriarch Charles Stillman, Jr. That friendship persisted through the intervening decades and grew ever more incestuous. Citicorp's head of legal affairs and future vice-chairman, Hans Angermueller, had been the senior Shearman & Sterling partner on the Citibank account until Wriston lured him onto Citicorp's payroll. And the chairman's second wife, attorney Katherine Dineen Wriston, had been associated with Shearman & Sterling from 1963 to 1968.

To better serve its largest client, Shearman & Sterling opened midtown offices on five floors of the new Citicorp Center, a gleaming white fifty-nine story tower with wedge-shaped super-structure that had only recently been completed. It was located at 153 East 53rd Street, across from the bank's head office at 399 Park Avenue, and the battalion of Shearman & Sterling partners and associates who moved there from the firm's principal offices at 53 Wall Street mainly were occupied on Citicorp-related accounts.

David Edwards, in the meantime, had not remained idle. Hoffman, it was true, liked to describe him as "the missing player." If he was "missing," however, it was only because Citicorp and its attorneys had banished him from their sight. But Edwards, convinced a cover-up was in progress, was advised by his lawyer, Geoffrey Shields, that

[5] Steven Brill, "What Price Loyalty?" *The American Lawyer*, August 1982. Hans Angermueller told the Oversight and Investigations Subcommittee of the House Energy and Commerce Committee that Shearman & Sterling's billings to Citicorp ran between $15–20 million a year, which Hoffman said represented 25 percent of the firm's total annual billings (ref. SEC and Citicorp, June 28, 1983 hearings, Serial No. 98–78, page 166).

if parking proved to be illegal, there was a moral, if not legal, obligation on the part of the employee who discovered the practice to report it to the authorities should the corporation itself not respond to a request for a hearing on the matter. So while Hoffman assembled a team to work on the special review, Shields advised Edwards to take his Blue Book to the SEC.

Ray Garrett, Jr., a former SEC chairman, acted as the messenger of these intentions.[6]

Garrett had returned to private practice and was a senior partner in the same Chicago law firm as Shields. Shields had spoken to Garrett about the Edwards case. Garrett provided Edwards with an introduction to Stanley Sporkin, who, as head of the SEC's division of enforcement, was the top watchdog of corporate morality in America.

Sporkin had enormous respect for Garrett and felt confident the Chicago lawyer would not send him a case unless it had merit. Not long afterward, Robert G. Ryan, a senior staff attorney in the SEC's division of enforcement, contacted Edwards and requested a meeting at the SEC headquarters so that Edwards could explain to the staff what the Blue Book was about. Immediately after that meeting, on March 17, 1978, Ryan called Shearman & Sterling and spoke to Hoffman. He told Hoffman of the allegations made by a former employee concerning Citibank's foreign exchange practices.

Hoffman, according to Ryan, professed no knowledge of these facts, but said he would look into them.

Ryan suggested that Citicorp might like to present its version at a meeting, which they fixed for March 28, 1978.[7]

Three days after receiving Ryan's call, Hoffman composed a letter formally engaging Peat Marwick to conduct the field audit work for the special review. The letter was dated March 20, 1978.

With this letter in hand, Hoffman and Angermueller met Ryan in Washington. They announced that they had already begun an investigation and proposed to keep the enforcement staff informed of the progress.

Back in New York, Hoffman marshalled his team. It included one other Shearman & Sterling partner, Danforth Newcomb, an associate attorney, Henry Weisburg, and a team of accountants from Peat Mar-

---

[6] Ray Garrett, Jr., was chairman of the SEC from 1973 to 1975. One of his first decisions as chairman was to make Sporkin the new director of enforcement.
[7] Memorandum to the commission from the division of enforcement, re: Citicorp, April 28, 1978, pp. 6–7.

wick. Also, Ed Pomeroy was seconded to Hoffman's staff as the official liaison officer.

They began to index and file the research product of their survey—9,000 documents by the time they were finished. Then they sat down and began planning the special review.

Early meetings between Shearman & Sterling and Peat Marwick consisted of a review of the Blue Book and discussions of the "appropriate methods" for determining whether there was any factual basis for Edwards's allegations. The Shearman & Sterling report, when it was released eight months later, became the only available source on how these "appropriate methods" were determined. The report, however, was vague. It stated:

> We decided that it would be appropriate to concentrate initially on the interbranch foreign exchange transactions conducted by Frankfurt, Milan, Paris and Zurich, inasmuch as these were the locations referred to in the Blue Book. (Later, after reviewing data in Citibank's internal management information system, and following further examination of documents and interviews with Citibank personnel, we expanded the geographic scope to include Amsterdam, Brussels and London.)
>
> We also made a tentative decision to cover a five-year period in our review. The Blue Book itself provided no useful guidance in selecting a time period, although all of the transactions it referred to took place in 1976. . . .
>
> Having made these initial decisions on the scope of the review, our attention turned to the development of an appropriate methodology. Our review would necessarily be based substantially on opinions from separate local counsel in each of the countries involved. Accordingly, every effort was made to insure that the procedures employed and the advice rendered with respect to each country would be as nearly comparable as possible. Without such comparability, synthesis by Shearman & Sterling of the local legal advice would be far more difficult and would reduce the value to the Committees of the review. In addition, the use of standardized procedures and techniques would provide the best method of insuring that the review was efficient, expeditious and thorough.
>
> We also recognized that the major source of factual information, at least at the outset, would be from interviews with Citibank employees and the examination of documentary material within the Bank. Further, it was apparent that the large volume of interbranch

foreign exchange transactions precluded a transaction-by-transaction review.

From these initial conclusions a basic sequential framework for the engagement emerged. . . . This sequence of procedures would . . . permit a uniformity of approach that would ease later comparisons and compilation.[8]

This was a lengthy way of stating that Hoffman had discarded the idea of investigating the four specific examples of parking provided by Edwards in the Blue Book. He and his staff decided instead to focus more generally on parking patterns used by Citibank traders at the seven European locations.

After further consulting with Citibank officials on how to proceed in the field, Hoffman's team drafted a questionnaire for the treasury heads of the seven Division III branches. The questionnaire was presented to them at a meeting in London in early April 1978.

As the treasury heads digested the questionnaire, in April and May 1978 Peat Marwick carried out its field survey. It showed that branch controls and auditing procedures were not uniform and often incomplete. It also confirmed that parking was "a relatively standard practice," which followed a few basic patterns, each with a number of variations.[9]

From the outset, then, Edwards's allegations were to some extent substantiated. This was not directly acknowledged, but the implication from the admission that parking was "a relatively standard practice" remained inescapable.

Shearman & Sterling failed to disclose, however, the consequences that the field survey provoked in Switzerland. These thoroughly vindicated Edwards's concern, at least as to the dangers of parking in that country.

In a random sampling of dealing-room blotters over a five-year period, the Peat Marwick auditors in Zurich uncovered some 875 parking transactions involving $22 billion. The snag here was that Peat Marwick were also the statutory auditors appointed under the Swiss Banking Act with a dual reporting responsibility to the shareholders of the bank and the federal banking authorities.

Concerned about the legality of these transactions, the senior Peat

[8] Shearman & Sterling Report to the Audit Committee of Citicorp and the Examining Committee of Citibank, November 20, 1978, pages 4–5.
[9] Ibid., page 8.

Marwick partner in Zurich reported them to the Federal Banking Commission, which opened an investigation. This investigation continued for the next sixteen months without the world at large being aware of it.

A standard for testing the bona fides of a transaction is whether it was conducted "at arm's length." One frequently cited definition states: "Parties are said to deal 'at arm's length' when each stands upon the strict letter of his rights, and conducts the business in a formal manner, without trusting to the other's fairness or integrity, and without being subject to the other's control or overmastering influence." [10] In other words, dealing at arm's length occurs when both parties act as independent buyers and sellers, each seeking his own best interest. It is not when one party writes both sides of a contract.

When multinational corporations transfer goods between affiliates in different countries, the generally applied standard for evaluating and taxing these transactions is the "arm's length" principle. Citibank knew that parking transactions had to appear to be at arm's length to claim a semblance of legitimacy. After the 1975 Natvig/Pomeroy survey, Citibank contended that parking was done at market rates— one of the tests in determining the arm's length principle. Citibank, however, equated market *rates* to the market *range* for any given day, which was not the same thing, as shall be explained later.

A second crucial factor in determining the arm's length quality of a transaction—whether both parties acted as independent buyers and sellers, each seeking his own best interest—was control. If control over a parked position remained with the party originating the transaction—i.e., if the party that parked a position could unpark it at anytime on whatever terms he wished—then it could hardly be said that the transaction was at arm's length.

From many Citibank documents it appeared that positions were parked and unparked solely on the instructions of the initiating branch, while the accommodating branch—i.e., the parkee—always acted passively. Shearman & Sterling's own report observed that Citibank's treasury and comptroller's division "increasingly saw the need for branches transferring positions to use rates within the prevailing market range on both the original and reversing contracts," but offered no opinion as to the adequacy of using rates within the market range to test the arm's length quality of the transactions.

---

[10] Henry Campbell Black M.A., *Black's Law Dictionary* (St. Paul, Minn.: West Publishing Company), fourth edition.

The argument Shearman & Sterling developed to refute the control issue rested on a theoretical possibility that the government of the sovereign state in which the parking-lot branch was located might decide overnight to freeze all foreign exchange assets. In this case, an act of state transferred the economic risk to the parkee and, according to Shearman & Sterling's reasoning, no act of "control" by the originating branch could alter that situation. Therefore, Shearman & Sterling maintained, effective control transferred with the position even if, at some later date, the position returned to the books of the originating branch.

While Shearman & Sterling obviously felt that parking was defensible, Hoffman said it would be presumptuous for the firm to opine on how foreign courts of law might interpret the monetary and fiscal regulations in force in their jurisdictions. And so, to support the thesis that parking was bona fide, Hoffman and his team developed ten "scenarios" that purported to describe typical kinds of interbranch transactions. Weeks of careful drafting went into them, and great importance was attached to every word. While the drafting continued, Shearman & Sterling selected local counsel in the seven European centers who were then asked to express their opinion as to the legality of the hypothetical transactions described in the scenarios.

The search for local counsel should have been aided by the fact that Robert Logan, head of Division III, had conducted a similar exercise the year before (see Chapter 13). Shearman & Sterling, however, claimed not to be aware of Logan's 1977 efforts to obtain opinions on parking. In only two cases did they retain the same counsel. These were the Liedekerke Wolters Waelbroeck & Kirkpatrick firm in Brussels and the Niederer Kraft & Frey firm in Zurich.

Instead of using Feddersen Kemmler Weiskopf in Frankfurt, they retained the Stuttgart firm of Haver & Mailänder.

Studio Legale Guglielmo Gulotta of Milan, which had been unequivocal in its 1977 opinion that parking was illegal under Italian law, was replaced by the Studio Legale Chiomenti in Rome.[11]

In Amsterdam they retained Caron & Stevens.

In London they used Coward Chance.

In Paris it was the law offices of S. G. Archibald.

In each case Shearman & Sterling furnished local counsel with in-

---

[11] The senior partner of Studio Legale Chiomenti, Pasquale Chiomenti, had the misfortune of accepting a seat on the board of directors of Bernie Cornfeld's IOS Ltd. just before it collapsed in 1970.

troductory comments to the scenarios, supplemented by additional information that local counsel themselves requested. They were also given, according to Hoffman, sections of the Edwards Blue Book relating to their country.

Shearman & Sterling made it clear to local counsel that they were not being asked to conduct any factual inquiry themselves. They were to use the scenarios and other information Shearman & Sterling furnished as the basis for their advice.

The scenarios and introductory descriptions made it appear as if the accommodation branch—i.e., the parkee—acted independently and that the positions, once parked, were no longer controlled by the branch that initiated the parking.

The scenarios also made it seem that parking was done at market rates when in fact the rate used to park a position was frequently identical to the rate used to unpark it.

The frequency of parking transactions was nowhere mentioned, and in most cases local counsel treated them as isolated occurrences.

These omissions shaded the manner in which local counsel viewed *parking*—a word which, in any event, was banished from the scenarios. Wearing these narrowly set blinkers, local counsel worked on their opinions throughout the summer and into the autumn.

Milan's Scenario No. 1 and explanatory comments were particularly misleading. The Chiomenti firm was told: "It is important to understand that Milan had no power whatsoever to compel any other branch of Citibank to accept and or enter into any of the foreign exchange transactions which are described in the draft scenarios. Such other branch always had absolute power and discretion whether to enter into such special transactions or not."[12]

The engagement letter hiring the Chiomenti firm stated: "Whenever Milan contemplated that it would have an exchange position at the end of the day and Milan believed that Citibank's worldwide profits would be increased by some other Citibank branch taking over such position, Milan would request that such branch take over the position. With only rare exceptions, such requests were agreed to by the other branch on the basis of Milan's good trading reputation. . . .

"The motivation for the Milan branch to initiate special transactions was that of maximizing the bank's income on a worldwide basis and to set the best possible record for the branch within the bank's

[12] Letter from Danforth Newcomb, Shearman & Sterling, to Phillip D. Sherman, Citibank Milan, September 14, 1978.

internal management information system (MIS)."[13]

The image given to Italian counsel by this description was that the Milan branch had such a good trading reputation, and was bountiful in making its expertise available to others, that should another Citibank treasury receive a call from Milan "requesting" it to take a position, it would quite willingly accept Milan's suggestion because it certainly would bring profit. Only once was Nassau mentioned as a possible counterparty. Milan's Scenario No. 1 was structured as follows:

Milan; Draft Scenario No. 1

GOAL: Citibank Milan wants to transfer its overbought dollar position to another branch, or assist another branch to transfer its position.

VARIATIONS I & II

A. *Transaction Steps*	*Results*
1. Milan purchases dollars on the open market at the market rate.	1. Milan is overbought in dollars.
2. On the same day, Milan instructs another Citibank branch to buy dollars from Milan spot or forward at the market rate.	2a) Milan is neither overbought nor oversold in dollars. b) The other branch is overbought in dollars.

B. *Removing the position from the other branch.*

3. At a later date, Milan buys the same amount of dollars from the other branch on the same value day and at market rate.	3a) Milan is overbought in dollars. b) The other branch is neither overbought nor oversold in dollars. Any profit occurs at the other branch and is recorded on the legal books of that branch. This step generates no profit or loss in Milan. (i) Assume Citibank's internal management information system reflects Milan's role in this transac-

---

[13] Confidential—Shearman & Sterling FX Engagement, draft 10/5/78, pp. 1–2; Citibank document 0024–0031.

tion. (ii) Assume Citibank's internal management information system does not reflect Milan's role in this transaction.

These transactions may be done with head office, European branches, or Nassau.

In a six-page *undated* opinion letter, Studio Legale Chiomenti was careful to point out, "If the transactions are read in the light of the preliminary guidelines to the draft scenarios, we believe that the transactions in question do not constitute any infringement [of Italian law]. . . . In fact the transactions in question fall within those which are generally authorized on the part of Italian banks, and, always based on the general guidelines to the draft scenarios, the Branch has no effective participation, either directly or indirectly (e.g., by way of a principal agency relationship) in the continuation of the holding and managing of the various exchange 'positions' envisaged in the scenarios."

This conclusion, although in line with the preliminary guidelines received from Shearman & Sterling, misrepresented the basic design of parking. The Milan branch had an "effective participation" in the "continuation" of the position because in practice the originating branch *always* was responsible for removing the position from the parking-lot branch. The Studio Legale Chiomenti opinion letter, however, made it seem that if Milan did repurchase a parked position, this was only a coincidental occurrence.

Frankfurt's Scenario No. 1 differed significantly from the "common pattern" described in Milan's No. 1 Scenario.

Frankfurt; Scenario No. 1

GOAL: Citibank Frankfurt wants to transfer its overbought Deutsche mark position to another branch.

VARIATION I

A. *Transaction Steps*	*Result*
1. Frankfurt has sold dollars on the open market at the market rate for delivery spot.	1. Frankfurt is oversold dollars and overbought Deutsche mark.

2. On the same day, Frankfurt buys dollars against Deutsche marks from Nassau in a spot contract at the market rate and so informs Nassau.

2.a) Frankfurt is neither overbought nor oversold in dollars.

b) Nassau is overbought in Deutsche marks and oversold in dollars.

B. *Removing the position from Nassau*

3. Sometime later (frequently after rolling over the position one or more times through swaps) Frankfurt buys dollars against Deutsche marks at the market rate.

3. Frankfurt is overbought dollars and oversold Deutsche marks.

4. Frankfurt sells dollars against Deutsche marks to Nassau on the same value date and at the market rate and so informs Nassau.

4.a) Frankfurt is no longer oversold or overbought in dollars or Deutsche marks.

b) Nassau is neither overbought nor oversold in Deutsche marks. Unless the market rate on the date the transaction is reversed is the same as the rate used in step No. 2 the profit or loss to Nassau is attributed to Frankfurt through Citibank's internal management information system but it is not recorded in Frankfurt's legal books. In the alternative, assume such profit or loss is not so attributed to Frankfurt.

Dr. Peter Mailänder, of the Stuttgart law firm of Haver & Mailänder, had considerable problems with this scenario. Instead of a five-page opinion, which his learned colleagues in Frankfurt had produced the year before, he constructed a complex and heavily hedged twenty-one page opinion letter. His concern for such thoroughness may have been influenced by the fact that he also served as chairman of the audit control board (Aufsichtsrat) of Citicorp's principal subsidiary in

Germany, Citibank AG, a detail that nowhere was mentioned but that apparently did not place in question his ability to function in the Shearman & Sterling special review with independent judgment.

While Mailänder's opinion did not reflect any awareness that the "Nassau" in question was merely a desk at head office, he pointed out that if the transactions were not properly documented arms' length transactions, they would be considered as "self-contracting" or "camouflage deals" and therefore risked running afoul of West German legislation.

His opinion letter noted that neither Scenario No. 1 nor the introductory material disclosed the underlying reasons for the transfer of Frankfurt's position to Nassau, and its subsequent return to Frankfurt. If the transfer of positions from Frankfurt to Nassau coincided with a shift of profits from Frankfurt to Nassau when these profits could have been incurred in Frankfurt, then Mailänder concluded that the transactions would be suspect under West German law.

The letter stated:

> If Frankfurt would restrict itself in its Transaction Step 2 to buy US$ against DM from Nassau with the understanding and commitment to sell US$ against DM to Nassau at a later date without any chance or risk remaining for Nassau, i.e., with the understanding that profits and losses from the final squaring out of the position would be for Frankfurt, we would have to deal with a parking scheme designed to get around restrictive ratio regulations. . . .
>
> As we have no indication that Frankfurt is committed to repurchase the DM positions from Nassau at any given date nor at any fixed rate other than the market rate, nor that Nassau is bound to retransfer this position to Frankfurt at any prefixed rate, the transfer in Transaction Step 2 does shift the foreign exchange risk involved to Nassau. . . . The internal booking for MIS purposes of profit or loss for Frankfurt does not have any impact on its financial condition.
>
> It is therefore to be concluded that Frankfurt by its transfer operation does not violate [the] text or spirit of the banking law. . . ."[14]

Should an audit of of foreign exchange transactions reveal that "the profitable ones were predominantly closed for Nassau and the losing

[14]Haver & Mailänder opinion letter of November 7, 1978; paras 3.1.2. and 3.1.3.; pages 9–10.

ones were primarily closed for Frankfurt," Mailänder warned that "the overall impression could reverse the foregoing conclusion."[15] In making this comment, Mailänder had touched upon the most striking short-coming of the scenario approach: the scenarios inaccurately described what was going on in the trading rooms.

The Zurich No. 1 Scenario was similar to, but not exactly the same as, the Milan and Frankfurt No. 1 Scenarios. And it also posed tremendous problems for Zurich counsel, the firm of Niederer Kraft & Frey.

The year before, Dr. Stefan Kraft had written a four-page opinion explaining that parking appeared to be a breach of Swiss monetary controls and income tax laws. Eighteen months later, Kraft and two of his partners, Walter Meier and Peter Isler, produced a seventy-eight-page opinion that came to the same conclusions. This massive document dealt with the Shearman & Sterling scenarios for Zurich in a heavily qualified fashion.

In a preface to their new findings, the Swiss attorneys stipulated: "Th[is] opinion is not supposed to be supplied to governmental or non-governmental agencies of any country nor to any other third parties. No part of the opinion shall be published." It added: "In any instance where . . . a quotation is made from this opinion, specific reference is to be made to the qualifications under which the opinion has been rendered."

Kraft and his collaborators wrote: "The mere fact that the same value date and the same rate as used in step No. 2 was applied for the removing of the position does not, in itself, raise the question of evasion of the law. If Zurich and Nassau did, however, not intend to enter into a 'real' contractual relationship with its risks and obligations, i.e., if the two transactions in steps 2 and 3 were purely simulated, a violation of the regulations relating to the banks' foreign exchange positions . . . would have been committed."[16]

The Zurich opinion letter had a final observation that cut through the legalese and squarely called into doubt the entire basis of the Shearman & Sterling special review: "The Scenarios (and the supplementary minutes) do not permit [us] to predict with desirable or even only approximate accuracy the tax and eventual penal consequences of potential non-compliances with the tax laws."[17]

[15] Ibid., pp. 19–20.
[16] Niederer Kraft & Frey opinion letter of November 7, 1978, page 46.
[17] Ibid., p. 77.

London's No. 1 Scenario described the parking of a position taken by the local branch against pounds sterling. But the word *parking* appeared nowhere, making it unclear whether from the outset the intention was to bring the short sterling position back from Nassau or whether it just happened to turn out that way. Local counsel, Hugh S. Pigott of Coward Chance, asked Shearman & Sterling about the frequency of such transactions.

Pigott was informed that about one hundred of them had occurred over the five-year period under review and that the average amount involved was $10 million per transaction. He discovered, however, that Citibank London had an authorized limit on net open positions set by the Bank of England of only $4 million. This admission, once again, seemed to confirm rather than disprove Edwards's allegations. The opinion expressed by Pigott was the most negative of the seven.

> In London it has long been the practice of banks to accept that the regulations of the Bank of England should be honored not only in the letter of the law but also in spirit. On its part, in our experience, the Bank of England has been prepared to accept that in exceptional circumstances its regulations will be breached inadvertently and in those cases to turn a blind eye to the offence. The Bank of England's attitude is, however, different where there has been a deliberate attempt to breach its regulations, whether in spirit or in accordance with the strict letter of the law.
>
> As a strict matter of law, the question whether [Scenario No. 1] is in breach of [the statutory limit] depends on whether there is a contractual obligation of Citibank's Nassau branch to sell back the sterling at the same rate. This is obviously a difficult question of law which, without more detailed knowledge of the facts and surrounding circumstances, it is not possible to express an opinion.
>
> But when the spirit of the Bank of England's regulations is taken into consideration, it seems to us that there is a marked difference between deliberately going above the prescribed limit and doing so inadvertently.[18]

With the opinion letters from the seven European counsel on the table, Hoffman and his associates began placing the finishing touches on a report of the investigation ordered by Wriston.

---

[18] Privileged and confidential letter from Hugh S. Pigott of Coward Chance to John E. Hoffman, Jr., November 7, 1978.

Chapter 22

"Paris Doesn't Park" —Part II

I don't give a shit what happens. I want you all to stonewall it, let them plead the Fifth Amendment, cover-up, or anything else, if it'll save it—save the plan. That's the whole point.

—RICHARD M. NIXON, MARCH 22, 1973

Shearman & Sterling refused to make public the texts of their foreign exchange scenarios. The reason given for this was that they were privileged as part of attorney-client communications.

The scenarios in fact did not describe the kind of parking exposed by David Edwards in his four Blue Book examples. The Blue Book examples were taken from real deals used by Citibank traders to transfer taxable profits to no-tax Nassau. Profit-transfer parking was the more offensive form of the art. Moreover, the scenarios only elliptically described the other form of parking, which indeed was the most common. This second form of parking essentially was a "wash," so termed because it enabled traders to make open positions disappear from their books. By using this second form of parking, traders could retain overnight control over open positions that exceeded local central-bank limits and return these same positions to the books again when needed. This practice gave the Citibank traders longer-term view of the market and an advantage over other traders, who respected the statutory limits. Because parking enabled them to avoid statutory limits, it also increased their potential for profit.

Edwards had taken his examples of profit-transfer parking from the cartons marked "parked positions" that he found in the operations department storeroom on the sixth floor at 399 Park Avenue. He had selected them from among thousands of similar transactions for their clarity in illustrating what he considered was a pattern of questionable activity.

Thomas C. Theobald, the head of the international banking group, had urged Edwards to bring to Citibank's attention any evidence "which would tend to substantiate your allegations" in December 1977. Edwards had responded in early January 1978 by sending Theobald the French example: a photocopy of a June 11, 1976, telex from Jean-Pierre de Laet in Paris to the Nassau desk in New York. Edwards told Theobald:

"The [June 11, 1976, telex] appears to be describing what is at least a questionable transaction. In my understanding of bank procedure, this message is prime documentation of what I have referred to as 'parking positions,' not what you refer to as 'placing positions.' I would be interested in how you perceive this transaction." [1]

The only answer Edwards received from Theobald was the letter terminating his employment. But when John Hoffman wrote to Edwards's attorney, Geoffrey Shields, on February 8, 1978, he noted, "While Mr. Edwards has been voicing his 'concerns' for over two years, it was not until January 1978 that he ever submitted any documentary material for our client's consideration—and that consisted merely of a copy of an internal Citibank telex communication reflecting a foreign exchange transaction some eighteen months ago."

This implied that Hoffman did not view the sample parking transaction from Paris as anything out of the ordinary. In fact, it described precisely what Edwards had alleged: that Paris was "cooking the books." A comparison of this Blue Book example with the hypothetical "scenario" Hoffman used to describe what he alleged to be the general pattern of parking by Paris was revealing of how the Shearman & Sterling report, when it appeared eight months later, was able to neutralize the Edwards allegations.

---

[1] Letter to Thomas C. Theobald from David Edwards, January 9, 1978.

Hoffman's scenarios described "the transfer of a foreign exchange position by one branch to a branch in another country." In true parking, the originating branch was responsible for removing the position from the parking-lot branch on terms dictated by the originating branch alone. In Hoffman's scenarios, the parked position came back to the originating branch, but the scenarios implied this occurred by happenstance rather than design. The scenarios mentioned as well that a profit might result from the transfer, in which case it could be credited, but not necessarily, to the originating branch by a MIS advisory.

The Blue Book example followed no such procedure. It began quite differently: "Please book for us the following transaction. . . ." This clearly indicated that Paris set the rates for both sides of the transaction—i.e., that Paris controlled the parking and the unparking of the position. That being so, it could not be construed as an arm's length transaction.[2] Moreover, the Blue Book example involved only two steps: the parking and unparking.

STEP ONE (parking):—"Citi Nassau buys from Citi Paris $6 million against French francs at the rate of 4.7275, value June 15."

STEP TWO (unparking):—"Citi Nassau sells to Citi New York $4 million against French francs at the rate of 4.7375, value June 15."
—"Citi Nassau sells to Citi Brussels $2 million at the rate of 4.7375 against French francs."

At this point, the impact was as follows: having jiggled the rates by 100 "pips," Paris "lost" FF 60,000 to Nassau. De Laet now began reversing the transaction—i.e., unparking it—in a first phase, squaring the books in Nassau. He transferred the position temporarily to New York and Brussels. In a later phase, presumably, he would return the position to his own books and then close it, though the telex did not mention this. As Edwards pointed out in his analysis: "It is reasonable to suppose that [Paris] instructed New York and Brussels to sell back the $6 million, at the same rate [of] 4.7375."

The Paris No. 1 Scenario that Shearman & Sterling submitted to French counsel reflected none of this.

---

[2] For a full text of the June 11, 1976, parking telex, see Chapter 11, pages 112–115.

Paris, Scenario No. 1

GOAL: Citibank Paris wants to transfer its oversold French franc position to another branch, or assist another branch to transfer its position.

Transferring a position was not the goal of the Blue Book example: it was to avoid taxes, or more specifically, to place a FF 60,000 profit in Nassau by causing Paris to "lose" a corresponding amount in a non-arm's length deal.

The Shearman & Sterling scenario continued:

VARIATION I

A. *Transaction Steps*	*Results*
1. Paris has sold French francs spot against the dollar on the open market at the market rate.	1. Paris is oversold in French francs.

This step one described a perfectly legitimate trade of a type which probably preceded the Paris-Nassau off-booking transaction referred to in Edwards's Blue Book. In fact the Paris Scenario step one was quite irrelevant to the Blue Book example and had nothing to do with what Edwards was alleging.

Step two of the Shearman & Sterling scenario stated:

2. On the same day, Paris buys French francs against dollars from Citibank Nassau at the market rate.	2a) Paris is neither overbought nor oversold in French francs. b) Nassau is oversold in French francs.

This corresponded more or less to step one in the Blue Book example, except that in the Blue Book version, Paris sold dollars to Nassau at an *arbitrary rate,* which may or may not have been selected from within the market range for the day. (The foreign exchange market had already closed in Paris when, at 5:27 P.M. local time, de Laet sent his June 11 telex.) The major divergence between the transactions only became apparent in Part B (step two) of the Shearman & Sterling scenario:

B. *Removing the position from the other branch*	
3. Sometime later, Paris sells the same amount of French francs	3a) Paris is oversold in French francs.

to Nassau on the same value date as in step No. 2 at the new market rate.

b) Nassau is neither overbought nor oversold in French francs. Since market rates are used to remove the position from Nassau, any profits or losses would appear on the books of Nassau.

c) The internal management information system attributes any such profits or losses to Paris but those profits or losses are not recorded on Paris's legal books.

d) In the alternative, assume the internal management information system does not attribute any such profits or losses to Paris.

Step three of the Shearman & Sterling scenario corresponded to step two in the Blue Book. In the Blue Book version, however, Citibank Paris removed the position from Nassau using a *second arbitrary rate* selected four days before the transaction was actually due to close. De Laet purposely avoided using market rates in order to leave a profit in Nassau.

For the scenario to state that ''since market rates were used to remove the position from Nassau, any profits or losses would appear on the books of Nassau'' was misleading. In fact, in the Shearman & Sterling scenario's step three a back-dated rate was used to remove the position. The scenario also suggested that losses might occur, when the goal of the Blue Book example was only to transfer profits. Allowing French counsel to assume that the objective was not specifically to transfer profits, though implying that from time to time this might happen, was a skillful dissimulation.

In rendering its opinion, the Paris law firm of S. G. Archibald also assumed ''that any such [parking] transactions were not frequent.'' And the opinion letter, signed by Sosthène de Vilmorin, further assumed that ''all interest and exchange rates used for the various transactions were the market rates then in effect.''[3]

---

[3] Privileged and confidential memorandum from the offices of S. G. Archibald, September 6, 1978, page 2.

De Vilmorin, however, was careful enough to caution that the transaction described in Scenario No. 1 could be in violation of exchange controls. "The authorities might argue that the effect of Citibank Paris having taken a position which it was officially unable to hold overnight, and having transferred that position for its account to another branch . . . was that Citibank Paris indirectly engaged in overnight speculation, although it was directly prohibited from doing so."[4]

De Vilmorin warned that if this view was adopted by the French authorities, attendant tax problems might develop as well.

In spite of this caveat, de Vilmorin's "privileged and confidential" letter demonstrated how the misleading nature of the Shearman & Sterling scenarios permitted European counsel to write ambiguous opinions. These ambiguous opinions in turn provided Shearman & Sterling at least with a plausibly defensible basis for their whitewash of parking.

[4] Ibid., p. 5.

Chapter 23

The Purging of Jean-Pierre de Laet

It is market practice that brokers remit gifts at the end of the year.

—JEAN-PIERRE DE LAET, APRIL 10, 1978

As the Shearman & Sterling team went into action, Jean-Pierre de Laet again became the focus of unwelcome attention. He was questioned repeatedly by Citibank's resident inspector in Paris, Neville Armstrong, about his dealings with two foreign exchange brokers, Degez & Cie. of Paris and Debeuckelaer & Cie. of Antwerp. His desk was searched, the dealing slips audited, and his bank files checked.

During one session, de Laet admitted almost jokingly that he had received two dozen bottles of wine for Christmas from his friend Jan Debeuckelaer, as he and his traders did every year.

Armstrong demanded details.

Well, de Laet explained, Debeuckelaer didn't get to Paris too often to do his shopping, so the Antwerp broker sent a check for FF 20,000 (equivalent to $4,210) and asked that de Laet buy twenty-four bottles of good French wine for himself and each member of his trading-room staff.

197

Had de Laet reported this?

No, he had not.

Why not?

It was customary at Christmas for brokers to give gifts of wine, champagne, or fine cognac to traders who did business with them. Every broker did it as a matter of course. There was no secret. It was the accepted tradition.

A check for FF 20,000?

Yes. De Laet had cleared it through his account at Citibank.

Could de Laet prove he bought wine with the money?

Certainly. He had an invoice from Nicolas S.A., the French wine shippers. It was for 290 bottles and totaled FF 14,280 ($3,000).

Armstrong checked the records of de Laet's account and found not one but two checks from Debeuckelaer, drawn on Banque Belge in London. The second was for FF 15,000 ($3,150). Oh yes, de Laet remembered, Debeuckelaer had given him a second check. De Laet had a special deal for buying wine through Nicolas at diplomatic prices. His former school buddy, the soft-spoken and bushy-moustached Debeuckelaer, had asked to be included in the scheme, too, and he paid de Laet with a check.

But the two checks totaled $7,360, and all gifts of more than $5,000 had to be reported. Why had de Laet made no report?

De Laet belatedly realized that the wine had turned sour. Armstrong was out to sink him. The resident inspector also questioned a FF 20,000 transfer from his brother. Finally, Armstrong uncovered a series of transfers by de Laet to the account of Esther Rebibo, his mistress, who also worked in the trading room.

During a heated session at the beginning of April 1978, de Laet started to cry. He said he would resign as he was no longer trusted.

On Monday, April 10, 1978, he wrote Young a memo attempting to explain the 290 bottles of wine and the FF 35,000. "First of all, I want to point out that I have always been very loyal to the Bank (11 years), that I am an honest man, nothing to hide. Second, that I would be the most stupid man in the world to credit my account with the Bank with kickbacks."[1]

Robert Logan, the head of Division III, thought de Laet had been treated harshly. Logan promised him an excellent letter of reference if he resigned. De Laet said it would only lend credence to the Edwards allegations. Nevertheless, he had made up his mind to leave,

---

[1] Citibank document 7894.

and on April 18, 1978, he sent Young his required three-month notice. This Young acknowledged in writing on June 12, 1978, offering a generous severance package. De Laet by then had an offer to become chief trader at a smaller American bank in Paris. As he was still negotiating for this job, Citibank said it would intercede to help him get it.

At the end of June 1978, French counsel working on the Shearman & Sterling scenarios contacted de Laet to ask for his clarification of certain parking procedures. De Laet was helpful and suggested amendments to Scenario No. 1 to make it more accurate. He left the bank's employment on July 18, 1978 and was given as a parting bonus six months of additional salary.

Weeks later, *The New York Times* contacted Citibank to ask if de Laet had been fired. A spokesman for the bank stated that de Laet had "resigned voluntarily" to accept a senior position with another bank. The spokesman declined to identify the other bank.[2]

In fact, there was no "other" bank, as de Laet did not get the job. Instead, seven months later he became treasurer for a group of companies in Paris controlled by Roger E. Tamraz, a Lebanese-American investment banker. The group included the Grand Hotel on the boulevard des Capucines, before it was sold to the Intercontinental chain. He remained with the group for one year, but left when Tamraz's plans to open a bank with Arab capital fell through.

De Laet remained out of work for the next nine months. In November 1980, he was interviewed by the personnel manager of Manufacturers Hanover Trust Company in Paris. Manny Hanny, as the fourth largest U.S. bank is known in the financial community, was looking for a chief trader for its Paris office. De Laet explained that he had had some problems at Citibank, which Manny Hanny checked, both in Paris and New York. Word came back that his record was clean and on November 21, 1980, he was hired for the new job. He spent the first week of December at the bank's head offices in New York and then immediately took charge of the trading room in Paris.

That same month, SEC investigators asked Shearman & Sterling whether Citibank had given de Laet a sweetheart severance package to keep him quiet. Henry Weisburg, an associate attorney working on the case, replied by letter that de Laet was given no special favors. The letter noted, however, that the bank had forgiven an outstanding

[2]Deborah Rankin, "Resignation of 2 Aides Disclosed by Citibank," *The New York Times*, August 3, 1978.

loan to de Laet on the grounds that he was unemployed and therefore could not meet the payments.

"At the time of Mr. de Laet's departure from Citibank, he was indebted to Citibank on a mortgage loan that had initially been in the amount of Belgian francs 1.5 million [equivalent to about $50,000]. No payments on this loan have been received since May 1979, as Mr. de Laet has been unemployed. Accordingly, this loan, presently in the amount of Belgian francs 1,218,000 [$39, 869 at the then-current exchange rate of BF30.55] has been carried on Citibank's books on a non-accrual basis," the letter stated.[3]

But Jean-Pierre de Laet was not unemployed. He was the new trading room boss of Manny Hanny in Paris and his salary was in the $50,000 range. Three years later he was promoted and transferred to Zurich where he became Manny Hanny's regional treasurer for Europe.

[3] Henry S. Weisburg, letter to Thomson von Stein, December 23, 1980.

Chapter 24

Order of Investigation

The SEC has the reputation of being the best agency—the most honest, most effective, with the most integrity—and I think that's largely because of Sporkin and his enforcement division. Commissioners come and go . . . but Sporkin represents the real drive and spirit of the SEC.

—SENATOR WILLIAM PROXMIRE, AS QUOTED IN *The American Lawyer,* NOVEMBER 1980

As director of the SEC's division of enforcement, Stanley Sporkin arguably wielded more power than any other person in corporate America. He had extraordinary courage and integrity, and although his salary was $65,000 a year (compared to Walter Wriston's $1.2 million), he was not only one of the most feared men on Wall Street, but also one of the most respected.

Sporkin, the son of a Philadelphia judge, came out of Yale Law School in 1957 and for the next three years served as clerk for the Honorable Caleb Merrill Wright, chief judge of the U.S. District Court in Delaware. He joined the SEC in 1961 as a staff attorney under the chairmanship of William L. Cary and became head of the division of enforcement in 1974 under Ray Garrett. His industry and creativity transformed the position into the most important law enforcement job in the country.

Sporkin, with his years of experience as top policeman of corporate crimes and prosecutor of executive-suite bandits, had developed a strong intuitive sense of right and wrong. In 1972, when he was the division's deputy director in charge of the Robert Vesco investigation, his instincts told him that $250,000 transferred by the New Jersey businessman from the Bahamas to New York was a payoff. His insistence that the money be traced led to the discovery of Vesco's secret contribution to CREEP, President Nixon's reelection committee, which ultimately financed the Watergate break-in. Vesco, then facing indictment, put a Washington, D.C., private detective by the name of Bud Fensterwald on Sporkin to dig up dirt. Fensterwald learned that Sporkin lived with his wife, Judy, and their three children in a modest home in Chevy Chase, Maryland, but he couldn't find the dirt.

Federal securities laws in the United States are based upon maintaining orderly markets through a system of full and fair disclosure. The philosophy of corporate disclosure as the best method for keeping the marketplace clean and safe was formulated by Supreme Court Justice Louis D. Brandeis in a series of articles that first appeared in 1914. "Publicity is justly commended as a remedy for social and industrial diseases. Sunlight is said to be the best of disinfectants; electric light the most efficient policeman," Brandeis wrote twenty years before the SEC was born.[1]

Between 1920 and 1933 some $40 billion of securities were sold in the United States. By 1933 half of them were worthless. That same year Franklin D. Roosevelt proposed to Congress that the Brandeis sunlight principle become the basis for federal regulation of the securities industry. Congress agreed, passing the Securities Act of 1933.

The 1933 act provides for "full and fair disclosure of the character of securities sold in interstate and foreign commerce and through the mails, and to prevent frauds in the sale thereof" by requiring corporations engaged in public underwritings to file a registration statement, as well as quarterly and other statements, setting forth specified information about themselves.

The SEC was created the following year by the Securities Ex-

[1] The articles were reprinted in Louis D. Brandeis, *Other People's Money* (New York: Stokes, 1932), p. 32.

change Act of 1934. The 1934 act provides for "the regulation of securities exchanges and of over-the-counter markets operating in interstate and foreign commerce and through the mails, to prevent inequitable and unfair practices on such exchanges and markets."

The 1934 act gave the SEC its structure: five commissioners, one of them chairman, appointed by the President and confirmed by the Senate, for staggered five-year terms. The commissioners presided over a staff divided first into three, and later five, operating divisions and an office of general counsel. The 1934 act also gave the agency its power of enforcement, and therefore its independence.

Roosevelt appointed Boston financier Joseph P. Kennedy as the agency's first chairman. Roosevelt believed that Kennedy, one of the great stock manipulators of the 1920s, would be effective because he knew the tricks of the trade. Although his chairmanship lasted only fourteen months, Kennedy instilled in the new agency a sense of dedication to the public interest that it retained throughout its first half-century existence.

New York securities lawyer Roberta S. Karmel, the first woman commissioner (appointed by President Carter in 1977), wrote that "the SEC has developed a highly competent staff with unusual esprit de corps. The staff's intelligence, dedication and willingness to work is really second to none in or out of government. Further, the SEC's independence as a prosecutor has given the Commission credibility and assisted in the efficient implementation of Commission policies."[2]

But Karmel did not see eye to eye with Sporkin. While she admired him for his "industry, integrity, creativity and even his ambition," she felt that the commissions under which he served had abdicated to him "a policy-making role that made him de facto head of the SEC in certain areas."

"What frightened me the most about Sporkin's power at about the time I became a commissioner was the fear he aroused of both him and the SEC. No unelected government official should wield that kind of power too long."[3]

Karmel thought that Sporkin was too flamboyant and that he curried the cult of personality. "Yet, the cult of personality in law enforcement can be a dangerous thing, both to the personality and to the institution to which he is attached. . . .

[2] Roberta S. Karmel, *Regulation by Prosecution: The Securities & Exchange Commission vs. Corporate America* (New York: Simon and Schuster, 1982), page 90.
[3] Ibid., p. 70.

"My complaint about the SEC at the time I was appointed a commissioner is that it had allowed its prosecutorial functions to overwhelm all its operations and policies. The enforcement division . . . was running the whole show instead of investigating and prosecuting cases in programs formulated by the Commission of the chairman."[4]

Sporkin's enforcement leadership, it was true, had broken a great deal of new ground in the disclosure of corporate wrongdoing. He had pushed for extending the SEC's involvement in corporate governance to include independent auditors and corporate counsel who failed to protect shareholders from greedy or self-serving management. More controversially, he had played a major role in extending the securities laws to require disclosure of questionable payments by U.S. corporations.

This came about after the office of the special Watergate prosecutor disclosed that several corporations and executive officers had used corporate funds to make illegal political contributions. The SEC, which had suffered its first serious scandal as a result of Watergate, forcing its newly appointed thirty-six-year-old chairman, Bradford Cook, to resign, reacted with what Karmel described as a show of "moralistic, perhaps even paranoid," indignation.

In March 1974, the SEC publicly expressed the view that nondisclosure of illegal political contributions was a violation of the federal securities laws. Investigations by Sporkin's staff led to injunctive actions against nine corporations during the following twelve-month period. All but one of these cases were settled by a consent to an injunction requiring the corporation to undertake a special review of the irregularities charged by the commission and to file a public report of the special review.

Investigations into illegal campaign contributions led to the disclosure of various kinds of payments to foreign government officials for the purpose of obtaining contracts abroad—so-called "questionable foreign payments," or more simply, "bribes abroad." Sporkin and his staff also decided that these, too, were evidence of poor corporate stewardship and should be disclosed to shareholders.

Sporkin, however, realized he did not have the manpower to bring injunctive actions against a sufficient number of companies suspected of making questionable payments to end the practice. Accordingly, he devised the "voluntary disclosure program," which virtually shamed corporations into cleaning up their accounts. More than four hundred

[4] Ibid., p. 97.

companies participated in this program, making a public confession of their "questionable" conduct. One of the most successful SEC enforcement programs, it became highly controversial and was detested by corporate America. It also made Sporkin more enemies than friends.

"While I might agree that the payment of exorbitant bribes to foreign officials by U.S. corporations was properly a matter of national concern, I do not believe it should have become the concern of an independent agency responsible for financial disclosure to investors," Karmel commented, capsulizing the counter-view to the "bribes abroad" program.[5] Many people agreed with her.

The point was, however, that no other federal agency showed any inclination to take the issue in hand. The "flamboyant" Sporkin, who was outspoken perhaps, somewhat naïve, and deeply principled, but hardly flamboyant, had filled a law enforcement void.

With the Citicorp case a feeling floated among the commissioners that Sporkin was attempting the same sort of extension of the SEC's jurisdiction into bank regulation.[6] More pointedly, some of the agency's leading critics asked if it was proper for Sporkin to use the federal securities law to compel obedience to foreign tax and exchange control laws. Sporkin contended that to the extent off-booking practices jeopardized Citibank's banking license in certain countries or exposed the bank to the possibility of incurring huge penalties, disclosure of these activities was required.

Robert G. Ryan, whom Sporkin assigned to look into the Citicorp matter, had handled many of the "questionable payments" cases. Ryan looked more like a tough Irish cop than a specialist in securities law. He was large and shuffling, with a boxer's nose, but gentle manner. Born and brought up in Buffalo, New York, he had obtained his law degree from the University of Buffalo in 1963. He joined the SEC in 1964 as a staff attorney, but left in 1967 to work for the Justice Department, becoming an Assistant U.S. Attorney on the Buffalo organized crime task force, helping to investigate and prosecute the local organized crime family run by Stefano Magaddino, then chairman of the national crime syndicate. Ryan returned to the commission in 1972.

Ryan was regarded by his colleagues at the SEC as considerate—a "nice guy"—but less than assertive. He smoked incessantly. Gray hair made him appear a decade older than his forty years. He was a

---

[5] Ibid., p. 90.
[6] One of the provisions of the Securities Exchange Act of 1934 is "to protect and make more effective the national banking system. . . ."

quiet, conscientious investigator with flashes of wit, one of a hundred attorneys who staffed Sporkin's division of enforcement.

The enforcement division handled an average of 1,400 investigations or administrative inquiries each year, resulting in up to 180 civil injunctive actions, half of them ending with criminal referral to the Justice Department. In the often rheumatic world of civil servants, this made Sporkin's enforcement staff among the most overworked and, by big law firm standards, underpaid. As far as Sporkin was concerned, there were never enough hands to go around. This was particularly so in April 1978, the month after David Edwards walked into the SEC with his by then infamous Blue Book. That month one of Sporkin's most experienced investigators, Thomson von Stein, quit the agency to become an assistant enforcement director at the Federal Energy Regulatory Commission (FERC).

Sporkin wanted to move ahead with the Citicorp case. He sensed it was important, involving new interpretations of the laws of disclosure as applicable to issues of corporate morality. He was impressed, also, that Edwards had put so much on the line for a question of principle; rather than compromise his integrity, the ex-Citibanker had sacrificed his career and this was the kind of ethical behavior that Sporkin wanted to see encouraged.

To help Ryan decipher the foreign exchange contracts contained in the Blue Book, Sporkin assigned Murray Garson, the division of enforcement's assistant chief accountant, to the case.

While Hoffman's team was busy drafting the foreign exchange scenarios, Edwards was badgering Ryan to move ahead on the case. He wanted Ryan to take a sworn statement from him, and he brought in a second volume of the Blue Book. As no formal investigation existed, Edwards could not be covered by a subpoena and so his testimony was taken "in private conference pursuant to voluntary appearance."

Edwards added little in his deposition beyond what was already contained in the Blue Book. But it nevertheless helped Ryan and Garson to better understand the nature of Citibank's off-booking practices. After completing the deposition, Ryan reported to Sporkin that a formal investigation—i.e., one in which Ryan and Garson could subpoena documents and witnesses—was warranted. Sporkin agreed and instructed him to prepare a written recommendation to the commission.

Ryan wrote a seven-page memo requesting a formal order of investigation to determine whether Citicorp had violated the disclosure statutes of the Securities Act of 1933 and the Securities Exchange Act of 1934. The memo stated that between 1972 and 1977, Citibank had reported $245.3 million in foreign exchange earnings and that an unknown percentage of this had been hidden from foreign tax collectors by constructing "sham" foreign exchange transactions within the Citibank branch network.

Ryan's memo also noted: "On March 17, 1978, the staff called outside counsel of Citicorp, the firm of Shearman & Sterling. The staff advised Shearman & Sterling in general of certain allegations made against Citicorp. In early February 1978, Shearman & Sterling had received the same information which the staff had received on March 17. Despite this, the attorney from Shearman & Sterling on March 17 professed to have no knowledge of the facts as presented by the staff of the Division of Enforcement. The staff invited Citicorp in for a meeting in order to let Citicorp present any explanation it might have for the above allegations. (The meeting took place on March 28, 1978.)

"At that meeting," the memo continued, "Shearman & Sterling and the general counsel of Citicorp stated they had begun an investigation of the activities mentioned above. They showed the staff an engagement letter with Peat Marwick Mitchell dated March 20, 1978, three days after they were contacted by the staff. . . .

"Based on the above facts, the Division recommends that the Commission issue a formal order of investigation naming Citicorp."[7]

Sporkin, Doherty, and Ryan appeared before the commission on Tuesday, May 9, 1978, where they met with chairman Harold M. Williams and commissioners Philip A. Loomis, Jr., and Roberta Karmel. The commission room in the old SEC headquarters at 500 North Capitol Street had been designed to convey the dignity of a judicial forum. The commissioners sat around a semicircular table, with the chairman in the middle. The staff sat at another semicircular table facing the commissioners. The staff were required to present their arguments for opening an investigation or recommending litigation and the commission judged the merits or, occasionally, argued against them.

Sporkin later reflected that he had worked under seven chairmen, but his relations with Williams were the worst. It was, Sporkin said, the most frustrating period of his career. Williams, who was appointed chairman by Carter in 1977, had come to the SEC with a

[7]Memorandum to the commission from division of enforcement re: Citicorp, April 28, 1978, pages 6–7.

background of varied accomplishments. Originally from Philadelphia, he had graduated from UCLA in 1947, age eighteen, and from Harvard Law School in 1949, age twenty-one. He practiced law for a while in Los Angeles, then served in the U.S. Army during the Korean War. In 1968 he was elected president of Hunt Food & Industries, Inc., which became Norton Simon, Inc., eventually becoming its chairman of the board. In July 1970 he was named dean of the UCLA Graduate School of Management.

Williams was against a continuation of the bribery cases, and he didn't want Sporkin to push him into any other new programs. "He couldn't make a decision," Sporkin said of his last boss at the SEC. The meeting on Citicorp was, as far as Sporkin was concerned, another example of Williams's lack of decisiveness. The chairman let the discussion bounce back and forth, and Sporkin, frustrated, had difficulty getting his viewpoint across.

Veteran commissioner Philip Loomis first voiced his misgivings about the Citicorp memo. A former SEC general counsel before being appointed commissioner by President Nixon in 1971, he was the dean and his view, infrequently expressed, was well respected by his fellow commissioners. "I have some problems with this. Mainly, the memorandum is so conclusionary that I can't tell exactly what it is," he remarked of Ryan's effort to set out the bare bones of the case based on the evidence then available.

Doherty tried to steer the discussion away from Loomis's remark by interjecting that on the previous Friday, commissioner John Evans had authorized a staff request to allow the Office of the Comptroller of the Currency access to the investigation files. Cooperation between the SEC and the comptroller's office was Sporkin's trump card.

"That was going to be my first question. I mean, what's the coordination with the comptroller?" chairman Williams asked.

"The people from their international unit were over yesterday and went through our files," Doherty continued.

Sporkin explained that on the previous Thursday, John G. Heimann, the Comptroller of the Currency, had called in a huff to ask why he hadn't been informed of the SEC's investigation of Citibank.[8]

Sporkin, surprised that the comptroller should know about it, told Heimann that his staff had only just received information from an informant and had made no determination about what to do with it.

---

[8] John G. Heimann was Comptroller of the Currency from 1977 to 1981, when he resigned to become deputy chairman of A. G. Becker Parisbas Inc.

Heimann asked if he could send someone over to look at the material. According to Sporkin, Heimann said, "You know, I know a little bit more about this area and it's tricky."

"I understand that," Sporkin assured him, having decided that the real issue, as far as the SEC was concerned, was whether Citicorp was "phonying up" the records. "Send someone over immediately," he suggested.

Still according to Sporkin, Heimann calmed down and mentioned that he'd like to work together with the SEC on the case. "That would be very helpful," Sporkin agreed.

"So, I think he's placated," he told the commissioners.

Ryan confirmed that the comptroller's people had in fact spent all of Monday afternoon going through the Edwards documents in his office. "Their conclusion was that, 'Well, you might have something here. We can't tell yet, but if we can help you in any way, we'll be glad to help you,' " Ryan reported them as saying.

Roberta Karmel commented: "Isn't this really banking violations? I mean, how are we in this? It seems to me the main burden should be on them, not us."

"Yes," Williams agreed.

Sporkin tried to reassert himself. "At this stage, if they're phonying up books and records . . . it is our jurisdiction."

The statutes were trotted out and verbally examined, some analogies given—the Bert Lance case, for one—and the newly drafted Foreign Corrupt Practices Act was mentioned. Sporkin said: "Somehow they think we ought to have some magic in how we're going to be policing this new act . . ."

"But you're not listing the new act here," Karmel observed, cutting him short. "You're listing proxy rules and reporting rules. Is this material?"

"Well, I say you don't know until you get the facts. Now, we could put in the Foreign Corrupt Practices Act, if you want," Sporkin replied.

As a result of the SEC's questionable payments program, the federal securities laws were amended in 1977 by the enactment of the Foreign Corrupt Practices Act. This law made the bribery of foreign government officials, political candidates, or their parties by SEC-regulated companies a crime. It also required all publicly listed corporations to maintain accurate books and records and to develop a system of internal accounting controls.

"Well, we'll add it on," Sporkin suggested. "But again, you don't know until you find out.'' As far as Sporkin was concerned, the question that most needed attention was how do you keep faith with someone like David Edwards, who brings in evidence of corporate wrongdoing because he has confidence that the agency will do something about it.

Sporkin maintained that ''one of the great benefits'' resulting from the bribes-abroad program was the show of support it prompted from small investors. ''We got all kinds of confidence out there,'' he said. ''People come to us . . . I had somebody come in on Israel bonds a week ago who says he will not take it to anybody in New York City because he doesn't trust that they'll do anything. And I said, 'Well, you know I'm Jewish.' And he said, 'Yeah, I know that.' But he says, 'I have confidence.' ''

Such sentiment did not stir Karmel. She said, ''I don't want us to end up, because of the Foreign Corrupt Practices Act, policing all violations of any statute.''

''Well, that just didn't cross my mind,'' Sporkin replied.

Loomis suggested that Citicorp probably transacted a ''vast amount'' of foreign exchange business ''and it's altogether probable that they would, in handling that business, endeavor to minimize their tax liabilities.''

Sporkin rejected this. ''Let me explain why this is different. It's not as if somebody here, down on the staff, ginned up and said, 'Hey, let's look into the foreign exchange transactions of Citibank; we think there might be something there.' You don't have that situation. You have an insider coming in here and saying, 'Hey, fellows, this is wrong. This is something I've been complaining about. They're doing it dishonestly.' That's what you have. . . . It seems to me that there is reason to move ahead. We've been very careful here. We weren't going to accept this man's, just his bald-faced statements. We said, 'We want to see support. We want to see facts. We want to see documents.' And he's given us those. . . .''

Williams was still not satisfied. ''You've got characterizations in here,'' he said, referring to the memo. ''Let me read you one sentence.'' And he reverted back to the original Loomis complaint about Citibank engaging in *sham* transactions to *park* its *illegal* foreign exchange positions.

Sporkin: ''Well, that's what the fellow is. . . .''

Loomis: ''Well, it's all so conclusionary. It's just adjectives.''

Finally, Williams repeated his main concern: ''I'm not sure we have the competence to judge it. . . .''

Loomis agreed.

Then Karmel asked: "How about the IRS? I mean, if this is really accounting fraud, shouldn't they be in on it?"

"Certainly at some point they'll be involved," Sporkin replied. "But we're not going to, you know, summon every government agency here and just say, 'Fellows, we got something. You know, what part of it do you want?' We're not syndicating this."

"It's not a matter of that," Williams corrected his enforcement chief. "I mean, they may have more knowledge and expertise as to whether we've got something. And I don't know—part of my concern is how are we going to know whether we've got something? And I just wonder whether we've got the expertise to know. That's the only reason I'm raising it now."

"All I'm saying to you is let us push ahead a little bit," Sporkin answered.

"It seems to me that this is a matter that either the IRS or the comptroller or both should be concerned with," Loomis repeated.

Sporkin had not anticipated such strong opposition. Under other chairmen, he usually had his way. And in the end, because he was the top securities watchdog in the nation and the commissioners rarely dared go against him, Sporkin's view prevailed. What the staff wanted, he explained, was to pressure Citicorp into hiring independent counsel to "go in and really do a thorough investigation," as in the questionable payments program, and file a Form 8-K report disclosing the full scope and context of its parking operation. Sporkin felt that the threat of administrative action would cause Citicorp to comply, the illegal foreign exchange practices would cease, and the interests of Citicorp shareholders would be protected.

"Well," Williams finally admitted, "I'm really not opposed to a formal order per se; I am really raising two kinds of questions. One, I do sense a degree of prejudgment here that troubles me. Number one. Number two, I have very serious questions as to whether we have the expertise to know whether—or to be able to evaluate what we find, and that's where I think we ought to have the comptroller more deeply involved and tell the IRS, too. . . ."

"I have trouble with the IRS," Sporkin interrupted. "We have problems bringing the IRS in at this time. Well, the reason is that, as you know, there's a Chinese Wall that's been developed between the IRS and the other agencies. . . . What concerns me is I would prefer to go down the road, get the information and give it to them. . . ."

"Do we grant the formal order?" Williams asked.

"Yes," Karmel answered. "But I really would go along with your caution to how the investigation is conducted."

"Yes," agreed Loomis.

"Okay, the formal order is approved on Citicorp," Williams ruled.[9]

[9]Excerpted from the minutes of the SEC meeting of May 9, 1978, as reproduced in *SEC and Citicorp*, Hearings before the Subcommittee on Oversight and Investigations of the Committee on Energy and Commerce, House of Representatives, Ninety-Seventh Congress, September 13 and 17, 1982, Serial No. 97–193, pp. 96–108.

Chapter 25

The Judge's Denial

Real progress has been made in finding the truth.

—RICHARD M. NIXON, APRIL 17, 1973

In June 1978, while Shearman & Sterling was still drafting its report, the SEC's Murray Garson subpoenaed Paolo Cugnasca to take his testimony in New York. Garson was following leads that David Edwards had given him. Edwards had assured both Garson and senior staff attorney Robert Ryan that Cugnasca could vouch for everything he had told them.

This assurance, Cugnasca later told Edwards, was the last thing he needed. Cugnasca's counsel, Norman S. Ostrow, wrote Garson, informing him that his client would invoke the Fifth Amendment and refuse to answer questions. This stymied Ryan and Garson, effectively blocking one avenue of inquiry, and halted progress on the case for most of the summer. It was also a blow to Edwards, who had hoped to call Cugnasca as a witness in the lawsuit he was planning against Citibank.

One month later—on July 14, 1978—Edwards sued Citibank in the Supreme Court of New York for wrongful dismissal. He was demanding $14 million in damages.

Wriston instructed Shearman & Sterling to defend the suit vigorously.

Edwards's New York attorney, Jonathan Lubell, argued that according to a section in the international staff manual, employment could only be terminated by resignation, retirement, or by Citibank-initiated action "for cause or for unsatisfactory performance."

Lubell conceded that conduct "detrimental to the best interests of Citibank" was a "for cause ground for termination." He pointed out, however, that Citibank had communicated to its employees that the bank's best interests required its business to be conducted in compliance with the laws of those countries where it operated. Lubell built his case around the contention that in 1975, when certain irregularities came to his client's attention, leading to his discovery of practices that appeared to violate the laws of several European countries, Edwards reported his concern to senior management. Citibank's response was to attempt to conceal these practices. When Edwards pressed executive management to examine and reconsider these activities and cease attempts to cover them up, he was fired.

The complaint relied upon the four examples of parking contained in the Blue Book and various other documents that Edwards had found in Cugnasca's office. The Blue Book and these other documents were attached to the complaint as exhibits.

Citibank responded by filing a motion for summary judgment against Edwards, which was assigned to New York Supreme Court Justice Martin Evans, and hearings began later in the autumn.

Suing Citibank in the Supreme Court of New York brought the issue into the public domain some four months before Hoffman was ready with his counter-artillery, the Shearman & Sterling report. While Hoffman prepared Citibank's defense, and at the same time was pressing European counsel to complete their opinions, the news media picked up the story and had a field day with it.

The moment was psychologically propitious for an attack on big banks for their manipulation of exchange rates. The dollar was in runaway decline, prompting Union Bank of Switzerland's foreign exchange department to comment that the U.S. currency was sinking "like a torpedoed submarine." Inflation in the U.S. was at 10.4 percent and rising, while President Carter was still months away from mounting a rescue operation to save the U.S. currency and the U.S. economy.

In the midst of the unfavorable press reaction, Tom Theobald circulated a memo to all Citibank officers, telling them that "a full and independent study'' of the Edwards charges by Shearman & Sterling was ''in progress and expected to be completed at the end of September.''

Theobald's memo continued:

To put Mr. Edwards's charges into perspective, you should be aware of the circumstances which led to the termination of his employment and subsequent $14 million lawsuit.

Late in 1974, Mr. Edwards was assigned to work in the foreign exchange trading room of the Bank's Paris branch. In the latter part of 1975, he accused one of the local senior officers in the branch of taking kickbacks. Although Mr. Edwards was unable to produce any substantiating evidence, the matter was promptly investigated and found to be without foundation.

Thereafter, Mr. Edwards accused the Paris branch itself of improperly transferring certain of its foreign exchange positions to other Citibank branches in violation of local French laws. Later Mr. Edwards made similar charges with respect to other European branches of Citibank.

Mr. Edwards was reassigned to Head Office in 1977 and was told that he would be working in the Government lending area. The memorandum which advised Mr. Edwards of his new assignment to this area was signed and returned by him with the following remarks:

This is unacceptable. I plan to remain in the
Treasury Group until we resolve this—D.E.

This was shortly followed by a letter from Mr. Edwards's lawyer stating that Mr. Edwards would be willing to terminate his employment with the Bank at the end of September 1978, on condition that (i) he be 'given support and resources by the Treasury Division in his research project to develop a program to stimulate an increased volume of US exports to overseas markets'; (ii) provided with Citibank's assistance to find him another job outside the Bank; and (iii) given permission 'to maintain his subsidized apartment in New York under the present arrangement with Citibank for the duration of his employment at Citibank.'

The conditions proposed by Mr. Edwards's counsel were rejected and, in the light of Mr. Edwards's behavior and attitude, he was requested to resign from the Bank.

Mr. Edwards responded by letter stating, among other things, ''I have no intention of resigning from the Bank until I have been given adequate answers to the serious questions I have raised.'

Shortly after receipt of this letter, Mr. Edwards was advised that his employment had been terminated.[1]

When Robert Logan received his copy of Theobald's memo, he exploded. His assistant, Saleem Muqaddam, had handed it to him with the remark that it was a "foolish" mistake.

"Logan looked at it and uttered an obscenity, then ran to Theobald's office. Theobald was giving significance to something which didn't warrant it," Muqaddam later said.[2]

Hoffman filed a motion for a gag order restraining Edwards from talking to the press. He also asked that all confidential bank documents filed by Edwards be placed under seal, as well as transcripts of discovery hearings. He wanted to quash a subpoena to take evidence from Walter Hanson, the senior Peat Marwick partner on the Citicorp account. He filed another motion seeking to have hearings held in camera whenever Citibank's products, services, methods, or systems were discussed.

Frank Church, senator from Idaho and chairman of the Foreign Economic Policy Subcommittee of the U.S. Senate Committee on Foreign Relations, had been following the Edwards case with interest. His subcommittee was investigating the reasons for the dollar's decline, and he viewed the possibility of a gag order with some alarm. In September 1978 he wrote Justice Evans, stating that his subcommittee was analyzing the causes and implications of the dollar's rapid decline, and he asked the judge, in what might have been construed as an act of meddling with the judiciary, not to stifle the parties to the action.

"There is growing concern, both in Congress and in the international finance community in general, with the wildly fluctuating dollar, sometimes falling as much as five percent in one day against various European currencies. A question has now been raised with regard to the role which U.S. banks may have played in exacerbating the dollar's decline. Mr. David Edwards . . . has made allegations concerning the impact of banks' foreign exchange trading practices on the dollar, allegations which the subcommittee believes it must investigate. . . . However, I understand that a motion has been filed by

---

[1] Memo to All Officers, from Thomas C. Theobald, E.V.P., International Banking Group, Re: Allegations of Foreign Exchange Violations, July 27, 1978; Citibank document 7218.
[2] Testimony of Saleem Muqaddam before the SEC, August 14, 1980, pp. 152–154.

Citibank enjoining all parties from discussing the case, and sealing all records. Because such an order, if broadly drafted, may inhibit Mr. Edwards and bank officials discussing Mr. Edwards' allegations with this Subcommittee, I respectfully ask that in making your ruling on this motion you take into account the Subcommittee's interest,'' Church's letter stated.[3]

Hoffman nevertheless was partially successful in his quest for confidentiality. Edwards was enjoined from talking to reporters. This, however, did not stop Larry Kramer of *The Washington Post* from writing a series of articles on Citibank and the Edwards allegations.

Kramer, who subsequently became metro editor of the *Post,* was a Harvard MBA, class of '74. As editor of *Harbus,* the graduate weekly, he had frequent contact with the dean of the Harvard Business School, Larry Fouraker.

Kramer read about the Edwards case in *The New York Times* and decided it was a story worth developing. The *Post* gave Kramer *carte blanche* to handle the international banking story as if it were a police-beat report. As Senator Church had pointed out, the foreign exchange markets were in turmoil at the time. "The U.S. dollar was down and bank regulation in a tizzy,'' said Kramer. "There was no international policeman to ensure that banks were keeping themselves in line.''

He got hold of a set of documents filed with the court. He found that the documents opened a window on the banks' practices of trading currencies and transferring profits. He quickly found that people at Citibank were "paranoid'' about the case. Everytime he tried to approach the bank, he ran into a stone wall. This whetted his appetite even more. He decided to visit Citibank branches in the major European foreign exchange centers. Before leaving for Europe, a source from the bank read his travel itinerary to him over the phone.

In Zurich, he was standing across the street taking pictures of the new Citibank offices on Seestrasse when a police van rolled up. He was bundled into it and driven to the local police station for questioning. Kramer said he was told that Citibank Zurich had complained that a "suspicious person'' was taking pictures of the premises. He was let go with a warning.

Larry Fouraker was once heard to remark that he considered Kramer one of the finest financial writers in the country. This was one issue on which Fouraker and Wriston disagreed. After studying the documents, Kramer became convinced that all the information wasn't

---

[3] Letter of Senator Frank Church to Mr. Justice Martin Evans, September 11, 1978.

getting through to the board, and he tried to tell Fouraker this. The dean wasn't interested.

A subsequent report to the Citicorp board noted that Kramer had written sixteen articles on the Edwards affair between August 1978 and May 1979, all of them from an "alarmist" viewpoint. The one that particularly angered Wriston appeared in the Sunday edition of May 6, 1979, under a comic-strip cartoon by Robin Jareaux entitled "$wapman."

The Jareaux cartoon showed a figure in sunglasses and bathing trunks lying under a palm tree on a Bahamian beach with a telephone at his side. The introductory caption was "How Citibank traded money among its branches on June 15, 1976." The eight-frame cartoon described the criss-crossing of exchange contracts between Paris, Nassau, New York, and Brussels, and "$wapman" ending his day in the sun with a FF 60,000 profit.

A month after Edwards filed suit, the SEC's Robert Ryan issued a subpoena addressed to Walter Wriston personally, demanding that the corporation produce from its files seven broad categories of documents relating to parking and the management information system. These included all manuals, correspondence, memoranda, and records showing parked positions or MIS credits, as well as all dealer tickets, confirmations, and telexes received through or sent from the numbers 423712, 236335, and 425848. These were the telex numbers listed in Cugnasca's parking manual.

Hoffman, on the one hand cajoling European counsel to complete their opinion letters, defending the Edwards action with the other, now had to contend with a sudden spurt of activity from the SEC. He took his initial stand on high ground and began stalling. His tactics were remarkably successful. He wrote Ryan suggesting that they get together "to talk things over." They finally structured a deal over the subpoenaed documents in January 1979. Hoffman had gained four months' breathing time, and he was able to impose his terms for a partial compliance of the SEC subpoena to Wriston. Ryan was allowed to consult certain documents at the Shearman & Sterling offices in New York. He was allowed to take notes from them, but he was not allowed to photocopy them. Rather than take issue by asking a federal judge to order Citicorp to comply with the subpoena, Ryan accepted this arrangement as a temporary expedient.

Meanwhile, one month before Shearman & Sterling filed its report with the SEC, the administrator of national banks at the Office of the Comptroller of the Currency finally began a separate investigation of

Citibank's foreign exchange operations. Sporkin had already written the Comptroller of the Currency, taking up the suggestion, previously made by John Heimann, to propose that the two agencies cooperate in their investigation. He received no reply.

The filing of the Shearman & Sterling report in November 1978 coincided with the transfer to Toronto of Charles Young.

Young later said his appointment as president of Citibank Canada came about because of his negotiating skills with governments. In Paris he had concluded several large loan transactions with French government agencies.

Canada was drafting new legislation governing the operations of foreign banks, which until then had been restricted in favor of the seven nationally chartered Canadian banks. Upon his transfer to Toronto, Young pitched in with the foreign banking community to squeeze the best deal possible out of Ottawa. No mention was made of the French tax investigation of Citibank Paris, which had commenced in July 1978.

The Edwards lawsuit dragged on for another seven months. In June 1979, Justice Evans dismissed it on grounds that under New York law, employment can be terminated for virtually any reason if there is no written employment contract. Edwards had no written contract.

The Edwards lawsuit dragged on for another seven months. In June 1979, Justice Evans handed down his decision on Citibank's motion for summary judgment. He held that Citibank was not bound by its own staff handbook, and that the personnel manuals and other documents it had issued did not constitute an employment contract for Edwards.

Claiming that there was no written employment contract, the judge concluded that New York law permitted Citibank to terminate Edwards for virtually any reason. Justice Evans thereby declined the opportunity to modify that rule of contract law, or recognize the tort of wrongful discharge and reinstate Edwards or award him damages.

Edwards appealed. But the Evans decision was upheld. The score was two-zero for Hoffman.

Chapter 26

"Whitewash"

The (S&S) Report . . . was, however, an elaborate expensive sophisticate's whitewash, from start to finish.

—VON STEIN REPORT, PAGE 102

These descriptions, called "scenarios" . . . are lessons in linguistics—good illustrations of what advocates can do and, arguably, what true investigators would not do.

—*The American Lawyer*, AUGUST 1982

Hi-tech transformed the foreign exchange market from a series of regional exchanges, as it was in Carlo Bordoni's day, to a single global market spanning the world's time zones.

The Milan trading room over which Bordoni ruled was, in 1963, the most active in the Citibank network. The room was furnished with one long table that had a row of twenty single-line telephones on it. He and his assistant trader, Francesco Redi, spent all day running from one end of the table to the other, manning the phones. Sophistication came slowly. First switchboards replaced single-line phones, then telex machines made their appearance in the trading rooms. But the major revolution came when the first television screens brought near-instant market rates onto the traders' horizon.

About the time David Edwards left Citibank, big banks were beginning to restyle their trading rooms to reflect the latest advances in communications technology, and trading desks became crowned with consoles that resembled the control panels for a NASA space launch. The expensive electronic gadgetry enabled a trader in Zurich, speaking with a counterparty in Hong Kong, to watch the market movement on one of the screens in front of him while another screen instantly plotted the rate changes on a graph showing not only the tick-by-tick range for the day but a twenty-one-day moving average for each currency. He could even split his screens and get, side-by-side, the latest bullion rates, world news flashes, or swap and deposit rates from one to twelve months forward.

The electronic gadgetry meant that a foreign exchange trader in Pago-Pago could play the market in New York, dealing from his screen, while positioning his profits in Nassau, and if he structured his bookkeeping creativity enough, the fiscal authorities in Pago-Pago would never catch sight of a mark, pound, drachma, or dollar of taxable revenue.

Shearman & Sterling appreciated the implications of the new technology in transferring positions and profits from one jurisdiction to another. Their report on Citibank's foreign exchange practices, finally completed in November 1978, described the flavor and complexities of the electronic marketplace:

> Markets in foreign exchanges are far more active than ever before, in terms of increased volume, number of participants, and locations where markets are centered. Banks, brokers and corporations around the world trade daily and in large volume. Trading centers are no longer confined to Europe and New York, but now include large markets in the Middle and Far East and in Central and South America.
>
> These changes have been accompanied by the introduction of new technological systems, which speed the conduct of business and the dissemination of information. Important participants are all closely linked by telephone and telex lines which permit instantaneous access to the latest exchange rate quotes. Further, international and domestic news, to which exchange rates are highly responsive, is spread quickly through this system, resulting in speedy reactions world-wide to significant events.

The result is essentially an efficient global network through which the huge volume of foreign exchange passes. It is a transnational market that never closes, as dealers are dispersed throughout the world, trading twenty-four hours a day. (New York is active after Europe has closed; Tokyo, Hong Kong and Singapore are active after New York has closed; next it is Bahrain; and then Europe is open again.)

It must be stressed, however, that the foreign exchange market remains a dealer market in which individual participants quote rates directly to one another. There is no central trading floor, no formal trading or clearing organization, and no single market rate.[1]

Hoffman was acknowledged as the report's principal author. He paid close attention to form, intending it to be a broadly circulated public disclosure document. To this end, it was divided into five parts.

The first part described the mandate and program followed by Shearman & Sterling in investigating Citibank's parking practices.

Part II consisted of a scholarly dissertation on the general background of foreign exchange trading, with sections on the monetary system created under the 1944 Bretton Woods agreements, the major upheavals in foreign exchange trading during the 1970s, and governmental response to the changing nature of the foreign exchange market.

Part III described the foreign exchange operations of Citibank, including a broad sketch of the management information system and a history of parking.

Part IV was headed "Factual and Legal Conclusions Regarding the Conduct under Review." It gave a summary of the legal opinions provided by local counsel in the seven target countries.

This was followed by a closing section, Part V, which gave "Some General Observations."

The report was skillfully written. Its historical section on foreign exchange trading was clear and concise, detailing the expansion of currency dealing occasioned by the growth in world trade following World War II, the breakdown of the Bretton Woods system in the 1970s, and with it the disappearance of fixed exchange rates.

It was full of nubbly facts, irrelevant to the main subject of the report, but which journalists could appreciate. For example, it ex-

[1] Shearman & Sterling Report to the Audit Committee of Citicorp and the Examining Committee of Citibank, November 20, 1978, pp. 17–18 of the printed version.

plained that "the growth in international trade and the volatility of exchange rates have led to a great increase in volume of foreign exchange trading, as participants in international trade need to acquire and dispose of foreign currencies. There are few reliable figures on the total volume of foreign exchange trading; however, a common estimate for 1977 is that it was approximately equivalent to 50 trillion dollars world-wide."[2]

Once the report was published, *The Wall Street Journal* picked this morsel and built a three-column article around the fact that according to Citicorp, "World-wide foreign exchange volume is placed roughly at $50 trillion a year."

The article quoted Citicorp's vice-chairman Al Costanzo as estimating that "maybe we do 10 percent of the business," or some $5 trillion a year (roughly four times the then current output of U.S. goods and services), to which Costanzo added, "we aren't initiating [the business], we're just sitting there taking orders."[3]

The report also mentioned different government efforts to restrict the speculative flow of currencies across and within their borders. These "sovereign limitations" were largely ineffective, the report pointed out, as ultimately, the basic economic strength or weakness of a country determines the market value of its currency.

Finally, on the twenty-second of forty-five pages, the report introduced the concept of parking:

"Citibank has engaged in foreign exchange transactions that have the effect of transferring a net foreign exchange position from one branch to a different branch in another country, *from which it may eventually be reacquired*. Transactions of this type are *sometimes* referred to as parking transactions."

The report described the development of parking through Citibank's European network during the early 1970s as a method for "complying" with restrictive overnight position limits set by local governments and central banks. "A position was generally transferred for a relatively short period of time, and then reacquired by the transferring branch at the same rate that had been used on the initial transfer. Therefore neither branch had a gain or a loss as a result of the transaction.

"During this period the volume of world trade continued its pattern of rapid acceleration. The adoption of floating exchange rates resulted

[2] Ibid., p. 17.
[3] *The Wall Street Journal*, January 15, 1979.

in wide fluctuations in the exchange markets. This, in turn, led to new exchange controls in many countries. The net effect of increased exchange trading, coupled with more stringent exchange limits, was an expansion in the practice of transferring positions to branches in other countries where they could be maintained. The practice of transferring positions was the individual branches' response to local regulatory conditions," the report explained.[4]

It related how, from almost ad hoc beginnings, parking procedures became institutionalized and standardized, first through other European branches, then through the Nassau desk at head office.

It also explained that some branches "considered it undesirable to realize large profits or losses as this could potentially raise questions by regulatory agencies and competitors as to the volume of foreign exchange transactions being conducted by the branch. It was therefore important to conduct interbranch transactions in such a way that any profit or loss would be realized at the transferee branches."[5]

This is where the management information system (MIS) came in. "Branches also became more confident in the operation of MIS, and were therefore more willing to transfer positions at rates within the prevailing market range, and to receive an MIS adjustment in recognition of their role in initially taking the position."[6]

The report stated that MIS ascribed "debits and credits against figures derived from actual accounting records of the various segments of the institution." It added: "If a profit is recorded on the books of one branch because the profit was realized at that location, but another branch had a role in initiating the profitable transaction, an MIS adjustment may be appropriate. In the context of foreign exchange trading, MIS adjustments are used to recognize the role of a branch in initiating an exchange profit or loss, even if the actual profit or loss is realized and recorded on the books of another branch. This reporting system provides an incentive for the various segments of Citibank to make their business decisions with an eye towards global or institutional concerns, rather than strictly along divisional lines."[7]

To compare and express an opinion on the legality of the different types of parking, the report explained that ten basic scenarios had been developed, "some [one] of which described transactions common to

---

[4] Shearman & Sterling report, p. 22, emphasis added.
[5] The report speculated that the Nassau desk was ultimately preferred for foreign exchange parking because "by transferring European positions to Nassau rather than New York, city and state taxes could be avoided." (Ibid, p. 22)
[6] Ibid., p. 24.
[7] Ibid., p. 21.

all of the branches under review, and some [eight] of which related to several [two] or just one branch. As the transactions described were all complex, and had many [up to five] steps, some [one] of the scenarios contain up to ten variations.''[8]

The report claimed that the scenarios included all the characteristics of classic parking transactions. The texts of the scenarios, however, were not disclosed.

In spite of the absence of the scenarios themselves, a paragraph described the exchange rates they used. This was interesting because it turned out to be one of the few explicit bodies of text in the report. It read:

''When an overbought or oversold position is transferred from one Citibank branch to another Citibank branch and is subsequently retransfered, as described in the basic pattern, different exchange rates may be used. if the same rate is used in both a transfer and a retransfer transaction, no profit or loss occurs at either branch as a result of those two transactions.

''A profit or loss occurs when there is a differential between the rates used in the two transactions. Such a differential can result from several circumstances: (1) the rates for each transaction are within the prevailing market range and those rates have changed between the transfers; (2) a rate within the prevailing range and a different rate outside the market range is used on the transactions; or (3) two different rates outside the prevailing market range are used. Citibank branches have entered into transactions with other Citibank branches using each of these possible combinations of rates.''

Immediately, the veil closed again. The passive voice and conditional tense were adopted: ''Where a profit or loss occurs at the transferee branch *there may be* a recognition within Citibank of the transfer branch's role in initiating the transactions by means of Citibank's Management Information System.''[9]

Finally, the report summarized the legal opinions of local counsel without giving their identity or disclosing the full texts of their opinion letters. The highlights are paraphrased below:

1. Amsterdam, the Netherlands

Local counsel concluded that if (1) ''ordinary'' market rates were used, (2) control of the positions actually passed to the parkee, and (3) the

---

[8] Ibid., p. 8.
[9] Ibid., p. 26, emphasis added.

Amsterdam branch could not predict the outcome of the reversal, "the transactions described in the scenario and related information did not violate the exchange regulations of the Netherlands."

2. Brussels, Belgium

Belgian counsel concluded that if (1) market rates were used, (2) applicable overnight limits were not exceeded, (3) the branch's books were kept in accordance with Belgian rules and regulations, (4) control passed to the parkee, and (5) MIS adjustments were only equivalent to "moral" credit or blame markers, "the transactions described ((in the Belgian scenarios)) do not constitute a violation by Citibank of any Belgian laws."

3. Frankfurt, Germany

German counsel based their opinion on two scenarios, which they analyzed in terms of three distinct categories of German law.

Under *contract law,* counsel opined that the validity of a contract that "transfers, rolls-over or closes a position" depends upon the express or implied approval of the parkee to accept the position on its books. "Such approval may be implied when the transferee accepts the position and does not act to frustrate the transaction. The approval of the transaction by the transferee will eliminate any problem that may be raised by the German law prohibition against 'self-contracting.' "

Under *banking law,* German counsel concluded that, because the scenarios gave no indication that Frankfurt was obliged to reacquire the position from the parking-lot branch, and because the parkee could realize a loss or gain on its books, "the transactions described do not violate the German regulations." However counsel pointed out "that transactions at rates outside of the prevailing market range may violate applicable German regulations."

Under *tax law,* a fundamental concern was the arm's-length quality of the transactions. If they were truly at arm's length, any profit recorded in New York or Nassau would not be taxable in Germany. Counsel expected, however, that Frankfurt would receive compensation for its services. Nevertheless, counsel cautioned that if the transactions were analyzed collectively rather than individually there would be "a severe risk" that income realized in Nassau might be attributable to Frankfurt during the period it was a branch—i.e., prior to

September 20, 1976, when Citibank AG was incorporated. Therefore, Citibank AG, as an independent legal entity subject to German law, would be taxed on all its income, regardless of territorial source.

In conclusion, German counsel stated that "properly recorded transactions that are truly equal to arms length transactions with third parties can be defended as proper under German law."

4. *London, England*

Shearman & Sterling reported that English counsel found "both the 'spirit' and letter of the exchange regulations are significant, and that the Bank of England is fully cognizant that a large bank with an active foreign exchange department cannot always adhere to the overnight position limit. However, an important distinction must be made between deliberate and inadvertent transgression of the regulations. Without more detailed knowledge of facts and surrounding circumstances as to the specific obligations of the transferee branch to resell sterling positions to London at the same rate, local counsel cannot express any more precise opinion as to the basic pattern."

5. *Milan, Italy*

Italian counsel's opinion was based upon three scenarios and related information provided to them by Shearman & Sterling, Peat Marwick, and Citibank personnel. On the basis of this information, counsel assumed that the Milan branch could not "compel" any other Citibank branch to enter into an exchange transaction, and that other branches had discretion to refuse these transactions but did so rarely.

Italian counsel also assumed that any gain or loss realized by another branch as a consequence of the transfer of a position by Milan would not appear upon the books and records of the Milan branch. Finally, they assumed that Milan was motivated to maximize Citibank's income on a worldwide basis, and to set the best possible record for the branch within Citibank's MIS. Counsel recognized that MIS was significant for the bank's internal managerial purposes, but had no bearing on the legal and financial posture of the branch. The report added:

> Italian counsel are of the opinion that the transactions engaged in by the Milan branch that are of the type described in the basic pattern do not constitute an infringement of the applicable regulations. . . . They are also of the opinion that the transactions of

this type do not constitute a breach of tax laws, notwithstanding the fact that Milan may have originated the transactions. . . . The operation of the MIS does not alter their opinion, and is not relevant with regard to compliance with either tax or exchange law.

6. Paris, France

French counsel noted from a review of three scenarios that Citibank Paris had applied French exchange control regulations "realistically and with an understanding of the practical exigencies of foreign exchange trading." They pointed out, however, that a fundamental rule of French law, which regulatory authorities might apply, is that "one cannot do indirectly what cannot be done directly." Based upon the statements of Citibank Paris personnel, local counsel assumed that all interest rates and exchange rates used in the scenarios were market rates. But it also added in this respect that Peat Marwick's field survey had noted this was not always the case.

Local counsel further opined that in transactions where Paris showed a loss "from virtually simultaneous non-French franc transactions," there was a risk that French authorities would find that these transactions not only violated French income-tax rules but also violated French exchange controls relating to the transfer of foreign currency out of France. Counsel warned that if such transactions were made at rates outside the prevailing market range, this risk would be significantly increased.

7. Zurich, Switzerland

Swiss counsel concluded that the transfer of an oversold foreign currency position taken against Swiss francs from Zurich to another Citibank branch and the subsequent reacquisition of that position by Zurich was not, by itself, a breach of Swiss exchange regulations, provided the limitations on forward contracts were complied with. "The transactions do not by themselves raise an issue of any evasion of law, provided that there were bona fide contractual relationships, with attendant risk and obligations, between Zurich and the transferee branch," Swiss counsel advised.

Swiss counsel were also of the opinion that the transfer of positions out of Switzerland, if conducted at arm's length, did not violate Swiss tax laws. Counsel noted this was not the case when exchange rates above or below the prevailing market range were used. Such transactions "may not have complied with" the tax laws. Counsel further explained that if a profit was recorded at the parking-lot branch "because of the use of such rates there may have been a division of income properly attributable to the Zurich branch." Counsel also noted that MIS adjustments, by themselves, were "irrelevant" to Swiss taxation.

The report failed to mention an investigation of Citibank Zurich's parking operations by the federal banking authorities. As it was covered by Swiss banking secrecy, it remained confidential. No mention of it appeared, either, in Swiss counsel's seventy-eight-page opinion, even though it commenced in August 1978, when Dr. Kraft and his associates were preparing their opinion, and continued through the period that Shearman & Sterling was drafting its final report.

The last section—Part V—was headed "Some General Observations." The observations were for the most part elemental, such as: "Most of the local counsel are of the opinion that the transfer of a foreign exchange position by one branch to a branch in another country may be effectively accomplished in a manner complying with local regulatory provisions."

Logically, that was so. But a simple "transfer of a foreign exchange position by one branch to another" was not a parking transaction. As long as no commitment existed for the removal of the position from the books of the receiving—i.e., parking-lot—branch on terms decided by the originating branch, the transaction could be a bona fide deal done at arm's length.

The report could not completely ignore the arm's length phenomenon. It conceded, on the second to last page, that "some" local counsel "referred to a necessity for 'arm's length dealing.' " The report added that "as the 'arm's length' quality of the [parking] transaction declines the likelihood of tax liability accruing to the transferor branch is increased."

Four paragraphs later, it noted: "While no institutional pattern of transferring tax liability from one country to another in violation of local tax laws was present, we have discovered some specific instances where local counsel advise that tax challenges involving particular transactions would appear to have a high probability of success."

By extrapolation, this implied that the four examples of profit-transfer parking given in the Edwards Blue Book were isolated cases, although nowhere in the report were the four examples set out. The move from specific examples to hypothetical ones—the so-called scenarios—had enabled Shearman & Sterling to use broader definitions and gave them greater freedom of interpretation.

While the report included a section on "Risks of Foreign Exchange Transactions and Their Control," this referred to control of risks and not physical control over open foreign exchange positions. The report did not deal with the issue of physical control over parked positions. As far as Hoffman was concerned, the premise that control was a deciding factor in determining the bona fides of a parking operation was incorrect. He considered it irrelevant under foreign law and therefore did not even bother to address the question. His view was that if the transfer occurred at rates within the prevailing market range, and the economic risk associated with the position actually went to the parking-lot branch, an effective and legal transfer had taken place.

In a final apologia, the report stated: "So long as Citibank engages in an active foreign exchange business through its overseas branches, it will continue to be involved with legal issues raised by the existence of a multitude of exchange control, tax and other laws promulgated by individual nations. These laws may frequently be in conflict. Recognizing the high standard of conduct set by Citicorp's corporate policy of adherence to the letter, spirit and intent of all relevant laws and regulations, we see no simple solution for this tangle of familiar problems."

The Shearman & Sterling report was filed with the SEC as a disclosure document on November 24, 1978. That same day, Citicorp issued a press release that stated in part:

The Report reached the following conclusions:

Eight months of intensive investigation revealed no pattern of violation of foreign exchange regulations in any country reviewed. The report noted, however, that certain transactions which on their face complied with local regulations could be viewed by local authorities as being in conflict with the spirit of that regulatory environment. . . .

The press release repeated Citicorp's newly seized upon theme that foreign exchange regulations were just too complicated to be obeyed. It stated:

In this connection, Citicorp vice chairman G. A. Costanzo pointed out that "there exist hundreds of pages of foreign exchange regulations in the countries involved. These regulations are constantly being changed and interpreted and none have the precision of a fifty-five-mile speed limit which one either exceeds or does not.

"In these circumstances, it is impossible for any organization, including Citicorp, to state categorically that none of its transac-

tions anywhere in the world violated an interpretation of some regulation. Conversely, no organization can state positively that all its
transactions worldwide are in total compliance. What we can state
is our policy and intent to comply in good faith with all applicable
regulations.''

Without acknowledging it, the report confirmed the essential accuracy of Edwards's allegations about parking. The report revealed
that ''a number of common patterns have been found that fall within
the colloquial rubric of 'parking transactions,' though it affirmed that
parking was not a ''manifest violation'' of local exchange controls or
banking laws. It found no contradiction in disclosing that because of
parking, Citibank had potentially serious tax problems in at least two
countries, and a less serious risk in three others, while British counsel
said they did not have adequate information on which to base an
opinion. It confirmed that Citibank traders, in exercising their duties,
had committed some excesses and that corrective action had been taken.
Citicorp's news release ignored these concessions, however, and took
instead a gratuitous slap at Edwards:

> As previously disclosed, the former Citibank employee whose
> allegations promoted the investigation also charged that one of the
> Bank's foreign exchange traders in Paris was taking kickbacks.
> Citibank's Comptroller, who reports directly to the Board of Di-
> rectors, conducted an immediate investigation of the charges and
> found no evidence of kickbacks. When the allegations were re-
> peated, a second audit was performed with the same results. De-
> spite repeated requests that he come forward with supporting
> evidence, Mr. Edwards never did so.

Part IV

THE INVESTIGATION

Chapter 27

"Back to Square One"

We have a policy that Nassau will always deal with overseas branches as . . . call it a last resort if you will. If a branch has an extra $10 million that they cannot lay off in the market they could always lay it off with Nassau. Nassau will always act as the repository of any branch's net position so that we don't lose the use of the funds.

—DONALD S. HOWARD, EXECUTIVE VICE-PRESIDENT, TREASURY, MARCH 27, 1980

For a year following the filing of the Shearman & Sterling report, the Citicorp investigation lay more or less dormant.

This was in part due to John Hoffman's refusal to comply with the SEC's subpoena for documents. Hoffman argued that Citicorp's banking secrets had to be protected. Robert Ryan, on the other hand, wanted to avoid a showdown on compliance because if the SEC's demand for documents was taken literally, Citibank might respond by sending seven moving vans of paper down to Washington and he would be buried under the *paperasserie* for the next seven years. Hoffman, though, mentioned that a lode of "refined" documents had been assembled for the Shearman & Sterling investigation. He and Ryan finally worked out an arrangement whereby the SEC could consult the "refined" documents at the Shearman & Sterling offices in Citicorp Center. But pursuant to this agreement, there was to be no photocopying of the documents and no verbatim transcriptions of them.

As far as Ryan was concerned, this represented "a temporary meeting of minds." Neither party was waiving privilege. "We had agreed not to fight until there was something to fight about. In cases like these, you take what you can get until you need more," he later explained.

Ryan spent a couple of days in the Shearman & Sterling offices reading through the "refined" documents and making "a library of notes." Shearman & Sterling neglected to furnish him with an index. He made none. The workings of the foreign exchange market baffled him, and he was the first to admit it.

Sporkin was impatient. "Damnit, Dave," he remarked one evening to his enforcement assistant, David Doherty. "We've got to get someone to help Bob on this case."

At the end of November 1979, Thomson von Stein dropped by the SEC offices after work to see his old boss, Sporkin. During his nineteen months as an assistant director of enforcement at FERC, von Stein had been responsible for the Tenneco gas diversion case. He recommended that the case be referred to the Justice Department, becoming the first criminal action initiated by FERC in thirty years. Ultimately, Justice cut a deal with the natural gas producer whereby Tenneco pleaded *nolo contendere* and was fined $1 million.

Von Stein had found the work at FERC uninteresting. He missed the more exciting white-collar fraud cases at the SEC. Sporkin called von Stein "the best investigative attorney in the business." Von Stein asked Sporkin if he could have his old job back.

"When can you start?" Sporkin asked.

"How about the beginning of the year," von Stein suggested.

Sporkin said okay.

The next day the matter assumed added urgency. *The Washington Post* completed a two-part series describing Mobil Oil Corporation's dealings with a London-based shipping company, Atlas Maritime, which operated a fleet of Mobil and Saudi oil tankers. Atlas Maritime was partly owned by Peter Tavoulareas, son of Mobil's president William P. Tavoulareas. The *Post* implied that Mobil's extensive business transactions with Atlas were a result of nepotism. Sporkin promptly asked Ryan to check whether Mobil had disclosed the family links with Atlas in its public filings with the SEC and, if not, whether grounds existed to initiate proceedings against the nation's second largest oil company and its chief executive officer.[1] That left the Citicorp investigation completely uncovered.

Sporkin immediately called von Stein at FERC and asked if he could come back sooner. "I've got a case for you," he said.

"What's the case?" von Stein inquired.

"Citicorp."

Von Stein, who had read Larry Kramer's articles in *The Washington Post* about the David Edwards affair, said he could be back working at the SEC in two weeks.

Von Stein agreed to take a civil-service grade cut, as there was no SEC opening for him at his FERC equivalence. But Sporkin offered him a pay raise by putting him near the top of the salary scale in the lower-grade SEC post. While von Stein cleaned up his affairs at FERC, Sporkin gave him the Shearman & Sterling report to read.

Sporkin's investigator was born in New York City in 1936, the second son of Charlotte and William von Stein. His father was a Park Avenue physician. He and his elder brother, Peter, moved with their mother to Colorado Springs in the late 1940s, where both boys attended Cheyenne Mountain High School. Young Tom played forward on the school's hockey team, the state champion Cheyenne Mountain Indians. He went back east to Williams College, played hockey there, then dropped out, eventually joining the U.S. Army. He served as an instructor in Germany for two years, teaching mathematics, history, and geography to non-commissioned officers. Before returning to the United States in 1959 to complete his bachelor's degree at Williams, he met his future wife.

At college, von Stein was known as eccentric, cynical, and droll, traits he retained in professional life. He graduated in 1961, the year that John Hoffman was admitted to the bar, and enrolled at Stanford Law School, obtaining his law degree in 1964. In January 1965, he and his wife moved to Washington, D.C., where he went to work for the Federal Power Commission. In 1968, the von Steins—the family now included four children: Peter, Jennifer, Thomas, and Christopher—moved back to Colorado Springs, where von Stein became a

---

[1] William Tavoulareas and his son filed a lawsuit against *The Washington Post* in November 1980, claiming the articles were "false and defamatory." Mobil later joined the action. The plaintiffs won a $2 million judgment, which was reversed on appeal. The SEC, meanwhile, continued to press Mobil to amend its filings and make full disclosure of the family connections.

Democratic candidate for the state legislature. With glasses, serious-looking, straight dark hair, and of medium build, he seemed cast from the perfect candidate's mold in spite of his thirty-two years.

"Tom Makes Sense . . ." his campaign pamphlet announced.

"Tom Makes Sense on Taxes . . ." it repeated, adding a quote from the candidate: "Those on low or fixed incomes pay too much of their income in taxes. Taxes must be set according to a man's ability to pay."

The pamphlet addressed a number of other basic campaign issues in this short, telegraphic manner, ending with:

"Tom Makes Sense on Crime . . ." and the candidate's rejoinder: "Law and justice are the foundations of a free society. We need both to prevent crime and its causes."

Unfortunately for von Stein, the Democratic Party was deeply divided and Nixon swept the state by 500,000 votes that November. Von Stein was defeated, and the Republican landslide ended his political aspirations.

The von Steins returned to Washington, and this time Thomson went to work for Stanley Sporkin as an attorney in the division of enforcement (then known as the division of trading and markets). Two years before, the SEC had permanently banned IOS Ltd., Bernie Cornfeld's renegade offshore financial services conglomerate, from selling its shares, services, or investment programs to U.S. citizens or American residents. Geneva-based IOS was then the largest mutual fund complex in the world and it represented a landmark case for the SEC.

Von Stein had been on the job for twenty-two months when the SEC became interested in Robert Vesco's efforts to wrest control of IOS from Cornfeld. In 1971, soon after achieving his objective, Vesco began dismembering the IOS empire and looting its mutual funds. Von Stein worked with Sporkin on the investigation that led to the indictment of the New Jersey businessman and five of his associates and their becoming fugitives from U.S. justice. He also handled the investigation of John M. King, founder of the ill-fated King Resources Company of Denver. King and his chief lieutenant were indicted for fraud, tried, convicted, and jailed. Von Stein then investigated Victor Posner, a Miami entrepreneur who was chairman of a number of public companies, including Sharon Steel. Posner consented to a securities fraud injunction and reimbursed $600,000 to the companies he headed. He was subsequently indicted for income tax fraud.

When he returned to the SEC in December 1979, von Stein was assigned an office on the fourth floor at 500 North Capitol, down the corridor from Sporkin's corner office, overlooking Union Plaza. Ryan's office was one floor above. Von Stein learned that the Citicorp investigation had the reputation around the division of being "a dog." Most of his colleagues thought the case was too obscure, the evidentiary problems too difficult. But the case was important. It didn't pass the "Sporkin stink test," which meant, according to von Stein, "if it smelled bad, it was illegal."

Sporkin described his "stink test" differently. He called it "an early instinct system." He said, "an aroma surrounds certain types of cases which, from experience, alerts you to the fact that something is wrong." This was the kind of gut reaction to law enforcement that drove Commissioner Roberta Karmel up the wall. She found it unseemly that "investigations and enforcement actions are begun and maintained out of an emotional reaction to particular factual situations," and it became part of the conflict that soured relations between Sporkin's enforcement division and the commission under chairman Williams.

In the mid-1970s, under Sporkin's enforcement leadership, greater emphasis had been placed on forcing the disclosure of information relating to management integrity. This involved stretching the scope of federal securities laws, which until then had provided that only "material" items need be disclosed. So what was material? Before Watergate, materiality was generally accepted to mean anything that was economically or quantitatively important to a company's wellbeing—a rule of thumb, for example, being 10 percent of earnings. But the materiality of management integrity was impossible to quantify.

In the mid-1960s the commission had begun to explore the notion that certain information that was not *quantitatively* material, such as evidence of poor corporate citizenship, might under certain circumstances be *qualitatively* material. In the post-Watergate era, qualitative materiality became the new battleground of disclosure.

Qualitative materiality is based on the notion that management of corporations are "stewards acting on behalf of the shareholders," that management which tolerates questionable practices, even though the practices may not be quantitatively material, cannot be trusted to exercise safe and proper custodianship of a corporation's assets, that questionable transactions have unpredicable repercussions, such as revocation of licenses or expropriation of assets.

The advocates of qualitative materiality argued that if a company violated the laws of the U.S. or of a foreign country or engaged in transactions that could be labeled "questionable," it was a matter of concern to investors. When the "questionable" activity had the potential to endanger the well-being of a company, management should be required to disclose it.

Defense attorneys who specialized in securities law argued that the SEC had exceeded its powers in adopting the qualitative approach to materiality. They contended that this was particularly true in the case of Citibank, where the offending transactions were trades in foreign currencies physically conducted by European branches outside the jurisdiction of the United States. Although the amounts involved in the parking transactions were large, to a bank with assets of $100 billion, they did not seem quantitatively material.

Von Stein understood that if he was to succeed in the Citibank case, he had to establish the following points: first, that the act of parking foreign exchange positions was an improper management policy; second, that deception had been used by management to cover it up; and third, that it was material, either quantitatively or qualitatively, to the well-being of the parent corporation, Citicorp, which was a publicly traded company subject to SEC regulation.

Von Stein liked to work alone. He had endless energy and was easily irritated by the delaying tactics used by the companies he investigated. He referred to such tactics as "the Wall Street waltz." He was a natural-born backyard mechanic, but he spent most of his time tinkering with violations of the federal securities law. To say that his interests were one-dimensional would be inaccurate, because he was deeply informed in all matters of public affairs and he read voraciously almost anything that came to hand.

He began his investigation by reading the case documents. It didn't take long. The investigation file consisted of the Blue Book, Edwards's testimony, the Shearman & Sterling report, the Ryan memo to the commission, some Citibank telexes and confirmation slips, and a Citibank binder containing some supposedly typical interbranch foreign exchange transactions. These intrigued him because Ryan had already explained that when the dealing slips, confirmations, and telexes referred to Nassau, this really signified a desk in Citibank's New York office.

One of his first conclusions was that the Shearman & Sterling report was itself questionable. The report was filed as a disclosure document—i.e., to clear up a problem. But to von Stein it was too vague, used too many semantic tricks, and in the end didn't disclose anything. He considered it dishonest. He mentioned this to Sporkin, who expressed interest in seeing the legal arguments for making the report part of the case. Von Stein said he would include them in his investigation report.

The reason the case file was so slim, von Stein learned, was because Hoffman had stonewalled Ryan with the argument that Citibank's business and banking secrets had to be protected by keeping the documents at the Shearman & Sterling offices in New York City.

Logically, the only way to determine the extent of Citibank's parking activities and judge their materiality to the bank's overall operations was to conduct a full audit of the foreign exchange records. For each branch, this would entail examining records in three separate locations: the branch itself, the off-booking center (i.e., Nassau), and the MIS department at head office. Obviously, this would take an army of accountants a considerable length of time. But the SEC only had a staff of four accountants. So von Stein realized this was not a viable proposition. He would have to settle for the 8,260 pages of documentation that Shearman & Sterling had assembled while preparing their report.

Although Ryan had already looked at them, von Stein decided to examine the documents himself. In early January 1980, he set aside two days to visit Shearman & Sterling's Citicorp Center offices. He was received coolly and taken to a small conference room. A paralegal brought in red expandable folders containing up to 800 documents each, taking back those folders he had finished reviewing. Shearman & Sterling did not produce their index of the documents. Von Stein made his own as best he could. Many of the documents were undated, unheaded, or unsigned. But at least each one had a Shearman & Sterling index number stamped on it. He described in his own form of shorthand the subject matter of each document, keying it to the Shearman & Sterling index number. He did not see Hoffman. He finished his notes as quickly as possible and returned to Washington.

At that point, the Citicorp investigation had been "open" for twenty months and the SEC still had no list of the "refined" documents at the Shearman & Sterling offices that supposedly formed the factual basis for the law firm's investigation. Von Stein's effort to produce a list was the SEC's first attempt. He noted that in addition to approximately 450 documents withheld from his inspection on grounds of attorney-client privilege and 850 documents that were not produced because they supposedly related to federal bank examinations, another 360 documents were missing. He pointed this out in a letter to Hoffman. The letter was ignored. It became one of several oversights forgotten in the long and shuffling investigation. From those documents that remained, von Stein selected more than 2,000 that he wanted delivered to the SEC in Washington. Even before the letter asking for the documents arrived on Hoffman's desk, foreknowledge that it was coming caused a stir, both in the enforcement division and at Shearman & Sterling.

The next week, Hoffman and Angermueller asked to see Sporkin. The purpose of their visit, Hoffman announced, was to report on the recent settlement of Citibank's problems with the Swiss authorities.

Sporkin had Doherty, Ryan, and von Stein attend the meeting, which was held in Sporkin's office. The enforcement chief, who rarely sat behind his desk, gathered the participants around his coffee table. Hoffman took a place with him on the overstuffed yellow-plaid sofa, which Sporkin had purchased himself. The sofa, some paintings by his wife, Judy, and photographs of persons with whom he had been associated during his career were the only items in the room not of government issue. Angermueller, Doherty, and Ryan sat in large easy chairs. Von Stein sat at the conference table, where it was easier for him to take notes.

Hoffman was affable. Wiry, with dark circles under his eyes, his brown hair pressed neatly into place, like the crease in his trousers, he was in sartorial splendor compared to Sporkin, who wore permanently crumpled two-piece suits, his tie often askew. Born in 1934, Hoffman was three years younger than Sporkin. He had gone to Princeton and Harvard Law School and had an air of self-assertiveness about him that bordered on arrogance.

Angermueller was more relaxed than Hoffman. He beamed through thin-rimmed glasses with the benevolent air of a college professor. Born in 1924 to an Austrian mother and a German father, Angermueller and his parents had immigrated to the United States when he was five. Educated at Harvard, where he obtained degrees in law and engineering, he came as general counsel to Citibank in 1973 from Shearman & Sterling, where he had been the highest ranking partner on the Citicorp account.

"We consider the Swiss reaction the key to European reaction," von Stein's notes of the meeting quoted Hoffman as saying. Hoffman handed Sporkin copies of two letters, one from Fritz Leutwiler, president of the Swiss National Bank, addressed to Wriston, and the other from the director and associate director of the Swiss National Bank's legal department, addressed to the Zurich senof. Hoffman explained that Wriston had just received the Leutwiler letter. Dated January 3, 1980, it read:

Dear Walt,
The Swiss National Bank has terminated its investigation at Citibank Zurich and placed the result on record in a letter to Mr. W.

Adams. The conclusion is that we abstain from taking further steps although from the point of view of our currency protection regulations various transactions do not appear to be beyond all doubt.

As far as we are concerned, the matter is thus settled; we now want to turn to the future again. I hope for good, undisturbed cooperation.

> With best wishes and kind regards,
> Yours sincerely,
> s/Fritz.

The other, a seven-page letter dated December 14, 1979, from Dr. Peter Klauser and H. Stabel, was not quite as sweet, but nevertheless, Hoffman represented it as an absolution letter clearing Citibank of any serious wrongdoing.

Hoffman explained that the settlement of the Citibank tax problems in Switzerland had cost the bank $5.6 million. The bank had paid $4.1 million to the canton of Zurich and $1.1 million to the federal authorities in Berne for 1974 back taxes, plus an "administrative fee" of $400,000. He said the Swiss had approved Citibank's 1973 and 1975–1978 tax returns. "We will file an amended tax return to get a credit for it in the United States," he said.

"Then why do it?" Sporkin asked, meaning Why avoid foreign taxes by parking if you get a U.S. tax credit in any event?

"We don't know," Angermueller replied.

"Has it stopped?" Sporkin wanted to know.

"Yes," Angermueller said.

Hoffman added: "The Swiss Banking Commission has closed its file. The Swiss National Bank has closed its file."

Hoffman, according to the notes, disclosed that investigations were still going on in France and Italy. But the fiscal authorities in Germany and the Netherlands had wound up their investigations without bringing charges.

The conversation turned to David Edwards. "Was he fired?" Sporkin asked.

"Yes," replied Angermueller.

"Was that fair? Here a guy brings matters to your attention," Sporkin said.

"In retrospect, it wasn't fair," the notes reflected Angermueller as saying. "There was a modicum of truth in what he said."

"You ought to do something about him," Sporkin affirmed.

"What about transferring long or short foreign exchange positions over local limits," Ryan asked.

"If we think it's okay as a credit matter, we'll continue to do it. The banking authorities know all Swiss banks do it," Angermueller replied.

"What do the Swiss say about that?" Sporkin wanted to know.

"We haven't specifically talked to the Swiss about transferring excess positions out of Switzerland at the end of the day," Angermueller answered.

"We want to know how high the knowledge of this went in Citibank," Sporkin said.

Hoffman intervened. "Freeman Huntington, the senior vice-president in charge of this area, was not well then. He was losing his grip. He's dead now. He reported to the treasurer, Don Howard."

"Did he know?" Sporkin pressed.

"Howard didn't know . . ." Angermueller said.

Sporkin brought the meeting to a close. "We don't know where [our investigation] will come out. We'll act as quickly as we can. We'll listen to any proposal you have," he said.[2]

Angermueller later claimed no recollection of having said of Edward's firing, "It wasn't fair." He and Hoffman flew back to New York on the Eastern shuttle that evening, and in the aircraft he made his own notes of the meeting.

"Was it fair to treat Edwards that way?" his notes showed he recollected being asked.

"On reflection, we might have dealt differently with the situation. We should perhaps consider new procedures that deal with things like whistleblowers," his notes indicated he replied.[3]

At the close of the meeting, von Stein informed Hoffman that he wanted production of approximately 2,700 documents, handing him a list with their index numbers, which he followed up three days later with a formalized request by letter.

Until von Stein's appearance, Hoffman had been under the impression that Sporkin was actually winding down the investigation. What more was there to investigate after the Shearman & Sterling report

[2] Extracted from memorandum to files, from Thomson von Stein, "Notes of Meeting, 1-14-80, with Citibank." For the record, Don Howard was sent the Natvig/Pomeroy report by Stephen Eyre in August 1975. He apparently read and digested it because Natvig recorded that "according to Don Howard, the proposals [for restructuring parking] are agreed to in principle, and the implementation will be worked out at the Oct. 1975 meeting of Treasury heads in New York" (source: Citibank document 1688).
[3] Transcript of hearings before the Subcommittee on Oversight and Investigations, House Committee on Energy and Commerce, Washington, D.C., June 28, 1983, page 75.

had set the record straight, after the Swiss had concluded their investigation, the Dutch and Germans, too?

One week later, having heard nothing from Hoffman, von Stein telephoned Shearman & Sterling to find out when the documents would be arriving.

Hoffman was not pleased. "It looks like the investigation is going back to square one," von Stein said Hoffman complained. Hoffman claimed he had not yet received von Stein's letter, but he took a firmly negative stand:

- He did not intend to photocopy the designated documents and send them to the SEC.
- The documents were available for inspection at the Shearman & Sterling offices, as per the agreement of January 31, 1979.
- He would have to reconsider what Citibank's response should be to this new direction of investigation.
- He would probably call Sporkin later in the week and ask for another appointment.

Von Stein told Hoffman that the SEC's highest priority was now to get the designated documents and that the SEC was prepared to issue another subpoena for them if necessary. He said that Sporkin had asked him to conclude this investigation as quickly as possible. He said the SEC would be able to begin taking testimony two weeks after receiving the documents.[4]

The battle for the documents lasted a month. Hoffman initially refused to comply and complained to Doherty that von Stein's request was contrary to the agreement he had worked out with Ryan. Doherty asked von Stein to explain why he needed so many documents. Von Stein said his notes of the documents indicated they were relevant to the case: they related to what Edwards had alleged, namely Citibank's use of foreign exchange trading to transfer profits and also the bank's avoidance through "parking" of exchange controls in Europe. Some of the documents, moreover, indicated that Citibank was parking out of Mexico and in Asia as well. He said he needed the documents to take meaningful testimony from Citibank staff and directors.

Doherty told him to reduce the number. Von Stein trimmed the list by more than a thousand. In the end, he limited the request to most of the Natvig work papers, the 1975 Natvig/Pomeroy report, the 1977

---

[4]Memo to files, from Thomson von Stein, call to John Hoffman, January 21, 1980.

audit of foreign exchange operations in Switzerland by Citibank's resident inspector, Edgar Giger's revealing correspondence with Freeman Huntington, examples of management profit reports, confirmation slips for parked positions, and post-facto approval requests.

When the shorter list was submitted, Doherty still wanted reassurance that von Stein was not embarking on some sort of evidentiary boondoggle. While the tussle for the documents continued, on February 8, 1980, von Stein subpoenaed Don Howard, the senior financial officer and once Huntington's boss; Bob Logan, the head of Division III; Stephen Eyre, the former comptroller, recently appointed corporate secretary; Ernst Brutsche, senior vice-president in charge of foreign exchange; Charles Young, the new senof in Toronto; George Vojta, in charge of long-range planning but soon to leave the Citi for other employment; Tom Theobald, about to be appointed vice-chairman; Sanford England, a former Swiss senof; Arthur Natvig and Ed Pomeroy, co-authors of the 1975 European Treasuries survey; and Victor Lee, the trading room clerk in New York.

The new demand letter, which accompanied the pruned list of 1,700 documents, was sent to Hoffman in mid-February 1980. Finally, at the end of February 1980, the first bundles of documents were delivered to the SEC. Other bundles followed during the next few weeks. In each case they were accompanied by a letter from Shearman & Sterling demanding their exemption from Freedom of Information Act disclosure.

Not content to wait for the SEC's decision on exemption, which ultimately denied confidential status for the majority of the documents, Shearman & Sterling marked each page with a specially cut stamp that read:

CONFIDENTIAL
18 USC 1905
EXEMPT FROM
FOIA DISCLOSURE

Chapter 28

Switzerland: Key to European Reaction

Parking? I'm not sure I know what it means.

—DONALD S. HOWARD, EXECUTIVE VICE-PRESIDENT, FINANCE, MARCH 27, 1980

Von Stein accepted Hoffman's suggestion that the Swiss findings were the key to the attitudes and reaction of European regulators and decided this would be a good place to concentrate his investigation.

At their January 14, 1980, meeting with Sporkin, at which Doherty, Ryan, and von Stein were also present, Angermueller and Hoffman had portrayed the Swiss National Bank letter addressed the month before to Citibank Zurich as absolving the bank of any wrongdoing. They had left Sporkin with an English translation of the December 14, 1979, letter and a note from Dr. Fritz Leutwiler, president of the Swiss National Bank, informing Walt Wriston that the Swiss investigation was closed.

Von Stein reread both these letters and concluded that the Swiss had not been all that conciliatory toward Citibank. He wrote to Dr.

247

Leutwiler, requesting copies of the correspondence between Citibank, their auditors Peat Marwick Mitchell, and the Swiss authorities. This correspondence was referred to in the Swiss National Bank letter, but Angermueller and Hoffman had not provided it to the SEC on the grounds that it was covered by Swiss banking secrecy.

While waiting for Dr. Leutwiler's reply, von Stein started piecing together everything he knew about the Swiss investigation to see if, as Hoffman maintained, it really was the prototype for reaction by other European regulators.

The key to understanding the Swiss situation was the triangular relationship between the independent auditors, in this case the Swiss affiliate of Peat Marwick, the bank, and the Swiss regulators. Under Swiss banking law, the auditors had a statutory obligation to report any suspect findings uncovered during an audit to the Federal Banking Commission. This triangular relationship was in many ways a model aspect of the Swiss law because it required auditors to be extremely vigilant or risk the same sanctions as the transgressor if they failed to report a breach of the banking act or such other legal provisions that might exist.

After some frustration, von Stein was able to form a clear picture of how, in Citibank's case, this statutory form of whistleblowing worked. He did it, however, without help from the Swiss, who jealously keep all banking matters confidential, even between regulators, as witnessed by the reply he received toward the end of April 1980 from Dr. Leutwiler.

April 17, 1980

Re: *Citibank Zurich*

Dear Mr. von Stein,

I am in receipt of your letter of March 25, 1980. You have been furnished—not by Banque Nationale Suisse, nor, as far as I know by the Federal Banking Commission—with a translation of our letter dated December 14, 1979 to Mr. William Adams, vice president of Citibank Zurich, and are now requesting me to send you copies of various documents referred to in that letter.

For legal reasons I am not in a position to comply with your request. Incidentally, I take it that you should have no difficulties in obtaining the required material from Citibank New York.

Yours sincerely,
s/Leutwiler

Following Leutwiler's suggestion, von Stein requested these documents from Citibank. Hoffman took the position that firstly, the documents were privileged and secondly, Citibank could not furnish them in any event as they were covered by Swiss banking secrecy. Von Stein found himself in a Catch-22 situation.

Von Stein reasoned that Shearman & Sterling, in hiring Peat Marwick as part of their investigative team, had meant to bring the auditors under the blanket of attorney-client privilege, thereby binding them to treat as confidential all material obtained while fulfilling their mandate.

But von Stein gathered from the Swiss National Bank's December 1979 letter—the "reprimand" letter—that Peat Marwick's senior partner in Zurich, Hugh Matthews, held the view that the statutory obligation took precedence over client-attorney privilege.

In July 1978, after completing the Zurich field audit for Shearman & Sterling, Matthews decided the Edwards allegations, as confirmed by the audit, were indeed serious enough to report to the Federal Banking Commission. His action provoked an investigation by the Swiss authorities, which began in August 1978 and continued for sixteen months. Matthews followed his initial report with a second, more detailed, letter to the Federal Banking Commission in November 1978. Von Stein knew of the existence of this letter because it was referred to in the December 1979 "reprimand" letter.

Von Stein was not able to obtain copies of the July or November 1978 letters. Shearman & Sterling persisted in maintaining they were covered by Swiss banking secrecy. Shearman & Sterling's position on this critical point was never challenged: no subpoena was issued to force their production.[1]

Although the SEC has subpoena-issuing powers, and a federal court has rarely denied a motion compelling compliance with an SEC subpoena, at this stage of the investigation Sporkin and Doherty did not want to rock the boat with such strong-armed and time-consuming tactics. Sporkin, for one, was tired of hearing complaints from corporate America and the securities bar that the SEC enforcers were bullies who abused the powers entrusted in them by the federal securities laws. Frequent criticism that he was too tough an enforcer had made him, over the years, more cautious, and this restraint, com-

---

[1] In June 1983, after being threatened with a congressional subpoena, Shearman & Sterling released the November 15, 1978 and April 20, 1978 Peat Marwick letters as well as the 1977 and 1978 legal opinions to the Dingell subcommittee. See Chapter 44.

bined with the limited investigation resources, weighed heavily on von Stein.

Had von Stein obtained copies of the Matthews letters, his investigation would have been significantly advanced by the revelations they contained. In the November 1978 letter, which was cosigned by fellow partner J. Fischer, Matthews described four examples of parking, accurately giving the intent of these "special transactions" for the Swiss banking commissioners. Unlike the Shearman & Sterling scenarios, Matthews's descriptions were simple and clear:

1. Citibank Zurich . . . has a large long position which it has to square to adhere to the Swiss regulations (reporting to the Federal Banking Commission when aggregate foreign exchange positions exceed 40% of equity). Zurich sells this position forward (per example, $20,000,000 at SF 2.05/1 US$, value May 23, 1977) to another branch (e.g. Nassau) or to Head Office with the result that the Swiss regulations are now adhered to. Some time later with a spot contract Zurich repurchases the same dollar amount at the same rate and with the same value date from the other branch or Head Office. As a result of this second deal Zurich again has a long position which can either be squared on the local market or transferred to another branch again.

   As can be seen from this example, the accounting records never show a foreign exchange position a the level (e.g. $20,000,000) which would require reporting to the Federal Banking Commission.

2. Zurich has a large short position in a foreign currency which has to be squared to adhere to Swiss regulations (Federal Council ordinance prohibiting speculative buying of Swiss francs and possibly the reporting of foreign exchange positions to the Federal Banking Commission). Zurich purchases dollars from another branch or Head Office at the same rate and with the same value date. The deals can be repeated. As both deals are transacted at the same rate and value date, the profit resulting from the speculation is recorded in the accounting records in Zurich although the position is held elsewhere for a time.

3. On November 20, 1974, the Swiss regulatory authorities established limits on future sales of Swiss francs to foreigners based upon balances at October 31, 1974, the higher limit of future sales of Swiss francs which can be made to foreigners. In the event that the balance at October 31, 1974 contained "parked"

transactions, the limit of future sales to foreigners is also higher.
4. Zurich has realized large exchange profits and is able to transfer a part of them to Head Office. . . . Zurich purchases, for example, US dollars from Head Office and sells them back on the same day at a lower rate, both deals having been executed with the same value date. As a result of this operation Zurich realizes a loss, whereas Head Office realizes a profit of an equal amount. This profit can be accredited to Zurich through the Management Information System. As a result of this deal Zurich has transferred profits.[2]

Peat Marwick's audit of Citibank's Swiss parking operations had covered a five-year period, commencing in January 1973. The audit was not comprehensive but selective, and was completed in six weeks. It uncovered 875 parking transactions, most of which were of the type described in the first two examples above. Their frequency on an annualized basis never exceeded 2 percent of the branch's total foreign exchange transactions, but in some years represented 10 percent or more of the total value of foreign exchange turnover (on one day—October 31, 1974—Zurich parked SF 400 million, equivalent to 57 percent of the total turnover for that day). In other words, the parking transactions were on average five times larger than normal day-to-day foreign exchange trades.

Matthews's insistence that the parking scheme be reported to the authorities provoked a rift in the accounting firm's Zurich office. To soften his statements, Peat Marwick's letter to the Federal Banking Commission included the opinion of another partner, who considered that Citibank's parking operations were properly documented transactions with a transfer of economic risk to the parking-lot branch. This view, which sounded as if it had been dictated by Shearman & Sterling, missed the authority of Matthews's arguments. His six reasons for claiming that the transactions "lacked substance" were the following:

a) Generally Zurich realized the profit or loss on positions transferred and later repurchased and would thereby appear to have also carried the risk during the period when the position was parked. In the event that profit was earned in the branch or Head

[2]Letter from H. N. Matthews and J. Fischer of Peat, Marwick Mitchell & Co. AG, Zurich to the Swiss Federal Banking Commission, November 15, 1978, pages 3–4 of the English translation.

Office where the position was parked it could be accredited to Zurich through the internal management information system.

b) The foreign exchange positions which were transferred to another branch or to Head Office were generally taken back under the same conditions (e.g. same rate and same value date) and occasionally on the same day. It can, therefore, be interpreted that there was an intention at the time of the original transfer to take back the position. This is not the case in a real foreign exchange deal.

c) The transfer of a position to another branch does not mean that the position no longer exists. On a consolidated basis it and the risk still exist. The transfer of a position seems, therefore, only to have a purpose when it is made for another objective (e.g. circumvention of local laws).

d) A deal lacking substance can also be properly documented from a legal point of view.

e) Many of the transactions were made in a complicated manner (e.g. through other branches) thereby complicating the possibility of detecting them.

f) The deals occurred frequently and in large amounts.

The Peat Marwick letter ended with this comment: "The leading auditor [Matthews] believes that the transactions classified as parking bear evidence that they were presumably only executed to avoid either filing a report or exceeding a legal limit or showing profit. As a result, in his opinion, the foreign exchange position of the bank was incorrectly shown, the profits not correctly stated, and it cannot be stated that the accounting records have been properly maintained."[3]

At this point, since the alleged misdeeds involved breaches of the central bank's currency-protection measures, the Swiss National Bank stepped in. Citibank was asked for its side of the story. At a meeting with the Swiss National Bank in March 1979, Citibank produced its own list of fifty parking transactions occurring between January 1973 to March 1978 (as opposed to the 875 examples unearthed by Peat Marwick), which it admitted deviated from market rates.

Matthews was asked to explain the discrepancy in numbers. He replied that simulated deals could be recorded within the trading range of deals done on any given day and therefore would appear to have been done "at market rates."

[3] Ibid., page 10 of English version. When von Stein finally was shown a copy of this letter in 1983, he said: "No clearer or more damning an assessment of parking could be written."

Matthews explained that "among the features noted [by the Peat Marwick audit] was the fact that [an] identical rate was used in the majority of the operations for both the transfer and repurchase. . . . Operations carried out at identical rates can nevertheless . . . be defined as having been executed at 'market rates [if they fall within the trading range for the day].' "[4]

Swiss National Bank inspectors visited the Citibank offices in Zurich on November 5, 1979, the day after Iranian extremists occupied the U.S. embassy in Tehran. Their findings were recorded in the seven-page "reprimand" letter sent by the head of the national bank's legal department to William Adams III, Citibank's new Swiss senof in Zurich. As the letter indicated that the Swiss had closed their investigation of Citibank's currency trading practices without initiating charges, Hoffman chose to interpret this as absolving Citibank of any parking sins and therefore left a copy with Sporkin. Von Stein, when he read the letter, retained these key points:

1. The foreign exchange bookkeeping at Citibank Zurich was not maintained in a manner "compatible with the requirements which must be met by a careful management. . . ."
2. The Swiss National Bank's review of the books confirmed Peat Marwick's findings that about 875 parking transactions had occurred over a five-year period. In the majority, "the repurchase was not within the daily trading range of the market. . . ." Citibank's claim that only fifty transactions deviated from market rates was therefore contested.
3. The Swiss National Bank found that the exchange rate risk for the parked positions remained with Zurich despite a temporary transfer of the position to another branch.
4. The federal decree prohibiting banks in Switzerland from speculating on an appreciation of the Swiss franc had been "undermined."
5. The number of parking transactions was "substantial."

The "reprimand" letter painted a picture of turmoil in the foreign exchange market during the period when Citibank was most actively parking. At the time, the Swiss franc was appreciating under speculative pressure, which imposed a heavy penalty on the Swiss export industry. Switzerland *must* export to stay alive. Its export industry

---

[4] Peat Marwick Mitchell & Co. AG, Zurich, letter to Dr. P. Ehrsam at the Swiss National Bank, April 20, 1979.

contributes 60 percent of the gross national product—more than any other industrialized country. With the Swiss franc rising against the dollar as well as other major trading currencies on an almost daily basis, Swiss industry found it difficult to maintain its share of the world market. Therefore, measures to shield the Swiss franc from excessive speculation were really measures to protect the economy as a whole.

"Under such circumstances," the letter asked, "was it sufficient for a foreign branch bank to comply with legal requirements at best in a formal manner—by squaring accounting-wise foreign currency positions without risk transfer—[which] from a material point of view . . . undoubtedly violated the 'ratio legis'?[5] To ask the question means to answer it negatively."

The Swiss National Bank reminded Citibank that when it sought permission to open its Zurich branch, it had assured the authorities it would respect Swiss monetary policy. The letter concluded: "We consider the foreign exchange practices of Citibank Zurich, particularly the 'parking' transactions during the years 1973 until 1978, as incompatible with this assurance and formal declaration of September 19, 1969." The Swiss National Bank, however, refrained from asking the Federal Banking Commission to initiate proceedings to withdraw the Zurich branch's banking license because:

(1) the statute of limitations had expired for transactions prior to 1976
(2) the emergency legislation to protect the Swiss franc had been repealed or relaxed
(3) Citibank had represented that it had changed its operating practices[6]

As far as von Stein was concerned, this was not a letter absolving Citibank Zurich of impropriety. He was puzzled, however, by the timidity of the Federal Banking Commission and the Swiss National Bank for failing to take disciplinary action against Citibank. One reason suggested to him by bank analysts in New York was fear by the Swiss authorities that any such action during a period of international crisis risked destabilizing the entire banking system.

---

[5]The "ratio legis" refers to the legally required ratio between a bank's capital and reserves and its open overnight foreign exchange position. A bank operating in Switzerland must report to the Federal Banking Commission when its overnight position in foreign currency exceeds 40 percent of its combined capital and reserves, in which case the banking commission may impose special measures upon the bank.
[6]Excerpted from Swiss National Bank letter, signed by Dr. Peter Klauser and H. Stabel, to William Adams III, vice-president, Citibank Zurich, December 14, 1979.

In February 1980, one month after Hoffman's and Angermueller's visit to the SEC, the Swiss Federal Banking Commission informed the Office of the Comptroller of the Currency in Washington of the results of its investigation:

It was . . . made clear [to Citibank] that the behavior of the Bank and its persons in charge was not in full accordance with the Swiss laws and practice.

In consideration of the fact that the Bank itself has restored the rightful conditions and that the expressed warnings will not fail to have the desired effect, the matter was . . . abandoned by the Federal Banking Commission.[7]

On February 26, 1980, the Federal Banking Commission informed Citibank Zurich:

[C]onsiderable irregularities did come to light. Under banking law, the foreign exchange transactions already criticized by the Swiss National Bank are especially objectionable. This reproach becomes even more important inasmuch as foreign exchange trading is one of the most significant activities of your branch and contributes considerable proportions of its profits. Your contention that this trading is carried out within written instructions which permit, without difficulties, the reconstruction of foreign exchange positions and the corresponding profit or loss calculations at any time, applies only to the present, and not to the 1973–1977 time span. As you yourself do not deny, during this time span . . . trading tickets lacking the date on which the transaction took place, omission of sequential numbers and time-stamping, all greatly contributed to the difficulties encountered by those conducting the investigation of the many transactions.

One of the pre-conditions to obtain permission to engage in banking activities (as per Article 3, par. 2 of the Revised Banking Act) is the existence of an administrative organization capable of supervising the business. As evidenced by the serious deficiencies in your conduct of foreign exchange trading, that pre-condition was not met by your branch during the years 1973–1977. In addition, your procedures did not comply with the "Universal Banking" law. We disapprove of your past conduct in the strongest terms. The

[7]Letter from the Swiss Federal Banking Commission to the Office of the Comptroller of the Currency, February 22, 1980; as reproduced in the SEC Division of Enforcement staff report; Re: Citicorp HO 1100, p. 133.

fact that in the meantime you have undertaken corrective action on your own has spared you from administrative measures on our part.

The National Bank has established that assurances given by your bank for the protection of Swiss monetary policy have not been observed. Only because of the reasons cited on page seven of the letter of December 14, 1979 [statute of limitation and a repeal of overnight position limits] has the National Bank abandoned its intent to have the Federal Banking Commission apply for the withdrawal of your banking licence. However, the Commission is still considering the possibility of taking less severe measures. In particular, a still unresolved question is, can persons responsible for the criticized foreign exchange activities—especially the "parking" activities—be trusted to conduct business in a lawful manner. . . .

However, it is assumed that the censure of the Swiss National Bank, which [we] endorse, will have the desired affect [sic] upon the responsible persons in your bank, and in the future can count on you to abide by Swiss monetary policy. In that regard, we hold you to your declaration at the close of your letter of January 22, 1980.[8]

Copies of the Federal Banking Commission letters were forwarded to von Stein almost a year later by the Office of the Comptroller of the Currency. Shearman & Sterling, however, continued to refuse him copies of the Peat Marwick letters.

Von Stein learned in the meantime that Eddie Giger had left Citibank. A few months after his June 1980 resignation, Giger formed E. A. Giger Consulting AG in Zurich and went into the business of advising private clients on how to manage their foreign exchange risk. Citibank refused to comment to von Stein on the circumstances surrounding Giger's resignation.

---

[8] Letter from the Federal Banking Commission to Citibank Zurich, February 26, 1980; as reproduced in the SEC Division of Enforcement staff report, pp. 133–134.

Chapter 29

"Rinky-Dink Deals"

I keep objecting to the use of this term parked position.

—EDWIN L. POMEROY, APRIL 15, 1980

On March 11, 1980, two weeks after receiving the first Citibank documents, von Stein and Ryan began taking depositions from Citibank directors and officers. As the Mobil case was occupying most of Ryan's time, the weight of the preparatory work fell on von Stein. Fortunately, he had no other investigation in progress.

Von Stein was conscious of the fact that if the SEC decided to file charges, the burden of proof would fall on the division of enforcement, not Citibank. Presenting the case in convincing evidentiary form would be a huge task. And he knew only too well that the division's resources were limited. He had no junior attorneys to assist him, no paralegals, and little secretarial help. He prepared his own synopses of documents, digests of testimony, and analyses of evidence.

The resources of Shearman & Sterling, on the other hand, were as large as Citicorp's litigation budget, and there was no way of knowing exactly how large that might be, although it was up in the tens of millions. Citicorp declared profits of $541 million in 1979. Its costs of doing business that year was $10 billion. The figure listed under "other expenses" was $723 million, so the scope was large. The SEC's operating budget, with nine regional offices, six branch offices, and a staff of two thousand, was $66 million—about equivalent to Shearman & Sterling's annual billing—and there were critics on Capitol Hill who complained even that was too large for the watchdog of all American securities markets.

Von Stein attempted to make up for the lack of resources by extending the hours he spent on the case. He was in the office by nine and rarely left before eight in the evening. He once remarked in apparent seriousness, "I can't conceive of anyone eating breakfast sitting down unless they're retired." He took a cup of tepid "iced" tea mix with him when he drove to work. That and an egg, consumed almost on his way out the front door, was his normal morning sustenance. Lunch was eaten at his desk.

When he went home to Rockville, in suburban Maryland, north of the capital, the Citicorp case went with him in his secondhand Chevrolet station wagon. He worked on the case on weekends and holidays. It was a single-minded existence. He and his wife had separated three years before. He looked after the children, whose ages then ranged from thirteen to eighteen. But the children were pretty well accustomed to looking after themselves. As a matter of form, von Stein posted a schedule of chores and code of behavior on two sheets of computer printout paper pinned to the door of the hall cloak cupboard.

One of the checklists also gave a few pointers on "privacy and courtesy." These included:

Do not go into anyone else's room unless *specifically* invited.
Do not criticize your siblings.
Answer phone politely and go to person's door who is called.
Sign the locator sheet.
Keep 15 cents to call if plans change.

The locator sheet was on a clipboard by the front door, and every time Pete, Jennifer, Tom, or Chris left the house, they were supposed to mark on it their whereabouts, time of departure, time of return, and the date.

The other sheet contained the list of chores. It was headed: *To Be Done Daily Before Any TV, Radio or Going Out*. It included directions for keeping the kitchen clean, bedrooms tidy, clothes folded or hung up and put away, the stairs swept, and putting out the garbage. Under a rubric marked "General" it stipulated, among other things:

Homework is to be done first after school (unless team practice is scheduled first).

Everyone saves *half* his earnings.

Do not use obscene words.

Do not break the law.

A final line noted:

List to be amended if circumstances so indicate. Private lists for individuals.

In the office, von Stein created and worked from a basic research document, the chronology, which set out everything he knew about Citibank relating to the case. It listed, by date and Shearman & Sterling index number, the relevant Citibank documents, giving a mini-digest of their contents, and later included in the same mini-digest form the Peat Marwick work papers, which he also subpoenaed. It took in related news items, important facts culled from testimony, and information from Citicorp reports filed with the SEC. The "chron" was regularly updated, extending in its last version to more than seventy pages of reduced, single-spaced type.

From the documents, a number of patterns became apparent. Natvig, for example, always wrote with the same small-print typewriter, leaving very little margin in order to cram a maximum onto each page. Natvig's notes were his traveling library. They had to be short and concise, he said, to fit into his briefcase. He fussed a lot. He was a perfectionist. He later explained that he thought his memory was failing and unless he put everything onto paper at once, he was unable to remember details of conversations that had taken place the day before. His memory, though sometimes selective, was in fact reasonably precise, even when he was in his late sixties.

Von Stein held off contacting David Edwards until he had a better understanding of the documents. But as the date for the first deposition approached, he called the ex-Citibanker at his apartment in New York. Edwards was then trading financial futures contracts for his own account.

As far as Edwards was concerned, the Citibank affair had been swept under the carpet by the Justice Department, the Senate Banking Committee, the Senate Foreign Relations Committee, and the Office of the Comptroller of the Currency. Moreover, by then he had come to regard even the SEC as part of unresponsive government. Mention of Ryan's name would make him despair, and he openly said he wanted

nothing more to do with Washington bureaucrats. For him, the issue
was dead.

Von Stein spent close to an hour talking with him on the phone
before he agreed to cooperate further. But it soon became clear to
von Stein that Edwards "only saw the tip of the iceberg." Still, he
was good on technical details. "He helped me understand the business," von Stein remarked.

One 19-page section of the documents supplied by Shearman &
Sterling was particularly interesting. It was neither dated nor signed
and bore no heading. Von Stein was taken by its florid language, but
he couldn't place it in any context and he puzzled over it for weeks.
At this stage he did not realize that Natvig and Pomeroy had written
their 1975 report.

The unheaded document described the function of a mysterious department inside the bank identified as FERA. It comprised a single
person and had been created after "the Herstatt failure in mid-1974
and also the Franklin exchange shenanigans and other exchange fias-
cos which broke at the same time." In part, the text read as follows:

> Senior management thought it a good idea that someone should take
> a look at what our overseas branches were doing in exchange and
> so Art Natvig, who was 'par excellence' the . . . Bank's exchange
> expert, was delegated to undertake this function with me in tow.
>
> Original idea was that we would take a swing through Europe, being
> the principal trading area, which would take about three months
> and that would be it. However, it was later decided to extend the
> survey to other areas and so the three-month project which began
> in January 1975 has . . . now become a permanent function. De-
> spite the impression that may have been given, it is not an exotic
> boondoggle which enables me to travel permanently on an expense
> account and see the world and the fact that the function has be-
> come a permanent one . . . reflects the importance which the
> Treasury has on the overall bottom line and also, of course, the
> specialized risks which it carries with it. . . .
>
> Although the unit is called Foreign Exchange Risk Assessment for
> the sake of brevity, this is really a misnomer in the sense that we
> cover the Treasury which encompasses the whole of the funding
> side—i.e., the money market as well as brokerage. . . .
>
> One of the principal purposes of our survey was to review what the
> limits imposed by the local authorities were and how we were ad-

hering to them. We attempted to summarize them. This was not an easy job as there are usually frequent changes announced by a succession of government circulars, incomprehensibly expressed, and the limits are hardly ever set down in any one place. We would like to see a more formalized requirement that our branches should set up specific files where the requirements are centralized and can be more readily comprehended by, say, an incoming senof or inspector. . . .

Post-Herstatt, and also because of exchange crises, strict regulations were imposed in various areas which restricted our trading, or rather restricted it as far as the exchange positions we were allowed to show on the branch books were concerned. . . .

The document described various techniques used by branch treasuries to circumvent the new regulations. It also mentioned "round-tripping," which, it said, was "really a rather euphemistic way of describing the rinky-dink deals . . . resorted to by our branches to get round the local regulations and any locally imposed limits. It covers a wide area ranging from parking of positions . . . to making deposit and placement deals which improve the bank's liquidity ratios according to local formulas. . . ."

The text also covered personnel dynamics in foreign exchange trading, under the heading of "Trading-room staff," which led to an exposé of position parking:

Trading is essentially a 'person-oriented business' since a trader can pick up the phone and, unlike most other areas of the bank, commit us to deals involving millions of dollars. As well as capability, integrity is obviously of prime concern. Overall appraisal of trading room staff is therefore very important, although . . . it is also one of the most difficult to do, particularly as far as integrity is concerned. There is continual talk of traders getting kick-backs from brokers, and their life-style . . . also gives rise to questions. We have to be alert to such rumors and attempt to evaluate them, but I have to admit that rarely does anything positive ever eventuate. . . .

Parking of Positions (Off-booking of positions enables the trader to comply with the letter—if not the spirit—of locally imposed limitations). In our European survey, this was one of the principal topics in our report and we had thought that we had finally prodded

Free Huntington to issue some specific instructions which would formalize the procedures for parking positions in those rare areas where the parking of positions was to be allowed to continue. For some reason this was never done but . . . a meeting was held in London recently which hopefully should resolve the situation. . . .

When talking of parking of positions, I'm really referring to the parking of overnight exchange positions, e.g., to stop the inflow of funds into Switzerland when the dollar and other currencies were under pressure, the Swiss authorities did not allow banks in Switzerland to have a net oversold position in foreign currency. . . . If our Zurich branch wished to go short in US$ against the Swiss franc, it was necessary for Zurich to transfer the position to another branch at the end of the day to reflect a balanced position. In effect, Zurich would buy dollars from, say, Nassau against Swiss francs and Nassau would then reflect a long position in Swiss francs and a short position in dollars.

Apart of course from the basic question of whether this type of business should be done at all (although there is a case for saying that Zurich is acting on behalf of Nassau in building up the position), this parking of the position results in difficulty in monitoring adherence to [the Bank's own] overnight limits. (If done properly, the department in Zurich responsible for monitoring adherence to limits wouldn't even be aware that Zurich really had a position.)

There is also the question of off-booking of profits. If the profits are brought back directly into Switzerland by buying back the position at the same rate at which it was originally transferred, the transparency of the deal is immediately revealed. (How can you show sizeable FX profits if your FX trading is supposedly severely restricted?)

If the profits are left offshore, the ethics of the situation are further compounded because of the question of tax evasion. In any event, the main thrust of our recommendations was that where such parking was to be allowed it should be done in such a way that we could scrupulously maintain that the branch in question was acting on behalf of Head Office or Nassau in building up and transferring (a rather nicer term than parking) the position. This would mean that if the position was brought back it would always be done at strict market rates prevailing on the day it was brought back and the parking should all be concentrated at one branch where proper limit policing could be done.

I'm not sure what the objections to our proposals were but, as previously mentioned, one of the top priorities of my visit to Head Office after this meeting will be to find out what has transpired and where the situation stands. . . .

Parking is obviously a delicate issue with many ramifications. The policy of parking should be continuously under review for each country involved and transactions suspended when there is significant possibility of conflict of viewpoint or downside risk with the local authorities. . . .[1]

Von Stein later learned that these were notes for a speech that Ed Pomeroy presented to a meeting of internal Citibank auditors in Athens in the spring of 1977. Pomeroy had prepared them only weeks after talking to David Edwards in Amsterdam. At their Amsterdam meeting, Edwards told Pomeroy that Paris was "cooking the books" by parking foreign exchange positions and profits in Nassau. This eventually led to Edwards's being interviewed in London by the bank's regional comptroller for Europe, after which he was told that no evidence existed to support his allegation.

As it happened, Pomeroy was the first Citibank employee to testify. But neither von Stein nor Ryan realized then that he was the author of the FERA notes. Nor did they immediately seize upon the significance of the admissions contained in the notes, which showed a total awareness of the ethical and juridical problems caused by off-booking in general—those "rinky-dink deals"—and the parking of positions in particular.

The night before Pomeroy's examination, which began on the morning of March 11, 1980—a Tuesday—in the Shearman & Sterling offices, von Stein mapped out the areas he wanted to cover in his questioning. For each heading, he had a few questions written out. Others would become apparent from the documents he hoped Pomeroy could identify.

Investigative depositions require different skills than trial examinations. In cross-examination, the trial attorney is supposed to know the answer before he asks the question. When taking a deposition, the

---

[1] Excerpted from Citibank document 7926–7946.

attorney is attempting to ascertain from the witness what the facts are. Von Stein's aim in examining the Citibank witnesses was to get them to flesh out the documents.

"I wanted to know from Pomeroy what was really going on. When I took his deposition I didn't even know what the Natvig/Pomeroy Report was. I got out the documents and asked him about them. Most of Natvig's work papers were undated and I couldn't make chronological sense of them. Speaking with Pomeroy helped," he explained.

Von Stein and Ryan agreed to take the depositions at the Shearman & Sterling offices in Citicorp Center rather than at the SEC's New York offices as an accommodation to the Citibank witnesses, most of whom were based at head office across the street, and also because Shearman & Sterling had a complete set of documents, which meant that the two SEC investigators didn't have to bring a set of their own from Washington.

Von Stein's first reaction was that the Shearman & Sterling conference room was more comfortable than the space allotted to them at the SEC regional offices in the Federal Plaza building in downtown Manhattan. Ryan noted that the quality of coffee was better too. Both were surprised when an ecclesiastic-looking individual, short and stocky, with a round face and glasses, in his mid-fifties, sauntered into the room. He was dressed in a cardigan and was accompanied by Hoffman's associate, Henry Weisburg.

The examination began with the administration of oath and the usual questions identifying the witness. When asked where he resided, Pomeroy replied, "I don't have a permanent address."

The first document von Stein brought out was a handwritten minutes of a meeting with Michael Conolly, managing director of International Westminster in France. Pomeroy confirmed that the notes were in his handwriting, but gave sparse details. "The occasion was a visit to Paris in November 1977. The visit was occasioned by the receipt of a letter addressed to Mr. Theobald and Mr. Sweeney, which repeated some of Edwards's allegations."

A second document was a scorecard for Paris treasury earnings in 1976, showing foreign exchange profits of $1,614,344, of which $936,000 was MIS'ed from Nassau. "The numbers were prepared at my request," Pomeroy admitted, adding that they had been assembled "in connection with the Edwards matter."

Pomeroy's testimony spanned three days and set the tone for the degree of cooperation the SEC investigators came to expect from

Citibank witnesses. Von Stein found Pomeroy very literal. "He was the kind of guy who, if you asked him, 'Is it five o'clock?' and it was one minute after, he would say, 'No.' "

Pomeroy explained that from November 1974, he had worked on foreign exchange and treasury matters, covering Citibank operations on all continents except Australia. But when asked if the Nassau branch had a foreign exchange trader, he replied, "I don't know." This struck von Stein as odd.

Von Stein asked when he first became aware of Edwards's allegations that Paris was transferring profits to Nassau.

"At the time of his letter [to Sweeney and Theobald] of November 1977," he replied. Then he partially corrected this by adding that at their Amsterdam meeting in March 1977, Edwards had "also alluded in some way [to] the incorrect internal record-keeping in Paris."

Pomeroy continued: "Edwards's knowledge of accounting was extremely poor. . . . He was not able to satisfactorily explain his allegations. . . . I tried . . . to get him to explain what he meant. . . . He could not understand the difference between a record that was kept purely for the trader for his own immediate reference purposes, and what was a record that would affect the financial position or the financial record-keeping of the books." [2]

Toward the end of the third session, which was held by conference telephone a month later, von Stein asked about parking procedures, to which Pomeroy snapped: "I keep objecting to the use of this term 'parked position.' "

Von Stein did not respond to Pomeroy's objection immediately. A few minutes later, however, he asked Pomeroy to refer to document 469—the Paris scorecard for 1976 treasury earnings. "Right-hand column under heading 'Nassau MIS'. Your handwriting?"

"Yes."

"Where did you get the figures that you put in under Nassau MIS?"

"[I]n the branch. . . . The precise person, I don't recollect."

"Two figures, $543,000 and $168,000, have the designation 'parking' marked beside them."

"Right."

"[H]ow is that different from the other transactions?"

"[I]n those days, I admit, I was using the terminology 'parking.' " [3]

[2] Ibid., pp. 287–288.
[3] Ibid., pp. 326–344.

Not only was Pomeroy using it "in those days," but his 1975 notes on foreign exchange operations at the Milan branch equated "parking" to one of the techniques used by convicted swindler Michele Sindona to falsify the books of his Italian banks.

"Since the Sindona bank failure (Banca Privata, Banca Unione, etc. in Italy, and Franklin National in New York), the Bofi [Bank of Italy] inspections have gotten better," Pomeroy warned. The Milan branch had to be careful when it "parked," he said.

"There is an awareness of parking and of circuitous routing of transactions to disguise their intent, because they were part of the Sindona syndrome," he concluded.[4]

Pomeroy did not mention that the master architect of the circuitous routing had been Carlo Bordoni, Sindona's foreign exchange wizard, who, for a brief period, had been Citibank's star trader.

[4]Citibank document 1741.

Chapter 30

More Evidence

We have a number of people who deal in foreign exchange in Nassau.

—DONALD S. HOWARD, MARCH 27, 1980

As soon as von Stein digested the Natvig/Pomeroy Survey of European Treasuries, he knew there had been a cover-up. "This essentially was a case based on the documents," he said. "They told the story. I hoped the witnesses would flesh out the documents."

He got no help from Stephen Eyre, whose deposition he took one day after receiving Pomeroy's first testimony. Citibank's former comptroller, recently relegated to corporate secretary, waffled on almost every issue. Unlike Hoffman, Eyre didn't think control over a parked position was irrelevant, but he claimed that it moved with the position to the parking-lot branch. He was asked whether it was the bank's policy, when branches dealt with each other, to do it at arm's length. He replied, "Yes."

When asked, "When you say 'arm's length,' are you referring to anything more than at market rates?" He replied, "That's correct."

Eyre testified that no difference existed between a parking transaction and any other foreign exchange deal that Citibank contracted with third parties. He testified that head office or Nassau could decline to accept a parked position. He testified that the originating branch was not required to take back a parked position. He testified that he was unaware whether Nassau actually had a foreign exchange dealer. He testified that he was unaware whether head office had approved higher overnight position limits for foreign branches than those authorized by local central banks. In fact Eyre claimed ignorance of an astounding amount of basic Citibank foreign exchange practices.

"I didn't know," von Stein later commented, "whether he was just jerking me around or if he really didn't know. I knew, however, that what he was telling me was contrary to what the documents said."

Von Stein did not realize at that point that Eyre was the person inside Citibank who guided the audit and examining committees through their deliberations on the Edwards affair. Consequently, he failed to ask questions about how the committees made their appraisal of the Blue Book. Eyre did allow, however, that the Edwards case had heightened the attention Citibank paid to "making sure that we operate according to [local] regulations."[1]

From the transcripts one could feel the distrust building up between von Stein, successive Citibank witnesses, and the attorneys from Shearman & Sterling. The brunt of counseling Citibank witnesses on how to respond to the SEC questions fell on Henry Weisburg. The conflict between von Stein and Weisburg became increasingly open as the depositions—a score of them in the end, with several witnesses being called back for further examination—continued over the next few months. But already during Eyre's deposition, Weisburg accused von Stein of making "nasty and suggestive comments" off the record.[2]

After Eyre, the next witness was Arthur Natvig. The "inspector-general," then retired and living on the west coast of Florida, struck von Stein as a "nice guy" who "tried to be honest."

Natvig was the first Citibanker to admit the true purpose of parking. He confirmed that "management of parked positions remains with the originating branch."[3]

This was also reflected in Natvig's 1975 working papers, the Natvig/Pomeroy report, and his correspondence with Eyre. But Natvig's

---

[1] Stephen C. Eyre, testimony before the SEC, March 12, 1980, page 50.
[2] Ibid., p. 60.
[3] Arthur Natvig, testimony before the SEC March 18, 1980, page 253.

testimony clashed with Eyre's on this point. Eyre maintained that the originating branch was under no obligation to take back a parked position.

"I would say that if it suits the book of the originating branch to take it back, and if it suits the book of the holding branch to give it back, then that would happen and it would go back," the former comptroller had testifed.[4]

Natvig also confirmed that there were two basic purposes for parking: "To bring the position within the locally prescribed limit. The other, to transfer profit."

"Did the transfer of profit raise a question in your mind as to its propriety?" von Stein asked.

"Yes," Natvig replied flatly.[5]

In spite of his apparent candor, Natvig claimed not to know whether the Nassau branch had a foreign exchange trader. This struck von Stein as an odd omission for someone who had been in charge of foreign exchange audit control.[6] He asked Natvig if he had attempted to refresh his memory before giving evidence by rereading his 1975 work papers.

Natvig replied: "I haven't studied them or anything, if that's what you mean. Mr. Weisburg told me it was advisable not to."[7]

This was the only instance where Shearman & Sterling's strategy for preparing witnesses came through in the deposition transcripts. Ryan and von Stein were perplexed that Citibank executives who had such responsible positions could not remember so much. The faulty memory syndrome that characterized the deposition process hinted at a stonewalling conspiracy that nagged the two SEC attorneys throughout the proceedings, though they could never document its existence.

Robert Logan, who followed Natvig, defended parking, if properly done—i.e., at "market rates"—as an acceptable banking practice. The position taken by Logan, and most other senior Citibank officers who testified over the next few months, was that the question of control over the parked position was irrelevant because they maintained that economic risk passed with the position to the parking-lot branch. This argument was developed by Hoffman, and von Stein had great difficulty in countering it.

Logan claimed that Fritz Leutwiler, president of the Swiss National

---

[4] Eyre, testimony March 12, 1980, page 25.
[5] Natvig testimony, March 18, 1980, pages 26–29.
[6] Ibid., p. 33.
[7] Ibid., p. 34.

Bank, approved the concept. At a meeting they supposedly had in Zurich, Logan reported that Leutwiler said to him, "As long as [parking] transactions are at market rates, there is nothing we can do or say."[8]

According to Logan, the Swiss objected to only two transactions, completed in 1974, that were put on Zurich's books at off-market rates in order to transfer a $7.5 million profit out of Switzerland.[9]

It wasn't until the following day, when von Stein and Ryan took the evidence of Victor Lee, a clerk in the Eurocurrency department, and Ernst Brutsche, senior vice-president in the treasury division, that they began to feel they had been led down the garden path by other Citibank executives.

Victor Lee, whose name was used as a code to signify "special transactions" on incoming parking telexes, had joined Citibank in September 1976 as a trainee currency trader.

Lee was responsible for transposing the booking information from parking telexes onto "dealer's tickets," which he then sent to the operations unit for processing.

Lee's description of how the parking deals—he mentioned six to ten a day—came in from Europe, often overnight, and were recorded on the books of the Nassau branch, "was a real breakthrough," von Stein said.

Lee deciphered for von Stein the "Attention Victor Lee" telexes that instructed the Nassau desk how to book "special transactions" to make them look like bona fide trades between counterparties dealing at arm's length. Lee explained that no contractual arrangement existed between the originating branch and Nassau, that each parking transaction was simply a temporary accommodation enabling the originating branch to off-book a position without the Nassau branch having any say in the matter.

[8] The Swiss National Bank informed the author by letter of August 30, 1983, that "the statement alleged to have been made by Dr. F. Leutwiler, 'As long as the parking transactions are at market rates, there is nothing we can say,' cannot be documented."

[9] The transactions referred to by Logan were summarized in Citibank document 1047, which showed that the Zurich branch had record foreign exchange profits in 1974 of $24,813,000, of which $17,313,082 was booked locally and $7,499,918 was MIS'ed from Nassau. The same document summarized Zurich's parking profits for other years as follows:

YEAR	BOOKED LOCALLY	MIS	TOTAL
1975	$7,814,969	$1,641,031	$9,456,000
1976	5,219,005	1,001,995	6,221,000
1977	6,130,776	4,670,224	10,801,000
Jan. 1978	1,958,000	3,000,000	4,958,000
Feb. 1978	289,000	1,000,000	1,289,000

"Lee established that no real deal was cut between the parkor and the parkee," von Stein said.

That afternoon, Brutsche, who some months afterward was transferred to Bankhaus Trinkhaus & Burkhardt, a Citibank affiliate in Düsseldorf, which he ultimately left to become group treasurer for Midland Bank in London, explained his three criteria for parking.

First, parking had to be done on the limits of the initiating branch. Second, each parked deal had to have senof approval. Third, parked positions had to be booked and unbooked at market rates—by which he meant within the day's market range.

If these three criteria were not met, the Eurocurrency department could refuse to accept the transaction. Otherwise, acceptance was automatic.

Brutsche also pointed out that positions were never parked directly with Nassau.

Why not? von Stein asked.

"Because there is no trader there." [10]

---

[10] Ernst Brutsche, testimony before the SEC March 20, 1980, page 9.

Chapter 31

How Parking Really Worked

At off-market rates, which is not our policy, you could do all sorts of things.

—WALTER B. WRISTON, JULY 9, 1980

As far as von Stein was concerned, April 24, 1980, was the day that he and Ryan nailed down the Citicorp case. After a three-week lull in taking testimony, the two SEC investigators returned to New York City to depose the eleventh and twelfth Citibank witnesses, Ralph Buenaga, Jr., and Michael J. Treacy, two medium-level foreign exchange managers.

The documents had already told von Stein how the parking of foreign exchange positions was conceived and practiced at Citibank. The clearest early reference came from the minutes of a treasury conference in New York in September 1973. The three-day meeting was organized by Freeman Huntington; Wriston, Costanzo, and Theobald had attended various parts of it to address the men from the field.

During that meeting there was a discussion of parking. Huntington

272

asked that until he had discussed the tax implications with the lawyers, head office not be used as an off-booking center. Pending more formalized procedures, he said, "positions should be parked with Nassau."[1]

In practice, nothing was changed by this arrangement. Nassau was not staffed to book and unbook foreign exchange transactions. Nassau, as Ernst Brutsche had pointed out, had no traders. Two telexes sent in February 1974 by Jean-Michel Ennuyer in Paris to Paolo Cugnasca in New York clearly confirmed that by "Nassau," Huntington had meant the "Nassau desk" at head office.

The telexes read:

> 2/27/74 11:56 EDT
> 423712 FNCB UI
> [PARIS] HI HI PALS
> PAOLO IN PSE FOR JM ??? + +
> [NY] HE IS TIED UP AT THE MOM CAN U LEAVE A MESSAGE PSE + +
> [PARIS] YES PSE   IT IS CONCERNING A SPECIAL TRANSACTION WE MADE WITH [CITIBANK] NASSAU
> WE WOULD LIKE TO BUY BACK OUR 10 MIONS DOLLARS POSITION FROM YOU AT A RATE OF 4 8285
> WE KNOW THAT DUE TO SWAPS THE COST OF THE POSITION IS 5 3285 BUT FOR SOME REASONS I WILL EXPLAIN
> PAOLO WE WOULD LIKE TO BUY BACK THIS POSITION AT 4 8285 VALUE MARCH 1 1974
> THE AMOUNT IN FRANCS WILL BE DIFFERENT AND YOU WILL BE OVERDRAWN WITH US BUT WE WONT CHARGE YOU THE OVERDRAFT INTERESTS

ENNUYER CAME BACK AN HOUR AND A QUARTER LATER, ASKING FOR CUGNASCA AGAIN, HAVING HAD NO RESPONSE IN THE MEANTIME.

> [PARIS] HELLO FRIENDS
> PAOLO IN PSE + +
> [NY] HELLO THERE WHO IS THIS PSE + +
> [PARIS] JM FROM CITY PARIS + +
> [NY] OK YES ONE TIC WILL SEE IF HE IS HERE + +

[1] Minutes of Treasury Division Heads Conference, New York, September 5–7, 1973, Citibank document 5346–5354.

[PARIS]	TKS+
[NY]	CAN U LEAVE A MESSAGE HELL BE RIGHT HERE IN A FEW MOM++
[PARIS]	NO JUST TELL ME ON THE TELEX WHEN HE WILL BE BACK AND I LL CALL HIM ON THE FONE PSE
[NY]	HE IS HERE BUT TALKING TO SOMEONE SO HELL BE ABLE TO [ILLEGIBLE]
[PARIS]	DID YOU ALREADY SEND HIM MY PREVIOUS TELEX PSE
[NY]	CIAO JM I SAW IT
	THIS IS GOING TO CREATE A LOSS FOR NASSAU COR-RECT+
[PARIS]	YES BUT FOR FISCAL REASONS YOU UNDERSTAND THAT I CANNOT PAY THE SAME RATE
	SO FOR MAKING UP FOR THE LOSS WHAT DO YOU SUG-GEST
	A SWAP OR SOME LOANS AND BORROWINGS WITH YOU AT DIFFERENT RATES++
[NY]	WELL I THINK THIS HAS TO BE DISCUSSED FIRST WITH SENIOR MGMT AS IT IS UNDESIRABLE FOR TAX PURPOSES TO HAVE LOSSES IN NASSAU
	I THINK A SWAP SHOULD BE THE BEST ALTERNATIVE HOWEVER AS A SWAP AT A FALSE RATE AND A SPOT AT THE WRONG MKT PRICE ARE THE SAME THING AS FAR AS EVENTUAL CONTROLS ARE CONCERNED I DONT SEE THE POINT
[PARIS]	WELL I LL DISCUSS TOMORROW THIS POINT BUT FOR THE TIME BEING WE BOUGHT BACK OUR POSITION AND DO NOT MIND FOR THE DIFFERENCE OF FRENCH FRANCS WHICH WILL APPEAR IN OUR BOOKS WE EVIDENTLY WILL COVER AND DO NOT CHARGE YOU INTERESTS FOR THE 5 MIONS FRANCS SHORT WITH US OK??
[NY]	BEFORE MY OPENING TOMORROW I WOULD APPRECIATE A TELEX DETAILING A SWAP TRANSACTION WHICH WILL OFFSET THE LOSS ON NASSAU S BOOKS+
[PARIS]	OK 6 MONTHS OK FOR YOU OR LONGER OR SHORTER ??++
[NY]	PREFERABLY SHORTER BUT I LEAVE IT UP TO YOU +
[PARIS]	OK TKS PAOLO[2]

[2]Citibank document 7061–7064

Von Stein understood from these telex conversations that Cugnasca and Ennuyer were discussing various methods for redirecting profits. He noted that the next day Ennuyer furnished the Nassau desk with the details of a swap transaction offsetting the loss on Nassau's books.

With the increase in Citibank's foreign exchange trading in 1974, Huntington attempted to improve the parking procedures. In July 1975 he circulated a draft of the new procedures to the treasury heads at the Amsterdam, Brussels, Frankfurt, London, Milan, Paris, and Zurich branches, authorizing them to park positions with the Nassau desk *without prior consultation.*

Once again, under these procedures, parking would be allowed with head office in New York. This was because some European treasury heads had protested that frequent use of a tax-haven counterparty might cause bank inspectors to look more closely at these arrangements. As an added safety feature, the new procedures also included use of a "formatted" telex, which began with a code word to alert the staff in New York that it was a "special transaction."

Natvig had reservations about Huntington's proposal, which he discussed with Brutsche. First, it was unclear what head office was supposed to do with the parked positions once received. He assumed head office in turn would off-book them at Nassau as separate deals, using exactly the same rates. Second, he observed that Huntington's draft instructions to the treasury heads stated: "*If* it is subsequently in your interest to repurchase such a position please dispatch a telex substantially in the form" of the recommended model.

"This gives the idea that the branch has some option, but in fact if the branch is responsible for the position it *must* repurchase it (or else separately arrange with HO to remove the position from the category of branch-risk positions)," he told Brutsche.[3]

The notion of "branch-risk positions" was interesting, because it seemed to confirm what von Stein suspected but Shearman & Sterling denied: that control of parked positions, as well as economic risk, remained with the branch that initiated the parking.

Brutsche confirmed that the "If" was just a mistake. "We will regard these positions as separate, and they *must* be reversed," he assured Natvig.[4]

Parking remained a serious audit-control problem, as Natvig and Pomeroy pointed out in their survey of European treasuries, and in

[3] Citibank document 2194; emphasis in the original.
[4] Ibid.

December 1975 Huntington issued a memo assigning Cugnasca to a special unit inside the Eurocurrency department with the task of establishing a "control mechanism for handling positions transferred to Head Office on a temporary basis by overseas branches."[5]

A copy of this memo went to Don Howard, who was regarded internally as Wriston's adjutant. Howard was an executive vice-president and the bank's chief financial officer, in overall charge of foreign exchange trading. He had received a copy of the Natvig/Pomeroy Survey of European Treasuries and Natvig had discussed with him recommendations for making parking harder to detect.[6]

Howard, accompanied by both Danforth Newcomb and Henry Weisburg, had given his testimony to von Stein and Ryan on March 27, 1980. At first he had claimed not to know what the term *parking* meant. He testified that Citibank's internal overnight position limits for Frankfurt, London, Paris, and Zurich conformed with local central bank limits. He testified that to his knowledge, no portion of Citibank Zurich's overnight position limits had ever been run through New York. He testified that a Citibank trader in Nassau could refuse to deal if he didn't like the rates given by Citibank's European traders. He testified that the Nassau branch was no different from other Citibank branches dealing in the foreign exchange market.

In late 1975 Cugnasca had drafted his parking manual, which he circulated to Howard as well as to European treasury heads. The manual was explicit: parking was done "either to comply with local regulatory requirements, or to transfer (taxable) profits generated abroad to a tax-haven area." It added:

> The responsibility for the management of these positions lies with the Parking Branch. Nassau Branch (i.e., the Nassau desk at Head Office) is advised by the Parking Branch of the contracts to be booked when the position is open and closed.

The manual included a new model for a formatted telex, and listed the numbers of three telex machines assigned to the Nassau desk in New York that the European branches were to use exclusively for transmitting their parking instructions.

The Shearman & Sterling report stated that the treasury heads had

[5]Memorandum to Department Heads, International Money Market Dvision, from Freeman H. Huntington, December 4, 1975; Citibank document 7925.
[6]Letter from Arthur Natvig to Stephen C. Eyre, October 2, 1975; Citibank document 1846–1849.

reservations about Cugnasca's manual and it was never adopted. Their justification for reporting this was that on April 7, 1976, Huntington told Cugnasca to hold the manual in his files.[7] Parking messages, however, began to flow through the three machines indicated in the manual, which suggested that at least some of its procedures were adopted.

The major flaw in Cugnasca's work was the design of a foreign currency control ledger. Soon after its inauguration, the system was paralyzed by chaos. Nassau and New York were supposed to keep parallel ledgers. New York would make the entries onto its control ledger as the transactions came in from Europe and then instruct Nassau what entries to make on its books. But the dual set of books, as Natvig and Cugnasca later explained (but not to von Stein), never tallied.

Although Nassau served as the booking center for all South American dollar loans, it was a relatively small branch, counting in 1976 approximately one hundred employees. Efforts were constantly made to upgrade the branch, but the upgrading never kept pace with the growth in demand for the branch's services. The Bahamian authorities, by their restrictive immigration policy, were partly to blame. They were loath to issue work permits to foreigners, as local unemployment was high. Natvig had testified that he supposed Citibank Nassau had a foreign exchange trader. "I never really knew," he claimed. But he must have known very well. Shortly before his retirement in March 1976, he was sent there to figure out what had gone wrong with Cugnasca's booking operation.

Nassau had no traders, as Brutsche stated. The bookkeeping staff was another matter. "They were local Bahamians and they kept putting things in the wrong columns. They didn't have much of a notion about accounting and couldn't have cared less. Some even came to work with six-packs of beer. It was a mess," Natvig later said.[8]

The problems with the Nassau branch were so bad that Citibank's chief accountant in Frankfurt had gone there as well to attempt to straighten them out. On the first reporting date, the head bookkeeper—"who had an 'Afro' out to his shoulders"—informed him that the month-end reconciliations were out by around $250 million. After hours of checking the entries, they were still unable to reconcile the accounts. Finally, the head bookkeeper suggested adding a line to

[7] Citibank document 7107.
[8] Interview with the author, November 10, 1983.

the month-end report that read: "Due from banks—$250 million." The accountant from Frankfurt, according to Cugnasca, almost went through the ceiling.

Citibank's traditional response to "rocks"—Citispeak for bottle-necks—in the system was to throw men and money at them. Ralph Buenaga was one of these rock removers. He was transferred to the Eurocurrency department in May 1976, at a time when both routes for parking were still in use. (Some European branches preferred to park through the head office trading room and have head office do the off-booking at Nassau, while others used the "Nassau desk," having no qualms about showing a tax-haven address as a counter-party.)

The choice of parkees only ended in July 1977, when Huntington and Logan issued their "tidying-up" letter. It instructed parkors to use the "Nassau desk," which they renamed International Foreign Exchange & Funding. Buenaga, whose testimony was scheduled for the April 24 morning session, gave evidence about the mechanics of parking after July 1977. Treacy, who was deposed that afternoon, testified about the parking procedures in force before the 1977 changes.

Buenaga appeared to von Stein as the archetype of a middle-level banking executive. He commuted to work each day from Red Bank, New Jersey, and had a master's degree in economics from New York University. Nothing about him stood out except his honesty. He had joined the management science department—an operations research unit—in 1966. He succeeded Cugnasca as manager of the Eurocurrency department. His desk was located on the fringes of the fourth-floor trading room at 399 Park Avenue. In addition to handling parking arrangements, his department was responsible for funding Eurocurrency loans that were booked through Nassau.

In spite of frequent objections, interruptions, and arguments by Henry Weisburg during the deposition of Buenaga, which von Stein interpreted as attempts to put the cork back in the bottle, during his three hours of testimony Buenaga unveiled the real nuts and bolts of parking.

"We [the Nassau desk] always dealt with Citibank branches. We never dealt with outside banks," he explained.[9] He confirmed that the parking telexes came in from the European treasuries with the instructions "Please book for us . . ." giving details and rates for the positions they wanted parked in Nassau.

Because of the difference in time zones, the parking instructions

---

[9]Ralph Buenaga, Jr., testimony before the SEC, April 24, 1980, page 30.

often landed in New York in the middle of the night and were only taken off the telex machines the following morning. Buenaga assigned a trainee, Victor Lee (and sometimes Robert Wexler), to watch the three machines and see that each transaction was properly processed.

Buenaga explained that for every deal received, Lee or Wexler made out a deal ticket and sent it to the operations unit. "We, representing Nassau, would have to write up a deal ticket. Every booking transaction has to have a deal ticket, otherwise it won't get recorded." [10]

In addition to transcribing them on the tickets, Lee also recorded the deals on a control sheet, showing the open positions.

Most interbank foreign exchange trading was done by phone, he said. But parking deals were *always* done by telex, never by phone. That was one of the distinguishing features of parking.

The operations unit wrote up confirmations for each parking transaction. The confirmations were batched together and sent out by mail at the end of the day. The actual booking instructions were telexed (or telefaxed) to Nassau all at one time, usually in the late afternoon.

Buenaga also said that Nassau did not have the authority to close out a position on its own. "The management responsibility [for parked positions] was with the [European] branches and it was their decision," he affirmed. [11]

Buenaga, temporarily, went to the top of von Stein's popularity poll. He was replaced in the number-one spot that afternoon by assistant vice-president Mike Treacy, a seasoned trading room pro, one of the few who hadn't burned out before the age of thirty-five.

The afternoon session began at 2:30 P.M., and for the next three hours von Stein and Ryan heard how parking had worked before 1977, when the transactions were routed through the head office trading room. The witness came across as very humble, and he spoke with a hint of an Irish brogue. He had a master's degree in business administration from New York University, class of '49. He had been with the bank for thirty-three years and had worked as a trader since 1952. "I guess I've traded really every currency in the world at one time or another," he said.

The parking telexes that came in from Europe were usually dropped on his desk by a clerk. The first time it happened, his boss called across the room: "Hey, Mike, make up those contracts," and so the

[10] Ibid., p. 109.
[11] Ibid., p. 51.

task of processing them fell to him, almost by default. He said it started in about 1972, and he found it an imposition.

"When you got a [parking] telex would you immediately write up the contract?" von Stein asked.

"No. If I got a telex, say, in the morning, let's say in the middle of our trading session somebody dropped one on my desk that, say, would require sixteen contracts, well, I'd just put it off to one side and do my trading. Then sometime in the afternoon I'd get to it."

Treacy would enter them as "special transactions" in the trading room's records. "[T]hey were all washes, and they were all washed out," he said. By that, he meant that New York received the parking instructions from Europe, recorded them on its books and then "passed" them to Nassau using the same rates so that no profit or loss showed in New York.

While "washes" they were, the way Treacy described them, the paper trail stopped dead in New York. No funds were actually transferred to Nassau. It was all done on accounting ledgers at head office.

After writing up the contracts, Treacy would have Mae Flynn, the trading room secretary, type a memo in his name to Freeman Huntington requesting approval for the deals, even though they were already booked.

Although Treacy did not mention it—von Stein didn't ask—this procedure was started by Jack Conlin after returning from vacation in 1972. Conlin, who was head of the foreign exchange trading department at head office from 1970 to 1976, found the first parking transactions had been parked with his department on behalf of Brussels during his absence. As Treacy had handled them, Conlin asked who had given him clearance.

Huntington, Treacy replied.

Conlin went to see Huntington. Since writing the tickets for each of these "trades" was time consuming, and the "trades" themselves were of no value to the New York foreign exchange desk, Conlin resented having to handle them.

Huntington instructed Conlin to continue booking them as normal transactions. Because he was given no choice, Conlin complied, but he didn't like it. He ordered Treacy to cover each parking deal with a memo indicating that it had been authorized by Huntington.[12]

---

[12] Conlin remained opposed to parking and was replaced as head of the foreign exchange department in New York in November 1976, after refusing to expand his dealing staff from a dozen to forty traders. "Brutsche wanted Citibank to lead the market in New York," he said. "I told him it couldn't be done." Conlin said he would be unable to supervise forty traders, that it was unsafe from a control point of view, and that the market in New York was too large for any one bank to lead. In March 1977, at fifty-five, Conlin elected to accept early retirement.

The memos, addressed to Huntington, became formatted. A typical one would read:

MEMORANDUM TO: Mr. F. H. Huntington
                      Senior Vice President

Please approve the following special transactions booked at the request of Citibank Milan, per attached cable.

Citibank New York buys from Citibank Nassau $10 million against Lire at 853.675 value June 22, 1976.

Citibank New York sells same amount, same rate and same value to Citibank Milan.

Citibank New York buys from Citibank Milan $10 million against Lire at 868.675 value July 22, 1976.

Citibank New York sells same amount, same rate and same value to Citibank Nassau.

                                          Michael J. Treacy
                                          Assistant Vice President

June 18, 1976[13]

Treacy said that at one point he was receiving anywhere up to sixteen parking transactions a day.

"But keep in mind," he added, "that this is a sort of a supplementary part of my job and it's something that is an onerous task, really. Say in a day you write up sixteen contracts. You have to check every one of those contracts."

Treacy explained that the "approval" memos went to Huntington with a copy that the head of IMMD was supposed to initial and return for Treacy to enter into his file. The memos all came back, but Treacy couldn't remember if any were actually signed by Huntington. The ones Pomeroy collected from the file when assembling material for the Shearman & Sterling investigation had not been initialed. When asked if Huntington ever disapproved a transaction, Treacy was formal. "Never," he said.

Ryan reverted for a moment to the theme of transaction approval. "When you prepared the contracts and wrote the memo to Mr. Huntington, did you also check the market price of the currencies to make sure that is the market price?" he asked.

---

[13] Citibank document 0079A. This particular memo was sent to Huntington only days before he flew to Paris for his heart-to-heart talk with David Edwards. At that meeting, according to Edwards, Huntington professed that he was more or less ignorant about parking.

"No," Treacy replied. "If it appeared to be off the market or something, that didn't concern me."

"Would it be possible for one of the European branches to deliberately take a loss on the transaction, let's say by shading the rates . . . so as just to put a profit in Nassau and take a profit out of its own branch?"

"Sure it would. It's possible."

Control procedure was picked up again by von Stein. "Do you recall it ever happening," he asked, "that somebody in your department checked to see whether or not the rates on the parking telex that was coming in were good market rates?"

"No."

"As of the time?"

"No. No, you really would just put these things through, and as I say, if some rate looked like it was some rate for another currency or something, then I would feel that, you know, it was my duty to say, 'Hey, did you make a mistake here on this? This rate isn't for Belgian francs, it's for something else.' "

"Something was out of the ball park?"

"Yeah. Way out . . ."

From the stack in front of him, von Stein picked out a document representing that at one point in August 1977 the London branch had a £4 million position parked in New York. He showed it to Treacy.

"Was this position then put in Nassau, to your knowledge?" von Stein asked.

"No, it was put right in our own books. Put in our own books and then taken out the next day."

"Well . . . let me read it with you. Document states, 'Attached contract represents Citibank London's position of four million pounds which has been parked with us. With contract dated August 16, '77, we buy four million pounds from Citibank London at the rate of 1.74, value August 18, '77. With contract dated August 17th we sell four million pounds to Citibank at rate of 1.74 value August 18, 1977.' Two contracts are being described, are they not?"

"Right."

"One of those contracts is dated the day after the memo is written. Is that correct?"

"Um-huh. Right."

"Is that a common way of doing a foreign exchange deal?"

"Is that—you'll have to repeat that."

"Yeah," agreed Henry Weisburg.

"Is it usual that you will write up a contract a day before the contract date?"

"Is that usual?" Treacy asked back.

"Yes," von Stein prompted.

"No, it's not usual."

"Were you aware that this was done in the case of the London parked position? For a period of time in '77? By Citibank?"

"Yes."

"Do you know the purpose of the transaction described on [document] 6499?"

"Why it was done this way? No, I don't know."

"Do you know what the transaction was?"

"It was done at the same rate. It goes in and out at the same price. So, for us, it was an absolute wash. Why, you mean, they did that?"

"No profit or loss?"

"Yeah. Absolute wash. Goes in at 1.74; goes out at 1.74. That's nothing."

"[On] August 16th, 1977, can you tell that the rate on August 17th, 1977, is going to be 1.74?"

"No."

". . . Do you have any idea why the contract would be written the day before the contract date?"

"He wanted to be sure that they would [not] forget to put that through, because the four million pounds goes into the trader's position today, he wants to be sure that it's taken out first thing in the morning."

"During 1977 did you have occasion to trade pounds sterling?"

"No."

"Do you know what a normal daily fluctuation would be in pounds? Or was?"

"In '77? I don't know. Half a cent."

"Don't guess," Weisburg instructed. "I mean, if you know, you know."

"Yeah," Treacy agreed.

"Yeah what?" Ryan wanted to know. "You're guessing or you know?"

"Well, I have the impression that you were just guessing," Weisburg said, trying to lead the witness back onto firm ground.

"I'm guessing," Treacy said.

"These gentlemen don't want you to guess," Weisburg admonished him.

"Right," Treacy said.

"Nor do I," Weisburg added.

"Educated guesses aren't bad," Ryan suggested.

Before signing off, von Stein asked one last question: "Have you ever seen a memo from Mr. Theobald which described three . . . principles or rules for foreign exchange trading? It was sometime in the last couple of years. Maybe the last three years."

Several senior-management witnesses had referred in their testimony to Theobald's "three principles," and von Stein was intrigued because nobody ever gave the same three principles.

"Rules for foreign exchange trading?" Treacy repeated.

"Yes. It's been referred to as a listing of three principles of foreign exchange trading. Have you ever heard of anything like that?"

"I don't recall it, but if you have a copy I could tell you right away."

"I'm dying to get a copy," said von Stein.[14]

The record was closed at 5:21 P.M. Sporkin's investigators were pleased. At last they had a description of how parking really worked, including the "batching" of contracts for transmission to Nassau, with the deals coming in from Europe in the morning and New York waiting until the afternoon to let Nassau know.

What Buenaga and Treacy, the two parking mechanics, told them in no way resembled what Fouraker, Theobald, and Wriston would tell them in testimony over the next four weeks. It also contradicted what Shearman & Sterling had told European counsel about parking almost two years previously.

[14] Excerpted from testimony of Michael J. Treacy before the SEC, April 24, 1980; pages 50–67.

Chapter 32

Fouraker and Theobald

"When I make a word do a lot of work like that," said Humpty Dumpty, "I always pay it extra."

—LEWIS CARROLL, *Through the Looking Glass*

On Monday, May 12, 1980, von Stein and Ryan returned to the Shearman & Sterling offices in New York to take the testimony of Dr. Lawrence Fouraker, who had just completed a ten-year term as dean of the Harvard Business School. Although von Stein had talked to him over the phone before, it was his first meeting with Fouraker. He found the professor, originally from Colorado, to be a tall, bluff man with a self-assured air.

The session began at 2 P.M. To the surprise of the SEC investigators, Fouraker was accompanied by John Hoffman. Henry Weisburg trailed behind. And behind him came a paralegal, Ms. Ruth Raymond. Fouraker was the only witness to be represented by Hoffman throughout the entire proceedings.

In the introductory questioning, Fouraker said he had been a Citicorp director for ten years and that he had been a member of the audit committee or its predecessor during all of that time. He professed not to have heard of the term *parking* in its foreign exchange context until he received the Edwards Blue Book.

"I had a general understanding of the nature of the transactions," Fouraker volunteered. "As an economist, I know how foreign exchange markets work and I have some idea of the movement of those markets with the sun around the world and the necessity of financial institutions to maintain continuous interchange, but I had not heard the specific term *parking* applied to any of those transactions, to my knowledge."[1]

Fouraker was repeating litany dear to the heart of Walter Wriston. The March 1979 edition of *Executive,* a monthly published by Cornell's Graduate School of Business Administration, quoted the Citicorp chairman as saying:

> As far as parking . . . is concerned, you can say that's an artificial transaction; but then you have to say it's artificial that the sun rises in the east and sets in the west. The foreign exchange market goes on twenty-four hours a day, and there may be a bank that doesn't hand its position off from London to New York to San Francisco to Singapore to Bahrain and then back to London—but I've never heard of one.
>
> We coined a sexy word called parking, in which you did hand the positions off. This had the effect of increasing U.S. taxes. We handle about four million transactions every day in a hundred countries. If you ask me whether some of them were wrong, I would say on an actuarial basis they had to be. Did we do something wrong intentionally? The answer is no.

This "handing-off" was a mischaracterization of parking as described by Natvig, Lee, Brutsche, Buenaga, and Treacy, although it may have been an accurate portrayal of how Wriston viewed the practice. Jack Conlin, who spent eighteen years in Citibank's foreign exchange trading room in New York, also was puzzled by Wriston's statement. He later remarked, "If Walt had asked me, I could have told him that from 1948 to 1976 Citibank never moved its foreign exchange positions" in this manner.

Von Stein didn't challenge Fouraker on it; he was interested in learning whether the professor thought parking was conducted at arm's length. Fouraker testified that Eyre had told him parking was an inevitable aspect of foreign exchange trading and that if done at

---

[1] Lawrence E. Fouraker, testimony before the SEC, May 12, 1980, pages 6–7.

arm's length, there was nothing wrong with it.

"What did you understand Eyre to mean by the phrase 'arm's length'?" von Stein inquired.

"That would mean transactions undertaken at 'market rates.' You have, inescapably, almost endless financial transactions among branches of an international bank. They're buying and selling currencies on contracts continuously. I have seen foreign exchange departments in operation and it's a very hectic experience. They are continuously involved in transactions with other banks, with branches of their own bank and with customers and it is in no way an improper transaction to have a sale or a purchase of . . . currency with another branch of the bank. As a matter of fact, it is very necessary."[2]

That was fine as far as it went, von Stein decided, but Fouraker had not answered the question. Moreover, the interbranch transactions Fouraker was attempting to describe had nothing to do with parking. He pressed for more detail: "Did Mr. Eyre indicate to you that if a transaction was done . . . at 'market rates' . . . this would mean that it was an arm's-length transaction?"

"There is a rough correlation, I think, between a trade at 'market rates' and 'arm's length.' That is, it's a trade that would occur with any other trader. . . . It's obviously improper, as . . . the Shearman & Sterling report indicates, to make a transaction outside of the market for purposes of transferring profits from one branch to another. . . ."

"Was there anything else beside a transaction being done at 'market rates' that you understood Mr. Eyre to mean when he used the phrase 'arm's length'?"

"That's the substance of it."

"At 'market rates'?"

"Yes."[3]

Fouraker, an eminent authority on business terms and practices, had just redefined "at arm's length," giving it a most permissive Citibank definition tailored to the situation. Digging further, von Stein asked: "When you first began to understand what 'parking' was in the context of Citibank foreign exchange dealings, did you understand that any particular branch was the normal, or inevitable, or usual booking branch?"

"I knew that Nassau handled a very large volume of exchanges

[2]Ibid., p. 18.
[3]Ibid., p. 20.

with European offices in particular. We had all sorts of problems [there]."

"You mean foreign exchange transactions?"

"Foreign exchange transactions. We had spent a good bit of time on the Nassau branch because they had difficulty in maintaining all the records involved in this large volume of business. Ultimately, I think, those transactions are booked and the records are kept in New York."[4]

Fouraker attempted to explain how seriously he took his responsibilities as a board member. Rather than rely on written reports or presentations to the board to form a judgment of Citicorp's operations, he said he often went into the field to see for himself.

"It was my practice—particularly in this period when I was chairman of these committees—to call on branches outside of the United States when I was there on other business . . . or on vacation, or for any reason, and I would normally spend a half day, or a day if it was a large branch, and go over the operations of that branch, particular problems they would have, opportunities they saw and try to meet as many of the officers as I could as a regular practice. . . . And I did that in, I would guess, several dozen instances in the five- or six-year period."

"Do you recall doing that with London?"

"I did it with London three or four times."

"From '75 through '78?"

"Yes, yes. . . ." And he explained that the last time in London he had spoken to the ACO about the Edwards allegations "because London is such an important area of the foreign exchange transactions."

And what did the ACO tell you? von Stein asked.

"He called in their chief trader, I believe a man named Redi, and I talked with him at length about the charges. We went into their foreign exchange room. I talked to some of the traders."

Redi, Fouraker testified, explained that London parked in order "to maintain a position in a currency after that market closed."

"Couldn't a man maintain a position in the currency after the market closed simply by buying it and keeping it on his book?" von Stein suggested.

"It depends on the local exchange rules and regulations, and they vary enormously from sovereign to sovereign."

[4] Ibid., p. 27.

"I see. In that case, when he said he wanted to maintain a position after the market closed, did he say that he wanted to maintain a position . . . greater than the local regulations permitted?"

If the local regulations placed a zero limit, as he affirmed some did, Fouraker said it was normal for the bank to retain the position by transferring it to another branch. He admitted that "in the aggregate" this might not seem consistent with the local exchange control regulations, but "it was my understanding from Mr. Redi that that had been reviewed by the Bank of England and by the monetary authorities who regulated and audited their transactions and found . . . to be appropriate."

". . . Well, what else can you recall that Redi told you about the Edwards allegations?"

"I think he was reassuring that this was a normal part of the transactions of a foreign exchange trader."

"Did Redi tell you that the Bank of England had reviewed the matter?"

"He assured me that they were under constant surveillance of the monetary authorities in England, as they are in all European countries, and this was not viewed as being an unusual or improper practice."

"By the authorities?"

"Yes."

"Did he indicate to you that the Bank of England was aware that Citibank London did park positions through New York in Nassau or with the New York office of Citibank?"

"The Bank of England examiners would have access to all of the transactions of the London office, and it would certainly be aware of any such exchanges as a normal practice."

"Well, is this your opinion or Redi's opinion or what?"

"I think it was both. It was my opinion after I had investigated this practice."

"But did Redi tell you flat out that the Bank of England was aware that Citibank London was parking positions with New York or with Nassau or whatever?"

"The impression that I had from Mr. Redi was that there was nothing illegal or improper or unwise about such a transaction, if done at arm's length, that is at market prices."

"But address yourself to my question, please. Did Redi say that the Bank of England was aware of this practice, good or bad, whatever? Did he?"

"I certainly had the impression that the Bank of England was aware of the practice, yes."

"After your conversation with Redi?"

"Yes. Yes"

"And from your conversation with Redi?"

"Yes."

"Did you also have the impression from your conversation with Redi that the Bank of England thought it was proper?"

"Yes."[5]

Throughout this exchange, Hoffman had not said a word. He hardly was in a position to tell Fouraker, his client, that English counsel was of a contrary view. Coward Chance, the London solicitors, had warned Shearman & Sterling two years before that the parking of sterling positions appeared to be a deliberate violation of Bank of England regulations. Von Stein was not aware of this detail either, as Hoffman had refused to turn over to the SEC the 1978 opinions of foreign counsel on grounds that they were privileged.

Von Stein questioned Fouraker again about the depth of his knowledge of parking. He learned, for example, that the dean had never seen the Natvig/Pomeroy report. Nor had Fouraker's curiosity been raised by the Cugnasca parking manual, even though a copy of it was included in the Blue Book. In fact, he admitted never having seen most of the base data for the Sherman & Sterling report.

But he had been to Zurich and talked with the ACO there. He remembered that because Larry Kramer of *The Washington Post* had just been through the Swiss banking center and reported that Citibank might have to pay $50 million in Swiss back taxes as a result of its parking from Zurich.[6]

"It was entirely spurious," Fouraker fumed, "a number he had arrived at by calling an officer of the bank, who said, 'I can't tell you what the number is, obviously, because we are negotiating with the Swiss authorities.'

"And Larry said—I've known Larry; he was a Harvard Business

[5] Ibid., pp. 32–38.

[6] "Banks Fear Swiss Probe Will Widen," *The Washington Post*, December 22, 1978. Fouraker was offended by the second and third paragraphs. They stated: "Earlier this week bank sources reported that Citibank might owe as much as $50 million in back taxes because of questionable international currency transactions.

"A well-informed source close to the case here said today that although the $50 million figure may be 'exaggerated,' the Swiss authorities are now investigating far more serious currency control and banking violations that grew out of [an] audit, conducted for the bank by Peat, Marwick, Mitchell & Co."

School graduate and was the editor of our newspaper at the school, and he's a darned good business reporter, but reporters are apt to be motivated by a need to have coverage and get a good headline—and as I understand the conversation between the two of them, Larry said, 'Well, is it a hundred million?'

"And the man said, 'Oh no, Larry, you're way out of the ball park. It's nothing like a hundred million.'

"And then Larry put in fifty million, which was equally as unreliable and that stirred up the Swiss authorities to the extent that, according to the ACO in Zurich, he had been the recipient of a substantial amount of increased activity from the central bank but I think we assured them that it was nothing like fifty million dollars."[7]

Fouraker was candid about giving the Blue Book short shrift. He never bothered to read the four examples of parking included by Edwards in the book. "My general impression of all that material was that these were examples that he alleged involved transfer of profits from one branch to another at artificial rates," he said.

"Did you or the audit and examining committees ever instruct anybody, namely Peat Marwick or Shearman and Sterling or the comptroller's division, or anybody else, to analyze the transactions?. . . ."

"That was part of the request we made to Shearman and Sterling in their organization of the investigation. Now the basic issue there, as I understand it, is that 'parking' at arm's length is an entirely legal and appropriate, even necessary transaction. Like any other appropriate, desirable, and necessary transaction, it can be used improperly, and at variance with regulations, both of the bank and of the local law."

Fouraker maintained that Shearman & Sterling had investigated "literally thousands of transactions, perhaps even hundreds of thousands" and found there were some instances when non-market rates were used which "seemed to be motivated by a purpose other than normal coverage of risk" and "we asked the bank to review its practices in that area and make certain that the practices were consistent with local law, and that was not a . . . request. That was a directive."[8]

Hoffman broke his silence to help Fouraker over the hurdle of whether Zurich's transfer of $1 million to Nassau via a series of foreign exchange contracts was ever investigated, stating that it was

---

[7]Fouraker testimony, pp. 40–41.
[8]Ibid., p. 52.

covered on page 39 of the Shearman & Sterling report.

"You're quite familiar, I'm sure Mr. Ryan is too, with the scenario approach that we took in putting our study together, and this particular one, I think, probably falls roughly with scenario one, variation seven, as described in our report and as commented on to the board," Hoffman said.

"Now we did not undertake to try to get into a dialogue with a missing player, namely Mr. Edwards, and deal specifically with his characterizations and mischaracterizations. Our assignment was to find out what the facts were and then to advise on the implications of those, and that we did," he added.[9]

Von Stein ignored Hoffman's interruption. Shearman & Sterling had refused to produce copies of the scenarios, and so he was unable to comment on whether Zurich's transfer of profits had been accurately portrayed under the scenario variation that Hoffman mentioned but didn't describe. Von Stein was confident that no adequate description of Zurich's profit-transferring techniques appeared in the Shearman & Sterling report, and this he considered misdisclosure.

The closest the report came to acknowledging that Zurich engaged in profit-transferring was a general admission that "Zurich has entered into transactions of the basic pattern [i.e., scenario one], sometimes at rates which have not been within the prevailing market range." The report added: "The rate used on the contracts may have been above or below the prevailing market range. Any profit or loss resulting from a difference in rates would be recorded on the transferee Branch's books, and Zurich would receive an appropriate MIS."[10]

Von Stein persisted in questioning Fouraker on whether he knew about the $1 million in trading profits that Zurich had transferred to Nassau at the end of 1976.

"We had discussion of this general range of issues," he said. "The exact amount and aggregate I do not remember as being a million dollars because that was given to us as an aggregate figure."

"I'm sorry?"

"Well, the amount that was transferred was much more than a half-million dollars. I'm quite certain of that."

When pressed further, he said he thought that during the five years covered by the Shearman & Sterling review, Zurich had transferred "a sizeable amount" to Nassau through "questionable transac-

[9]Ibid., p. 57.
[10]Shearman & Sterling Report to the Audit Committee of Citicorp and the Examining Committee of Citibank, November 20, 1978, pp. 39–40.

tions"—in the range of five to six million dollars, he finally ventured.

"Mr. von Stein, let me say this, and perhaps I haven't made this clear, that the clear impression that the committees had of these transactions that involved transfer of profits from one branch to another were that these were aberrations. They were of the nature of needles in the haystack of transactions that were looked at. There was no pattern that we could discern of systematic deliberate uses of that device of 'parking' as a device to minimize taxes in one country and maximize them in another. These are a handful of transactions."

"Fine. Let me point out to you . . . that for 1977, according to document 1569, the foreign exchange earnings booked locally [for Zurich] were $6.1 million and [there was] a MIS credit for another $4.67 million. . . . Did you ever learn during [your] investigation that something in the nature of . . . forty-five percent of the total [1977] foreign exchange earnings for Switzerland were earnings represented by MIS credits [i.e., off-booked in Nassau]?"

Fouraker admitted he did not know the breakdown "of these numbers in this way." Then he tried to extricate himself by claiming, "MIS—right. Has relatively little importance to regulatory authorities because it's essentially an internal management score-keeping device and its relationship to overall profits as defined legally is at best a tenuous one as far as I know. It would be almost as appropriate to call those 'beans' or 'stars' or—whatever." [11]

Finally von Stein maneuvered Fouraker into giving his understanding of the mechanics of parking. Fouraker, after all, had painted himself as an expert in foreign exchange, having visited trading rooms and talked with "various trading officers" in the Citibank network.

"I think," he said, that parking "is a standard transaction where a trader would pick up the telephone and call his counterpart and say, 'What's your quote on dollars,' and he'd say, 'I want to buy or sell one million dollars.' Then he hangs up the telephone and answers his other telephone and he's doing this continuously all day long. These are enormously demanding jobs. People burn out at about age thirty-five. . . ."

"Well, is it your belief that the Zurich trader, when he wished to park a position in Nassau, would call up and ask for quotes from the New York trader?"

"That would be my understanding of a normal transaction." [12]

[11] Fouraker testimony, pages 63–64.
[12] Ibid., pp. 72; 75.

It was then after 5 P.M.—they had been at it for more than three hours—and Hoffman announced that time was up.

"I just don't think that's right to cut off like that. I have more questions," von Stein protested.

Hoffman ignored him.

"I do not force a man to stay here if you're taking him out," von Stein remarked, but he was peeved at Hoffman's arrogance.

Fouraker made a short closing statement praising the Citibank staff and Shearman & Sterling for their diligence. "I have had experience as a director in a number of situations of this sort. I know of few cases that have been disposed of and implemented as thoroughly as this one."

"That will close the record," von Stein said. He intended to request Fouraker's appearance at a later date.

The two SEC attorneys were back in the Shearman & Sterling offices on Friday, May 16, 1980, to take the testimony of Thomas Theobald. The session began at 9:15 A.M. Theobald was accompanied by Danforth Newcomb and Henry Weisburg.

The tenor was set in the opening minutes, when von Stein asked if parking had ever been a topic of discussion in the bank's policy committee, of which Theobald was a member. The future vice-chairman's reply was startling: "I don't know what you mean by 'parking' of foreign exchange positions. It's not a term that is a standardized definition of anything."

Von Stein immediately brought out the Shearman & Sterling report—which Natvig had referred to in his testimony as "that little slick booklet"—and read the definition of parking which appeared on page 11:

> In the context of the foreign exchange business, parking is loosely used to refer to the transfer of a specific position from one branch of an organization to another branch of that organization located in a different country, where the position is maintained so that it may later be transferred back to the first branch, or to a third location.

Theobald corrected himself. Although head of the international banking group, with its 27,000 employees, he said he had not been aware of position parking by foreign exchange traders until the Shearman & Sterling report was issued. He added that he had no recollection of parking having been discussed at his November 1977 meetings with Edwards or at any other time. Von Stein tried another approach.

"I had previously been told that you had enunciated three principles relating to foreign exchange trading. Is that the case?"

This was a subject that Theobald didn't mind talking about. He became almost verbose: "I had in mind three statements that I made repeatedly to my associates that may have been identified as three principles. . . . First, we should make sure that transactions undertaken do not transfer reported profitability or loss from one period to another period; secondly, that we should be careful not to transfer profits or loss from one location to another, in terms of financial books [and] tax books; and third, we should be careful on any kind of transaction to make sure that it does not have inadvertent or unthought of tax consequences."

"When [did] these statements evolve?"

"I don't recall the precise circumstances, but the general concept was that the Shearman and Sterling investigation suggested that people at a middle level in the organization might initiate a transaction that they really didn't think of all the consequences on, with regard to those three principles." [13]

Von Stein finally referred Theobald to his December 14, 1977 letter asking for Edwards's resignation, and he wanted to know the basis for Theobald's claim that "neither our investigators nor you have to date been able to provide any substantive, factual corroboration of the allegations you have made."

He said he had signed the letter after discussing with Steven Eyre whether his investigations had produced anything to support Edwards's charges. "He assured me they had not and so I was acting on that basis."

[13] Thomas C. Theobald, testimony before the SEC, May 16, 1980, pages 36–37.

Chapter 33

Dear Mr. von Stein

We conducted a textbook operation.

—JOHN E. HOFFMAN, AS PARAPHRASED BY THE SEC
STAFF, AUGUST 5, 1982

SHEARMAN & STERLING
Citicorp Center
153 East 53rd Street
New York 10022

(212) 493-1000
Telex: 126698

Thomas von Stein, Esq.,   June 2, 1980
Securities & Exchange Commission
Division of Enforcement
500 North Capitol Street, NW
Washington, DC 20549

Dear Mr. von Stein:
I have your letter dated May 20, 1980 asking for another one-half
day to take further testimony from Dean Lawrence Fouraker of the

Harvard Business School, a Citicorp director. This request follows your other examinations of 13 officers of Citicorp and Citibank. These prior witnesses have included Citicorp's Chief Auditor, its senior officer for all treasury and foreign exchange operations, its senior officer for all international operations, its senior officer for all European operations, as well as six other officers with the rank of vice president or above. In addition, we are currently scheduling the depositions of Walter B. Wriston, Chairman of Citicorp, and G.A. Costanzo, Vice Chairman.

Under the circumstances, we must respectfully decline to produce Dr. Fouraker for another session. The transcript of his testimony thoroughly demonstrates that you had more than adequate opportunity to pursue all relevant topics at Dr. Fouraker's deposition on May 12, and that a follow up session is not warranted.

Sincerely yours,
s/
John E. Hoffman, Jr.

Chapter 34

Wriston

Citibank . . . has built its business . . . on the bedrock of institutional integrity.

—WALTER B. WRISTON, JUNE 28, 1983

On Wednesday, July 9, 1980, von Stein and Ryan finally met in person the chairman of the board of Citicorp and America's premier banker. They were ushered into Shearman & Sterling's main conference room for the occasion. For von Stein it was a chance, his only one, to find out what Wriston knew about parking, when he first came to know about it, and if he had approved the parking operation.

Wriston was an imposing figure. Six feet four, with cold eyes, a biting voice, and clear diction, he had revolutionized banking, making it a leading American growth industry. His philosophy had transformed the staid institutions whose principal purpose once was to safeguard people's savings, using the deposits entrusted to them to finance local commerce or extend personal loans that benefitted the community, into monster electronic credit organizations no longer tied to a customer deposit base, but able to create instant liquidity and finance their own loans to governments or foreign potentates. Wriston had become a power broker himself; he entertained ambassadors and dined with presidents. He could be haughty or humble, sarcastic or witty. He was a man of culture and charm.

He was accompanied by Danforth Newcomb and the ever-present Henry Weisburg, arriving a few minutes behind schedule. He was placed under oath, and the deposition began with the standard questions about his background and early career. After ascertaining in general terms his knowledge of foreign exchange trading, von Stein asked, "Are you familiar with the concept of parking as used in the context of foreign exchange trading?"

"Well," he replied, "parking has been a generic term—invented by I don't know who, for moving positions originally as they followed the sun around the world. If I can remember, London has moved positions to New York to San Francisco to Hong Kong to Bahrain, because the market is open twenty-four hours a day. Where the term originated I don't know, but it has been around for quite a while."

Von Stein pondered over this statement. The oracle himself seemed to be admitting that London controlled a position as it moved from time zone to time zone around the globe.

Von Stein decided to let Wriston elaborate on this. He asked: "Would London control the position [and] give instructions to . . . Hong Kong to sell it to the [branch in the] next time zone?" In other words, who called whom? Who had control?

Wriston must have realized he had said too much, and now pulled back. "Well," he replied, "the person who owned the position would make the decision of what to do with it. It is conceivable that London would come in and want to buy it back, and it's conceivable that the rate they offered would be bettered by somebody else, so the trader who owned the position is the one who is responsible for selling it, covering it, or doing whatever." [1]

By suggesting now that Citibank London *might* be interested in reacquiring its position, in which case it would have to bid for it at market rates when London reopened for trading next morning, Wriston had altered the implication of his first statement that the Citibank trader in London moved the position through the marketplaces overnight in order to recapture it next morning.

Von Stein realized only too well that Wriston's modified answer did not correspond to the way Buenaga and Treacy had said parking worked; he sensed something was wrong.

[1] Walter B. Wriston, testimony before the SEC, July 9, 1980, page 19.

"Did you ever become aware of parking in the sense that the London branch at Citibank would instruct the New York branch of Citibank or the Nassau branch of Citibank . . . that it had made a particular contract for the purchase or sale of a particular currency and that London would be responsible for that, even though it was on New York's books or Nassau's books?"

"I don't have knowledge of that, no."

"Did you ever come to understand parking to mean that the initiating branch would control a position once it was on another branch's books?"

"I never understood it that way, no."

". . . Did you ever understand parking to mean the transfer of a profit from one branch of Citibank to another?"

"No."[2]

Von Stein asked about the Natvig/Pomeroy report. Wriston didn't remember receiving it, even though he acknowledged that he had sent a note back to Eyre asking him to follow through on the report's recommendations.

He denied knowing about round-trip transactions. He denied knowing that Milan kept a foreign exchange trader in London to handle "special transactions." He denied knowing that Switzerland had split limits: one declared to the regulatory authorities, and one at head office. He said he didn't know about the Cugnasca parking manual until he read it in the Blue Book, but he added, "As far as I know, this memorandum was never issued by Citibank." He said he had never heard the phrase *special transactions* used in connection with parking transactions, nor had he heard of a "World Trading Position."

"Did you ever learn or do you know that the Nassau branch of Citibank was used as a repository for parked positions by other Citibank branches and that the Nassau branch held such positions on its books even though it did not control those positions?" von Stein inquired.

"I don't know that to be true, no," Wriston replied.

"Do you have any opinion as to whether or not it is true?"

"Well, I assume they control their own positions."

"Do you happen to know if Citibank Nassau has any foreign exchange traders?"

"I assume they do. I haven't been there in fifteen years."

"Why do you assume that they do?"

[2] Ibid., pp. 21–22.

"Because they have foreign exchange positions." [3]

Von Stein asked what Wriston thought about the Blue Book.

"[It] was a collection of various allegations, unissued memorandums, and other items," Wriston replied. "The whole book was inconsistent with the way I believed we were trading in foreign exchange and I think my impression of that was borne out by the audit committee's report."

He added: "It's just full of all kinds of inference, which only an audit committee, if they spent a million dollars, could possibly sort out—which they did." [4]

The Blue Book was nothing more than one hundred pages of internal Citibank documents with five one-page analyses by Edwards of specific groups of these documents. The documents were not forgeries. Even Citibank acknowledged this.

Von Stein asked whether interbranch parking was done at arm's length.

"I have seen nothing in the audit reports to indicate otherwise," Wriston replied.

"Maybe not, but you might have some knowledge other than the audit report."

"I do not."

Ryan asked: "What do you understand 'arm's length' to mean?"

"Are you asking in the context of foreign exchange trading?" Wriston wanted to know.

"Anything. . . ."

". . . At market rates."

"Anything other than market rates?"

"I beg your pardon?"

"Does anything other than market rates come within your perception of arm's-length trading in the context of foreign exchange deals?"

"No." [5]

Von Stein took over again: "Do you know whether or not it is possible for one Citibank branch to transfer profits to another Citibank branch by doing foreign exchange transactions with that other branch which are, although what can be called market rates, so structured as to transfer profits?"

"I couldn't tell you that, no."

All in all, Wriston answered negatively to or professed no knowl-

[3] Ibid., pp. 35–36.
[4] Ibid., pp. 45–48.
[5] Ibid., pp. 68–69.

edge of more than ninety questions. One of the last von Stein thought to ask was "Has the Blue Book or any other action by David Edwards caused any changes to the way Citibank transacts its foreign exchange trading?"

". . . What the Blue Book did was cause us to spend a lot of our shareholders' money to go out and conduct an enormous investigation and mail that to every central bank in the world and every newspaper and the SEC."

At that point the telephone rang. Newcomb took it. "Tom," he said after putting the receiver down, "that call was the receptionist saying they have a waiting line for this room starting at noon."

"Tell them the chairman of the board is in here," von Stein shot back.

"The receptionists don't pay attention to the senior partner. I don't know why the chairman of the board of our largest client should be any different," Newcomb remarked.

One last question: "Did you ever learn that Citibank had withheld information from its statutory auditors, Peat Marwick, in Switzerland?"

To which Wriston responded with a final, "No."

Chapter 35

London-Nassau
Round-trip

Shady practices have pervaded Citibank.
—*Multinational Monitor,* OCTOBER 1982

Two days after taking Wriston's testimony, von Stein and Ryan took evidence from the vice-chairman, G. Albert Costanzo. It was more of the same "I don't know." Then, in August 1980, they took testimony from Saleem Muqaddam, Robert Logan's assistant.

"We were attempting to dance as fast as we could," said von Stein, who spent the next year "writing up the case," a report that ultimately extended to 70,000 words. The report, he noted, went through about twenty "expansions" and became, during its gestation period and for a considerable time thereafter, the focal point of his life.

While von Stein wrote the report, Ryan often discussed it with him. Both investigators considered the parking of foreign exchange positions to be an ongoing practice at Citibank, and both thought it was material to Citicorp's operations, which meant that it should have been disclosed to shareholders. During this time, they tried to keep Stanley Sporkin and his associate director of enforcement, David Doherty, apprised of their progress.

On September 15, 1980, von Stein completed his first draft of the report. Ryan had some reservations about parts of it. Doherty thought it was too diffused. Von Stein returned to the drafting board with it. A month later, Sporkin wanted to know what was happening on the case. Election Day was approaching and it seemed increasingly certain that Ronald Reagan would be in the White House come January. Wriston was a member of Reagan's inner council, and there were rumors around Washington that he was being considered for Secretary of the Treasury.

Sporkin, because of the erosion of his operating discretion under chairman Williams, found it more difficult to take strong positions of enforcement. The constant tugging at him from all sides—hearings in the Senate, a hostile commission, a securities bar that was out to curb his power, and, in his words, a "gung-ho staff" that wanted to move forward on important enforcement issues—was draining his strength. He had been hospitalized earlier that year for surgery, and he feared it would only be a matter of time before he collapsed altogether. He had dark circles under his eyes and looked exhausted.

Sporkin's instincts told him that Hoffman would be in one day to talk settlement. Hoffman had impressed Sporkin in a much earlier case involving insider trading of McDonnell Douglas stock because Hoffman, the youngest member of the defense attorneys working the case, broke ranks with the pack and settled one of his clients out, thereby, in Sporkin's words, "saving the firm $1 million in legal fees."

Toward the end of October 1980, von Stein wrote Sporkin a memo setting out his thoughts on the case. He recommended taking evidence a second time from Eyre, Pomeroy, and Howard because of their conflicting testimony the first time around. He also suggested commencing formal proceedings against Citicorp.

Knowing that this would provoke an outcry, Sporkin wanted to be sure von Stein had the goods on Citicorp in proper evidentiary form. He was being extra cautious. Rather than press ahead, which had been his style under more supportive commissions, he opted for building up the record by taking more evidence.

Sporkin was not helped by the ambiguous findings of the Comptroller of the Currency in his investigation, announced in early December 1980.

The national bank examiners on the comptroller's staff had not found the practice of parking foreign exchange positions to be unsafe or unsound in principle. "We believe that parking in response to local regulatory position restrictions can be perceived as an acceptable practice

provided that it is consistent with policy and done under strict operationally effective controls,'' they said in their report.

The Deputy Comptroller for Multinational Banking, Billy C. Wood,
noted in his letter to Citibank's board of directors, however, that his
inspectors had determined that the methods used by Citibank branches
for parking avoided sound prudential controls.

Wood's letter also vindicated David Edwards. It stated that the bank's
own internal investigations into his allegations had left much to be
desired, and it attacked the impartiality of the Sherman & Sterling
report.

''Many of the Citibank foreign exchange transactions that were reviewed essentially accomplished what David Edwards, a former employee, alleged; namely, foreign exchange transactions were conducted
at off-market rates. The practice of booking foreign exchange contracts at off-market rates is not a normal banking practice in that it
has serious audit as well as safety and soundness implications. Some
of the transactions in question had the effect of shifting profits from
one jurisdiction to another. Other transactions reviewed had as their
result, the avoidance of stamp taxes on foreign exchange contracts,
the avoidance of local exchange restrictions, and, in some cases, failure to properly reflect profits on the bank's books.

''We believe that these types of transactions are more serious than
portrayed in the Shearman & Sterling report. We recognize that such
practices do not comport with Citibank policy; however, we understand that certain members of senior management of the bank were
aware of the existence of these transactions. Certain officers were
alerted to the potential problems with interbranch foreign exchange
dealings at off-market rates as early as 1975 by the bank's own
comptroller's division. It does not appear that sufficient action was
taken to correct, prohibit, or eliminate the aforementioned practice at
the time of its disclosure in 1975. The question of why the practices
were not eliminated when initially disclosed to Bank management is
not clear. It also raises questions concerning the effectiveness of the
then existing audit procedures.

On the one hand, Wood wrote that the Shearman & Sterling report
appeared to be ''a fair and accurate presentation of the circumstances.'' But he immediately followed this with a statement that it
did not ''fully address why certain transactions and operations existed.'' Moreover, he noted that Shearman & Sterling had not fully
apprised local counsel of all the facts.

In this respect, Wood noted the following:

- Shearman & Sterling indicated to local counsel that once an exchange position was parked, no legal commitment existed between the initiating and transferee branch and that the initiating branch had no legal responsibility or authority regarding that position. *Institutional practice indicates, however, that the responsibility for the position remained with the initiating branch. Local counsel was not made aware of this fact.*
- Shearman & Sterling developed "factual transaction descriptions" which were commonly referred to as scenarios. These scenarios were submitted to local counsel and served as a basis for the legal opinions rendered. Our investigation indicated that there may have been additional scenarios which were not submitted.
- *The intent or objective of a transaction, even if known, was not disclosed or discussed with local counsel.*

We believe that a number of foreign exchange transactions reviewed *were inconsistent with sound banking principles* and exposed the bank to penalties and assessments levied by foreign supervisors. Although not precisely a quantifiable risk, satisfactory relations with foreign sovereign licensing authorities is viewed as critically important to the corporate operations of Citibank.[1]

The Comptroller of the Currency exacted no sanction. Wood merely requested that Citibank revise its policy regarding the conduct of foreign exchange policy and then "vigorously" enforce it.

"After a review of existing policy, and the development of the requisite instructions, please provide this Office with copies of the policy statement, a copy of the Board resolution implementing the policy, and a description of the actions taken to ensure bank-wide compliance with that policy," was all that Wood demanded.

By then von Stein had received through subpoena some Peat Marwick work papers. They opened a window on another aspect of the case, those "rinky-dink" deals that Pomeroy had mentioned, which until then had received little attention.

The "rinky-dink" deals were in fact another form of parking, or off-booking, but instead of involving foreign exchange positions, they transferred money-market deposits and placements. They were also known as "round-trip transactions."

[1] Letter from Billy C. Wood, Deputy Comptroller for Multinational Banking, Office of the Comptroller of the Currency, to the board of directors of Citibank N.A., December 8, 1980; emphasis added.

A first reference to round-tripping appeared in the 1975 Nat-vig/Pomeroy Survey of European Treasuries. It stated:

A *variety of round-trip transactions is done* by the European branches, mainly for the following reasons:

- Window-dress local balance sheets to improve ratios (e.g., liquidity, capital adequacy, etc.).
- Avoid or reduce obligatory reserves.
- Reduce tax liability for Bank and customers.
- Fund and borrow from the DM "Jersey Pool."
- Fund and lend through Nassau-Germany.

Strictly confidential treatment is necessary. In general, European management does not foresee serious reprisals if discovered; but disclosure could mean instructions to discontinue, and might involve tax claims and penalties. Reportedly other banks in Europe do comparable transactions.[2]

The Natvig/Pomeroy report gave a brief description of each type of round-trip transaction, starting with London, which was the most extreme case, by the volume of money involved and since, to hide it, the bank had falsified its tax returns to UK Inland Revenue. The report described the London-Nassau round-trip as follows:

Deposit-placement transactions to transfer money-market gap positions and related profits (or possibly losses) to Nassau branch: London places dollars with Nassau at call (earning at the now relatively low *market* call rates) and borrows dollars (i.e., takes deposits) from Nassau at about six months (paying interest at the relatively high *market* six-month rates). The effect is roughly to cover the liquidity gap on London's books which arises from money market dealings with other banks, and to transfer it to Nassau's books. Nassau's books then show not only the gap risk (i.e., the risk that the interest cost of the call money will rise substantially), but also the interest-differential profit (or loss if call rates should rise substantially). Present amounts (June 1975) are about $300 million falling due in months 4, 5 & 6 (originated mostly from April onwards), for an overall total of $900 million; and at present rates the net interest income spread is about $1 million per month (profit for Nassau). Institutionally the gap risk falls under London's Maxi-

[2]Citibank document 1699; emphasis in original.

mum Cumulative Outflow limits, and the profits (or possibly losses) are transferred to London by MIS entries at Head Office. The net institutional effect is that the risk and the expected profits are booked in tax-haven Nassau.[3]

To understand the round-tripping practices better, von Stein subpoenaed Citibank vice-president John Gardner. Gardner, who had worked for UK Inland Revenue before becoming a banker, was the Citibank tax expert who in April 1976 first told David Edwards about the "epidemic" use of parking by Citibank treasuries in Europe. At a meeting in Paris, he allegedly showed Edwards a memo headed "£10,000 fine, and/or two years imprisonment," which was the penalty for falsifying UK tax returns.

Edwards said that at their Paris meeting, Gardner claimed that he and a colleague had dreamed up the round-tripping of deposits to generate compensatory income for large real estate losses incurred in 1974 by the London branch.

During testimony on January 21, 1981, Gardner claimed that in early 1975, Citibank's senior financial vice-president Don Howard had suggested to Ernst Brutsche, then treasurer in London, that he should place part of London's large "gap" in Nassau. Gardner told Brutsche that as long as the transactions were done at market rates, there was no UK tax problem.

The "gap" is the difference between maturities when a banker borrows short-term money and lends it as longer-term money. London, at the time, was borrowing call money (24 to 48 hours) in the interbank market and lending it out for six months or longer, to take advantage of the higher interest rates for the longer-term funds. This was a calculated bank strategy, as the London treasury was then paying about 2 percent less for the call money than it was charging for the six-month loans. By putting the gap on Nassau's books, Citibank London transferred its profit on the interest-rate differential to the Bahamas.

Citibank calculated that the call rate would stay below the six-month rate, which it did. The operation was described in internal bank documents as "extremely profitable."[4]

According to the figures in von Stein's report, from February 1975 to April 1977, Citibank London deliberately lost at least $33.7 mil-

[3] Citibank document 1701; emphasis in the original.
[4] Citibank document 2076.

lion to Citibank Nassau by placing up to $1.5 million in Nassau at call rates and taking the same money back as six-month deposits, paying to Nassau the market rate for six-month money. He drew his information from a memo written in 1977 by Gardner's successor as Citibank tax manager in London.[5]

Gardner by then had been transferred to the corporate tax department in New York. One of his first assignments, following a senior management decision to stop using the London-Nassau round-trip, was to help execute the decision and sanitize the books.

Gardner explained in a memo to Muqaddam that when he rendered his 1975 opinion, he expected that the transactions would be (1) of limited duration, (2) only a handful of people would be aware of the arrangement, and (3) the procedures were such that the transactions would be almost impossible to identify. But, he noted, this method of reducing London's tax liability "was too good to abandon" and the volume increased. "While some allowance could be made in defense of this operation, *there is no doubt in anybody's mind that if all the facts were to emerge we would not have a case.*"[6]

Gardner told von Stein that the head of the corporate tax department, William M. Horne, instructed him not to send out this memo as it was too explicit. Gardner replaced it the following week with a more anodyne eleven-line memo, explaining why the practice must cease.[7]

Citibank's UK tax returns for 1975 were understated by $12 million because of the London-Nassau round-tripping, Gardner disclosed to von Stein. The 1975 tax returns were filed with the UK authorities in November 1978, before the decision to end round-tripping had been put into practice. The London branch's financial statements for 1976 and 1977 also reflected the loss to Nassau on the back-to-back deposits. But when Citibank filed its 1976 and 1977 tax returns, sometime after November 1978, revenues were reported as if the back-to-back deposits had not occurred.

"This retroactive un-MIS'ing is contrary to all of Citibank's current arguments attempting to legitimatize parking and the income transferred to Nassau by parking," von Stein noted in his draft report.

[5] Handwritten notes attributed to Roy Groves, tax manager, London; Citibank document 477A–482A.
[6] Draft memo of April 6, 1977, to Mr. Saleem Muqaddam, vice-president, re: Nassau Funding; Citibank document 473A–475A; emphasis added.
[7] Memo from John C. Gardner to Saleem Muqaddam, re: London-Nassau funding, April 12, 1977; Citibank document 476A.

To avoid taxes and lending requirements in Germany, Citibank Frankfurt made use of a funding "trick," which Natvig referred to as the "Jersey Pool." It worked as follows:

> *Citibank Frankfurt finds DM deposits to fund the "Jersey Pool,"* *which are returned to Citibank Germany free of reserves as long-* *term deposits:* the interposition of Jersey . . . has the effect of exempting this funding from normal German deposit reserves (because the placements with Germany are under legally binding contracts for over four years). It also improves the German-branch liquidity for compliance with local ratio requirements.[8]

By 1978, the "Jersey Pool" consisted of $619 million of loans that Citibank Channel Islands Ltd. (located on the Island of Jersey, off the coast of Brittany) made to Citibank AG, which Citibank's German subsidiary used to supplement its working capital. Pomeroy detailed the procedures in a March 1978 memo entitled "Treasury Guidelines—Germany."

"To avoid maintaining reserves with the Central Bank, Citibank AG has formal contracts with Jersey that show maturities greater than four years," the memo explained. "The Central Bank does not require reserves against deposits of this tenor."

In reality, the maturities on the Jersey loans to Citibank AG were nowhere near the required four years, the memo noted. It said that the loans were done at maturities of one to three months, while in the reports to the Bundesbank the borrowings from Jersey were shown in the "over four years" category.[9]

The "Jersey Pool" paid off for Citibank. By using this strategy, the bank avoided tying up $124 million, without interest, in additionally required reserves, one study estimated.

While the "Jersey Pool" allowed Citibank AG to borrow funds off-book, von Stein discovered that another ploy enabled it to loan funds off-book.

According to the documents, Citibank AG routinely booked its commercial loans to local German residents at Citibank Nassau or Citibank Monaco, but would control the funds from Frankfurt. Citibank's auditors, Peat Marwick, advised the bank in September 1977 that this trick was probably illegal. "We feel the German tax authorities would have good arguments to attribute the entire Nassau oper-

[8] Citibank document 1702; emphasis in the original.
[9] Citibank document 1787–1823.

ations to the German branches for this period," Peat Marwick wrote in a letter to Robert Logan.[10]

Peat Marwick warned that the tax inspectors might wake up to this trick. "It appears that the German tax authorities do not fully understand, yet" what Citibank was up to. "It is impossible to evaluate the progress of the education process of the German tax authorities," but the letter remarked that conceivably, they would take issue with the legality of the loan off-booking.[11]

This evasion netted Citibank a fortune. In 1977, the total assets and liabilities for Citibank Nassau and Monaco attributable to Citibank AG Frankfurt amounted to $2.7 billion, according to the Pomeroy memo. This prompted SEC associate director of enforcement, Irwin Borowski, to ponder whether the profitability of Citicorp AG's operations depended "disproportionately on its ability to evade domestic reserve requirements." If the answer was affirmative, then this was certainly a "material" matter.

Borowski followed the Citicorp investigation with interest, but from a discreet and secondhand vantage point. Although he was one of three deputies to Sporkin, Borowski's supervisory responsibilities at the agency covered other enforcement efforts. Nevertheless, he was a member of the car pool in which von Stein occasionally participated, and on the days they shared a ride, Borowski would ask von Stein how the Citicorp case was progressing. Von Stein invariably obliged by sharing the latest developments with Borowski. It was like a running corporate soap-opera serial, and at the time it was absorbing all of von Stein's existence.

---

[10]Tax opinion prepared by the Frankfurt office, Peat Marwick Mitchell & Company: "German Tax Treatment of Offshore Lending and Funding," page 4.
[11]Ibid., p. 6.

Chapter 36

Von Stein's Report

Perjury is an awful hard rap to prove.

—RICHARD M. NIXON, MARCH 23, 1973

In difficult cases, Sporkin always advised: "First get the facts, and the law will follow."

This was Sporkin's way of telling his staff that first and foremost, they should concentrate on assembling all the evidence. Once the evidence was digested, they could proceed with the law: At that point it would be more readily evident which statutes had been violated—if indeed violations had occurred.

Von Stein followed Sporkin's advice when he started writing his long report. He wanted to record every scrap of evidence he had uncovered in his investigation of Citibank's foreign exchange and money market operations. As it developed, the report became a running narrative, starting with events in 1973, when parking first became widespread at Citibank, and ending in 1980, when senior management finally claimed that parking had ceased.

As it evolved, von Stein's report was based entirely on the documents assembled by Shearman & Sterling for its own "special review" and which the big New York law firm had consented to release to the SEC, some Peat Marwick Mitchell work papers, and the testimony of twenty-four Citibank and Peat Marwick witnesses.

All in all, with the base documents and transcripts of testimony covering the most esoteric of banking operations—funding and foreign exchange—the total body of evidence spread over 16,000 pages. This mass of documentation, sometimes contradictory, always confusing, was almost incomprehensible to a layman. It was not easy to digest. Working under pressure from Sporkin, who by then was uninterested in the mechanics of the case but wanted some sort of final determination, von Stein reduced the evidence to 138 draft pages, including his write-up of relevant case law. He was proud of this achievement.

The draft was rough. Several secretaries had worked on it. It was marred by typing errors, dropped words, and incorrectly transcribed evidence. Von Stein's findings, though sometimes hard to follow, were nevertheless reasonably clear:

"From at least 1973 to at least April 1980, Citibank branches in Europe and, to a lesser extent, Asia [he omitted Mexico], have engaged in a variety of inter-branch transactions recorded as normal arm's length contracts between two or more Citibank branches but which were in reality transactions simply dictated by one branch. As such, these transactions enabled the dictating branch to evade (1) local exchange control laws, (2) local reserve requirements, and (3) local taxes. The transactions were known as 'round trip' and 'parking' transactions." [1]

The draft report alleged that Citibank's senior management, and not just the heads of treasury at branches in Europe, condoned the circumvention of local tax, exchange control, and reserve requirements "whenever they interfered with earning profits." It alleged also that the bank's own internal controls "were principally concerned with disguising the transactions from local regulators."

The draft report charged that "these practices and the risks to Citibank were not disclosed to shareholders." [2]

The introductory summary regarding Shearman & Sterling's role was blunt: "The November 1978 Shearman & Sterling Report, supposedly a report to answer Edwards's allegations and to describe Citibank's foreign exchange trading, was false and misleading. The S&S

---

[1] SEC staff report draft, p. 1.
[2] Ibid., p. 2.

Report was essentially a cover-up, failing to disclose the key facts about Citibank's past and then on-going practices. A careful analysis of the S&S Report, based on an accurate factual understanding of parking, as practiced by Citibank, and of Citibank's internal accounting system, known as the Management Information System ("MIS"), confirms that Citibank violated local laws in several European countries. The legal opinions from counsel in such countries, which were the key to the S&S Report, were, however, not based on an accurate factual understanding of parking or the MIS, nor did the report itself give an accurate and complete description of parking, its extent or purpose."[3]

Von Stein noted that Shearman & Sterling's definition of *parking* was incomplete. He preferred to paraphrase Citibank's own documents, defining *parking* as "the off-booking of foreign exchange positions at a unit other than the unit which initiates and controls that position."[4]

He also cited as more accurate a description of parking that Citibank Germany gave in response to a Shearman & Sterling questionnaire on foreign exchange practices. It defined *parking* as, "A party keeping a position for 'B' for the account and under the responsibility of 'B.' "[5]

The criticism of Shearman & Sterling in the main body of von Stein's report was sharper. The section dealing with the Form 8-K report was headed: *CITIBANK CAPS ITS MISLEADING DISCLOSURE OF ITS FOREIGN EXCHANGE TRADING WITH THE GRANDEST MISDISCLOSURE OF ALL: CITIBANK FILES SHEARMAN & STERLING REPORT ON PARKING AS AN 8-K WITH THE SEC AND VARIOUS CENTRAL BANKS.* In part, it stated:

"The report, in great measure, exonerated Citibank from Edwards's allegations. The report was, however, an elaborate, expensive, sophisticated whitewash, from start to finish. The S&S Report appears to be a gamble, i.e., disclose enough so as not to appear to be an obvious whitewash, but don't disclose anything meaningful," von Stein concluded.[6]

Von Stein detailed the different modes of parking and the mechanics of parking, then gave an indication of their materiality. The figures he was able to cull from the documents were incomplete. But

[3] Ibid., p. 2.
[4] Citibank documents 1687; 1912.
[5] Citibank document 4310.
[6] Ibid., p. 102.

the documents available to him showed that the total income transferred to Nassau for the years 1974 to 1978 by parking and other forms of round-tripping was at least $75 million, and this excluded income from Amsterdam, Brussels, and Paris, for which his information was fragmentary.[7] During this period, Citibank's earnings from foreign exchange totalled $417 million.

His discussion of case law was meager, only covering four pages. It was meager, he said, because few management-integrity cases ever made it into court. They were usually settled by a consent to an injunction which avoided "adjudication," a favorite Shearman & Sterling catchword.

As the SEC's position on deceitfully conducted special investigations, von Stein cited *SEC* v. *ITT,* a civil action brought in 1978 in which the SEC considered ITT's "internal investigation and special report" relating to questionable payments to be "false and misleading due to its incomplete and inaccurate nature."

In *United States* v. *Stirling,* a 1978 judgment held that "once [the company] decided to make representations concerning its labor relations, it should have described them accurately." Von Stein's contention was that once Citicorp described Citibank's foreign exchange operations in its annual reports to shareholders and in filings with the SEC, such as the Shearman & Sterling report, it was obliged to describe them accurately.

He also mentioned a 1980 judgment in *SEC* v. *Falstaff Brewing Corporation,* where it was ruled that mention of a nonexistent audit committee in reports to shareholders was false and misleading. The analogy here, von Stein said, was that Citibank never made it clear that the oversight provided by the comptroller's division was "directed principally at disguising parking transactions, not stopping them or informing the Board of Directors, and therefore mention of the Comptroller's supposed activities was false and misleading."

Finally, he referred to *SEC* v. *Schlitz Brewing Company,* wherein the court held that information concerning Schlitz's alleged improper marketing practices and transactions with its Spanish affiliates, which transactions involved violations of Spanish exchange control and tax laws, was material and thus was a required subject for disclosure.

---

[7] Von Stein's figure of $75 million included almost $35 million earned through the London-Nassau back-to-back deposits set up in 1975 to take advantage of the gap in interest rates between call money and three-month money. Profits parked in Nassau through simulated foreign exchange contracts therefore was at least $42 million for the five-year period, according to von Stein's calculations.

Ryan and von Stein agreed that the originating branch in a classic parking transaction continued to control the position while it was off the books. But Ryan didn't think this was always the compelling legal issue. "I thought we had to look at the arm's length aspect. If the price was right—at market—then I thought the transaction might be all right. I did not think that control alone was the determining factor. This was the *only* area of disagreement between Tom and me," he said later.

Doherty, however, thought von Stein's language was too strong. He didn't like the same characterizations that Commissioner Loomis had objected to in 1978—"sham deals" and "illegal transactions"— and he tried to steer von Stein away from them.

In any event, a 138-page report of any investigation was too long for the commission. Even Sporkin, his interest waning, didn't read it all. Doherty instructed von Stein to write a summary memo to the commission.

Sporkin had his own problems at the time. He was under fire for his management-integrity cases and a target for many Republican supporters. But now that Reagan had triumphed over Carter, Sporkin's old boss, William J. Casey, a chairman of the SEC under Nixon, was back in the anteroom of power. Of all SEC chairmen he had worked under, Sporkin considered Casey had the best record on enforcement. Casey, he said, was a straight arrow. Others said that Casey owed Sporkin a favor for steering him clear of White House meddling in the Vesco investigation.

Reagan, as everyone knew, was for confrontation in the secret war against the Soviets and, at home, deregulation in almost every sector, including the securities industry. To lead the secret war against the Soviets he chose, as the new head of the Central Intelligence Agency, his friend and campaign manager Bill Casey. To deregulate the securities industry he cast around for a new SEC chairman.

A "transition team," set up by loyal Republicans to advise Reagan on what to do with the SEC, prepared a devastating report recommending a 30 percent cut in staff and budget over a three-year period. "One of the principal objectives to be encouraged by the Reagan Administration is the elimination of unnecessary impediments to capital formation. It is only with effective capital formation that the goals of the Reagan administration for economic growth and greater productivity can be fully achieved.

"While the Securities & Exchange Commission by no means has a major role to play in capital formation, the SEC can and does raise artificial barriers in certain circumstances to the free accumulation and formation of capital."[8]

The hardest hit by the economy measures proposed by the transition team would have been the division of enforcement. The authors of the report recommended cutting the enforcement staff from the more than 200-level to "not more than 50." The enforcement program also came under heavy criticism for its "proliferation of meaningless enforcement activity directed at minor infractions."[9]

The team recommended that the commission curtail "less desirable unfocused broad-ranging investigations" and the "needless proliferation of enforcement investigations by informal means or by formal subpoenas which result in years of staff time being expended with the net result of a meaningless array of consent injunctions which have little, if any, significance to the investing public or to the individuals involved in the matter."[10]

Large-scale changes in personnel were recommended. Noting that many of the senior staff directors were appointed by previous Democratic administrations, the transition team said the new commission chairman "should make sweeping changes in senior staff promptly." It said that "in virtually every area the leadership of the various divisions is unsatisfactory either because of philosophic incompatabilities or competence."[11]

In a separate memorandum to Edwin Meese III, Reagan's chief of staff, the team endorsed its own coordinator and author of the transition report, Washington attorney Daniel J. Piliero, for the chairmanship. Piliero had served as special counsel to former chairman Casey and was an associate director of the Division of Market Regulation from 1973 to 1977. The memorandum to Meese said that Piliero possessed all the "essential qualities" for a SEC chairman under the Reagan administration: "commitment to the concept that the size of government, including the SEC, must be reduced and that the regulatory burden must be lightened through simplification and deregulation, where the interests to be protected are not harmed."[12]

When Sporkin was given a copy of Piliero's report, he took it personally, as a slap in the face. He circulated copies of it. Responding

---

[8] The Final Report of SEC Transition Team (the "Piliero Report"), as reprinted in No. 587 of The Bureau of National Affairs, Inc.'s *BNA News & Comments*, Jan. 21, 1981, page K-27.
[9] Ibid., p. A-1.
[10] Ibid., p. K-9.
[11] Ibid., p. K-28.
[12] Transition Team memorandum, as reprinted in *BNA News & Comments*, No. 581, Jan. 21, 1981, p. A-1.

to the report, a group of securities lawyers under former commissioner A. A. Sommer, Jr. produced a "countertransition document" urging the appointment of a chairman whose "integrity, experience, maturity and ability to relate to others at the Commission be unquestionable." [13]

The candidate finally chosen by the Reagan White House was John S.R. Shad, a vice-chairman of the E. F. Hutton Group, one of Wall Street's largest investment houses.

Shad, a minor Citicorp shareholder and an acquaintance of Wriston, was said to have remarked, "What am I going to do with Sporkin?"

Casey had a solution. He suggested taking Sporkin with him as general counsel to the CIA. Problem solved. Exit Sporkin as the nation's most effective law enforcement officer.

---

[13] *BNA News & Comments*, No. 591, February 18, 1981, p. A-3.

Chapter 37

Now, Therefore, Be It Resolved That . . .

Conceptually, the practice of parking foreign exchange positions is not considered unsafe or unsound. However, the actual manner in which Citibank's branch units parked their exchange positions violated principles of sound internal control.

We believe that parking in response to local regulatory position restrictions can be perceived as an acceptable practice provided that it is consistent with policy and done under strict operationally effective controls.

It is Citicorp's stated policy to conduct business dealings in accordance with the spirit and intent of relevant laws and regulations. It would appear that parking positions were not consistently conducted in accordance with this policy.

—COMPTROLLER OF THE CURRENCY'S REPORT ON CITIBANK FOREIGN EXCHANGE INVESTIGATION, NOVEMBER 1980

The Deputy Comptroller of the Currency for Multinational Banking, Billy C. Wood, told the Citibank board of directors in suitably non-alarmist terms, "We believe certain actions [relating to Citibank's foreign exchange practices] on the part of the directorate would be appropriate." More specifically, Wood asked that the bank clearly set forth its policy concerning currency trading and that instructions be given to the appropriate corporate officers to "vigorously enforce" the new policy statement.

The deputy comptroller asked that his office be provided with copies of the policy statement, the board resolution implementing it, and a description of the actions taken to ensure bank-wide compliance with that policy.

Citibank had already started a process of tightening its internal controls prior to receiving the deputy comptroller's letter. A statement of "Enhanced Management Systems Within Citicorp and Citibank" disclosed that in 1980, Citicorp underwent a management reorganization to strengthen its internal control functions. The most important of these was the restructuring of the comptroller's division. It was renamed the audit division, and the comptroller was given the new title of chief auditor. Stephen Eyre, who was criticized by the Deputy Comptroller of the Currency in his report on Citibank's foreign exchange operations for his handling of the Edwards investigations—"Certain allegations and assertions made by Edwards were not fully investigated"—was transferred to the position of corporate secretary in November 1980. He had already been replaced as chief auditor in August 1980.

An accounting and control department was created to oversee the function of the audit division. Independent of any line operations, it was placed under the direction of Paul J. Collins, who was promoted to the rank of executive vice-president.

Finally, at an April 20, 1981 meeting of the Citibank board of directors, a resolution was adopted along the lines requested by the deputy comptroller of the currency. The resolution and its preamble was a masterpiece of corporate mumbo-jumbo, showing the extent to which there was a near-senseless veneration of legalese in high executive places. It avoided all mention of parking—the word had been truly scrubbed from Citicorp's lexicon. Thus, upon motion, and duly seconded, it noted:

WHEREAS, Citibank, directly and through subsidiaries, is engaged in foreign exchange and money market activities in countries throughout the world; and

WHEREAS, many of these countries have adopted legal, tax, accounting and regulatory provisions applicable to foreign exchange and money market activities within their jurisdictions; and

WHEREAS, the legal, tax, accounting and regulatory provisions applicable to foreign exchange and money market activities in one country wherein Citibank does business may be at variance, and occasionally in conflict, with those of another country in which Citibank does business; and

WHEREAS, Citibank has adopted internal policy and procedural limits and guidelines with respect to the conduct of its global foreign exchange and money market activities; and

WHEREAS, consistent with its fundamental policies, Citibank recognizes its obligations to comply with applicable laws, rules and regulations of host countries:

NOW, THEREFORE, BE IT

RESOLVED, that the following statement of policy be distributed to and enforced by senior officers responsible for supervising Citibank's foreign exchange and money market activities.

The Board of Directors note and reaffirm:

- That it is Citibank's policy to decentralize management decision making over foreign exchange and money market activities, and to centralize the monitoring, reporting and internal control of such practices.
- That it is Citibank's policy that all foreign exchange and money market activities be conducted in a manner which conforms to applicable legal, tax, accounting and regulatory provisions of the countries within which it conducts such activities, as well as with Citibank's own internal policy and procedural limits and guidelines.
- That it is Citibank's policy that foreign exchange and money market transactions shall be executed at rates which conform to applicable legal, tax, accounting and regulatory provisions, as well as with institutional internal policies and guidelines.
- That it is Citibank's policy that all foreign exchange and money market activities be conducted in a manner susceptible to required review by local and other appropriate legal, tax and regulatory authorities and that transactions or procedures which local Citibank management believes may be challenged by local authorities be reviewed and approved by local and other appropriate legal, tax and/or accounting experts of recognized standing prior to their implementation.

In order to ensure that these policies are correctly applied, the Board of Directors direct that senior management report material matters regarding the internal accounting and control of foreign exchange and money market activities through the Chief Auditor to the Audit and Examining Committees.[1]

Although the resolution nowhere mentioned his name, and it made no reference to off-booking, the resolution was, in effect, a tribute to David Edwards. It came almost four years after he first raised the issue with Freeman Huntington, and it was the closest he would come to being congratulated for his integrity and perseverance.

[1] Resolution of the board of directors of Citibank N.A., April 20, 1981.

Chapter 38

Fifth Denial

PRESIDENT: *You think we want to . . . go this route now*
[and] let it hang out, so to speak?
DEAN: *Well, it isn't really that—*
HALDEMAN: *It's a limited hang out.*
EHRLICHMAN: *It's a modified limited hang out.*
DEAN: *What it's doing, Mr. President, is getting you up*
above and away from it. And that's the most important
thing.

—MEETING IN THE OVAL OFFICE, MARCH 22, 1973

John Sigsbee Rees Shad, then fifty-seven, was sworn in by Vice-President George Bush as the twenty-second chairman of the Securities & Exchange Commission on May 6, 1981. He was the second chairman in the SEC's history to come from Wall Street, and critics fully expected he would be soft on the industry to which he owed his fortune and had so recently left.

Shad had joined the securities industry in 1949, immediately upon graduating from Harvard with a master's degree in business administration. He was flat broke then and borrowed $500 from the student loan program to cover his moving expenses to a shared apartment in New York's Greenwich Village. He went to work for Value Line as a securities analyst, raised $5,000 more, and bought stock in a company called Associated Transport, then selling for 2½, and sold it at 9. With the proceeds, he shorted the Boston & Maine Railroad just as its share price collapsed and found that he had the modest beginnings of an investment portfolio.

Shad remained a securities analyst for the next fifteen years, watching his investment portfolio compound at a rate of 30 percent annually, which he unabashedly admitted was astounding. In 1959, he obtained a law degree from New York University while working at Shearson, Hammill & Company (later Shearson/American Express, Inc.), where he became a partner and initiated the firm's investment banking activities. He joined E. F. Hutton, then only a retail broker, in 1963 and directed that firm's entry into the investment banking field.

By the time he resigned from the vice-chairmanship at Hutton to become chairman of the SEC, Shad had amassed a personal fortune in securities alone of $17 million, which he placed in a blind trust over which he exercised no control. At the SEC he quickly gained a reputation for being a deregulator and a cost-cutter. He was intent, he said, on "reducing the regulatory burden of the regulated."

Shad, like Wriston, never had high regard for government bureaucracy. Two years after becoming SEC chairman, he told a group of securities traders: "The other day I was asked if I knew what a 'Damn Shame' is. I learned that a 'Damn Shame' is a busload of government officials going off a cliff—with five empty seats."[1]

George Ball, a former president of E. F. Hutton, considered Shad as one of the Manhattan money barons. "In what I would call the inner sanctum of Wall Street, banking and the securities-related lawyer fraternity—a totally informal and nondefined clan—John was well known, well thought of and an active participant," Ball told one reporter.[2]

Unlike most Wall Streeters, Shad was an early Reagan supporter— earlier, even, that Wriston—perhaps the only senior Wall Street figure to come out for Reagan prior to the 1980 primaries.

As a Reagan camp insider, Shad became friends with Fred Fielding, John Dean's assistant during the Nixon days and later White House

---

[1] Address to the National Securities Traders Association, Boca Raton, Florida, October 9, 1983.
[2] "Different Path for Investors' Watchdog," by Stephen M. Aug, *Nation's Business*, November 1983, p. 30.

counsel to President Reagan. Upon being nominated for the SEC job, Shad moved his family to an estate on Long Island and he became a weekly commuter to Washington. Bachelors in the nation's capital, he and Fielding frequently dined together—at least once a week, according to one Congressional staffer.

Sporkin resigned when Shad was sworn in. He left the SEC convinced that the Citicorp case was about to be settled. "We had certain preliminary discussions with Shearman & Sterling," he said, "and while we had not reached any definitive understanding, it was my best professional judgment that . . . the matter would be settled."[3] Shearman & Sterling, however, flatly denied that any such discussion had taken place or that their client had any intention of settling a case whose status seemed to wobble from inactive to barely active and back to inactive. Sporkin, just before leaving, had instructed the staff to wind up the investigation and recommend to the commission that Citicorp be ordered to correct its public filings.

Sporkin's move across the Potomac to the general counsel's office at the CIA marked the end of an era at the 47-year-old securities agency. There comes a point, economist John Kenneth Galbraith once said, when regulatory agencies become either senile or captives of the industries they regulate. Some observers feared that the SEC had reached such a point.

The person chosen to replace Sporkin was John M. Fedders. Then forty years old, Fedders was born and raised in the northern Kentucky city of Covington. "My parents," he said, "were very modest folk. My dad was a laborer and my mom a housewife."

Fedders once thought he wanted to be a journalist. He took a B.A. in journalism at Marquette University, where he played basketball. Then he decided more power and prestige accrued to lawyers. He took his law degree at the Catholic University of America School of Law.

After graduating from law school in 1966, he became an associate with a large New York law firm, and then, about to turn thirty, he became executive vice-president of Gulf Life Holding Company (later Gulf United Corporation) of Dallas. He left Gulf in 1973 to become a partner with the blue-ribbon Washington law firm of Arnold & Porter. He came to the SEC well qualified. He was active in the American Bar Association, serving on two of its subcommittees dealing with federal regulation of securities and white collar crime.

---

[3] Stanley Sporkin, testimony before the House Energy and Commerce Subcommittee on Oversight and Investigations, September 13, 1982 (page 16 of Serial No. 97–193).

Fedders literally stood head and shoulders above his predecessors at the SEC. At six feet ten, he had to bow every time he entered or left his office, to avoid hitting his head on the door frame.

He first became interested in Sporkin's job in mid-May 1981. On June 25, 1981, Shad told him it was his. On June 29, 1981, his appointment was publicly announced, and on July 20, 1981, he slipped into the harness of what he described as "the greatest law enforcement job in the world today."

"Within two or three days of walking in here, I knew that one of the big decisions I had to make was what to do with the Citicorp case. I had an inventory of open cases that was over 800. Citicorp was one of the biggest," he said.

"I had a series of briefings with von Stein and Ryan. Then Doherty and Ryan brought me the draft report. Ryan, I think, said, 'Don't waste your time reading it.' But I took it and the Wriston transcript home anyway. After reading them, I knew we had problems. Once through the Wriston transcript, I saw that we couldn't make our case. Of course the transcript raised questions in my mind. But by then we had been on this thing for three and a half years and hadn't gotten it tied down. I decided it was time to cut it off."[4]

Within a month of Fedders taking over as head of enforcement, Shearman & Sterling filed a "Wells submission" with the commission, setting out in a legal memorandum reasons why the Citicorp case was abusive and should be dropped. A Wells submission permits an individual or corporation under staff investigation to appeal directly to the five commissioners when informed that an enforcement proceeding will be recommended.

The submission argued that the initiation of proceedings against Citicorp would be an inappropriate use of the SEC's recources in view of three significant developments: (1) Citicorp filed the Shearman & Sterling report as a Form 8-K, calling it an "extensive report which thoroughly disclosed the factual background of this matter," (2) bank regulators have meticulously reviewed the matter, and (3) in the meantime Citibank had strengthened its numerous management and prudential control systems to prevent any recurrence of the few "white ravens" that the Shearman & Sterling review had uncovered.

The submission also stated that the issues involved were not material and therefore further action would waste the assets of Citicorp and the commission toward no profitable objective for the enforcement of federal securities laws.

---

[4] John Fedders, interviewed by the author, Washington, March 26, 1984.

The staff—i.e., Doherty, Ryan, and von Stein—pointed out that the submission, the bulk of which consisted of a reprint of the Shearman & Sterling report, did not mention, much less dispute, any of the underlying facts or evidence in the case. Fedders by then had already decided he would recommend to the commission that the Citicorp investigation be dropped.

"Sometime in the fall we began to reach decisions, and I said I was going to oppose bringing the Citicorp case. But as I knew how much work von Stein had put into his report, I said I would let it go up to the commission. I felt this was being fair. I could have killed it right there. But I didn't. I was that confident of my position," he said.[5]

That autumn, Fedders's old law firm of Arnold & Porter was hired to review a private investigation conducted by Pittsburgh lawyer Charles Queenan into questionable payments made by Ashland Oil Inc. The payments went to a wealthy Libyan with ties to the sultan of Oman to assure Ashland a ready supply of Omani crude. Queenan's six-month investigation, commissioned by the Ashland board, was completed in August 1981 and hastened the resignation of Ashland chairman Orin Atkins.

Eight years before, Ashland and Atkins had already been fined for channeling $100,000 to Richard Nixon's 1972 reelection campaign, and in 1975 Ashland signed a consent decree with the SEC in which the corporation agreed it would not report false information or launder its financial records to conceal questionable payments.

The Queenan report concluded that Ashland hadn't violated the Foreign Corrupt Practices Act in the Omani affair. The Arnold & Porter review concurred with this finding and, consequently, no disclosure was made of the questionable payments. Part of the reasoning for this was that in fact the payments in question had been retrieved from the Libyan at the insistence of the board's outside directors.

Meanwhile, echoes of the $1.3 million "rescinded bribe" had reached the enforcement staff, three of whom commenced an informal probe to see if the matter warranted further attention. Fedders heard about it in November 1981. He immediately called the three staff members into his office and dressed them down. "Haven't I told you we aren't bringing foreign-payment cases anymore," he was quoted as saying.

Fedders later admitted in an interview with *The Wall Street Journal* that his remarks were somewhat less intemperate. In any event, the

[5] Ibid.

staff told him they weren't only looking into foreign payments allegations, but also reports of insider trading violations. On that basis the Ashland probe was permitted to continue, but at a pace even slower than the Citicorp investigation. [It took another fifteen months before any SEC investigators were allowed to look at the Queenan report, and the SEC staff didn't request the power to subpoena Ashland's records until May 1983.]

Fedders later told the commission that he didn't know about Arnold & Porter's involvement in the case until the month after he scolded his staff. He said he would disqualify himself from any other matters involving Arnold & Porter—about fifteen cases in all.[6]

In preparation for the commission hearing on the Citicorp matter, von Stein had prepared a 28-page summary memo setting out the basic facts of the case. Fedders attached to this memo his reasons for recommending that it be dropped. The summary memo recommended, as Sporkin had suggested, an administrative proceeding to compel Citicorp to correct its filings and discuss a possible settlement before commencing injunctive action.

The memo stated: "During 1974–1978, Citibank earned $417 million from foreign exchange, at least $46 million of which was generated by parking transactions. The detail, risks, and ramifications of these activities were not disclosed to Citicorp shareholders."

The memo's analysis of the Shearman & Sterling report said it was written "as if the hundreds of internal Citibank documents in their possession did not exist, documents which show how senior management directed its procedures, including using false documents to hide it from the authorities, documents which show the non-arm's length nature of parking deals, documents which show its wide use for several years, and documents which show management knew it was done to circumvent local laws."

The memo further disclosed that in October 1979—one year after the Shearman & Sterling report was filed—Citibank's comptroller reported to the audit committee that his inspectors had found "off-market rates [were still being] used in foreign exchange transactions in Citibank's branches in Japan, Hong Kong, the Philippines, Singapore, Malaysia, Indonesia, India and Saudi Arabia."[7] This indicated that Citibank was continuing to rely on parking to boost its foreign exchange earnings.

---

[6] "Ashland Oil Criticizes Its Payments to Libyan to Get Oman's Crude," *The Wall Street Journal*, May 24, 1983; and "Fedders Criticized SEC Probe of Ashland While His Old Law Firm Was Involved," *The Wall Street Journal*, May 27, 1983.

[7] SEC Division of Enforcement staff memo to the Commission (undated), pp. 16; 18.

Unlike von Stein's draft report, with its direct language and colorful characterizations, the memo to the commission had the full support of Doherty and Ryan.

Fedders's recommendation that no action be brought was based on his exercising "prosecutorial discretion." In exercising that discretion, he said, "you must make five judgments whether the illegality is material."

You have to ask yourself, he said, whether the supposed illegality was material to:

1. assets
2. earnings
3. liabilities
4. sales
5. potential foreseeable adverse consequences arising from the misconduct.

Once you are satisfied there is no quantitative materiality, then you examine the qualitative aspects to materiality: does the course of conduct indicate that management is incapable of carrying out its fiduciary responsibilities in an honest way?

In the Citicorp case, Fedders concluded that, first, no one ever suggested the quantitative effect of parking was material and, second, it was never a seriously considered foreseeable consequence that Citibank could be kicked out of any country.

This last conclusion, he noted, was based on eighteen years' experience as defense counsel, including five years of specialization on questionable payments cases. "The one thing it taught me was that regulators are always prepared to fine offenders, but never to disbar them. In my judgment, there was no foreseeable likelihood that this was ever going to happen with Citicorp."[8]

His written recommendation, annexed to the memo, stated:

1. *Illegality.* We have not established that the conduct in question was illegal, except to a limited extent. We may be able to accomplish this with additional effort. . . .
2. *Quantitative Materiality.* Assuming that Citicorp's conduct was illegal, this fact alone is not sufficient to have required disclosure or to justify the initiation of an enforcement proceeding.

    Citicorp disclosed a version of its conduct in a Form 8-K. . . .
    The report was widely disseminated, including to government

[8] Interview with the author, March 26, 1984.

instrumentalities in the countries where the conduct occurred. Since that 1978 dissemination, we cannot demonstrate that the disclosures have had a material impact . . . on Citicorp's overall operations or on its operations in the respective countries. . . . (I do not subscribe to the theory that a company that violates tax and exchange control regulations is a bad corporation, and disclosure of illegal conduct should be forced as a prophylactic measure. This is not within our authority under the Federal securities laws. . . .)

While I do not condone Citicorp's conduct, if illegal, I am not persuaded that such conduct is "material" to investors or shareholders unless it results in significant economic harm to Citicorp. There must be at least a reasonable likelihood that the conduct will have a material affect on earnings, assets or liabilities. If not, the information is unlikely to affect the market price of the issuer's securities and, therefore, should not be a required item for SEC disclosure. . . .

3. *Qualitative Materiality*. We cannot demonstrate the conduct, if illegal, reflects on the integrity of Citicorp's management. . . . We have not established that senior management "participated" in any illegal conduct which reflects on its ability to exercise its fiduciary responsibilities or carry-out its stewardship.[9]

Fedders was more outspoken on the shortcomings of the Shearman & Sterling report. "I am troubled by the Shearman & Sterling report," he wrote. "Even though Citicorp's conduct may not have been material, . . . once Citicorp and Shearman & Sterling undertook to describe the conduct they had to do so in an accurate manner. The Shearman & Sterling report lacks clarity and precision. It [makes] several incomplete statements and omissions. Whether they are material misstatements or omissions is not clear. [But] I do not believe that the shortcomings are sufficient for the SEC to initiate an enforcement proceeding based on inadequacies in the Form 8-K."

Fedders concluded, "I believe we would be subject to criticism to initiate an enforcement proceeding more than three years after the filing of the Citicorp Form 8-K. It should not take us three years to make enforcement determinations."[10]

Ryan later said that he and Doherty did not agree with Fedder's

[9] SEC Division of Enforcement staff memo to the commission: Discussion and Recommendation of Director of Division, p. 28.
[10] Ibid., p.30.

judgment. "We considered parking to be an ongoing practice and we thought it was material," he said.

The SEC's office of general counsel, under Edward B. Greene, and division of corporate finance, whose newly appointed director was Lee B. Spencer, jointly sent a "supplemental memo" to the commission. (The memo was signed by John T. Shinkle, the associate general counsel, and Spencer.) It found the lack of disclosure in the Shearman & Sterling report troublesome, but it did not think that proceedings were warranted. The memo expressed a remarkable standard for disclosure:

"Even if we could establish [the] facts, Citicorp apparently had no obligation to disclose them since the Enforcement staff has identified no affirmative representations in its filings as to the honesty or integrity of these persons." Von Stein found this ironic because Citicorp had made several such representations which he quoted in detail in his report.

The office of general counsel, it turned out, had a completely different interpretation of the documents that von Stein relied on in his report. "We read the documents cited in the Enforcement Memorandum as showing no more than that Citicorp management made a reasonable and standard business judgment. The risk that a given course of action would result in a sanction (discounted for the probability that sanctions would result) was compared with the potential return from such a course, and management pursued what it thought likely to be the most profitable course, so long as it did not clearly violate the law. We do not believe that the reasonable investor would find such conduct to be dishonest or immoral."

When Fedders took over as director of enforcement he instituted routine weekly meetings with Shad to keep the chairman abreast of upcoming enforcement issues. Shad didn't want to be surprised by major cases falling into his lap about which he knew nothing. It was logical, then, that within this framework Fedders would have discussed the Citicorp case with Shad before it reached the commission. Fedders denied that he ever discussed it with Shad. Nevertheless, when the Citicorp package finally went before the commission on December 22, 1981, Shad let Fedders do most of the talking. Fedders acted as the principal adversary against the case.

Five commissioners were present, but Barbara Thomas, at thirty-five the youngest and the last commissioner to be appointed by the Carter administration, recused herself from participating in the deliberations for reasons that have never been disclosed. The rest of the commission—John R. Evans, Bevis Longstreth, and Philip A. Loomis, Jr.—remained relatively passive, while chairman Shad conducted what amounted to a trial of the enforcment staff.

Loomis spoke only four times during the ninety-minute session, once to remark, "I can't quite hear you." John Evans, whom Shad insisted on replacing when his term came up for renewal two years later, also spoke only four times, as did Bevis Longstreth, the newest member of the commission. Longstreth was a former partner in the New York law firm of Debevoise & Plimpton, which handled some of Citibank's legal work, but he did not mention this to his fellow commissioners.

The commission had previously thrown out Ryan's Mobil case, which concerned similar issues of non-disclosure. It had done so even though Mobil's attorneys had prepared a report, which the staff had reviewed and found satisfactory, and which the company was ready to file as a Form 8-K, spelling out the incestuous links with Atlas Maritime, the London shipping firm which operated a fleet of Mobil tankers.

Doherty handled the staff's presentation of the Citicorp facts, giving a good overview of why he, Ryan, and von Stein considered them to be material. Shad let him proceed without interruption. Doherty concluded:

"In my view, all of these factors put together, not analyzed separately but all of them, comprise a course of conduct that reflects on the integrity of the management involved; it would reflect on the integrity of the books and records and accountability system; and it could, to some degree, reflect on the quality of the earnings; and it exposed the corporation to significant business risk."

Fedders then summed up his reasons for wanting to drop the case. "I think my arguments come into three categories; and if you would accept any one of the three, I suggest to you that this case should not be brought. Two of the arguments that I would make are legal, and the third is from a commission enforcement policy.

"The first argument, and I think the most persuasive, is the sufficiency of our evidence. We can't prove this case. We have no ability to establish today that the conduct engaged in by Citicorp was illegal. We have circumstantial evidence; we have evidence that tends to indicate that there may have been improper conduct. But we could not walk into an administrative proceeding or to a court today and establish this case, that there was illegal conduct."

Shad interrupted to observe that he had missed the point. ". . .

We have to establish illegality, and I would say to you that we cannot establish that any of it is illegal today,'' Fedders insisted.

"It would be very difficult to reconstruct . . ." Ryan agreed.

"I think you can. . . " von Stein started to say.

"Let me finish," Fedders demanded, cutting him off. "I would suggest to you, from my careful reading of [the von Stein report], it does not establish that there was approval, acquiescence, or anything with regard to involvement by Citicorp. Tom vehemently disagrees with that; I read the evidence very carefully as to what senior management saw, and I suggest to you that it does not establish that they approved it or that they acquiesced in it. There may have been some casual understanding of parking; but to say and to be able to establish that they understood, approved or acquiesced that it was illegal conduct, I don't believe the sufficiency of the evidence is there. That's point number one. I think if you agree with it, any one of the two subparts fails.

"Secondly, the legal issues which everyone has really written to at greater length, and I'll be short on, and that's materiality. I don't believe it's material; I don't believe it's quantitatively material or qualitatively material.

"And from the third point of view, it goes to the length of the investigation; and, from my point of view, it is equally as important as the first two. This investigation was begun in May 1978, three and one half years [ago]. I suggest to you that it would be an embarrassment for this commission to institute a proceeding three and one half years after it began."

Shad asked why there had been this "extraordinary" delay.

Ryan volunteered an answer. "Number one, the first delay was the commission. The commission told us to wait until Shearman & Sterling finished their report."

"Well, but that was in '78," Shad countered.

"That was the first delay, sir. The second delay was Shearman & Sterling and Citicorp in delaying getting documents to us and arranging witnesses. Third, the complexity of the case; and fourth, quite frankly, disagreement among the staff as to the scope of the case."

Just about everyone present had something critical to say about the Shearman & Sterling report. John T. Shinkle, the newly appointed associate general counsel, agreed that the case was "a little unsavory. It's a huge corporation. It's, I gather, the largest foreign exchange trader in the world. It had a variety of practices which we look at today and . . . they don't look very good. But, in the end, it's difficult to see. The quantitative test is reasonably clear; the qualitative test, the materiality, the absence of clear illegality—there's no adjudications; the enforcement posture of the other countries has to be taken into account; the fact that our own comptroller went through this—all those things suggest that this isn't a case of rampant management fraud. . . ."

"Jack, why is it unsavory?" Shad wanted to know.

". . . It smacks of sharp practices; and, I think, likewise, the Shearman & Sterling report was one which, clearly . . . it was carefully drafted by lawyers as attempting to protect the position of their client and not, necessarily, with an idea of making an entirely clean breast of things," Shinkle replied.

"I don't suggest that they attempted to violate the law," he continued. "I don't think they did. But I think the sense that you get when you go through this is that this is a very large corporation engaging in practices fairly close to the line. They probably weren't illegal, or at least there's no establishment—it hasn't been established that they were illegal. But it makes you uncomfortable a little bit. . . ."

Von Stein protested. "We could still find out if it's illegal. I don't think it would be—"

Shad cut him off. "Well, they're now exposed, aren't they? I mean, the governments have reacted to them now."

"That's true," von Stein said. "The governments have reacted; but I suggest that the governments didn't know one-tenth of what we know about it."

"Even now?" Shad asked.

"Even now. Because the governments involved—"

"We don't know that for certain," Fedders said.

Loomis finally spoke up. "I agree that what Citicorp did here was questionable [but] I quite agree with Mr. Fedders, in the exercise of discretion, not to bring this."

Shad asked for Evans's view.

"I find this a very difficult case. I think that the activities involved in here by Citicorp, to me, were an obvious attempt to evade . . . In my view senior management certainly did know what was going on. I don't know how you could possibly say they didn't know what was going on, and the fact that they didn't stop it, I think, is the same thing as approving it. . . . I think the report that Shearman & Sterling did was very misleading in its content, and I think it was intended that it be misleading. They were paid to do that, and I think they were not paid to make it look like Citicorp had done something that was improper. . . . And I think that disclosure here was inadequate, in my opinion. I think that the fact that they made affirmative comments in Shearman & Sterling documents is probably the most difficult and probably the most likely thing where they went wrong. Had they done nothing, I think it would not have been as good a case. I think, all combined, I would be inclined to bring a 15(c) (4)."

Shad asked for Longstreth's opinion.

"I share the agonies around the table because it is a tough case, an awfully tough case. I guess my bottom line is that I, in the exercise of prosecutorial discretion, I guess I wouldn't bring the case," Longstreth said.

"Would not?" Shad asked.

"Would not. I think, and I say that because quantitatively I think it's hard to show materiality in terms of the money made and also in terms of the risk. I think that evaluating the risk is within a business judgment; and if you operate within a business judgment and you don't feel the risk was material, I don't see, I think it's very hard for the SEC to prove that you were wrong, at least in a case as fuzzy as this. . . . I think you do [have a qualitative materiality problem here], but we don't have the case that quite gets there, in my judgment, because you don't know the top management knew about it, and if they didn't, they may have been advised that it's, in other words, it may have been within the business judgment rule to decide that the law's unclear and what we're doing may be okay. So it doesn't quite all come together, although I agree with the comments that have been made here about the sleazy character of this thing. It does have an odor to it, I think, and the odor is made stronger by the Shearman & Sterling [report]. But that's so cleverly done you can't really get a handle on it."

Loomis agreed. "It's very hard to get a handle on it."

"I mean, that's what I'd like to get a handle on, frankly, because it's not a forthright report. . . . And I don't like the idea that the passage of time can mean that our hands are tied because that's certainly frustrating. That just encourages people to delay. . . . But having said all that, I don't think it's a good case now to bring for the various reasons introduced," Longstreth added.

Shad concurred with Longstreth and Loomis. "I think it is a close case in many respects, but I really had a lot of problems with bringing it on the basis of the sufficiency of the evidence. . . . Without protracting on this, I think that the Shearman & Sterling report is a real problem. But taking all the other facts we've got—also, even though it's circumstantial, it doesn't bother me in terms of if we decide to bring it. We bring plenty of things on circumstantial evidence—but it's a question of whether we can sustain the case with the lack of good evidence and the lack of materiality, in my opinion, and so—yeah?''

"The evidence is there," von Stein protested. "There are hundreds of documents which describe the practice."

"The evidence is arguably there," Shad answered. "In your view, it's there, and in the opinion of the other two divisions, it's questionable."

"I'm the only person in this room who has read all the documents, and I'm telling you," von Stein insisted.

"I've reviewed the case and I stand by what I said," Fedders cut in.

"You said that with a little more work you could probably show that they were illegal," Evans prompted.

"A hell of a lot more work," Fedders cut in. "This was an enormous case to prove illegality. That's the important thing. You've got to go in with that premise. The first thing the judge should say, whether administrative law or civil judge, is 'Okay, prove your case.' We don't have any proof that the conduct was illegal. We think we can obtain it, but after three and one half years we don't have it. That's what concerns me, and I suggest to you that it's numerous months because the letters Tom wants to get from foreign countries, we got to get through the State Department, the Department of Justice. It's a very lengthy process, and I question—the word that was used at the table is more correct than any other word: it was *questionable* practices. In the so-called questionable payments area, the commission was involved with dealing with illegal practices—bribes, payoffs, kickbacks, and the things—but these are none of those. These are questionable practices, and I suggest to you that we don't have evidence that they are illegal."

Shad agreed with Fedders.

"On that basis," he said, "I concur with the other two commissioners. Thank you very much."[11]

---

[11] Excerpted from a transcript of the December 22, 1981, meeting of the Securities & Exchange Commission, as reprinted in Hearings before the Subcommittee on Oversight and Investigations of the Committee on Energy and Commerce, House of Representatives, September 13 and 17, 1982, Serial No. 97–193, pages 305–326.

Chapter 39

Materiality

All I am saying is that the issue was irrelevant.

—JOHN E. HOFFMAN, JR., JUNE 28, 1983

The Shad Commission did not consider the most compelling argument on materiality. It was expressed by no less an expert than the deputy comptroller of the currency for multinational banking, and it contradicted the views of John Fedders on the subject with the sharp crack of authority.

First, the deputy comptroller, Billy Wood, listed the wrongful acts that his inspectors confirmed that Citibank traders had committed:

- conducting foreign exchange transactions at off-market rates;
- shifting profits from one jurisdiction to another;
- avoiding local income taxes on foreign exchange by off-booking transactions;
- avoiding stamp tax on foreign exchange contracts;
- parking positions to avoid local exchange restrictions;
- failing to properly reflect trading profits on the bank's books.[1]

---

[1] Letter from Billy C. Wood to the board of directors of Citibank N.A., December 8, 1980.

Although most of this activity was clearly illegal—avoiding taxes, for example, and failing to keep proper books—none had been adjudicated, so to speak, which didn't bother the deputy comptroller. He simply wanted Citibank to put a stop to it because it was unsound and unsafe banking practice. But Wood's list was expert confirmation of everything von Stein had highlighted in his draft report. As far as the deputy comptroller was concerned, the proof existed, and if it was good enough for him, it should have been good enough for Shad and his fellow commissioners.

But the real meat of Wood's findings was the materiality of these deeds. These "unsound" practices "exposed the bank to penalties and assessments levied by foreign supervisors," he pointed out. "Although not precisely a quantifiable risk, satisfactory relations with foreign sovereign licensing authorities is viewed as *critically important* to the corporate operations of Citibank N.A."[2]

The U.S. Supreme Court, in a 1976 decision, provided a simple yardstick for defining materiality:

An omitted fact is material if there is a substantial likelihood that reasonable shareholders would consider it important in deciding how to vote. . . . Put another way, there must be a substantial likelihood that the disclosure of the omitted fact would have been viewed by the reasonable investor as having significantly altered the "total mix" of information made available.[3]

Any practice that—as the administrator of multinational banks expressed it—risked upsetting Citibank's *critically important* relations with foreign governments was manifestly material, considering that more than 60 percent of Citibank's earnings came from abroad.

Some doubt at the SEC obviously persisted on this issue. While the Citicorp case was now shelved, and virtually dead, it was not officially closed as no closing memo, standard procedure at the commission, was entered into the files. The case was condemned to a roosting place in SEC limbo.

---

[2] Ibid., p. 3; emphasis added.
[3] *TSC Industries Inc.* v. *Northway Inc.*, 426 U.S. 438 (1976).

Part V

THE LEAK

Chapter 40

Gerth's Scoop

> *Despite our system of checks and balances, the press remains largely accountable only to itself and, therefore, depends critically on the responsibility of its reporters. It is troubling that in the Citicorp matter that responsibility was missing.*
>
> —BEVIS LONGSTRETH, MARCH 1, 1982

SEC associate director of enforcement Irwin Borowski, a Democrat, did not get on with John Fedders, his new boss. He did not like Fedder's enforcement politics. Borowski had helped structure many of the management-integrity cases under Sporkin. Fedders made it clear that he intended to bring very few of this type of case.

Borowski resigned from the SEC in September 1981, two months after Fedders took over as head of the division of enforcement. He became counsel of the Subcommittee on Oversight and Investigations of the House Energy and Commerce Committee. Both the subcommittee and its parent, the House Energy and Commerce Committee, were chaired by Congressman John D. Dingell, Democrat, from Michigan.

While at the SEC, Borowski had followed von Stein's investigation of Citicorp. He had not played any part in shaping the case, as it came under Doherty's supervision and not his, but he considered it important. He disagreed, however, with the way von Stein concentrated on foreign exchange parking. Nevertheless, Borowski thought "the evidence of materiality was there, if you looked for it." If Fedders couldn't see the materiality of parking, Borowski thought it was because the new enforcement chief had not read the report very carefully.

Instead of focusing on the amount of foreign exchange earnings parked in Nassau—the $42 million—Borowski felt that von Stein should have paid more attention to the total volume of Citibank's parking of loans as well as foreign exchange and money market positions. This would have reached astronomical sums, he said.

Referring to a Peat Marwick work paper, Borowski pointed out that in 1978, one-fifth of Citibank's total assets of approximately $75 billion was booked through Nassau. Considering Nassau was only one of Citibank's offshore booking centers, the total amount booked through accommodation branches had to be much larger. "Maybe as much as one-half of the bank's balance sheet was run through offshore booking centers," he speculated.

One of Borowski's first tasks as counsel to the Dingell subcommittee, which had oversight responsibility for the SEC, was to find out why the Shad Commission had not proceeded with the Mobil case. In January 1982, he called Ryan to the subcommittee offices in the Rayburn House Office Building for questioning. Ryan came accompanied by John Shinkle, from the SEC's office of general counsel. As assistant general counsel, Shinkle was newly appointed under the Shad administration. Peter Stockton, the subcommittee's investigator, handled the questioning of Ryan. He asked the SEC attorney whether it was unusual for the commission to turn down a staff recommendation.

Shinkle volunteered that it wasn't unusual at all. He said the commission had just turned down another staff recommendation for action against "a major New York bank." Borowski, without saying anything, took note. He knew that the only case the SEC had against a major New York bank was the Citibank case.

On the way back to the SEC headquarters, Shinkle asked Ryan if Borowski could figure out that the "major New York bank" was in fact Citibank.

"Of course Irwin could," Ryan said.

Borowski, in fact, had already heard through the grapevine that the commission had turned down the staff recommendation on Citicorp. This and the killing of the Mobil case indicated a shift in the commission's attitude to management-integrity issues. He mentioned it to Michael F. Barrett, Jr., the subcommittee's staff director and general counsel. Barrett, like Dingell, was interested in how Shad intended to deregulate the securities industry. Here was clear indication that major corporations were no longer a primary target of the SEC's enforcement efforts. Dingell asked Barrett to find out exactly what had happened.

About this time, veteran *New York Times* investigative reporter Jeff Gerth visited the subcommittee offices in search of information concerning another, unrelated, matter. He met Borowski and told him he was working on two SEC stories. Borowski asked if Citicorp was one of them. Gerth was sufficiently vague that Borowski, two years later, could not recall with certainty the reporter's reply. Borowski's question, however, sparked Gerth's interest.

A member of the *Times*'s Washington bureau, Gerth was a thoughtful and meticulous journalist who was a frequent critic of inept government. He had helped, for example, expose the Libyan connections of two former CIA agents, Edwin P. Wilson and Frank E. Terpil, who were suspected of acting with the connivance of senior CIA officials. Gerth knew the SEC had an investigation of Citicorp in progress because in his clipping file he had a 1978 *Wall Street Journal* article that mentioned the Citibank probe.

This article had intrigued Gerth because it quoted a Citibank spokesman as denying any impropriety by the bank in its foreign exchange operations. The spokesman said that Citibank had ordered a study by outside attorneys and auditors to *certify* that this was so. "We believe, of course, we were in accord with applicable laws, and the purpose of the study is to confirm this," it reported.[1]

The statement indicated to Gerth that Citibank had commissioned the Shearman & Sterling study with a precise objective in mind and therefore had predetermined the results.

When Borowski mentioned that the commission had killed the Citicorp case, he said Gerth seemed to know about it already. "I didn't give him any documents, because I didn't have any."

Gerth, like Borowski, wondered whether the commission's decision reflected a new political orientation. He decided to go after the

---

[1] "Citibank's Activities Being Probed by the SEC," *The Wall Street Journal*, July 27, 1978.

documents. After a lot of hard work, he got hold of the package that went to the commission—von Stein's summary memo, with Fedders's counterrecommendation incorporated, and the joint memo from the office of general counsel and the corporate finance division. He was not able to put his hands on a transcript of the commission meeting, as none had been typed up. Only a tape had been made. Gerth never disclosed the source of the documents other than to comment that "they didn't come by the obvious route."

All fingers pointed to von Stein. But the documents had been circulated to about fifty people—the five commissioners, the agency's secretary, the executive assistant to the chairman, all senior staff officers, nine regional administrators, and the heads of the six branch offices. Gerth did not get a copy of von Stein's main report, as it had an extremely limited circulation.

Concerned that someone else might be working on the story, Gerth wanted to complete his inquiries as quickly as possible. He contacted Citibank for comment and received a one-page typewritten statement from the public relations department. The statement cited the complexity of international tax laws and said that nearly four years before, the bank had "ordered changes in procedures wherever we felt there was any room for misunderstanding or dispute" and had "reallocated profits among several country operations, where earlier allocations had been questioned or might be opened to question."

Gerth's story appeared on page one of *The New York Times* of February 18, 1982, under the headline: "SEC Overruled Finding by Staff that Citicorp Had Masked Profit." Aside from a recital of the facts, the article stated:

> The commission's decision, made in a closed meeting, has dismayed some current and former commission officials. They described the Citicorp case as the most dramatic example of how the Reagan Administration's philosophy of deregulation is turning the commission away from its statutory duty to protect investors and toward protecting the interest of the publicly held corporations that it regulates.
>
> The Citicorp case, these officials say, represents an abrupt reversal of SEC policies in the 1970s, which held that disclosure of questionable payments by corporations, even relatively small amounts, was vital because it addressed the issue of management integrity. Under Federal securities laws, the SEC's principal regulatory weapon is its power to require publicly held companies to disclose important matters.

The critics, who are still in the Government and asked that they not be named, said their dismay stemmed not simply from the commission's overruling of its enforcement staff, which they concede has become a more frequent occurrence in recent years.

Instead, the critics point to the evidence uncovered during the investigation—which they consider as yet unrefuted—and to what they say is an abdication of the agency's responsibility to enforce basic standards of honesty in corporate behavior.

Between three and four in the morning that Thursday, February 18, 1982, unable to sleep, David Edwards was staring at the ceiling of his private hospital room in Wichita Falls when the telephone rang. David had broken his back playing touch football that winter and spent the next three months lying flat on a bed without springs.

The accident marked a new low for David. He was overtaken by insomnia and for the first time knew what it was like to lie awake all night contemplating the world and his misfortune. At first he had thought a lot about Citibank, the institution he had once felt so proud to be a part of, but gradually he stopped reliving the pain of the cover-up, the indignity of being lied to and thinking he was at fault for not properly expressing himself, and finally the guilt for having acted so naïvely, and for some weeks it had been out of his mind.

He reached for the phone, grateful for the break it offered in the monotony of waiting for daybreak. A former girl friend from New York, who was also an insomniac, was on the other end of the line. She had just read the Gerth story on the front page of *The New York Times*. She spent an hour on the phone reading it to him.

Fighting senior management at Citicorp had cost David his banking career and wiped out his savings of $50,000. But now the cover-up was exposed, and he suddenly felt elated again. It was a turning point in his depression.

Gerth followed his initial report with two others, one on the following day disclosing the private investigation by the Office of the Comptroller of the Currency's national bank examiners into Citibank's parking operations. It noted that two subcommittees of the House Commerce Committee, which had oversight over the SEC, said they intended to investigate the commission's handling of the Citicorp case. One was the Subcommittee on Telecommunications, Consumer Protection and Finance. It was holding hearings on the Foreign Corrupt Practices Act. The other was the Dingell subcommittee.

The third article appeared on March 1, 1982, under the headline: "SEC Vote On Citicorp Questioned." It began:

Bevis Longstreth, one of three Securities & Exchange commissioners who voted against bringing an enforcement action against Citicorp for inadequate disclosure of its foreign currency trading practices, says he once represented the bank and was a partner in a law firm that has long had Citibank as a client.

Mr. Longstreth testified last July at his confirmation hearings that he intended to withdraw from 'any enforcement proceedings in which my former firm was involved in any way in representing a party.'

Mr. Longstreth said in a telephone interview that his Senate pledge was meant to apply only to clients his former firm, Debevoise, Plimpton, Lyons & Gates, represents before the SEC, not to general representation as is the case with Citibank. . . .

Mr. Longstreth also says that he thought about disqualifying himself from the commission decision because it might appear that he had a conflict of interest, but thought it was more important that the commission hear his views on the matter. . . .

Mr. Longstreth, according to sources familiar with the commission's deliberations, argued that Citicorp had acted properly by measuring the risk of getting caught against the potential profits to be gained by the questionable currency transactions.

'I think that it's hard to show the materiality in terms of the money made and also in terms of the risk. I think that evaluating the risk is within a business judgment,' Mr. Longstreth reportedly argued. . . .

The article disclosed that Longstreth had represented Citibank in the mid-1960s, when it invested in a subsidiary of Penn Central, and again briefly in the early 1970s, when the bank was involved in the railroad's bankruptcy proceedings. The Debevoise Plimpton firm also represented the personal estate and trust department of Citibank, an account which, the article pointed out, was "not insignificant" for the law firm.

"Mr. Longstreth is the newest commissioner, filling out the final year of the term of Stephen J. Friedman, who left the agency last June to become a partner again in Debevoise, Plimpton.

"Mr. Longstreth, in his confirmation proceedings, said he had no present plans to return to his old firm. However, he still maintains some links to the firm. Until January 1988 he will be receiving his share of the firm's profits . . . and while at the SEC, the trustee of his blind trust is a Debevoise, Plimpton partner, according to Mr. Longstreth's financial disclosure forms."

Longstreth reacted sharply to Gerth's article. He immediately dispatched a letter to the *Times* protesting that Gerth's reporting "does no credit to the *Times*'s reputation for responsible journalism."

As the headline suggests, Mr. Gerth's goal is to question my integrity in participating in the Citicorp matter. Clever splicing of selective portions of my statement to him on the telephone with comments from his unidentified sources seeks to serve this goal. I'd like to set the record straight.

- Mr. Gerth persists in misreading the oral and written statements on disqualification that I made to the Senate. The written language has been used by other commissioners. It means exactly what it says. When my former law firm is representing a party in an SEC enforcement proceeding or is seeking exemption from a rule or statute, I will recuse myself. This was not the case here.
- As Mr. Gerth states, I did consider disqualifying myself on the basis of a possible appearance of conflict of interest. But I also told him that the Citicorp matter involved important policy issues that I thought I ought to be involved in, barring an actual conflict. I stressed my view that I had a duty to act on as many commission decisions as possible. . . .
- In describing my brief representation of Citibank over a decade ago, Mr. Gerth does not point out that Citibank was just one of three clients and the representation was limited to handling their investment in secured notes of a Penn Central subsidiary. . . .

Over all, the publicity given by Mr. Gerth to the Citicorp matter—through internal documents leaked in violation of law—contains bias and innuendo calculated to impeach the commission's processes. The commission cannot respond without being unfair to others and further injuring its processes. Yet the cost to our effectiveness may be significant. . . .[2]

In spite of having told the Senate at his confirmation hearings that he had "no present plans" to return to his old firm, Longstreth did not seek to renew his term as commissioner when it expired three months later. He returned as a partner to Debevoise, Plimpton, which continued to do a sizable amount of work for Citibank's personal trust division.

[2] Letter to the Editor, "Of Citicorp and an SEC Commissioner," *The New York Times*, March 5, 1982.

Chapter 41

Search for the Leaker

"The SEC has for many years had an enviable reputation as the premier regulatory agency in Government."

—JOHN D. DINGELL, SEPTEMBER 13, 1982

The Citicorp case would have died and been forgotten had the Gerth articles not appeared. Deeply stung by their publication, the Shad Commission reacted in an unprecedented manner. Contrary to Longstreth's affirmation that the SEC "cannot respond . . . without further injuring its processes," four days after Gerth's article impugning the Longstreth vote, the commission issued a press release explaining its decision to spare the omnipotent Citicorp the embarrassment of an administrative proceeding. Some said it was undignified for the commission to explain in public a decision made in a closed hearing around the commission table.

For Immediate Release: Friday, March 5   82-19
CITICORP
The Commission has released the following statement concerning an investigation involving Citicorp:
There have been recent press reports concerning the Commis-

sion's decision not to take action against Citicorp for not disclosing alleged foreign exchange trading improprieties to avoid foreign taxes and currency exchange controls.

Certain members of the enforcement staff believed that Citicorp violated the Commission's disclosure rules. However, the Director of the Division of Enforcement, the Office of the General Counsel and the Division of Corporation Finance were of a contrary opinion. The factors that influenced a majority of the Commissioners' decision not to bring the case included the following:

1. The allegations were not adequately established.
2. Even if established, the alleged amounts for the years in question were not material to Citicorp.
3. The Comptroller of the Currency had concluded that no action was warranted under U.S. banking laws.
4. The law concerning disclosure of unadjudicated allegations is unclear. There would have been a serious possibility of court reversal of the Commission's action, which would have been bad precedent.
5. The matter was essentially a banking or tax case, not a securities case.
6. The case was old. The practices in question occurred in 1973 to 1978.

The illegal disclosure to the press of confidential Commission proceedings is also a serious cause of concern. It violates the rights and interests of private parties, inhibits the Commission's ability to obtain essential cooperation of the private sector in its investigations and undermines the candid debate of critical issues by members of the Commission and the staff necessary to well considered decisions. It is for these reasons that the Commission normally does not comment on actions not brought.

In view of the distorted impressions created by statements in the press, the Commission would welcome the opportunity to provide a full account of its handling of the Citicorp matter before an appropriate Congressional committee.

Responding to the commission's professed desire, Congressman Dingell's subcommittee invited the SEC to supply it with the relevant documents in the Citicorp case so that it could begin preparing for hearings. After some initial concern over what should be made available, the SEC sent its entire Citicorp file to the subcommittee offices on Capitol Hill.

The commission, though, was still irked by the leak of its non-public documents and, in a mood of growing paranoia, ordered its own investigation to find and punish the leaker. Such matters are handled by the SEC's ethics counsel, staff attorney Myrna Seigel. She interviewed Ryan and von Stein several times.

Ryan told Seigel the story of his visit to the Dingell subcommittee offices with John Shinkle and Shinkle's comment about "a major New York bank." She drafted an affidavit for Ryan to swear, which stated that "a member of the staff may have mentioned the matter to the subcommittee."

Ryan did not like the inference that a member of the enforcement division might have been the culprit and before signing the affidavit changed it to read "a member of the staff in the Office of General Counsel. . ."

Von Stein swore an affidavit in which he affirmed he did not know Gerth, had never met him, had never communicated in any way directly or indirectly with him, and had no knowledge of how Gerth obtained the commission documents.

He did state that on February 5, 1982, he had invited Stanley Sporkin and his wife to dinner at his home and that Citicorp may have been mentioned in the conversation during the course of the evening, but that he had no recollection either way.

A number of other persons were required to swear similar affidavits as the staff, with morale sinking, became engulfed in the commission's paranoia.

Seigel even went outside the agency in search of the leaker. She asked Borowski to swear that he was not responsible for providing Gerth with the documents. He assured her he was not, but refused to give a sworn statement because it would set a precedent that might be used against Congressional staff members in future investigations. Next, Seigel went across the Potomac to the CIA in Langley, Virginia, and asked Sporkin to swear that he was not the leaker. Sporkin was deeply offended but agreed.

Sporkin had not leaked the documents on behalf of von Stein to *any* member of the press. That was not his style. In any event, both he and Borowski had left the agency months before the documents came into existence. Still, Seigel persisted. What about the dinner party? she asked. What dinner party? Sporkin wanted to know. The one at von Stein's home in early February: two "reporters" were among the guests, Seigel reminded him. Sporkin had forgotten about the "dinner party." The two other guests Seigel referred to were a British television producer and his associate producer for a three-part series on the Rise, Fall, and Rape of IOS. One year later, the associate producer began writing this book, but he can assure Ms. Seigel that the topic of Citicorp never came up.

The leaker was never uncovered. No one owned up to the deed, which had the effect of resuscitating a case that, according to the commission's scenario, should already have been dead.

Part VI

THE UNRAVELING

Chapter 42

The Dingell Hearings

In any organization of 60,000 people, whether it be a corporation or a small city, there will always be a handful of people who do not follow the rules. As President Kennedy remarked, when an Air Force pilot flew a mission near Russian Siberia during the Cuban missile crisis, "There is always some guy who doesn't get the message."

—WALTER B. WRISTON, JUNE 28, 1983

Citicorp under Mr. Wriston has made the sort of big decisions that would give other bankers heart attacks. It has also made the sort of spectacular boners in foreign exchange dealing and in Latin American lending for example that bring smiles of smug satisfaction to conventional banking lips.

—The Times (LONDON), JUNE 21, 1984

John David Dingell, Jr., a lawyer from the industrial suburbs of Detroit, former cloakroom page, and the son of a New Deal congressman, was chairman of the oldest committee on Capitol Hill, the House Committee on Energy and Commerce, and with it, the Subcommittee on Oversight and Investigations.

Dingell, then fifty-six and a twenty-six year veteran of Congress, was regarded as one of the most powerful and best legislators in the House. He was respected for his ability to treat his opponents fairly, move legislation, deal with the Senate, and protect his Energy and Commerce power base—and its constellation of six subcommittees—among the busiest and best staffed on the Hill.

Many crucial decisions made in Dingell's Energy and Commerce diocese affect the lifestyles and habits of American consumers in domains as basic and diverse as health and welfare, entertainment, investing, sports, and nuclear power. In an average session of Congress, between 30 and 35 percent of the bills introduced in the House fall under Dingell's jurisdiction.

The burly, six-feet-three Dingell felt that the Citicorp matter was worthy of attention. The SEC's handling of the case had the whiff of political partisanship to it. After requesting the SEC to turn over its files, in mid-June 1982 Dingell wrote Wriston and announced that his Oversight and Investigations Subcommittee was "reviewing Citicorp's foreign exchange trading activities and the disposition by the SEC of its investigation into these matters."

Dingell requested that Citicorp make available to the subcommittee by the end of the month all documents, memoranda, correspondence, and drafts in the possession of Citicorp or outside counsel relating to:

(1) Opinions obtained in 1977 regarding the legal or other risks involved in the parking of foreign exchange positions.
(2) the Legal opinions of foreign counsel obtained by Shearman & Sterling during their investigation in 1978.

Dingell's staff realized that taking on Wriston and Citibank would be no small enterprise. Since Wriston had been named Citicorp chairman in 1970, his stature in the world of banking had grown apace with the bank's assets, which had more than quadrupled—fom $25.5 billion to $110 billion in 1982. This still placed Citibank second to Bank of America, but not for much longer.

Citicorp—the concept of a bank-holding company was Wriston's brainchild—was already the number one financial institution in the United States in terms of earnings, which were $555 million for 1981. Citicorp's total capital was $4.3 billion; at year-end '81, its loans to foreign governments and official institutions were equal to its capital, while its loans to the third world in general—both the public and private sectors—exceeded $8 billion. Fully two-thirds of its income was generated from outside the United States.

Troubling, but unnoticed amid the concern over the SEC's refusal to force Citicorp to be more forthcoming in its public disclosure, was the thirty-percent increase during 1981, a year of "ferment in the financial marketplace," according to Wriston's letter to stockholders, of Citibank's non-performing loans. At a chilling $800 million, they were equivalent to one-fifth of its capital and were soon to increase even more dramatically.

Wriston, *sans souci,* had powerful friends. Shuttling back and forth to Washington, he advised President Reagan on economic affairs—indeed he was about to be appointed chairman of the President's Economic Policy Advisory Board. He attended White House dinners for visiting heads of state, and his public image had gone from banker-philosopher to statesman-banker.

"There's even a theory," one pundit reported, "that he was passed over for Secretary of the Treasury in the [first] Reagan Administration not because of any possible conflict of interest (Citibank's empire is so vast it would be impossible for Wriston to extricate himself from all issues touching his bank) but because he would have outshone Reagan in his embodiment of those all-American virtues [hard work, ambition, and achievement]—not to mention intellectual prowess."[1]

Wriston's eye was more and more drawn to Washington. He was two years away from Citicorp's mandatory retirement age of sixty-five. Preparing for his succession (Citicorp vice-chairman Al Costanzo had already retired; Citibank president Bill Spencer and executive committee chairman Edward Palmer were about to retire), in June 1982 Citicorp announced the three top contenders for Wriston's job—Hans Angermueller, Thomas Theobald, and John Reed, who was in charge of Citicorp's consumer banking—had been elevated to the equal rank of vice-chairman.

Realizing the ride was not going to be as easy with the Democrat-dominated Dingell subcommittee as it had been with the Republican-dominated SEC, Citicorp hired the Washington law firm of Wilmer, Cutler & Pickering to deal with the demons on the Hill. The firm's senior partner, Lloyd Cutler, was a staunch Democrat who had been

[1] Fran R. Schumer, "Banking on the Future," *Barron's,* April 12, 1982.

Washington counsel to Jimmy Carter. He was imagined, therefore, to have the right kind of pull with Big John Dingell.

Citicorp, in its first move of a strategy to delay the subcommittee's inquiry as much as possible, waited until the appointed deadline before responding to Dingell's letter. Then, on June 30, 1982, Michael Klein, a partner in the Wilmer Cutler firm, met with the subcommittee staff—counsel Irwin Borowski and investigator Peter Stockton— to test the waters, so to speak. Klein requested that the subcommittee itemize the areas of inquiry it was interested in pursuing.

While Dingell's staff drafted such a list, Citibank executive vice-president Charles E. Long replied to Dingell's initial request by supplying only the names of European counsel retained by Shearman & Sterling in 1978. Long said that Citicorp had taken note of the request for other documents concerning the 1978 special review, but that counsel was still determining whether legal imperatives permitted their release.

In mid-July, Dingell responded to Klein's suggestion by furnishing a list of twelve areas the subcommittee was interested in exploring and asked that the corresponding documents be made available by the end of the month, a deadline Citicorp also finessed.

As Dingell's staff pondered how to win Citicorp's compliance short of issuing a subpoena, Wriston's bankers were busily syndicating a $45 million Eurodollar loan that Citicorp International had concluded in May 1982 with Petroleos Mexicanos, the Mexican state oil company. The Pemex loan was a standard short-term credit facility. It fell due at the end of October 1982. Like all big banks engaged in syndicating Eurodollar loans, Citibank "sold" participations in these loans to smaller banks.

Thus, as an example, on July 12, 1982, Citibank sold 11 percent of the Pemex loan, representing $5 million in principal, to the Michigan National Bank of Detroit. For Michigan National, it represented a sure-fire profit of around $250,000 come October, when the loan was scheduled to be repaid. Mexico, after all, was awash in new-found oil reserves and the syndicator was Wriston's pristine Citicorp, an institution to be trusted. Citicorp also sold participations in the Pemex loan to First City Bank of Dallas, Banc One of Columbus, Ohio, Siam Commercial Bank, Los Angeles, Banca Catalana, New York, and Asian International Bank, New York.

At the time, only a handful of doomsayers cried reckless the lending policies of Citicorp and other multinational banks to developing nations. In fact, by lending so generously to the third world, Citibank and the other big banks were viewed by some in government and international finance as actually bolstering the system. The big banks were, it was true, providing much needed liquidity to the system, albeit without thought of a master scheduling plan and only their own commercial interests in mind. All aspects of the problem considered, third world lending was merely an extension of the petrodollar recycling that major multinational banks had been required to undertake in the mid-1970s—a role that arguably should have been assumed by governmental or international agencies.

Dingell's staff were oblivious to any pending debt crisis. But they were concerned whether Citicorp would meet the new deadline for producing documents. On July 28, 1982, Citibank's Long, while protesting "the greatly expanded range of subjects [covering] matters that encompass the principal dynamics of the international banking system," suggested that the subcommittee staff might like to consult a large file of more than 12,000 pages of materials—the lode of "refined" documents, slightly enhanced, which the SEC staff had reviewed at the Shearman & Sterling offices in New York. Borowski, like Ryan and von Stein before him, made the pilgrimage to the Shearman & Sterling offices at Citicorp Center, where he was shown, file by file, the documents from which he was allowed to make notes but not photocopies. In a letter to Citicorp's attorneys a few days later, Borowski requested that several hundred of the documents be turned over to the subcommittee. These were finally released sometime in February 1983.

A monkey wrench was thrown into the works at this point by the publication of a critical article in *The American Lawyer* about Shearman & Sterling's efforts to absolve its largest client of the wrongdoings alleged by the troublesome Edwards. The article, by editor Steven Brill, remarked that the Shearman & Sterling report "raises anew the old question of how far a lawyer, or law firm, should go for its client."[2]

The basis for the article, it turned out, was leaked by a staff member of the Dingell subcommittee, though at first Hoffman suspected it was the work of the original SEC leaker. It quoted extensively from that section of von Stein's 138-page draft report discussing the adequacy of Shearman & Sterling's work. Brill also uncovered shortcomings in the Shearman & Sterling report of which von Stein had not been aware.

Von Stein wrote a memo to Doherty, who took it up with Fedders,

[2]Steven Brill, "What Price Loyalty," *The American Lawyer*, August 1982.

recommending an investigation of Shearman & Sterling based on the new disclosures in the Brill article. Fedders felt sufficiently threatened by the article to do something about it.

The article hinted that Fedders had done Shad's bidding in recommending the Citicorp case be dropped. His thirteen paragraphs attached to the staff memo that went before the commission "probably represented the Reagan-appointed commissioners' position as well as his own," the article stated.

Fedders invited Hoffman to a meeting at his office on August 5, 1982. He also had present, in addition to Doherty, Ryan, and von Stein, two members of the general counsel's office, Paul Gonson, the SEC solicitor, and Russ Stevenson, a deputy general counsel. Hoffman was accompanied by Robert Carswell, a senior Shearman & Sterling partner who had worked on the Citibank account for twenty-five years, and another senior partner, Joseph T. McLaughlin.

McLaughlin said nothing throughout the meeting. But Hoffman was disturbed because it seemed that just about everyone had a copy of the von Stein draft report [he assumed Brill had one, when in fact Brill only had extracts from the report] but Citicorp and Shearman & Sterling. When Shearman & Sterling asked the SEC's Office of General Counsel for a copy, the request was refused.

Hoffman and Carswell were curious as to how Brill had obtained the names of European counsel. Von Stein said it was not from the SEC, because the staff had never learned their identities. Hoffman replied: "I'm not so sure."

The Brill article concerned Hoffman for several reasons. He said it was painful to have his firm's name dragged through the gutter. He considered the 1978 Shearman & Sterling report, which he had authored, "a textbook operation." He cast doubt on Brill's integrity as a reporter, a point of view that Fedders seemed to credit.

Carswell stated that he once had thrown Brill out of his office. He also said that European counsel whom Brill had contacted had refused to talk with him. This didn't prevent Brill from quoting Jacques de Liedekerke, who had written the Brussels opinion, even though de Liedekerke claimed to have told Brill to get lost. Brill, who had previously written extensively about Shearman & Sterling, also quoted a source inside the law firm. Hoffman said as far as he knew, Brill had no Shearman & Sterling source.

In a discussion of the scenarios, which Brill attacked for telling "less than the full story," Hoffman burst out: "I don't know where Brill gets his facts."

A staff memo summing up the meeting recorded that the SEC participants did not feel Hoffman was "as responsive as he could have been" to their questions. "The whole discussion regarding whether Shearman & Sterling told European counsel the full [and] relevant story . . . was somewhat unreal, in that S&S was describing bits and pieces here and there of the scenarios or other documents relating to what S&S told European counsel, without the staff having the whole document. Such documents exist, S&S paraphrased them, and the opinions based on them in the S&S report, but we have not seen them," the SEC memo stated.

The real irony, Brill had pointed out, was "regardless of whether securities laws require a company to voluntarily reveal that it is skirting foreign exchange and tax laws, there is little debate that an 8-K filing—a disclosure document—is supposed to disclose accurately and fully the conduct it purports to be disclosing. Put differently, even if Citicorp's conduct didn't violate securities laws, Shearman & Sterling might have violated those laws if its report about Citicorp's conduct was deceptive."

Shad had already stated that he considered the Shearman & Sterling report "a real problem," and Fedders concurred. After the Hoffman meeting, the commission suggested that the office of general counsel look more closely at it. But nothing resulted. The file remained buried in the solicitor's office, and no recommendation was ever made.

Two weeks later, the world's second largest debtor, Mexico, informed its creditors that it was unable to service, let alone repay, its existing foreign debt. Mexico had borrowed from foreign banks, governments, and official institutions $80 billion upon which it now declared a temporary payments moratorium.

How the world's fifth largest oil producer and thirteenth largest economy, with a population of seventy million people, had reached that point was not easy to explain. Citibank had $3.2 billion tied up in Mexican loans—including the short-term credit to Pemex, which only six weeks before had looked so secure—and this amount was equal to more than two-thirds of its capital.

Citibank took a leading place among the 115 international banks whose representatives met that Friday, August 20, 1982, at the Federal Reserve Bank of New York with Mexico's minister of finance to find a way of averting disaster. The Bank for International Settlements in Basle, a sort of European central bank for central bankers, agreed to provide Mexico with an emergency loan of $1.5 billion; the

U.S. Treasury chipped in another $2 billion; and the International Monetary Fund provided $3.6 billion to tide Mexico over its liquidity crisis. Eventually, the commercial banks made a commitment to pump another $5 billion into the Mexican economy in fresh loans while rolling over for six more months the $10 billion (including the $45 million from Pemex) in existing loans that had fallen due.[3]

The Dingell subcommittee suddenly realized with the debt crisis it had a hot number on its hands. The subcommittee expanded the scope of the hearings, now firmly scheduled, in an initial phase, for mid-September. Finally, on Wednesday, August 25, 1982, while the bankers were still working out the details of a Mexican rescue package—and more than two months after Dingell's original request—Citibank's Long responded with a list of the European legal and tax advisors who counseled Citibank about parking in 1977. But Citibank still declined to turn over the 1978 legal opinions and the Shearman & Sterling scenarios.

In order to permit Citicorp "to begin to provide the subcommittee staff with copies of documents," William Perlik, another Wilmer Cutler partner, drafted a ten-page "Memorandum of Understanding Concerning Non-Disclosure and Confidential Treatment," which he asked Congressman Dingell, staff director Barrett, and investigator Stockton to sign. A paragraph on sanctions, in addition to those imposed by the law, required the immediate dismissal of any "investigator or agent" of the subcommittee who violated the agreement.

The memo went into Borowski's filing cabinet and remained there, unsigned and unacknowledged.

The hearings opened at 10 A.M. on Monday, September 13, 1982, in the second-floor committee room of the Rayburn Building. The room, with its French empire-style blue and gold decor, was crowded with onlookers, one of whom, Henry Weisburg, picked up one of the copies of the von Stein report, which were stacked up on the press table to the left of the witness table. For the first time, Shearman & Sterling had in its hands a copy of the document that had rendered its own report notorious as "the greatest misdisclosure of all."

Dingell, described as "the man with the Delphic smile," rapped the table with his gavel and began by explaining the program for the

---

[3]Michigan National Bank initially refused to consent to an extension of the due date for the Pemex loan and sued Citibank and Citicorp International Bank S.A., a Panamanian corporation, in the U.S. District Court for the Eastern District of Michigan. According to Shearman & Sterling, Michigan National finally accepted the debt restructuring and "the lawsuit became moot and was dismissed."

planned four days of hearings. For the first day, Dingell had called as witnesses the three principal SEC attorneys responsible for handling or overseeing the Citicorp case: Sporkin, Doherty, and von Stein. Ryan, who was interviewed several times by Dingell's staff, was not called to testify. At a second hearing on Friday, Dingell scheduled three banking and accounting experts to place Citicorp's practices within the context of current monetary, economic, and regulatory conditions. "Thereafter," he explained, "we will invite Citicorp and then the commissioners of the SEC."

Dingell explained that the SEC's role in assuring a high level of management integrity was vital to the smooth functioning of the free enterprise system. "It would be one thing if the Citicorp case were an isolated instance. However, a clear pattern of events has emerged showing there was a fundamental shift in the attitude of the commission toward its responsibilities. There is now an emphasis on such things as trading on inside information and stock price manipulation with hardly any mention of the management fraud issues. In an internal list of enforcement priorities containing some nineteen items, the management-integrity-type issues are placed at the bottom.

"Inside information may be important, but corruption, particularly when it occurs in the executive offices and board rooms of major American corporations, is a threat to the whole system. It is a cancer which one day manifests itself as 'cooking the books,' on another occasion in paying bribes, and still another occasion in the issuance of false financial information."

Dingell called Sporkin as the first witness. The former head of enforcement said that if his position had prevailed, the commission would have ordered Citicorp to disclose the full facts concerning the bank's parking practices and correct its filings with the commission, at the same time undertaking publicly not to engage in such practices in the future. To suggest that Citicorp had no obligation to disclose dishonest practices because management had made no representation of moral conduct to stockholders, as the new office of general counsel and division of corporate finance directors had suggested, was "laughable" and, along with a similar notion that no action should be commenced unless there was intervening adjudication of the wrongdoing, would relegate the agency to the status of irrelevancy.

Sporkin explained that "certain preliminary discussions with Shearman & Sterling and representatives of Citibank" had already taken place, and "while we had not reached any definitive understanding, it was my best professional judgment that the proposal I . . . was contemplating would be found to be satisfactory to Citicorp, and the matter would be settled.[4]

"Based upon these views, I directed the staff . . . to finalize the case and proceed along these lines. It was at this time, May 1981, that I left the commission. At that time my instructions on the case to the staff . . . were to wind up the matter and send it up to the commission."

Von Stein, who sat to Sporkin's left at the hearing table, had bought a new suit for the occasion. Albert Gore, Jr., Democrat from Tennessee, did most of the questioning. He referred to the Nassau branch as "an electronic bagman." Discussing the 1975 Natvig/Pomeroy report, he asked whether it had been given to top management.

Von Stein affirmed that it had.

"Mr. Wriston evidently made a note on his copy of the report telling the comptroller to follow up on the matters in the report, which included suggestions to disguise the transactions. Is that correct?"

"Correct."

"Yet he later disavowed knowledge of the report?"

"He didn't recall receiving it. . . ."

Dingell took over the questioning for a moment. He concentrated on establishing the image of Citibank as the largest foreign exchange dealer in the world—twice as large as the number two dealer, von Stein told him—in some instances controlling 20 percent of the world supply of a given currency.

"So with this volume of money, they could significantly affect the flows of currency throughout the world and by using parking transactions . . . they could confer . . . a singularly large benefit upon themselves, could they not?"

"I assume that, but I can't say for sure."

"This amount of money can be moved in defiance of national currency limitations. There is a possibility for adversely affecting the national policies of some of the nations in which those currencies originate, is there not?"

"That is correct."

The chairman yielded the floor to Bob Whittaker, a Republican from Kansas. Whittaker ignored Sporkin and von Stein and addressed a series of leading questions to Doherty. He hinted, for example, that there had been disagreement among the staff over the drafting of the final report and that this was the reason why Ryan had not been invited to testify.

[4]Shearman & Sterling senior partner Joseph T. McLaughlin later denied that any discussion of settlement took place.

Doherty denied there had been any disagreement over the facts, but admitted some differing views concerning the conclusions that could be drawn from the facts. This, he said, was normal in large and complex cases. He was supported by Sporkin.

". . . This was a massive undertaking, and I must take my hat off to Mr. von Stein and Mr. Ryan to be able to do this in the short time in which they did it. You really needed fifty to one hundred people to do this kind of investigation. The reason it takes three and a half years is because you have two people doing a job that fifty to one hundred people ought to be doing," Sporkin said.

Whittaker then had Doherty confirm that the enforcement division had not sought an injunction against Citicorp prohibiting future violations of the law, but only a hearing to determine whether they had complied with the SEC's disclosure requirements. As this was so, hadn't Citicorp fulfilled their requirements by filing the Shearman & Sterling report as an 8-K document?

"We asserted that [the Shearman & Sterling] report was deficient; that it did not comply with the requirements of the Federal securities law," Doherty replied.

Dingell intervened to find out why the report was "deficient."

Doherty explained that the report had not adequately disclosed the nature and scope of the parking transactions, had not adequately disclosed the manner in which they were booked, and had not adequately disclosed management's involvement in the transactions. "I would also say [that] while it contained a number of opinions of local counsel dealing with the legality of the parking transactions, we had significant concern that the information . . . provided to local counsel upon which they based their opinions was not complete."

"Are you saying to us . . . that the information that was provided by Citicorp to the local counsel was not adequate for them to properly characterize the legal character of the behavior of Citicorp with regard to the parking transactions?" Dingell asked.

"That is correct."

". . . Were the full copies of those local counsels' opinions made available to the SEC?"

"They were not."

"Why were they not made available?"

". . . My understanding is that we asked for those materials and the attorney/client privilege was asserted and they were not provided."

Dingell had just touched upon the major weak point in the SEC investigation: their failure to go after the 1978 legal opinions. There was considerable case law to support the argument that once Shearman & Sterling had paraphrased the opinions in a document and made that document public, the privilege was waived and the opinions themselves rightfully should have entered the public domain.

Sporkin admitted later in the hearing that the failure to go after Shearman & Sterling for the opinions was his error. "I took the position that I would prefer to go as far as I could without them, because of two things. One, I didn't want to put more time on the investigation unnecessarily. Two, [von Stein] and I had different views concerning how far we would go in exploring the Shearman & Sterling report. He wanted to go further, and probably was right. I decided . . . to cut it off and get the case moving."

Dingell turned the floor back to Whittaker, whose next approach was to support Citicorp's materiality argument. "Is it true," he asked Doherty, "that the administrative proceedings you recommended would have required the commission to prove that Citicorp failed to comply with the federal securities law reporting requirements in a material respect?"

"Yes."

After hearing that cases concerning the materiality of unadjudicated allegations had been decided either way, Whittaker suggested that acts of unproven wrongdoing could be considered material only when it was deemed likely that a reasonable investor would consider them important in making an investment decision.

"I certainly agree with that," Doherty replied coolly.

Next, Whittaker sought and obtained Doherty's confirmation that in the case of Citicorp, no adjudicated findings existed. Dingell intervened, wanting clarification of the tax claims that Citicorp had settled.

"My recollection is it came up to $10 or $11 million in fines or additional taxes . . . stemming from foreign authorities inquiring into parking-type activities of Citicorp," Doherty specified.

Whittaker then obtained Doherty's admission that $42 million in earnings over a four-year period from an unadjudicated practice was not quantitatively material to Citicorp's operations.

"But that was not the strong position we were taking," Doherty pointed out. "Our view was that all of these elements combined, not discussed independently, but rather the practice, the dollars involved, the risk, and certainly in terms of risk you can get potentially the materiality concern—management involvement, falsification of the records—comprised a course of conduct that did give rise to a disclosable event."

Whittaker ignored Doherty's logic. Instead, he turned and addressed the chair. "Mr. Chairman, could I note that parking, by itself, done at arm's reach, is not illegal and if Citicorp were astute enough to generate a revenue producer, it was to the benefit of their stockholders."

The record was so charged, and Whittaker returned to his assault on Doherty: "Mr. Doherty, according to a June 1982 report of Citicorp's audit committee, all of the payments [for back taxes] except for $1.2 million have been credited against Citicorp's U.S. tax liability. Mr. Doherty, Shearman and Sterling gave you that report, didn't they?"

"Yes, they did."

"Mr. Doherty, would that make the net payments resulting from these transactions five-hundredths of one percent of Citicorp's earnings during the period in question?"

"You will have to do the arithmetic. I have no reason to believe that is not the case, although I would say that what you have to look at in these kinds of things is not just the amount of—"

"But whether they are material—"

Ignoring the interruption, Doherty continued: "—the amount of actual payment, but the risk to the business that comes about by virtue of the practice, and if as Tom indicates, some of the offices were earning up to thirty percent of their foreign exchange earnings through this practice, if it were to be disclosed or be required to cease, that could have a significant impact . . ."

Dingell interrupted and brought up the "domino effect." He read from a "private and confidential" letter Natvig had sent to Eyre in May 1975:

> Logan phoned today. He said Giger has been to the banking authority to answer an allegation by another Swiss bank that he has somehow broken the rules and taken positions against the dollar. . . .
>
> According to Logan, Giger was able to reply satisfactorily, but he also got a warning to the effect that if anything "funny" is going on, the banking authority would have no hesitation in lifting Citibank's license. . . .
>
> We cannot dismiss the possibility of severe reprisals, that central bank action in any one country would almost certainly trigger checkups in all countries, and that in general the Bank has a great deal to lose.

"That indicates some materiality of concern on the possibility of loss of license by Citibank, does it not?" Dingell asked von Stein.

"Yes," von Stein agreed.

"And it further indicates the possibility of a domino effect taking place, cancellation of a license or a proceeding to eliminate a license in one nation . . . would very probably trigger similar inquiries in all other nations, who might feel that then their banking laws, their currency laws, the laws relative to taxes and parking and foreign exchange might be violated; isn't that correct?"

"There are documents which show that Citibank was concerned about that very thing," Von Stein answered.

". . . So that would tend to indicate substantial reason to believe that these might then be material to the investments of the stockholders or potential investors in Citibank, isn't that right?"

"Yes."

Dingell turned the floor back to Whittaker. He reminded Sporkin that in May 1978, because of the commission's fears that the staff lacked expertise in banking matters, he had said the staff would work closely with the comptroller of the currency.

". . . Did the comptroller of the currency conclude after its lengthy investigation that there had been any violations of any . . . laws?" Whittaker asked.

Sporkin was visibly fuming. As far as he was concerned, the comptroller of the currency had refused to cooperate with the SEC after indicating he would. "I don't recall what they concluded. I know what my conclusion was, and there were many instances, Mr. Whittaker, in which we had disagreements with the comptroller.

"First was the [Bert] Lance case, where, as you know, they could find no violation by Mr. Lance and we did, and we brought the case. Later they went in with us.[5]

"There was also a case with Mr. C. Arnholt Smith in San Diego, in which for many years the comptroller of the currency permitted that bank [U.S. National Bank of San Diego, which collapsed in 1973 with $297 million in loans outstanding to companies controlled by Smith, the bank's principal stockholder and chairman] to operate, so I don't know what they did. All I know is what my own views, [based] on . . . sixteen years . . . of experience, told me this was a case."

Dingell took the floor and asked Sporkin if Citicorp had "a potential tax liability . . . of several millions of dollars in each of at least

[5] Mr. Lance consented to an injunction.

four countries: Italy, Germany, Switzerland, France?''

"Yes," Sporkin replied.

"There is potential here of penalties, interest in addition to the tax, isn't that correct?''

"That is correct.''

"There is potential of criminal penalties, criminal prosecutions in each of the countries, is there not?''

"That is correct.''

"There is potential here for jailing of officers of the corporation, and civil and criminal liabilities against the officers of the corporation, is there not?''

"That is correct.''

"There is potential here of loss of licenses to do business as Citicorp was warned in its internal documents, by its people in the field, is that not a fact?''

"That is a very important fact.''

"That is a very important fact, because that could be the entire loss of earnings and the trading in that particular nation, is that not correct?''

"That is correct, Mr. Chairman.''

"And if that were a major nation like Switzerland, which is a major banking center widely used by every country in the world, including the Communist bloc countries, that becomes a very significant fact, does it not?''

"That does.''

Sporkin had a final point to make about Whittaker's seeming contention that no case should be brought unless prior adjudication existed. If that were to become the standard, he said, "then I think the commission will become an irrelevant agency." He cited the Equity Funding insurance fraud scandal, where the SEC had suspended the stock from trading pending the conclusion of its investigation.

"Imagine . . . in the Equity Funding case, we were not going to sit around and wait for the insurance commissioners of California to determine whether they had phony insurance policies. . . . This would have taken three or four years . . . , and a disclosure system is based upon a corporation making immediate disclosure of the facts which they are aware of. Remember, it is the corporation and its officers and officials that have the burden of making those disclosures, and disclosures must be made by them, not on the basis of something that is adjudicated, but on the basis of what they know the facts to be.''

And there the matter rested. After the hearing, Sporkin, Doherty, and von Stein were struck by the detailed expertise that Whittaker had shown. His command not only of the facts but the concepts of law that rendered them important, if not to say material, had impressed them. They supposed, as did members of the subcommittee staff, that he had been fed the questions by Henry Weisburg, who was observed going into the minority members' caucus during a break in the hearing. This assumption was strengthened by his line of questioning, which followed very closely the Citicorp position as formulated by Shearman & Sterling.

But the questions, it turned out, were not fed to Whittaker by Citicorp. It was Fedders himself who disclosed that he had prepared them. Through Whittaker, he said, he was able to show that his staff had not made their case and that his judgment had in fact been correct.

Chapter 43

Banking Against Disaster

Among the world's bankers, Mr. Walter Wriston is the number one, standing figuratively and usually literally head and shoulders above the rest. His achievement is to have made Citicorp the most courageous, outrageous, admired, envied and disliked of all international banks.

—*The Times* (LONDON), JUNE 21, 1984

The newspapers on Tuesday morning, September 14, 1982, carried reports that were generally unflattering to Citicorp and Shearman & Sterling. *The Wall Street Journal* focused on the "too cozy" ties between the law firm and Citicorp and noted that an unrelated decision earlier in the year of the U.S. Court of Appeals in New York City had suggested that lawyers closely involved with a company may be "torn between a desire to see the firm prosper and their professional and legal obligations." When wrongdoing is suspected, the court added, "the wiser course may be to hire counsel with no other connection to the corporation to conduct investigations. . . ."[1]

[1] "Was Law Firm's Study of Citibank's Dealings Abroad a Whitewash?" *The Wall Street Journal*, September 14, 1982.

Jeff Gerth's article in the same day's *New York Times* quoted Sporkin as testifying that the SEC would become "irrelevant" if it adopted some of the arguments it used in deciding not to bring proceedings against Citicorp.[2]

A provocative article on significant banking issues appeared on the Op Ed page of the same issue of the *Times*. It was written by Walter Wriston.

"Over the years," it stated, "a lot of intellectual capital has been invested in the proposition that massive defaults by developing countries will eventually cause a severe world financial crisis. Those who took that view in 1973–1974 have been proved wrong, and those of us who believed that the market would absorb the shock of skyrocketing oil prices proved correct. Despite this, the perception remains that some form of disaster is inevitable. It is not.

"To see why, it is only necessary to understand the basic facts of government borrowing. The first is that there are few recorded instances in history of government—any government—actually getting out of debt. Certainly in an era of $100 billion deficits no one lending money to our Government by buying a Treasury bill expects that it will be paid at maturity in any way except by our Government's selling a new bill of like amount."

The author pointed out that when problems of debt service arise in a country, as they had done in Poland or Mexico, "they are problems of liquidity, not insolvency."

Countries do not go bankrupt. "Bankruptcy is a procedure developed in Western law to forgive the obligations of a person or a company that owes more than it has. Any country, however badly off, will 'own' more than it 'owes.' The catch is cash flow and the cure is sound programs and time to let them work."[3]

To ensure that its cash flow problems were in hand, Mexico, the week before, had nationalized private banks on grounds that the bankers had masterminded a $39 billion capital outflow that had landed the country in its present liquidity bind. [Citibank documents showed that from 1976 to at least 1979, its Mexico City branch's month-end parked positions in Nassau ran from a few hundred thousand dollars to almost $10 million.]

When Congressman Dingell opened the second day of hearings that

---

[2] "SEC Is Criticized For Citicorp Stand," *The New York Times*, September 14, 1982.

[3] "Banking Against Disaster," by Walter B. Wriston, *The New York Times*, September 14, 1982. The article was a rewrite of a speech given by Wriston at an International Monetary Conference in Lausanne, Switzerland, on June 4, 1982.

Friday, September 17, 1982, he mentioned the Wriston article with some distaste. He gathered from it that Wriston did not believe the normal inhibitions on credit extension applied when dealing with government lending and that a bank could continue to roll over debt and add to it indefinitely without concern for the ability of the borrower to repay. Dingell said this attitude was "disturbing" and may "to a large extent be responsible for the difficulties we now face . . . in the international financial markets."

The second day of hearings was intended to address the larger question of bank prudence and controls. The first witness was Abraham J. Briloff, professor of accounting at City University of New York. He was a noted critic of inconsistent and incongruous accounting practices used by some of the nation's largest corporations. Briloff's testimony described Citibank's "rinky-dink deals" as "money laundering practices" similar to those used by organized crime syndicates.

"I must say that if I were not told that these transactions were undertaken by one of the most prestigious major banking institutions around the world, I would say that these were manifestations of what is going on in the underground economy or by some syndicate committed to international crime.

"The money-laundering that went on, the ways in which communications were to be off the record, the way in which documents were created, phony documents created, it is shocking, shocking to think that undoubtedly moral men could lend themselves to the creation of such crucially immoral decisions, decisions which, according to the record, and I believe the record makes it abundantly clear, were overtly and knowingly in violation of the tax laws and the banking laws of various governments with which we have maintained very cordial relationships," Briloff told the subcommittee.

Hiring Shearman & Sterling to do an internal investigation, he said, was like "sending a goat to guard the cabbage patch." He termed the reasons given by the SEC for not proceeding against the bank or their counsel as "the Greshamization of our precepts of corporate governance."

The next witness was Dr. Richard S. Dale, an economist and lawyer then with the Brookings Institution under a Rockefeller Foundation fellowship. Dale was a specialist on multinational banking and he was particularly intrigued by the way Citibank had used its offshore network—including branches in Bahrain, Channel Islands, Monaco, Panama, Cayman Islands, and Nassau—to circumvent national regulations. He pointed out that some of Citibank's circumventions were made possible by a lack of parity in legal and supervisory concepts in the major financial centers. And while fragmented supervisory arrangement invited window dressing and other deceptions, there was in any case a tendency by multinational banks to concentrate their risks in permissive banking centers, such as Nassau or Panama.

The last witness of the day was Karin Lissakers, a fellow of the Carnegie Foundation and wife of financial writer Martin Mayer.

"In authorizing and carrying out the transactions which have been described in the SEC staff report and the internal Citibank documents released by the subcommittee last Monday, Citibank managers and officers have shown a total disregard for . . . legitimate government responsibilities [to maintain a sound and orderly financial framework within which a nation's economy can prosper]. Citibank has in effect put itself above the law in certain countries where it has established banking operations," she told the subcommittee.

In a highly internationalized, integrated financial environment, Lissakers found that a government's ability to influence multinational banks was extremely circumscribed. "Comprehensive bank legislation that was passed in this country in the 1930s has really been rendered in large part ineffective by the existence of this huge international capital market: the trillion-and-a-half-dollar Eurocurrency market. Banks and funds now move freely across national borders, but bank regulation is still largely limited to national jurisdictions."

Citibank, she said, appeared not to have been content with a high degree of freedom accorded to banks in the international marketplace and sought to exploit the existence of its branches all over the globe "to play off one regulatory jurisdiction against another, and manipulate funds between its branches to escape those limited local controls that do apply to international operations."

Parking foreign exchange positions enabled Citibank to speculate against the local currency and violate prudential rules on open foreign exchange positions, she explained. But just as serious was "the laundering of maturities, taking three-month funds locally, passing them through an offshore center and bringing them back miraculously transformed into four-year money." Both practices meant that Citibank was evading local regulations and undermining the monetary policies of the host government.

Lissakers told the subcommittee: "It is absolutely essential that bank regulators and central banks coordinate their policies and cooperate closely in supervising and regulating the international banking system. We learned in the 1930s what could happen when there is in-adequate supervision and too limited public disclosure of private bank activities. It is a lesson we should not have to learn again in the 1980s.''

The one absent witness was David Edwards. He had declined the subcommittee's invitation to come to Washington. He did not believe it would accomplish anything, he said.

While the hearings remained recessed, *Fortune* published an article by senior staff writer Roy Rowan, assisted by researcher Sarah Bartlett, that described Edwards as ''a smart but stubborn Texan [who] by the time he was 30, in 1974, had bootstrapped his way into a senior Citibank slot in Paris, in charge of *les cambistes,* as the fast-and-furious foreign exchange traders are called. His cowboy boldness and calculator-quick mind equipped him well for this high-pressure operation.''

The article explained how Edwards, ''the maverick who yelled foul at Citibank,'' had discovered that Jean-Pierre de Laet was ''cooking the books'' by parking foreign exchange positions in Nassau, and how weeks later Edwards had reported this to Huntington, and then a year later to the internal auditors, to executive vice-president Vojta, and finally to Vojta's successor, Thomas Theobald, only to be fired.

Citibank had refused to allow its executives to be interviewed, and Wriston had even brought pressure on *Fortune*'s editor-in-chief, his friend Henry Grunwald, not to run the article. Grunwald, who normally does not get involved in the details of any story, took a keen interest in Rowan's article. He remarked to a member of his staff: ''Wriston seems to have a blind spot.''

The article, in the January 10, 1983 issue, prompted a six-paragraph reply from Citibank, which pointed out, among other things, that ''Edwards was a junior officer rather than 'in charge of' the foreign exchange department in Paris,'' and ''the assertion that currency trading represented $265 million of Citicorp's pretax earnings of $855 million does not take into account the operating expenses necessary to generate foreign exchange revenue as well as other revenue. A more appropriate comparison would be foreign exchange revenues of $265 million, compared to total revenues of $3.8 billion.''

The letter ended with the assurance that ''we look forward to the time in the near future when we may present the actual facts in their entirety.''

Citicorp dropped $1 million in advertising from forthcoming issues.

Dingell was eager to give Citicorp an opportunity to present the facts in their entirety. He requested the appearance of five Citicorp witnesses for the third hearing, which was initially scheduled for the third week in February 1983. The five were Wriston, Angermueller, Theobald, Fouraker, and Hoffman. In addition to the matters set forth in the SEC report, the subcommittee wanted to question the five on Citicorp's international lending activities and the extent to which they had been monitored by the audit and examining committees and disclosed to the public.

On February 3, 1983, Lloyd Cutler's partner William Perlik finally released a six-inch-thick batch of documents to the subcommittee, representing most of the material Borowski had requested in August 1982. But Citicorp and Shearman & Sterling still refused to produce the 1977 and 1978 legal opinions of foreign counsel. Then, on February 8, 1983, claiming that scheduling problems made the February hearing impossible, Perlik suggested it be rescheduled for a later date. In addition to Angermueller and Hoffman as witnesses, Perlik proposed Darwin E. Smith, chairman of Kimberly-Clark Corporation and current chairman of the audit and examining committees, and George J. Clark, an executive vice-president in charge of the bank's cross-border lending to third world countries. Perlik added that it was "not necessary" for Wriston, Theobald, or Fouraker to appear before the subcommittee.

This was unacceptable to Dingell. He insisted on Wriston's appearance. Citicorp, meanwhile, hired a Washington lobbyist, Franklin R. Silbey. The large and ebullient Silbey had worked as an investigator for John E. Moss when the California Democrat was chairman of the subcommittee.

Citicorp paid Silbey a starting retainer, according to the staff, of $10,000 a month, but soon raised it to $30,000. Silbey had been a partner of Max Hugel, the New Hampshire businessman who resigned as deputy director of the CIA amid controversy over his stock dealings. Silbey recommended that Citicorp provide the subcommittee with the documents it requested.

A new hearing date was scheduled for the end of June 1983. Early that month Perlik and Cutler paid a visit to Barrett in an attempt to tie the staff director down to an agreement on the scope of the hearing. Only with such an agreement, they implied, would Wriston agree to appear. Barrett drafted a letter stating the parameters—dropping all reference to the international debt crisis and the parking of loans.

"It was an unusual procedure," Borowski commented. "It was a slow, bleeding process," Stockton agreed.

Interest in the Citicorp hearings was waning as the staff was investigating a far "sexier" case, the "political manipulation" of a $1.6 billion Environmental Protection Agency fund to clean up toxic wastes. What they uncovered here led to the resignation of the fund's administrator, Anne Burford, and the laying of criminal charges against hazardous waste program chief Rita Lavelle.

With only a few weeks remaining before the new hearing date, Citicorp finally furnished copies of the 1977 and 1978 legal opinions. Then, days before the event, Wriston himself paid a "courtesy" visit to Congressman Dingell at his Rayburn House offices. The primate of American banking had come, humbly, to pay his respects to the man with the gavel. They reached a gentlemanly entente.

Chapter 44

Final Denial: The Dingell Hearings —Part II

[The Edwards affair] made me unhappy because it was so incorrectly shown, and I was very happy to go down [to Washington] and put the record straight, which we did with some great documentation. It all came up what the true facts were. That was a mess, because there were so many errors and omissions and commissions, and that made me unhappy. We had millions and millions of transactions, and they found 26 of them that were clearly wrong, and we paid $1,200,000 in fines, which wasn't a penny a share. We had 19 separate investigations and no one has ever found anything more than that to stick.

—WALTER WRISTON, AS QUOTED IN *Euromoney*, OCTOBER 1983

It had dragged on for too long. The Shad Commission killed the Citicorp investigation in December 1981 and it was now the summer of 1983. The international debt issue had moved into a second phase, with undeclared defaults by Brazil and Argentina. The International Monetary Fund bailed out Brazil, temporarily, with a $5.5 billion loan.

Argentina remained on the critical list. Congress had approved a $8.4 billion increase in the U.S. contribution to the IMF. And here was the Dingell subcommittee still discussing events that essentially had occurred in the 1970s. The third act of this side-show was scheduled to take place on Tuesday, June 28, 1983. A fourth act was still to follow.

Citibankers reacted to the Dingell hearings with a yawn. They felt the show was largely a creation of the press, and if they could point their finger at any particular culprit, it would have been Jeff Gerth. But Citibank's real *bête noire,* after David Edwards, was Thomson von Stein, that "junior" and "incompetent" SEC staff member—the same adjectives they used for Edwards.

The subcommittee staff decided to preempt Citibank's PR forces by releasing their curtain-raiser material—a memo from Dingell to the subcommittee members—to selected reporters on the Wednesday of the week before the hearing. The normal practice—and the one Citibank anticipated—would have been to release the material over the weekend for Monday's papers.

Gerth got his copy of the Dingell memo and prepared his opener: "Representative John D. Dingell . . . said today [June 23] that Citicorp documents obtained by his staff had lent 'substantial additional weight' to accusations that [Citibank] and its lawyers failed to adequately disclose information about the legality of some currency transactions in the 1970s." Dingell, Gerth explained, was specifically referring to the 1977 and 1978 European legal opinions and a Peat Marwick letter of November 15, 1978, to the Swiss Banking Commission.

Silbey, at Citicorp headquarters in New York for a strategy meeting, was in Wriston's office when he heard about the subcommittee's preemptive coup. He called the subcommittee staff on a speaker-phone to find out why they had released the material so soon. The subcommittee receptionist passed him to Stockton, who laughed. "We really shoved it up Wriston's ass this time," he told Silbey. The lobbyist had neglected to warn Stockton that he was on a speaker-phone and among those present in the chairman's office was the chairman himself.

The Citicorp camp moved to Washington for the weekend. On Sunday, two days before the hearing, Silbey and the attorneys organized a dress rehearsal, which was attended by the four Citicorp witnesses: Wriston, Angermueller, Darwin Smith, and Hoffman. A panel of surrogate congressmen asked the four participants all manner of questions that could be expected from the subcommittee.

When Wriston walked into the hearing room on Tuesday morning, surrounded by a phalanx of aides and legal advisors, he looked supremely confident. In addition to Silbey, attorney Lloyd Cutler, and Citicorp senior numbers man Don Howard, about forty Citicorp and Shearman & Sterling personnel fluttered around Wriston like ballet dancers as he and the three other witnesses took their seats at the witness table.

Dingell opened the hearing with the usual pomp. "Today's hearing has been delayed for nearly nine months due to Citicorp's continued reluctance to produce documents requested by the subcommittee, and we will inquire about that today. Citicorp still has not produced all the documents we requested. But those we have received show the importance of the 1977 and 1978 legal opinions that Citicorp obtained from foreign counsel regarding the legality of billions of dollars in foreign exchange transactions in the mid- to late 1970s. . . .

"It is obvious why Citicorp attempted to withhold these opinions and continues to withhold the other requested documents. Contrary to Shearman & Sterling's claims, several of these opinions shed a completely different light on the legality of Citicorp's foreign exchange manipulations presented in the Shearman & Sterling report. In particular, various 1977 opinions conclude that Citicorp's parking practices were illegal, either because of currency regulations or tax laws or both. The Italian opinion, for example, warns that the manipulations may give rise to potential criminal activity with fines and penalties rising into the billions of dollars if all the facts were made known to the regulators."

Only days before, Perlik had furnished the subcommittee with a copy of an Italian Treasury Ministry decision exonerating the Milan branch of charges that it had illegally exported $350 million through phony foreign exchange contracts. Citicorp was intent on parading the "judgment" because in it the Italian Treasury accepted the argument that economic control passed with the parked position to the parking-lot branch. The passing of economic risk was said to render the parking transaction a bona fide arm's length deal.

"We are intrigued by the fact that this document [dated March 4, 1982] was withheld until literally the very last minute. Apparently, no public disclosure has been made heretofore on this matter. The delivery of the document to us at this late hour makes it impossible for us to inquire into the circumstances surrounding its issuance," Dingell remarked.

The document revealed that the Italian authorities had brought criminal charges against the bank and its Milan traders in January 1981. This, Dingell said, appeared to be a material fact that should have been disclosed to Citicorp's shareholders. "Since under Italian law it appears the amount of penalties that can be imposed may be a multiple of the amount involved, we do not see how this amount would not be material. We may have to ask the SEC to look into the matter to determine whether failure to disclose the [Italian] proceeding . . . violated their regulations."

When Dingell finished his introductory remarks Wriston was called as the first witness. He was mildly indignant, not abusive, but disdainful of David Edwards, and he belittled the investigative work of Thomson von Stein. His coolness was impressive. He told the subcommittee he was proud of the Citi's record.

"In good times and bad," Wriston said, Citibank "has built its business both here and abroad in almost one hundred countries on the bedrock of institutional integrity."

The men and women who work at Citibank know that banking is built on "trust and honesty," he affirmed. And all Citibank officers are instructed "never to lose sight of the fact that we are guests in countries abroad." This was the guiding policy behind Citibank's success and prestige.

Mistakes happen, of course, and aberrations occur not only in market rates but in human behavior. Wriston, however, put most of the blame for Citibank's mistakes in foreign exchange trading on the turmoil that existed within the monetary system following the collapse of the Bretton Woods agreements. The cacophony in the foreign exchange market was not caused by the traders but by central bankers and regulators.

When the Bretton Woods system broke down, there was no other currency which could be substituted for the dollar. This led central banks to experiment with diverse forms of exchange control regulations. Few if any currency traders had experienced a comparable situation. In fact nobody had—not governments, not central bankers, not regulators, and certainly not the young men and women manning our trading desks, working to recycle petrodollars. . . .

It is also necessary to understand that central bank regulation in Europe has traditionally been more informal than comparable regulation in the United States. Here, federal regulators publish thousands of regulations and interpretations; in Europe, many regulatory positions are provided orally to bankers at meetings which occur on a regular or occasional basis. This fact, together with the singular increase in exchange rate fluctuations after 1971, made it almost impossible at times for anyone to know what current local laws required. Central banks in Europe began to develop new techniques, approaches, and new rules and regulations for banks to operate in foreign exchange markets on almost a weekly basis. These rules and regulations changed many times on short notice and without prior consultation. It was a period of trial and error; a learning experience for everybody, including the regulators. The velocity of change during that period was greater than at any time since World War II.

"In that environment, it would have been virtually impossible for any bank's foreign exchange practices not to deviate occasionally from the fluctuating wishes of some central bank.

Wriston remarked that in spite of the confusion and disruption, European central bank inspectors could only find twenty-six transactions over a five-year period that were "the basis for fines or penalties."

Given Citibank's enormous volume of foreign exchange trading activities during this petrodollar recycling period—which amounted to hundreds of billions of dollars—this is a remarkably low incidence of error. Contrary to impressions previously given this subcommittee, no pattern or scheme of improper transactions by Citicorp has ever been found by any of the numerous authorities which have examined the accusations. . . .

Citicorp has never, to my knowledge, knowingly conducted its business in violation of foreign laws or regulations. At the same time, we do not argue that none of our 60,000 employees operating in almost one hundred countries has ever made a mistake in judgment. Some have.

We have no serious disagreement with the observation made by the Office of the Comptroller of the Currency in his letter of December 8, 1980, to the Citicorp board of directors that booking foreign exchange contracts at off-market rates is not a normal banking practice. It is, in fact, totally against our policy, and we could not agree with the comptroller more. That these things did occur in a few instances some years ago is a fact that we regret. . . .

I have one final note: in some nine years there have been some twenty separate inquiries and an expenditure of millions of dollars. While some issues were raised by European government agencies, *no authority has ever adjudicated that out of the millions of trans-actions a single one was unlawful;* twenty-six specific transactions were the subjects of voluntary settlements. None of the adjust-ments in these transactions changed the earnings of Citicorp by as much as a penny a share. . . .

Reviews of our operations in many major markets revealed we operated properly, honorably, and devoid of abuse. I am proud of our record in that regard.[1]

Wriston turned the floor over to vice-chairman Hans Angermueller, who set out to undermine the credibility of the von Stein report. He said it was "full of factual errors, unsupportable assumptions, mis-representations, distortions, and significant omissions." More sim-ply, it was "not a highly professional job."

Angermueller was most indignant about the suggestion in the re-port that Wriston had been unconcerned about the issues raised in the 1975 Natvig/Pomeroy Survey of European Treasuries. Within eight days of its delivery, he said, "Mr. Wriston returned his copy of the report to Citicorp's chief comptroller with a specific written instruc-tion, noted on the cover, to '[b]e certain to follow up on these points.' The chairman's note clearly instructs the comptroller to make sure that action is taken to implement the various matters dealt with in the re-port." Angermueller admitted, however, that it took two years to be-gin to do anything about those "matters."

Angermueller annexed an "Analysis of Division of Enforcement Report of Investigation" as Exhibit 1 to his testimony. This fifty-two page document listed the "major" flaws by category: misstatement of evidence; unsupported assumptions of illegality; unsupported as-sumptions of materiality; unsupported attacks on the integrity of man-agement; and a distorted description of Citicorp's management information system. They are summarized as follows:

Misstatements of Evidence
over sixty quotations do not indicate deletions from the quoted ma-terial, ranging from single words to lengthy passages.

over fifty quotations contain variations in language from the quoted material, ranging from minor to substantial, sometimes distorted and sometimes paraphrases set forth as quotations.

---

[1] Statement by Walter B. Wriston, hearing before the Subcommittee on Oversight and Investi-gations of the Committee on Energy and Commerce, House of Representatives, June 28, 1983, Serial No. 98–78, pp. 14–17; emphasis added.

in over twenty quotations from Citicorp documents, language has been omitted which conflicts with the conclusion the draft report reached.

over fifty miscitations to the documentary evidence (in about fifteen cases the correct citation cannot even be identified).

over one hundred citations do not fully support the proposition for which they are cited, ranging from minor to major innacuracies; and

approximately five quotations from deposition testimony contain language from the question set forth as if it were the witness' answer.

Unsupported Assumptions of Illegality

The central accusation under this heading was that von Stein had adopted as his main thesis "the contention that virtually any transaction between two Citibank branches is inherently suspect, if not illegal *per se*." The analysis did not indicate that von Stein's report only examined one type of interbranch transaction, which Citibankers themselves classified as "round-tripping." Parking was the most prevalent form of round-tripping. Von Stein in fact pointed out in his report that interbranch transactions, if at arm's length, were perfectly legal.[2]

Unsupported Assumptions of Materiality

The analysis maintained that the $42 million figure mentioned in von Stein's report as representing earnings from parking was irrelevant. "It only represents adjustments ascribed through Citicorp's Management Information System, which are not the same as debits and credits to the legal accounting records." But even if the $42 million figure were relevant, "it would not be material." Between 1974 and 1978— the years to which the $42 million figure related—Citicorp had total revenues [as opposed to earnings] of $11.296 billion, of which foreign exchange trading revenues amounted to $470 million—or 0.37 percent of the total.

---

[2] The von Stein report, on page 86, stated: "If Citibank branches actually dealt with one another at arm's length, i.e., as independent buyers and sellers, each seeking its own best economic interest or, as Citibank's Swiss counsel described it, two entirely separate parties dealing under conditions and at prices prevailing in the open market (S&S report, page 42), then no government could claim that Citibank was violating either exchange control or tax laws; there would be no question about which party had the risk or responsibility of a position, no question that the initiating branch's books are incorrect in not reflecting off-book positions [which] the branch controls, and no question of transferring credit or profits."

Unsupported Attacks on the Integrity of Management

This section criticized von Stein's slurs on Wriston and accused him of twisting the context of some Wriston quotations. The only substantive example was taken from the minutes of a 1973 treasury conference, which stated: "Wriston told the traders that management knows the risk in foreign exchange." The risk referred to was apparently economic risk, while von Stein's interpretation, according to Angermueller, made it relate to parking. Von Stein's report on this issue was ambiguous and could have been read either way.

Distorted Description of the Management Information System

Angermueller objected to von Stein's characterization of MIS as "a second set of books." He referred instead to a magazine article entitled "MIS in Banking" which reported that such systems were a modern, accepted and even necessary management tool.[3]

Angermueller's critical review of the von Stein report concluded: "The draft report exemplifies the very two flaws which the commissioners of the SEC identified before the staff's investigation commenced: lack of expertise regarding the activities being reviewed, and prejudgment or bias. Accordingly, those who rely on the draft report risk being seriously misled."

Angermueller also provided the subcommittee with a country-by-country review of the tax and exchange control investigations to which Citibank had been subjected in Europe.

In France, the exchange control authorities spent two years (1978–1980) examining the Paris branch's books and finally focused on twenty-four transactions occurring between April 1976 and March 1977. The French authorities concluded that these transactions "may be in violation of foreign exchange rules." Although Citibank challenged these conclusions, following a hearing with the French authorities it decided to settle the claims for $880,000. Citibank paid another $275,000 to the French tax authorities for back taxes and penalties. No adjudication.

In Germany, the federal banking authorities conducted a six-month audit of Citibank's foreign exchange operations and found, according to Angermueller, "no irregularities." In 1980, however, the federal

[3] Steven A. Machlis, "MIS in Banking—The State of the Art," *Bankers Magazine*, November 1982. Machlis was a consultant for Deloite Haskins & Sells in the Management Advisory Services Department; the article in fact explained the workings of a MIS model that was somewhat different in format to the one used by Citibank.

tax authorities conducted a general audit of Citibank AG's foreign exchange activities from 1974 to 1978 and concluded that back taxes were owing. In 1982, Citibank agreed to "a *tentative* tax settlement of $3.7 million relating to interbranch foreign exchange transactions." No adjudication.

In Italy, there had been investigations by the Bank of Italy, the Italian Foreign Exchange Inspectorate, and the Italian fiscal police. Their findings were reviewed by the Ministry of the Treasury, which found that "parking transactions" were lawful because "they were genuine transactions made at market rates on the dates reflected in the records." Under a tax amnesty law, Citibank voluntarily paid additional Italian taxes for the years 1976 through 1981 of $615,000, thereby absolving itself of any additional tax liability. No adjudication.

In the Netherlands, Citibank's Amsterdam senof was called to the Dutch central bank in 1979 for a discussion of the local branch's foreign exchange dealings, but the matter went no further.

In Switzerland, Citibank settled a tax claim by the cantonal and federal authorities concerning two transactions that had occurred in April and May 1974. The full amount of the settlement, including "administrative fees," was $5.7 million. No adjudication.

At the time of the hearing, a tax inquiry by Inland Revenue in Britain was continuing.

Thus, up to June 1983, Citibank had been required to pay a total of $11.2 million in back taxes and penalties in four countries. In one country [Germany] the settlement was only "tentative," while in a fifth country [Britain] an investigation was still ongoing.

Darwin Smith, the new chairman of the audit and examining committees, praised Citicorp's reaction to the Edwards allegations and the manner in which Shearman & Sterling had conducted its special review. He neglected to mention that his company, Kimberly-Clark Corporation, owed Citibank $28 million.

John Hoffman, on the other hand, was fiery. He defended the integrity of his report. "The luxury of hindsight permits us now to reaffirm, as our report stated, that there was no general pattern of unlawful conduct. The transactions we investigated did not bring into question the integrity of Citicorp's management, the fairness of its financial statements, or the adequacy of its reports to stockholders. We did, however, identify certain potentially troublesome trading activities that required management attention."

He gave no credit to David Edwards for bringing the "potentially troublesome trading activities" to the bank's attention. "From our review, I believe that . . . the first time that Mr. Edwards brought up the subject of parking [was] late in 1977,'' he told one Congressman. [Edwards said he first mentioned parking to Huntington in June 1976, to Pomeroy and Claman in March 1977, and again to Sweeney in May 1977.]

Hoffman clashed with Congressman Gore over whether control of a parked position remained with the originating branch.

"The key,'' Hoffman insisted, "is whether the position was, in fact, transferred. If you take the example of a transferring branch, and assume that you are correct, that the transferor has control, but he has a position which, if you want to use the terminology, was 'parked' in Nassau, if overnight either Nassau or, say, Switzerland, if we are using a Swiss example, adopted regulations which prohibited the return of those positions, all the control in the world would not get it back to Switzerland.''

"That is a rather unlikely hypothetical,'' Gore responded.

"It is hardly unlikely,'' Hoffman corrected him.

"Does Switzerland normally pass laws with no notice overnight?''

"Switzerland, like many of the European countries, has adopted exchange control regulations with great frequency and no advance notice.''

Hoffman said that in the 1970s new exchange controls "grew up like mushrooms all over the place, and nobody knew where the next one was going to pop up. It was a very difficult job for people to keep up with this.''

This was too much for Gore. "Let me come back to the original question. I asked you, isn't it correct that the Shearman & Sterling report did not disclose that control of the parked position was left with the parking branch? And you said, no, that is not correct. Can you tell me, can you point to me where in the Shearman and Sterling report you disclosed that control of the parked position was left with the originating branch?''

"Certainly not, because your premise is incorrect. I never said that. All I am saying is that the issue was irrelevant.''

Finally, Gore said, "Now if you can both show me the courtesy, both you [Mr. Angermueller] and you, Mr. Hoffman, of not making me wade through all these grammatical hoops—well that is a mixed metaphor—but if you will just be candid and forthright with me and answer my questions in common English—the fact of the matter is, is it not, Mr. Angermueller, that control of the parked positions was left with the parking branch, right?''

"I don't agree with that. I think that the economic risk was transferred. Had there been a law or regulation imposed by New York or Nassau, which prevented whatever the understanding might have been, which I think you describe as synonymous with control, as preventing the Nassau branch from complying with its obligation, then—"

"Let's talk about the laws that existed rather than hypothetical laws that did not exist. Under the laws that existed at the time of the transaction, the laws—not hypothetical laws, but the laws that applied to the transaction—control of the parked position was left with the parking branch, correct?"

Angermueller: "No."

Gore: "Why not?"

"Because I think there was an effective transfer of the ownership of that position to Nassau, and Nassau had the right, during the period that it held it, to transfer that position to anyone it wanted. . . ."[4]

It was late now and Dingell turned the floor over to Borowski so that he could ask a few final questions. Borowski referred to a note that Natvig had made of a conversation with Wriston and asked Wriston to read it. The text was only six lines.[5]

"It is apparently a note that Natvig made of a conversation with me . . . eight years ago."

Wriston read it out loud: " 'He [Wriston] doesn't see how we can be criticized for taking Swiss franc positions in Nassau, even if the Swiss dealer does it. Of course if we undo at the same rate as we originally did the deals, we are looking for trouble.' That is correct. 'It may be that in Switzerland we will be told not to do commercial business. If so, we will have to comply with the central bank rules, but this would be a new rule entirely.' "

When he had finished reading, Wriston looked up at the subcommittee table and announced: "That is further evidence that everything that I have done in my life for the last thirty-five years says you will obey the law."

"I am asking a narrower question than that," Borowski informed him.

"I am addressing a broader question," Wriston insisted.

"I want you to just respond to my question."

"I did," Wriston assured him, although Borowski hadn't yet asked his question.

[4] Hearing before the Subcommittee on Oversight and Investigations of the Committee on Energy and Commerce, House of Representatives, June 28, 1983, Serial No. 98–78; pp. 175–179.
[5] Citibank document 1683.

"The question I have is you specifically state that if parking and unparking is done at the same rate that we are looking for trouble."

"That is what his note says. I have no recognition of the conversation."

"Do you agree with that proposition?"

"Sure."

"So you would accept the Peat Marwick analysis [that 875 parking transactions violated Swiss regulations because they used identical rates]."

Wriston saw Borowski's trap and drew back. "What kind of trouble we are looking for was not specified, certainly not legal. What I am saying is—"

"The whole paragraph is about legal authorities."

"No one has ever found parking illegal in any foreign country," Wriston asserted boldly.[6]

At this point Dingell cut the hearings short. He requested that Citicorp supply the subcommittee with documents concerning the British tax inquiry, which Citicorp never did. He also reassured a nervous Lloyd Cutler that "it is not our intention to go into the broader banking practices of [Citicorp]. I want that very clear."

Dingell lowered his gavel and the Citicorp hearings were laid to rest, never to be reconvened.

[6] House Energy and Commerce Subcommittee on Oversight and Investigations, June 28, 1983, Serial No. 98–78, pp. 224–225.

*The banking system is held together by psychological,
rather than market forces. . . . If enough people believe
a bank is in trouble, the bank will be in trouble.*

—CONGRESSMAN CHARLES E. SCHUMER (D., NEW YORK),
MEMBER OF THE HOUSE BANKING COMMITTEE, JUNE 7,
1984

*All banking is built on trust and honesty. Men and women
who come to work with us know that. From a purely
business point of view, we are always aware that we are a
guest in each country in which we operate, and can be
ejected by any sovereign with the stroke of a pen.*

—WALTER B. WRISTON, JUNE 28, 1983

While Wriston was testifying before the Dingell subcommittee, SEC
enforcement chief John Fedders spent the morning similarly engaged
before the Senate Banking Committee's Subcommittee on Securities.
He found himself in the embarrassing position of having to deny to

the Senate subcommittee that he had done anything "wrong or improper" in assisting Southland Corporation in 1978, while he was still a partner at Arnold & Porter, with an internal investigation of possible bribery.

Fedders was the subject of a grand jury investigation into a conspiracy by the Dallas-based Southland, several of its officers, and a New York attorney to bribe state tax officials. The very authority who told his enforcement staff that he wasn't interested in bringing any more bribery cases was himself a key figure in not one but two such cases.

Southland, which operates the nation-wide 7-Eleven convenience store chain, one of its vice-presidents, and the attorney Eugene Mastropieri, a former New York City councilman, had been indicted in May 1983, and were later convicted, for the bribery and cover-up conspiracy.

Fedders had been asked by Southland to review the findings of an internal probe undertaken in 1978 in response to an SEC threat to investigate certain matters it deemed suspicious. In the documents he reviewed, Fedders uncovered reference to a $96,500 payment made in 1977 to attorney Mastropieri. But the company report of the probe's findings, which Fedders vetted and approved, omitted any mention of the Mastropieri payment.

Fedders explained to the Senate subcommittee that he had come across a bill submitted by Mastropieri for legal expenses and found it "unusual and frankly suspicious." Mastropieri had wanted the $96,500 billed as an airplane lease instead of legal fees. This request was denied by the company, and the money, which in fact was used to constitute a secret slush fund, was eventually paid to him by check against an invoice for services rendered.

Fedders, then thirty-five and a partner at Arnold & Porter since 1973, agreed with Southland's in-house lawyers that "there was unsubstantial evidence on which to base a conclusion of illegality." Still, the payment had looked fishy, and Fedders allowed it to pass under the carpet. He rationalized that as Southland had wanted to keep costs low by having its own in-house legal department do the investigative legwork—he was only required to review their findings—it was not for him to probe deeper. "I reviewed no memoranda of interviews or any corporate documents gathered during the investigation," Fedders told the subcommittee. "My advice could be based only on information obtained by others and repeated to me."

At trial a year later, which convicted the company and Mastropieri

(Southland vice-president Eugene DeFalco had already pled guilty), Fedders was called as a defense witness. The Southland affair had been a time-consuming worry for the new SEC enforcement chief. In addition to appearing before two Congressional committees, he had been called to testify before the New York grand jury, had been interviewed by his own SEC staff, and he appeared at trial. This was a heavy burden to bear for having relied on management's word that the facts were as management portrayed them.

Fedders had been through a similar situation once before, when executive vice-president of Gulf Life Holding and a director of its subsidiary, Gulf Life Insurance. Gulf Life Insurance had offered a Florida state insurance commissioner a below-market-rate mortgage on a shopping center in which the commissioner was to hold a secret interest. The commissioner accepted the mortgage. He was later indicted for income tax evasion and went to prison.

After Fedders joined Arnold & Porter, he continued to serve as outside counsel for Gulf Life. Two years later he was asked by Gulf Life to do a special investigation. He failed to reveal in the subsequent report that he had been the number two corporate officer and a director of the company he was investigating at the time the suspect mortgage was proffered.

At the request of Dingell, the Shad Commission held an internal SEC inquiry that eventually absolved Fedders of any malpractice in the Southland case. The Gulf Life affair never resurfaced. But the Southland matter remained an open sore that kept Fedders on the defensive. He constantly sought justification.

"My decision not to bring the Citicorp case represents the highest form of enforcement integrity," he said in 1984. "No single act I have ever performed has received more praise and congratulations."

While this was surely an exaggeration, Fedders expressed disappointment that Dingell had not given him an opportunity to tell his side of the Citicorp story. "My statement is prepared. I'm ready," he said nine months after the last subcommittee hearing. But he was also satisfied that the questions that he admitted he prepared for Congressman Whittaker had set the record straight.

"Whittaker's cross-examination took the case away from [Sporkin, Doherty, and von Stein]. . . . Doherty conceded . . . they failed to make the case." Moments later, he added: "Integrity is my most important word."[1]

---

[1] John Fedders, interviewed by the author, March 26, 1984.

John Shad's investment in Citicorp stock, when it came to light, also caused consternation. His $150,000 holding was uncovered as a result of a Freedom of Information Act request by Jeff Gerth. The issue by itself was unimportant. Dingell's staff, however, said that when Shad was asked by his fellow commissioners why he had not mentioned the holding before, he claimed his wife had purchased the stock without his being aware of it. But the brokerage records showed the stock was in his account and later it was transferred to his blind trust.

As it turned out, the SEC's Citicorp decision did not herald a wholesale retreat from enforcement. The yearly totals of enforcement actions brought during the first four-year tenure of Shad and Fedders actually increased over those of their predecessors. But critics, including Barrett and Borowski, maintained that the numbers were deceptive, that they hid a marked reluctance to prosecute major corporations.

"Under Shad," Barrett affirmed, "only the little guys get hammered."

Fedders engendered little loyalty from the old-timers on the enforcement staff. Doherty found the atmosphere too oppressive and left, joining Sporkin as associate general counsel at the CIA. Von Stein stayed, though no warmth existed between him and Fedders. Finally, after forty-two months in the top enforcement job, Fedders abruptly resigned in the wake of publicity over a divorce action in which he admitted having beaten his wife. He was replaced by the one remaining deputy, Gary G. Lynch, who had served under Sporkin. Lynch, then thirty-four, had joined the enforcement division in 1976, one year out of Duke Law School.

In his departing letter to the commission and staff, Fedders had high praise for the people he had worked with. He called them "good, honest, and tireless women and men. Folks with pride and determination. A team that has learned there are no hopeless situations. What appears as an unsolvable problem to some is actually a rather exhilarating challenge to the enforcement staff. You are people who inspire others because you see invisible bridges at the end of dead-end streets."[2]

Sporkin, meanwhile, was tiring as legal advisor to the cloak-and-dagger fraternity. He was for more openness in government, not less,

[2] Letter from John M. Fedders to the chairman, the commissioners, and the staff, especially the Division of Enforcement Staff, Securities and Exchange Commission, Washington, D.C., March 4, 1985.

and there was certainly very little of it to be found at the CIA. The agency's director, Bill Casey, asked President Reagan to nominate Sporkin, at fifty-two, to a seat on the U.S. District Court for the District of Columbia, which the President did in June 1984. But Sporkin's enemies sabotaged the nomination and it was withdrawn three months later.

Looking back on the Citicorp case, Sporkin said he was surprised it was never settled. He had learned from Felix Rohatyn, the investment banker whose financial wit helped save New York City from bankruptcy, that a fair settlement gives something to everyone. "If everybody had acted in an honorable way," said Sporkin, "Citibank would have been out of the heat and the Edwards story would have been forgotten."

Was it ethical for John Fedders to feed hostile questions to a tame member of the Dingell subcommittee? Sporkin thought it was analogous to a football coach giving his team's plays to the opposing side.

As for John Hoffman's performance as principal author of the Shearman & Sterling report, Sporkin said he would like to hear Hoffman's explanation on a number of points before making judgment.

Hoffman wasn't talking. One of his partners indicated, while patting a printed volume of the subcommittee hearings, that everything anybody would ever need to know about the case had already been placed on the record. But the controversy over whether law firms should investigate their own clients persisted. No less an authority than the chairman of the American Bar Association's ethics committee, H. William Allen, suggested they should not. "The good practice," he said, "is to hire an independent law firm." [3]

Citicorp's attitude was that far too many executive work hours had been wasted on the Edwards affair to engage in any new discussion of it. Charles Young, Citibanker on Toronto's Front Street, suggested there might be another reason. "Citibank considers the David Edwards affair a 'no-win' situation. Our policy has been, really, not to talk about it," he said.

When Wriston retired on September 1, 1984, John S. Reed, who succeeded him, was the only one of the three contenders not to have been involved in, or tainted by, the Edwards affair.

Wriston had transformed the Citi into a bank without walls, serving customers twenty-four hours a day through electronic tellers. A total of 12 million people—equivalent to half the population of Canada—had learned to appreciate the benefits and risks of credit-card

[3] *Business Week*, July 11, 1983.

banking, which Wriston's Citi pioneered through control of the Visa, MasterCard, and Diners Club organizations. Besides commercial banking, the Citi also sold insurance, was involved in discount brokerage, underwrote various federal, state, municipal, and corporate securities, and offered mortgage financing in huge amounts.

The Wriston revolution had introduced the notion that money was like any other commodity that banks could go out and "buy"—which they did by issuing certificates of deposit. This enabled them to lend more. But it also caused the cost of money to soar and contributed to the surge in interest rates. Along the way, Citicorp became the world's biggest private lender. But the legacy was heavy: $12.3 billion of its loans were, in 1984, to troubled debtor nations.

Wriston's critics, and there were many, perceived that he had somehow led the entire banking system into crisis. His legacy was that big banks, the multinational mammoths, had become so big that they could neither be regulated nor allowed to go bust. If one of them collapsed, the risks were high that the whole system would follow like a house of cards.

Citibank's nonperforming loans had grown during Wriston's last full year as chairman by $1 billion. By mid-1984 they totalled $2.6 billion, half of them concentrated in Mexico, Brazil, Argentina, and Venezuela.

As Argentina hovered on the brink of disaster, the bitter realization began to sink in that the banks really had been having a very good time of it. According to *The Wall Street Journal,* "While the bankers were pumping $40 billion in loans into Argentina, we understand, the Argentinians were taking $30 billion out to park abroad."[4]

The Argentinians, naturally, were not "parking" these deposits with their own banks. They were parking the cash with the same money-center banks that extended the loans, through their offshore booking centers.

While the multinational giants had demonstrated they could surpass existing prudential safeguards and regulatory controls with disconcerting ease, and had greater resources than most central banks, Wriston, the champion of deregulation, wanted still greater freedom for banks.

The U.S. Treasury headed by Donald T. Regan, a former chairman of another Wall Street giant, Merrill Lynch & Company, shared Wriston's views. The U.S. Treasury under Regan wanted to let bank-holding companies like Citicorp establish subsidiaries to offer finan-

---

[4]"The Creditors' Club," an editorial in *The Wall Street Journal,* June 20, 1984.

cial services prohibited by the fifty-year-old Glass-Steagall Act. These would include the selling and underwriting of securities and mutual funds, insurance brokerage and dealing, and real estate equity investment, development, and brokerage. Citicorp, through one loophole or another, was already engaged in much of this business.

The Federal Reserve, led by conservative technocrat Paul Volcker, was strongly opposed to such freedom, contending that the financial system was too important to be exposed to such risks as real estate speculation. Volcker believed that imposing conditions on holding-company activities was crucial to the regulatory efforts.

The basic structures to license and regulate U.S. banks were put in place in the 1930s, when multinational banking was all but unknown. Four agencies rather than one regulate various parts of the industry. The Federal Reserve Board, the nation's central bank, was given the responsibility of setting monetary policy and examining state banks which are members of the Federal Reserve System. The Office of the Comptroller of the Currency examines federally chartered banks. The Federal Deposit Insurance Corporation examines state banks that are not members of the Federal Reserve system but have FDIC coverage. The Federal Home Loan Bank Board regulates all federally insured savings and loan associations.

The Federal Reserve Board, the Comptroller of the Currency, the SEC, and the Dingell subcommittee had shown reluctance to take the Edwards case in hand and impose sanctions against the institution or its officers. Both the SEC and the Comptroller of the Currency had found evidence of wrongdoing but virtually did nothing. A central consensus seemed to say that too much attention drawn to relatively minor evasions of good banking practice could undermine the remaining confidence in an already shaky system, regardless of whether the evasions themselves covertly undermined the system.

There was no adjudication of wrongdoing, Wriston insisted. "No country has ever found parking illegal."

Shearman & Sterling's scenario for parking by Citibank's branch in London was a perfect example. The Bank of England, when asked by the author, refused to comment on it even though it contained evidence of misconduct.

London Scenario No. 1

GOAL: Citibank London wants to transfer its oversold sterling position to another branch.

VARIATION I

A. *Transaction Steps*	*Result*
1. London has sold sterling on the open market at the market rate.	1. London is oversold in sterling.
2. On the same day, London buys sterling from Nassau in a spot or forward contract at the market rate.	2a) London is neither overbought nor oversold in sterling. b) Nassau is oversold in sterling.

B. *Removing the position from the Nassau branch*

3. Sometime later, London sells the same amount of sterling to Nassau on the same value date and at the same rate as in step 2.	3a) London is oversold in sterling. b) Nassau is neither overbought nor oversold and has no profits or losses.

VARIATION II

These transactions are also done with Citibank's Head Office in New York or another European branch.

The goal, as stated, was in fact achieved at the end of Step A. It was, therefore, not the real goal. "Only when Step B is completed does it become an immoral transaction," said a respected British foreign exchange expert who, because of his past association with Citibank, asked not to be named.

The travesty of the scenario approach only really became apparent when two necessary assumptions were added to place the scenario in proper context. These were:

1) Citibank's limit for open overnight positions as authorized by the Bank of England was, at the time, $4 million.
2) In every instance, the parked positions exceeded the authorized limit and, according to Shearman & Sterling's own clarification to British counsel, averaged $10 million.

An internal SEC document, prepared by Robert Ryan, indicated that the British authorities did not take action because the government was concerned that "Citicorp might remove its leasing operations from the United Kingdom" at a time when the British economy was in the worst depression since the 1930s.[5]

[5]Draft memo from Robert Ryan to David Doherty, re: Citicorp HO-1100, January 5, 1981.

Switzerland was the only country that considered and rejected stern action. The Swiss banking authorities found that Citibank had indeed been "bidding up the franc," contrary to Eddie Giger's earlier assurances that this was not the case. Giger resigned. The Swiss then invoked the excuse that the statute of limitation had expired for not seeking adjudication in a criminal court. In, fact, parking continued in Switzerland until 1980.

The Swiss, however, had a final word about the integrity of Wriston's affirmation that in the regulatory environment of the 1970s "it was virtually impossible for any bank's foreign exchange practices not to deviate occasionally from the fluctuating wishes of some central bank."

"From the point of view of the Swiss National Bank, we would have to protest against Mr. Wriston's thesis. . . . The Swiss National Bank has always tried to word its currency protection rules clearly and practicably. Modifications of the executive regulations were each time discussed in advance with the banks in a representatively composed group," said Dr. Peter Klauser, eminent jurist and one of three Swiss National Bank general managers.[6]

Angermueller, according to von Stein's contested notes, had tried to shift the onus for parking's permissibility onto the Swiss. He was quoted as telling Sporkin: "the banking authorities know all Swiss banks do it."[7]

Credit Suisse's chief dealer, Edgar Peng, laughed at the suggestion. "We never parked. Nor do we believe any of the other big three banks did. When the central bank introduces new measures, you make sure you abide by them."

The British clearing banks, too, felt it their duty to cooperate with the Bank of England in refraining from undermining the pound. Nor has any managing director, treasurer, or chief financial officer of a major British bank ever suggested that in the turbulent seventies, it became "virtually impossible not to deviate from the fluctuating wishes of some central bank." William Batt, treasurer of National Westminster Bank before retiring in 1984, said flatly, "We don't park. We go by the rules."

According to Shearman & Sterling, Citicorp Leasing International, Inc., conducts "a modest equipment leasing operation in the UK."

[6] Letter from Swiss National Bank general manager Dr. Peter Klauser to the author, August 30, 1983.

[7] Memorandum to files by Thomson von Stein: Notes of a Meeting with Citibank, January 14, 1980.

Epilogue

*We're not here to discuss what is right and wrong; we're
here to discuss the facts.*

—EUGENE SWEENEY TO DAVID EDWARDS, JUNE 13, 1977

On January 5, 1982, almost four years after he fired David Edwards
for acting "in a manner detrimental to the best interests of Citibank,"
Thomas C. Theobald sent the following memo to all "Country Corporate Officers" of the bank:

> I am happy to be able to tell you all that today the last of the in-
> vestigations by various governments into our Foreign Exchange ac-
> tivities have been terminated.

> The support that our legal and regulatory advisors were given by
> our staff was critical and very much appreciated, proving once again
> that we have highly professional and seasoned people who can cope
> with unusual and demanding situations.

> This has been a most loborious [sic] and difficult exercise which,
> looked at positively, serves to remind us that all our staff must be
> totally familiar with the legal and regulatory environment in which
> they work, adhere to that environment scrupulously, and always
> operate in a manner which maintains the highest level of business
> standards which the world is entitled to expect from us. Please pass
> on our thanks to everyone involved.

The irony of Theobald's memo was not immediately evident. There was, in fact, no end in sight to the Edwards affair. Senior vice-president Robert Logan referred to the U.S. Federal Reserve's new foreign exchange reporting requirements as another example of "the high cost of David Edwards," while other highly placed Citibankers preferred to will the Edwards matter out of existence. But with all their dissimulation, or more probably because of their dissembling, the Edwards affair wouldn't go away.

Theobald, who was about to be named vice-chairman but was still head of the international banking group when he wrote the memo, did not disclose which "last" investigation had just been terminated. To be perfectly frank, when the memo was circulated there were tax investigations on-going or about to get under way in New York City and Britain. Moreover, a fourteen-month-old criminal investigation in Milan had recently entered a new phase. The Guardia di Finanza reported to the public prosecutor in January 1981 that Citibank's Milan traders had illegally exported enormous amounts of capital through parking. This was reaffirmed in a second Finanza report three years later, which included as an annex the von Stein opus. In June 1984, the Milan prosecutor issued eleven indictments. The trial opened in September 1984, and, after an initial adjournment, it resumed in April 1985, this time under a new court president assisted by two assessors.

Once resumed, the trial lasted three days. The judges found Citibank's two senior officers in Milan during the height of parking—Baron Hans von Fluegge, a German national, and Rafael Moreno Valle, originally from Mexico City—guilty, and sentenced each of them *in absentia* to one year in prison. The judges acquitted Philip Sherman, who succeeded von Fluegge as Milan senof, and four other members of the Milan trading room staff. They accepted the argument of "extenuating circumstances" for Francesco Redi, his chief trader Franco Riccardi, and two other traders, and absolved them of responsibility.

In addition, the judges fined von Fluegge and Moreno Valle a total of lira 2,425,810,000 ($1,254,000 at current exchange rates) and condemned them to pay lira 240 million ($124,000) in court and administrative costs.

Appendix

THE WORLD'S BEST FOREIGN EXCHANGE DEALERS

RANKING	BANK	% MARKET SHARE ESTIMATES
1	Citibank	9.08
2	Chase Manhattan	5.50
3	Morgan Guaranty	4.93
4	Continental Illinois	4.85
5	Bank of America	4.25
6	Harris Trust and Savings Bank	3.23
7	Standard Chartered Bank	2.48
8	Dresdner Bank	2.38
9	European American	2.25
10	First National Bank of Chicago	2.20
11	Lloyds Bank	1.95
12	Bankers Trust	1.90
13	Toronto Dominion	1.80
14	Barclays Bank	1.75
15	Mellon Bank	1.65
16	Credit Industriel et Commercial	1.63
17	Hill Samuel & Co.	1.38
18	Bank of Tokyo	1.13
19	Banque Nationale de Paris	1.10
20	Manufacturers Hanover Trust	1.08
	TOTAL MARKET SHARE OF 20 BANKS	56.5%

Index

403